# MISSION
# IN THE NEW TESTAMENT

*American Society of Missiology Series, No. 27*

# MISSION IN THE NEW TESTAMENT

## *An Evangelical Approach*

**William J. Larkin Jr.**
**Joel F. Williams**
**editors**

ORBIS BOOKS

**Maryknoll, New York 10545**

The Catholic Foreign Mission Society of America (Maryknoll) recruits and trains people for overseas missionary service. Through Orbis Books, Maryknoll aims to foster the international dialogue that is essential to mission. The books published, however, reflect the opinions of their authors and are not meant to represent the official position of the Society.

Copyright © 1998 by William J. Larkin Jr. and Joel F. Williams.

Published by Orbis Books, Maryknoll, New York, U.S.A.

Manufactured in the United States of America.

Manuscript editing and typesetting by Joan Weber Laflamme.

Library of Congress Cataloging-in-Publication Data

Mission in the New Testament : an evangelical approach / William J. Larkin Jr., Joel F. Williams, editors.
   p. cm. — (American Society of Missiology series : no. 27)
   Includes bibliographical references.
   ISBN 1-57075-169-2 (alk. paper)
   1. Missions—Biblical teaching. 2. Missions—Theory—Biblical teaching. 3. Evangelization. I. Larkin, William J. II. Williams, Joel F. III. Series.
BV2073.M55 1998
266—dc21
                                       97-38902
                                            CIP

# Contents

## PART FOUR
## THE GENERAL EPISTLES AND JOHN'S WRITINGS

# *Preface to the ASM Series*

The purpose of the ASM (American Society of Missiology) Series is to publish—without regard for disciplinary, national, or denominational boundaries—scholarly works of high quality and wide interest on missiological themes from the entire spectrum of scholarly pursuits relevant to Christian mission, which is always the focus of books in the Series.

By *mission* is meant the effort to effect passage over the boundary between faith in Jesus Christ and its absence. In this understanding of mission, the basic functions of Christian proclamation, dialogue, witness, service, worship, liberation, and nurture are of special concern. And in that context questions arise, including, How does the transition from one cultural context to another influence the shape and interaction between these dynamic functions, especially in regard to the cultural and religious plurality that comprises the global context of Christian mission?

The promotion of scholarly dialogue among missiologists, and among missiologists and scholars in other fields of inquiry, may involve the publication of views that some missiologists cannot accept, and with which members of the Editorial Committee do not agree. Manuscripts published in the Series reflect the opinions of their authors and are not understood to represent the position of the American Society of Missiology or of the Editorial Committee. Selection is guided by such criteria as intrinsic worth, readability, and accessibility to a range of interested persons and not merely to experts or specialists.

The ASM Series, in collaboration with Orbis Books, seeks to publish scholarly works of high merit and wide interest on numerous aspects of missiology—the study of mission. Able presentations on new and creative approaches to the practice and understanding of mission will receive close attention.

The ASM Series Editorial Committee
James A. Scherer, chair
Mary Motte, FMM
Charles Taber

# Contributors

*Clifford H. Bedell* (M.A., Wheaton College; M.A., University of Georgia) teaches New Testament and intercultural studies at Columbia Bible College.

*Martin Erdmann* (Ph.D. cand., Brunel University) is a graduate of Columbia Biblical Seminary. He is the founder and president of Online Communication Systems, Inc.

*John D. Harvey* (Th.D., Toronto School of Theology) teaches New Testament and Greek at Columbia Biblical Seminary and Graduate School of Missions. He is a graduate of Columbia Biblical Seminary.

*Don N. Howell Jr.* (Th.D., Dallas Theological Seminary) is assistant dean and a member of the New Testament faculty at Columbia Biblical Seminary and Graduate School of Missions.

*Andreas J. Köstenberger* (Ph.D., Trinity Evangelical Divinity School) is an associate professor of New Testament at Southeastern Baptist Theological Seminary and a graduate of Columbia Biblical Seminary.

*William J. Larkin Jr.* (Ph.D., University of Durham) teaches New Testament and Greek at Columbia Biblical Seminary and Graduate School of Missions.

*Ferris L. McDaniel* (Th.D., Dallas Theological Seminary) teaches Old Testament and biblical languages at Columbia Biblical Seminary and Graduate School of Missions.

*Robertson McQuilkin* (M.Div., Fuller Theological Seminary) is the president emeritus of Columbia International University.

*Johnny V. Miller* (Th.D., Dallas Theological Seminary) is the president of Columbia International University and its constituent schools, Columbia Bible College and Columbia Biblical Seminary and Graduate School of Missions. He also serves as a member of the New Testament faculty at Columbia Biblical Seminary.

**David P. Seemuth** (Ph.D., Marquette University) is on the pastoral staff of Elmbrook Church, Brookfield, Wisconsin. He is a graduate of Columbia Biblical Seminary.

**Joel F. Williams** (Ph.D., Marquette University) teaches New Testament and Greek at Columbia Bible College.

# *Preface*

## Robertson McQuilkin

You have in your hands an unusual volume—a serious study on missions not from missiologists but from New Testament scholars. Missions courses in our theological schools, if present at all, traditionally have been relegated to the "practical" division of studies, not the "scholarly." Resulting from this, or bringing it about, few biblical studies seem to have recognized what this volume so ably demonstrates, that the New Testament is about mission, the mission of our redeeming God. These ground-breaking studies should help correct the church's near-sighted view of scripture, recapturing the worldwide intent of God.

However, there is another reason this volume is greatly needed. At a time of unprecedented advance in world evangelism and of great ferment in new ideas about how it should be done, the need is for a careful examination of the foundation for a church on mission, the New Testament documents themselves. *Mission in the New Testament*, read carefully by missiologists and missions activists, could prove an antidote to anti-biblical fads in the world of missions and, simultaneously, help provide focus on biblical principles and priorities.

It should not be surprising that these ground-breaking biblical studies come from a group of New Testament scholars associated with Columbia International University and that the impetus for producing the volume should be the seventy-fifth anniversary of that missionary-sending institution. I join the authors in prayer that this volume may be used to advance the cause of world evangelism.

## Previously Published in
## The American Society of Missiology Series

# Abbreviations

| | |
|---|---|
| AB | Anchor Bible |
| AnBib | Analecta Biblica |
| *ANRW* | *Aufstieg und Niedergang der Römischen Welt* |
| BECNT | Baker Exegetical Commentary on the New Testament |
| *BFCT* | *Beiträge zur Förderung Christlicher Theologie* |
| *Bib* | *Biblica* |
| *BJRL* | *Bulletin of the John Rylands Library* |
| *BSac* | *Bibliotheca Sacra* |
| *BT* | *The Bible Translator* |
| *CBQ* | *Catholic Biblical Quarterly* |
| *CurTM* | *Currents in Theology and Mission* |
| *DJG* | Joel B. Green and Scot McKnight, ed., *Dictionary of Jesus and the Gospels* |
| *DPHL* | Gerald F. Hawthorne and Ralph P. Martin, ed., *Dictionary of Paul and His Letters* |
| EMS | Evangelical Missiological Society |
| *EvQ* | *Evangelical Quarterly* |
| *ExpTim* | *Expository Times* |
| *FB* | *Forschung zur Bibel* |
| HNTC | Harper's New Testament Commentaries |
| *HTR* | *Harvard Theological Review* |
| *IBS* | *Irish Biblical Studies* |
| ICC | International Critical Commentary |
| *IDBSup* | *Interpreter's Dictionary of the Bible: Supplementary Volume* |
| *Int* | *Interpretation* |
| *ISBE* | *International Standard Bible Encyclopedia* |
| *ITQ* | *Irish Theological Quarterly* |
| IVP | InterVarsity Press |
| *JBL* | *Journal of Biblical Literature* |

| | |
|---|---|
| *JES* | *Journal of Ecumenical Studies* |
| *JETS* | *Journal of the Evangelical Theological Society* |
| *JSNT* | *Journal for the Study of the New Testament* |
| *JSNT*Sup | *Journal for the Study of the New Testament* Supplement Series |
| *JTS* | *Journal of Theological Studies* |
| LSJ | Liddell, Scott, and Jones, *Greek-English Lexicon* |
| LXX | Septuagint |
| MT | Masoretic Text |
| NAC | New American Commentary |
| NICNT | New International Commentary on the New Testament |
| NIGTC | New International Greek Testament Commentary |
| NIV | New International Version |
| NKJV | New King James Version |
| *NovT* | *Novum Testamentum* |
| *NRT* | *La Nouvelle Revue Théologique* |
| NSBT | New Studies in Biblical Theology |
| NT | New Testament |
| *NTS* | *New Testament Studies* |
| OT | Old Testament |
| *RevExp* | *Review and Expositor* |
| *RTP* | *Revue de Théologie et de Philosophie* |
| SBLDS | Society of Biblical Literature Dissertation Series |
| SBLMS | Society of Biblical Literature Monograph Series |
| *SBS* | *Stuttgarter Bibelstudien* |
| SBT | Studies in Biblical Theology |
| *SEÅ* | *Svensk Exegetisk Årsbok* |
| *SJT* | *Scottish Journal of Theology* |
| SNTSMS | Society for New Testament Studies Monograph Series |
| *ST* | *Studia Theologica* |
| *TDNT* | G. Kittel and G. Friedrich, ed., *Theological Dictionary of the New Testament* |
| *TLZ* | *Theologische Literaturzeitung* |
| *TS* | *Theological Studies* |
| *TynBul* | *Tyndale Bulletin* |
| *TZ* | *Theologische Zeitschrift* |

| | |
|---|---|
| VT | *Vestus Testamentum* |
| WBC | *Word Biblical Commentary* |
| WEC | *Wycliffe Exegetical Commentary* |
| WMANT | Wissenschaftliche Monographien zum Alten und Neuen Testament |
| WTJ | *Westminster Theological Journal* |
| WUNT | Wissenschaftliche Untersuchungen zum Neuen Testament |
| WW | *Word and World* |
| ZNW | *Zeitschrift für die Neutestamentliche Wissenschaft* |

# Introduction

## William J. Larkin Jr.

### AIM AND RATIONALE

This volume aims to present a comprehensive articulation of the New Testament teaching on the theme of mission. Such a study hopefully will contribute to a fresh statement of the biblical foundations of mission and serve as a catalyst for the completion of the church's universal mission in this generation.

Consideration of this theme leads us to a central aspect of New Testament theology.[1] The New Testament is a missionary document, containing preaching (the Gospels), model mission history (Acts), and letters written primarily by missionaries while on mission. Although a majority of the documents are addressed "in house," to Christians, it must be remembered that these were first- or second-generation Christians in church bodies that were the product of first-century missions. The documents themselves, more often than not, are aimed at encouraging these Christians in mission.

A curious aspect of New Testament studies is that, since World War II, little attention has been given to the theme of mission. Only two books have appeared in English that deal comprehensively with this theme.[2] David Bosch and Elisabeth Schüssler Fiorenza have found

---

[1] Donald Senior and Carroll Stuhlmueller, *The Biblical Foundations for Mission* (Maryknoll, N.Y.: Orbis Books, 1983), 4.

[2] Ferdinand Hahn, *Mission in the New Testament*, trans. Frank Clarke, SBT, no. 47 (Naperville, Ill.: Alec R. Allenson, 1965); Senior and Stuhlmueller, *Biblical Foundations*. Two collections of essays have a few articles, but neither deals comprehensively with the New Testament. See Paul Beasley-Murray, ed., *Mission to the World: Essays to Celebrate the Fiftieth Anniversary of the Ordination of George Raymond Beasley-Murray* (Didcot, England: Baptist Historical Society, 1991); Wayne C. Stumme, ed., *Bible and Mission: Biblical Foundations and Working Models for Congregational Ministry* (Minneapolis: Augsburg, 1986).

reasons for this paucity in the practice of the historical-critical method.[3] Historical-critical scholars have tended to read their own established church situation back into the New Testament. They have treated the first-century history represented in the New Testament books as "confessional history," inner church doctrinal struggles among various factions and theologians. Further, their strong historical consciousness produces a lack of incentive for finding material in the New Testament teaching on mission that is directly applicable to today's very different historical setting. The theme of mission has also been neglected in evangelical New Testament studies. Aside from John Piper's exposition of the supremacy of God in missions and the forthcoming volume by Peter T. O'Brien and Andreas Köstenberger on mission in the New Testament, all comprehensive work by evangelicals in this area has come from missiologists.[4] The time is past due for evangelical New Testament scholars to turn their attention to the study of mission.

Indeed, the current situation of mission advance in the universal church calls for such a study. The leadership and drive from the two-thirds-world church through the A.D. 2000 movement seems to assume the biblical foundations as it concentrates on strategic planning. The movement's recent Global Consultation on World Evangelism in Seoul, Korea, attended by four thousand evangelism leaders from 186 countries, was self-confessedly a strategy working session. According to participant Samuel Kameleson of World Vision, however, the consultation showed a "lack of theological reflection."[5] Motivation and action are vital to fulfilling the Great Commission in our day, but for the action to maintain itself and avoid becoming aberrant it needs to be carried out within an articulated biblical theological framework. Conservative evangelical reflection on the biblical foundations of mission has an essential contribution to make to such a framework.

---

[3] David J. Bosch, "Mission in Biblical Perspective," *International Review of Missions* 74 (1985): 532; Elisabeth Schüssler Fiorenza, "Miracles, Mission, and Apologetics: An Introduction," in *Aspects of Religious Propaganda in Judaism and Early Christianity*, ed. Elisabeth S. Fiorenza (Notre Dame, Ind.: University of Notre Dame Press, 1976), 1.

[4] John Piper, *Let the Nations Be Glad! The Supremacy of God in Missions* (Grand Rapids: Baker, 1993); Andreas J. Köstenberger and Peter T. O'Brien, *Mission in the New Testament*, NSBT (Grand Rapids: Eerdmans, forthcoming); George W. Peters, *A Biblical Theology of Missions* (Chicago: Moody, 1972); J. Herbert Kane, *Christian Missions in Biblical Perspective* (Grand Rapids: Baker, 1976); Roger E. Hedlund, *The Mission of the Church in the World: A Biblical Theology* (Grand Rapids: Baker, 1991); Philip M. Steyne, *In Step with the God of All Nations: A Biblical Theology of Missions* (Houston: Touch Ministries, 1991).

[5] Doug Koop, "Mobilizing for the Millennium," *Christianity Today* (17 July 1995), 53.

The situation in North America also calls for a biblical study on mission. With the increasing strength of isolationist voices after the fall of communism in the late eighties, this generation's task of making the missionary mandate of the church its own becomes all the more difficult.[6] Yet that task is all the more urgent, for the wave of World War II–generation missionaries is now retiring and recruits need to be found to fill the ranks. Comprehensive and foundational biblical study on mission will be an invaluable resource in helping younger generations to see clearly their missions responsibility. Such a study fits well with recent calls for evangelical missiology to rediscover its theological roots.[7] And there is also the "great new fact of our day": America as a mission field. Craig Van Gelder correctly sees that.[8] All pastoring in the post-modern, increasingly post-Christian North American environment has become either church planting or church revitalization. In order to undertake their new missionary role, pastors must learn what mission is and how it is done, starting with the biblical foundations.

## DEFINITION

In the Bible, "'mission' is the divine activity of sending intermediaries whether supernatural or human to speak or do God's will so that God's purposes for judgment or redemption are furthered."[9] The concept of mission comprises six elements. (1) There is the sender, along with the sender's purpose and authority in sending. That purpose is God's accomplishment of salvation for humans and God's application of it to them. (2) One must consider the act of sending, a commissioning or authorization that leads to movement. To be on mission is to respond to the sender's call and commission and go to those to whom one is sent. (3) Further, study must be done on "those who are sent": the various agents God employs, and about their stance: obedience. In the foreground of this study will be the church, that divinely ordained agent for applying salvation blessings to humanity. (4) Another element is the particular task of those on mission, which in the New Testament focuses primarily on the proclamation in word and deed of

---

[6] Paul Borthwick, *Youth and Missions: Expanding Your Students' World View* (Wheaton: Victor Books, 1988); Annette Elder, "Boomers, Busters, and the Challenge of the Unreached Peoples," *International Journal of Frontier Missions* 8 (1991): 51-55.

[7] Edward Rommen, "The De-Theologizing of Missiology," *Trinity World Forum* 19 (Fall 1993): 1-4.

[8] Craig Van Gelder, "A Great New Fact of Our Day: America as Mission Field," *Missiology* 19 (1991): 409-18.

[9] William J. Larkin Jr., "Mission," in *Evangelical Dictionary of Biblical Theology*, ed. Walter A. Elwell (Grand Rapids: Baker, 1996), 534.

God's saving work. Especially important in this area is what the New Testament has to say about that task's universal scope. (5) The result of mission must be explained. How does the kingdom of God advance as the church fulfills its mission? What constitutes a completion of the task, and how are those successful results accomplished? (6) Finally, there is mission's comprehensive historico-theological framework. The whole study must view mission within the framework of God's salvation history, whereby God does the covenantal work of judgment or redemption.

Since the present study is intended to contribute to a clear understanding of the biblical foundations for mission, in the foreground of all our considerations will be the concept of the universal mission of the church, that is, mission as salvation applied through the church to the nations to the ends of the earth. For the sake of comprehensiveness and a proper perspective, the study must also consider other "sent ones" and their role in salvation accomplished, as well as applied. If, however, the teaching on mission is to be useful for the church—as the New Testament writers originally intended—the universal mission of the church must be at the center of our considerations.

## METHODOLOGY

The general approach adopted involves three steps: (1) investigation of historical background, (2) analysis of New Testament documents, and (3) synthesis of findings. In order to understand the New Testament teaching, the work of each writer must be viewed within its historical setting and within the larger context of precedent thought. The teaching on mission in the Old Testament and intertestamental Judaism must be examined, as well as the teaching of Jesus and the early church. With that background established, this study will proceed in roughly canonical order, with some adjustments for chronology, to analyze the thought of Paul, Matthew, Mark, Luke-Acts, the General Epistles, John, and Revelation. A concluding synthesis can then draw together the strands of teaching uncovered.

The specific research method for each New Testament writer will first of all probe the historical setting for his thought, so that the historical and situational factors that led to his distinctive expression of the mission concept may be understood properly. The study will then seek evidence for the writer's view of the theme of mission. Word studies of *apostellō, pempō, erchomai, poreuomai, kērussō, euangelion, ethnos, basileia,* and cognates as appropriate will be the starting point. In the light of a basic profile on mission, an attempt will be made to discover the way in which the writer's manner of composition manifests his desire to highlight this theme. The basic profile will also lead to the identification of key passages that must receive detailed treatment. For example, key texts from various authors for the church's universal mission are Matthew 10:1-42; 28:16-20; Mark 13:9-13; Luke 4:16-30; 9:1-6; 10:1-16; 24:44-48; John 3:13-19; 4:1-42; 20:21-23; Acts 1:8; 20:13-35; 26:16-18; Romans 1:1-5; 15:14-33; Galatians 1:11-17; 1 Thessalonians 1:9-10; Hebrews 13:13; 1 Peter 2:9-12; 1 John 4:9-11.

## INTERPRETATIONAL ISSUES

In addition to the contribution that such a comprehensive study can make through a synthetic presentation of New Testament thought on mission, there is also an opportunity to address certain standard interpretational issues involved in this issue. Hahn and Senior/Stuhlmueller have already brought to our attention some of these. First, there is the question of whether any of the New Testament books may be properly classed as missionary documents, that is, works intended to further mission because they have an evangelistic purpose and are addressed to non-Christians.[10] Related to that question is the matter of which books do or do not have a mission concern. Normally, Paul's prison and pastoral epistles, together with certain of the General Epistles, are judged to a greater or lesser degree to contain the mission theme.[11]

Second, there is the matter of the roots for the early church's commitment to a universal mission. In what way does the Old Testament prepare the way for it? Put more candidly, does the Old Testament itself have the concept of mission? Again, Hahn and Senior/Stuhlmueller give varying assessments.[12] Did Judaism in the intertestamental period manifest a sense of spiritual mission to the nations?[13] Further, during his earthly ministry, what was Jesus' understanding of his mission and that of his disciples, especially with reference to its universal character? What relationship did this have to the universal mission that the early church undertook?[14]

---

[10] Fiorenza ("Miracles," 2) says that they should be viewed as propaganda; Senior and Stuhlmueller (*Biblical Foundations*, 162, 211) consistently say that they should not, although they do see the gospels as "mission documents for the church itself, meant to justify, renew, and motivate the church's claim on the heritage of Jesus' boundary-breaking ministry" (211).

[11] Hahn (*Mission*, chap. 6) finds less "mission" in these, while Senior and Stuhlmueller (*Biblical Foundations*, chaps. 8, 13) find more.

[12] Hahn, *Mission*, chap. 1; Senior and Stuhlmueller, *Biblical Foundations*, chaps. 1-5.

[13] See Scot McKnight, *A Light among the Gentiles: Jewish Missionary Activity in the Second Temple Period* (Minneapolis: Fortress, 1990).

[14] S. McKnight, "Gentiles," in *DJG*, ed. Joel B. Green and Scot McKnight (Downers Grove, Ill.: InterVarsity, 1992), 259-65.

Third, how are we in this generation to understand the nature of the connection between church and mission? Given the fact that New Testament documents representing the second and third spiritual generations seem to show a separation of church and mission, Hahn concludes that each spiritual generation is responsible to raise and answer this question anew.[15]

Hahn and Senior/Stuhlmueller have also left us with some unfinished business. Senior/Stuhlmueller explicitly stated two "unanswered questions" that have yet to be satisfactorily addressed: (1) the relationship of the worldwide mission of the church to the unique role of Israel in salvation history; and (2) the relationship of Christianity's unique and exclusive offer of salvation to the non-Christian religions' positive values and salvific claims.[16] Though New Testament scholars have recently given attention to these issues,[17] they remain within the purview of any study of mission in the New Testament.

The historical-critical method approach of Hahn and Senior/Stuhlmueller naturally calls for a conservative evangelical study to "continue the conversation," especially concerning historical reconstructions. The articulation of Jesus' understanding of mission recovered from form and redaction-critical analysis must be tested and adjusted to yield a profile that squares with a historical reconstruction compatible with a confidence in the historical reliability of the gospel accounts. The same testing and adjustment must be pursued with reference to the reconstructed Palestinian-Jewish and Hellenistic-Jewish-Christian approaches to mission. The conservative evangelical acceptance of the explicit testimony to authorship found in New Testament books means dealing with historical settings different from those proposed by Hahn and Senior/Stuhlmueller. The category of canonical deutero-pauline literature becomes unnecessary. As for the Synoptic Gospels and Acts, most conservative evangelicals place these books in historical settings before 70 C.E., taking seriously the early external evidence for authorship, setting, and composition, as well as internal evidence for the closeness of author and composition to the events.[18] This

---

[15] Hahn, *Mission*, 170.

[16] Senior and Stuhlmueller, *Biblical Foundations*, 344-46.

[17] Craig A. Evans and Donald A. Hagner, *Anti-Semitism and Early Christianity* (Minneapolis: Fortress, 1993); Joseph B. Tyson, ed., *Luke-Acts and the Jewish People: Eight Critical Perspectives* (Minneapolis: Augsburg, 1988); Andrew D. Clarke and Bruce W. Winter, eds., *One God, One Lord: Christianity in a World of Religious Pluralism* (Grand Rapids: Baker, 1992); Edward Rommen and Harold Netland, eds., *Christianity and the Religions: A Biblical Theology of World Religions*, EMS Missiological Monographs, no. 2 (Pasadena, Calif.: William Carey Library, 1995).

[18] Cf. D. A. Carson, Douglas J. Moo, and Leon Morris, *An Introduction to the New Testament* (Grand Rapids: Zondervan, 1992), 66-79, 92-99, 113-18, 185-99.

also differs from the Hahn and Senior/Stuhlmueller starting points. Since a biblical theology looks to historical setting/background as a key component in the unfolding of scripture's theological thought, these differences in settings will lead to a different articulation of the mission theme.

Paul Bowers describes previous studies in the biblical theology of mission, as they relate to Pauline research, as tending "more to offer summary and synthesis of scholarly findings than to break new ground."[19] As this study is able, it will seek to "break new ground" as it attempts to expound the concept of mission in each portion of the New Testament. For example, according to Bowers, E. P. Sanders originally identified as one of the primary convictions that shaped Paul's theology the fact that he "was called to be an apostle to the Gentiles."[20] Although some have seen the formative place the Gentile mission holds in Paul's theology,[21] Sanders's suggestive pointer has, in the main, been undeveloped as scholars have concentrated on Sanders's other concern: the relation of Paul to the Law and Judaism.[22] There is, then, still a need in Pauline studies to address "questions surrounding the place of Paul's mission in his theological reflection."[23]

## OCCASION AND CONTRIBUTORS

The catalyst for this study comes not only from the factors listed under "Aim and Rationale" above. Columbia International University and its constituent schools, Columbia Bible College and Columbia Biblical Seminary and Graduate School of Missions, are celebrating a seventy-fifth anniversary in 1998. Alumni live in ninety-seven countries, the vast majority serving in foreign missions.

The New Testament faculty members of Columbia International University believe that an appropriate way to mark that occasion is to further the understanding of the biblical foundations of mission. We have gathered together New Testament scholars, either Columbia educators or alumni, to add our voices to the discussion in the hopes that a church more faithful to the last great command of the Lord will complete the task of evangelizing the world in this generation.

---

[19] W. P. Bowers, "Mission," in *DPHL*, ed. Gerald F. Hawthorne and Ralph P. Martin (Downers Grove, Ill.: InterVarsity, 1993), 614.

[20] E. P. Sanders, *Paul and Palestinian Judaism* (Philadelphia: Fortress, 1977), 441-42.

[21] N. T. Wright, "The Paul of History and the Apostle of Faith," *TynBul* 29 (1978): 61-88; J. D. G. Dunn, "The New Perspective on Paul," *BJRL* 65 (1983): 95-122.

[22] Stephen Westerholm, *Israel's Law and the Church's Faith: Paul and His Recent Interpreters* (Grand Rapids: Eerdmans, 1988); Frank Thielman, *Paul and the Law: A Contextual Approach* (Downers Grove, Ill.: InterVarsity, 1994).

[23] Bowers, "Mission," 618.

*PART ONE*

# BACKGROUND

# 1

# *Mission in the Old Testament*

## Ferris L. McDaniel

Whenever a study appears concerning one of the biblical testaments, it is customary for the other testament to provide a foreword (for New Testament studies) or an appendix (for Old Testament studies). The prefix furnishes the antecedent background to whatever New Testament concept or action is probed. A New Testament suffix gives the fulfillment, continuity, or discontinuity of the Old Testament analysis. In this study, the Old Testament will play handmaiden to the New.

Of necessity an OT preface to a NT theme could be painted with broad strokes or the canvas might be smaller, showing more detail but less scope. The present treatment is of the more limited variety. The NT action is that of the missionary enterprise; its study is a theology of mission. Many biblical theologies of missions present the OT material in a more comprehensive way. This study will portray just part of the picture. Jesus was raised from death and promised an empowerment to the disciples for mission. His commission reduces to this: God sends. The question must arise, Is there any anticipation of this action or any informing theology in the OT for the action of God sending? In this study, the link between the testaments will be lexical. The Greek word for sending, *apostellō*, almost always translates the Hebrew *šālaḥ*. And happily there are over eight hundred uses of *šālaḥ* in the Hebrew Bible, with just over two hundred of these taking God as the subject. In those passages with God as subject, the LXX uses *apostellō* or a compound of it to translate the Hebrew *šālaḥ* in three-quarters of its usages.[1] The

---

[1] The LXX translates the Hebrew with the uncompounded *apostellō* well over one hundred times when God is the subject. In over thirty references *exapostellō* is used. In the LXX's translation of the books of the Hebrew Bible, *apostellō* is used over five hundred times and translates the Hebrew

Jews of Jesus' day would have linked his action of sending with the OT word.

I will divide the present portrait into two parts. The first part presents parallels between the "secular" uses of *šālaḥ* (human sending) and the divine uses (God's sending).[2] The second part examines, in particular, divine sending in the OT by showing the story of God's work of sending.

## PARALLELS BETWEEN SECULAR AND DIVINE SENDING

The study of *šālaḥ* in the Hebrew Bible yields a variety of non-theological idioms and nuances. To understand divine sending, we must consider these secular uses of the word. By analogy, they will provide a picture of divine sending.[3]

The first feature of "sending" is so obvious as to be consistently overlooked: the sender purposes to do something. Sending is a product of the will. The organic connection of *šālaḥ* to the will is seen in the "sending" or "stretching out" of the hand so as to accomplish the will of the sender.[4] Abraham reaches for the knife (Gen. 22:10), Jael the tent-peg (Judg. 5:26), and Samson the jaw-bone (Judg. 15:15). Noah reaches to receive the dove into the ark (Gen. 8:9) and Uzzah to steady

---

*šālaḥ* in all but thirty texts. In this study I will not differentiate the LXX passages using *apostellō* from those using *exapostellō*. The usages for both overlap to a great degree. For example, in 2 Samuel 22:15 and 17 the LXX uses *apostellō* while for the same text in Psalm 18:15(14) and 17(16; LXX Ps. 17:15, 17) it uses *exapostellō*. In a number of texts one LXX manuscript will use one and another the other. Only when some other Greek word is used to translate *šālaḥ* will it be noted. Also, when the English verse number does not match that of the Hebrew Bible, the Hebrew reference will be placed first in the listing. For references to the LXX, see Alfred Rahlfs, *Septuaginta*, 2 vols. (Stuttgart: Württembergische Bibelanstalt, 1935).

[2] For this breakdown of the use of *šālaḥ* illustrated in the book of Isaiah, see P. Bernard Wodecki, "*ŠLḤ* dans le livre d'Isaïe," *VT* 34 (1984): 482-88.

[3] I will not discuss every nuance of the verb *šālaḥ,* because not every use has a divine parallel. These are mostly having to do with familial contexts, for example, sending a son to find a wife (Gen. 28:5), giving a departing family member a proper send-off (Gen. 31:27), sending a son to check up on his brothers (Gen. 37:14), sending goods to one's father (Gen. 45:23), and so on. One familial use does have a divine parallel—the sending away of divorcement. The Law gives instructions regarding divorce (Deut. 22:19, 29; 24:1, 3, 4). The prophets use the figure of the bill of divorcement for the action of God sending the people into captivity (Isa. 50:1; Jer. 3:8). When God sends in the Old Testament, however, it is usually in a context that parallels the action of a political or religious authority figure.

[4] Most often the LXX translates this idiom using *ekteinō*.

the Ark of the Covenant (2 Sam. 6:6 [hand unexpressed]). These illustrate sending as a purposeful act.

The LORD also "stretches out his hand" to perform his will. He will do this to force Pharaoh to let Israel leave the land (Exod. 3:20). His punishment against unfaithful Judah is his hand sent forth (Ezek. 14:13). Likewise Satan entices God to "put forth" his hand against Job (Job 1:11-12; 2:5). It is the LORD's outstretched hand that touches Jeremiah's lips as God puts his words in Jeremiah's mouth and commissions him to be his spokesman (Jer. 1:9). God's stretching out of his hand is a graphic metaphorical picture of action performing his will.

Another idiom reveals the connection with the will of the sender. Although rare, this word is used of an enemy "sending fire" (setting fire) to a foe's defenses.[5] The enemy purposes to destroy his foe (Judg. 20:48; 2 Kgs. 8:12; Ps. 74:7 [LXX 73:7]). The LORD also sends his fiery arrows (2 Sam. 22:15/Ps. 18:15[14; LXX 17:15]) against David's enemies and fire against Israel's foes (Amos 1:4, 7, 10, 12; 2:2, 5). Psalm 144:6-7 uses the LORD's sending of arrows and lightning (LXX Ps. 143: *astraptō*) as well as the LORD's stretching of his hand to describe the rescue of the psalmist. Throughout the other nuances of this verb, the aspect of sending as a willful act will also be present. This is illustrated in the number of times it is used with the Hebrew *lāmed* with the infinitive construct, often the construction for a purpose clause.[6]

A second observation growing out of the hundreds of "secular" sendings involves the authority of the sending party. In over three hundred uses, it is a judge or other person of rank, especially a king, who sends.[7] In many instances a nuance of "command" or "give orders that/to" would be an acceptable translation.[8] This authority is seen in the context of sending out spies (e.g., Num. 13:2, 3; Deut. 1:22; Josh. 2:1; 1 Sam. 26:4 [LXX 26:5]). It lies behind the expulsion of Abram and Sarai (Gen. 12:20 [LXX: *sumpropempō*]) from Egypt. God sends Moses (Exod. 3:10) to ask Pharaoh's permission to let the children of Israel go (literally, "send them," e.g., Exod. 4:21; 5:2; 9:17; 10:20). This is a contest of two wills; God will remove his people by rendering the will (literally "heart") of Pharaoh obstinate (Exod. 4:21; 7:3, 13; 9:12; 14:4). In scores of other references, a king or ruler issues com-

---

[5] Perhaps this indicates that the fire was hurled by means of some device. Fire was used in the defense of a city at the time of Sennacherib. See James B. Pritchard, ed., *The Ancient Near East in Pictures* (Princeton: Princeton University Press, 1969), 130-31, 293-94.

[6] In over two hundred references *šālaḥ* is followed with an infinitive construct.

[7] The LXX translates with *apostellō* in two-thirds of these contexts. If *exapostellō* is added to these, the number is almost total.

[8] J. Ellington, "Send!" *BT* 45 (1994): 228-38. In Jeremiah 23:32 and 1 Samuel 21:3(2) "send" is placed parallel to "command."

mands to be carried out by subordinates. For example, the king of Jericho sends to Rahab concerning the spies (Josh. 2:3).[9] Joshua sends warriors by night toward Ai (Josh. 8:3). Saul sends messengers to watch for and seize David (1 Sam. 19:11, 14, 15). David sends ten men to Nabal to request aid (1 Sam. 25:5). Solomon sends Benaiah to kill Joab (1 Kgs. 2:29). Everywhere in royal narrative kings use their authority to perform their will.[10]

Similarly divine sending displays the authority of the LORD. He sends Adam and Eve out of the Garden (Gen. 3:23), thrusts the Canaanite from the land (Lev. 20:23), sends out Rezin against Judah (2 Kgs. 15:37), prepares to send Hananiah to his death (Jer. 28:16 [LXX 34:16]), and sends his horsemen to patrol the earth (Zech. 1:10). In the contest of authority with Pharaoh, the LORD sends Moses to declare his demand for the release of Israel (Exod. 3:10, 14-15), but God also sends foreign agents to destroy Judah and capture his people (2 Kgs. 24:2; Jer. 16:16; 43:10 [LXX 50:10]). Solomon recognizes that the LORD might send his people out to war (1 Kgs. 8:44 [LXX: *epistrephō*]). God's sending prerogative mirrors that of an earthly king's, and this parallel is probably intentional. God is seen as the king exercising his will over the affairs of earth.[11]

A third part to the OT picture emerges logically from the first two. Because sending is an expression of the will of an authority figure, there is reluctance on the part of the one sent to disobey. The OT has few who refuse such a commission. David is obedient to go wherever Saul sends him (1 Sam. 18:5). Jonathan must endure the wrath of his father for questioning Saul's command to send for David so he could kill him (1 Sam. 20:31-33). The third captain of fifty is sent to encounter Elisha, knowing that the first two bands sent had been destroyed by fire from heaven. He obeys, but pleads with Elisha for his life and the life of his men (2 Kgs. 1:9-14).

There are two examples of men who were reluctant to be sent of God. Moses desires that someone else be sent to bring the children of Israel out of Egypt (Exod. 4:13). For this he must endure the anger of the LORD (v. 14). The irony is he addresses God as 'ădōnāy, by which he claims that God is his master. Similarly, Jeremiah, said to be sent by God no fewer than six times (Jer. 1:7; 19:14; 26:12, 15 [LXX 33:12, 15]; 42:21 [LXX 49:21]; 43:1 [LXX 50:1]), tries to stifle the proclama-

---

[9] Even though subordinates are not mentioned, a truly intransitive use of šālaḥ would be unusual, suggesting the sending of messengers. See Ellington, "Send!," 228-29.

[10] Likewise, the NT centurion recognizes that summoning and sending assume authority (Matt. 8:9; Luke 7:8).

[11] Interestingly, Jesus prefaces his commission with a declaration of universal authority (Matt. 28:18).

tion of the message and finds that he cannot (20:9). The price of his obedience causes him to curse the day of his birth (20:14-18). It is understood that the sending of God is a commission requiring obedience. As recorded in the OT, it is rarely disregarded or questioned.

A final observation of "secular" sending involves the use of messengers. Persons in authority, especially kings, use envoys in the process of diplomacy. The sending of messengers (Hebrew *mal'āk*, Greek *angelos, presbus*)[12] from kings or governors is recorded over two dozen times. For example, Moses sends messengers to request passage (Num. 20:14; Deut. 2:26). Gideon summons Israel by sending messengers (Judg. 7:24). Jephthah sends them to the king of Ammon (Judg. 11:12, 14). Ahab and Ben-Hadad exchange words through messengers (1 Kgs. 20:2, 9 [LXX 21:2, 9]). Amaziah "picks a fight" this way (2 Kgs. 14:8).

A context similar to the sending of messengers is the sending of letters or a word. This idiom is found more than twenty times in the OT. Pharaoh sends and calls Moses and Aaron (Exod. 9:27). Balak sends word to Balaam (Num. 22:10). The kings of Jerusalem and Hazor sent word to other kings for help against Joshua (Josh. 10:3; 11:1). David sends a letter by the hand of Uriah (2 Sam. 11:14). Solomon and Hiram exchange words (1 Kgs. 5:16, 22[2, 8]). Jezebel sends letters in her plot against Naboth (1 Kgs. 21:8, 11 [LXX 20:8, 11]). Elisha sends warning of a Syrian threat (2 Kgs. 6:9). Sennacherib sends words of reproach against the LORD (Isa. 37:17). Jeremiah sends instruction to various kings (Jer. 27:3 [LXX 34:3]). Mordecai is authorized to send letters to all the districts in the name of the king (Esth. 9:20). In all of these the sending is an official pronouncement stating the will of the sender.

It is against this background of authorized communique that the messengers and words the LORD sends may be viewed. From Moses throughout the prophetic tradition, the prophets are the sent of God. Over thirty times the OT speaks of God's sending of a prophet (especially Moses and Jeremiah), with at least eight of these speaking of the sending of God's servants, the prophets. In addition, God often sends angels to do his bidding.[13]

In summary, the process of sending in the OT often involves an authority figure commanding a subordinate. It is an official act by which the intentions and desires of the sovereign are performed or communicated. In these ways, the instances of divine sending parallel human sending.

---

[12] Both Hebrew *mal'āk* and Greek *angelos* can be translated as "messenger" or as "angel." A king's sending of a messenger is paralleled by God's sending of an angel or messenger.

[13] A fuller discussion of these will appear later in the study.

## THE STORY OF DIVINE SENDING

A study of the similarities between secular and divine sending provides clues to the emphases of *šālaḥ*, but this does not show the "story" of God's sending through the OT period. To observe this we must view the categories of usage for divine sending in particular. The OT presents a picture of God as the divine sovereign LORD who sends in order to convey and accomplish his will upon the earth. Perhaps no passage illustrates this as well as Isaiah 55:11. The LORD says concerning his word (*dābār*) that it will accomplish that for which he would send it. The LXX caught the force of this by translating it, "until whatsoever I have willed shall have been accomplished."[14] This divine word almost takes on a force of its own, working the will of the LORD in history. The divine word (*dābār*) sent against Jacob "falls on Israel" (Isa. 9:7[8]).[15] It will destroy the plans they have to build up their defenses. Psalm 107:20 (LXX 106:20) states that the LORD sent his word (*dābār*) and it healed them and delivered them from destructions (literally "pits"). When God says that he will send his word, it is a statement that God purposes to accomplish his will in history.[16]

Another aspect of God's sending in the OT has to do with his exiling of sinners. The LORD sends Adam and Eve out of the Garden of Eden (Gen. 3:23). For resisting God's word, God will send (remove by death) Hananiah (Jer. 28:16 [LXX 35:16]). On the corporate level, God casts out the debauched nations of Canaan before the children of Israel (Lev. 18:24; 20:23). However, God will also send his people out of the land for their sin (Jer. 15:1; 25:9). This sending away is likened to a bill of divorcement (Isa. 50:1; Jer. 3:8). Those who sin are sent away, exiled by the offended deity.

The LORD sends a variety of agents to punish wrongdoing. In the case of Sodom and Gomorrah, God sends angels (Gen. 19:13, cf. v. 1). In his contest with Pharaoh, the LORD sends plagues, his burning anger, destroying angels (Exod. 9:14; 15:7; Num. 20:16; Pss. 78:45, 49;

---

[14] *heōs an suntelesthē hosa ēthelēsa.*

[15] The LXX uses *apostellō* but says that it is death that is sent (Isa. 9:8).

[16] The creation account of Genesis 1 testifies to the force of the accomplishing word; all things were created when God spoke. This anticipates the New Testament teaching that the Word, who is Jesus Christ, created all things (John 1:1-3; cf. Col. 1:16; Heb. 1:2). He is also the effectual sustainer (Col. 1:17), upholding all things by the word of his power (Heb. 1:3). Peter speaks of the word that created all things and is now reserving the present heavens and earth for a future flood of fire (2 Pet. 3:5-7). See Warren A. Gage, *The Gospel of Genesis* (Winona Lake, Ind.: Carpenter Books, 1984), 32-33. In the giving of the Law, the LORD gives the "ten words" (Deut. 10:4). These moral words are statements of God's absolute will.

135:9 [LXX 77:45, 49; 134:9]), and darkness (Ps. 105:28 [LXX 104:28]). God promises that an angel will drive out the people of Canaan (Exod. 33:2 [LXX: *sunapostellō*]). In the conquest, he will also send ahead of them his terror and hornets (Exod. 23:27-28; Deut. 7:20; Josh. 24:12). He sends an evil spirit between the men of Shechem and Abimelich to punish his treachery (Judg. 9:23). God sends lions on those whom Assyria had exiled to the promised land because they did not fear the God of that land (2 Kgs. 17:25, 26).

Similarly, if Israel sins against its God, he will send his agents. He sends fiery serpents upon the people in the wilderness (Num. 21:6) and wasting disease (Ps. 106:15 [LXX 105:15]). If they disobey the covenant, God promises to send beasts, pestilence, famine (Lev. 26:22; Deut. 32:24; Ezek. 5:17), the curses of the covenant (Deut. 28:20), and enemies against them (Deut. 28:48). Israel does not obey. God warns them by sending locusts (Joel 2:25). He sends a plague to cause them to return to him (Amos 4:10). God sends Rezin (2 Kgs. 15:37) and bands of enemies (2 Kgs. 24:2) against Judah. He sends them stubborn hearts (Ps. 81:13[12; LXX 80:13]). Through his prophet, the LORD promises to send the sword to kill them (Jer. 9:15[16]) along with famine and pestilence (Jer. 24:10), wild beasts and serpents (Jer. 8:16 [LXX 8:17]; Ezek. 14:21). He will send fire against the cities (Hos. 8:14; Amos 2:5). The LORD will send Assyria against his godless people (Isa. 10:6). He will send for Nebuchadnezzar to rule over the land (Jer. 43:10 [LXX 50:10]). Ultimately, it will be his anger he will send against them (Ezek. 7:3 [LXX 7:7]). The Lord ('*ādôn*) will send a famine of his word (Amos 8:11).

However, it is not only against Israel that the LORD will send agents of calamity. After using Assyria as a club in his hand, the Lord ('*ādôn*), God of Armies, will also send a wasting disease among Assyria's troops for its arrogance (Isa. 10:16). The LORD sends Jeremiah against the nations with a cup of wrath, a sword he will send against them (Jer. 25:15-17, 27 [LXX 32:15-17, 27]); he will send a sword against Elam (Jer. 49:37 [LXX 25:37]) and foreigners to devastate Babylon (Jer. 51:2 [LXX 28:2]). He will send pestilence and blood against Sidon (Ezek. 28:23). The Lord ('*ādôn*) will send fire upon Magog (Ezek. 39:6) and against Hazael, Gaza, Tyre, Teman, and Moab (Amos 1:4, 7, 10, 12; 2:2). God will send agents to "tip over" Moab (Jer. 48:12 [LXX 31:12]).

The Old Testament reveals that Israel's God has the prerogative to send calamity upon his people and all peoples. This sending to covenant and non-covenant peoples alike is a strong statement of his purposeful sovereignty over all of the nations of the earth. Yet the disposition of the LORD is to save. He receives no delight in destroying the wicked; he would rather they repent (Ezek. 18:23; 33:11).

Not surprising, then, the LORD sends benefit and salvation. With respect to his people, God sends in order to establish and preserve them. He sends his angel to help Abraham's servant find a wife for Isaac (Gen. 24:7, 40). God sends Joseph to Egypt to preserve his people (Gen. 45:5, 7, 8; Ps. 105:17 [LXX 104:17]). He promises to send an angel to guard them and bring them to the promised land (Exod. 23:20). The ordaining of the covenant is a sending of salvation from the LORD (Ps. 111:9 [LXX 110:9]). In the wilderness he sends abundant food (Ps. 78:25 [LXX 77:25]). He sends a prophet to predict victory over the Midianites and sends Gideon against them (Judg. 6:8, 14). The judges are sent by God (1 Sam. 12:11). The LORD sends Saul to Samuel to be anointed king of his people (1 Sam. 9:16; 15:1), and later God sends Samuel to anoint David (1 Sam. 16:1). God sends Saul to subdue the Amalekites (1 Sam. 15:18, 20). After the locust plague, the LORD promises to send grain, new wine, and oil (Joel 2:19). Even the captivity, which is a sending of calamity for the nation, is a beneficent sending for the good captives (Jer. 24:5).

On the personal level, God sends Lot out of the city before he destroys it (Gen. 19:29). Samson's father asks that God send the man of God (revealed as the Angel of the LORD) to instruct them regarding their unborn son (Judg. 13:8). David blesses the LORD, who sent Abigail with her wise counsel (1 Sam. 25:32). David praises God, who had in times of difficulty sent arrows (lightning) scattering David's enemies (2 Sam. 22:15/Ps. 18:15[14; LXX 17:15]) and who had sent and taken David out of difficulty (2 Sam. 22:17/Ps. 18:17[16; LXX 17:17]). The congregation prays that the LORD send the king help in battle (Ps. 20:3[2; LXX 19:3]). The psalmist prays that God send his light and truth to guide him (Ps. 43:3 [LXX 42:3]). The psalmist is also confident that God will send his lovingkindness and truth to save him (Ps. 57:4[3; LXX 56:4]). The directness of the LORD's helping the psalmist against his enemies is seen in its description as a sending of his hand (Ps. 138:7; 144:7 [LXX 137:7: *exeteinō*; 143:7]). Nebuchadnezzar blesses Israel's God who sent his messenger to deliver the three from the fire and Daniel confesses that his God sent an angel to shut the mouths of the lions (Dan. 3:28 [LXX 3:95]; and 6:23[22; LXX 6:23 Theodotion]; both Aramaic *šĕlaḥ*).

Throughout the OT the sovereign God is sending that which benefits his people, but that also speaks of his sending with respect to the world as his creation and his relationship to mankind generally. Rain is the sending of his command (Ps. 147:15 [LXX 147:4]) and at the sending of his word snow and ice melt (Ps. 147:18 [LXX 146:7]). He sends forth springs and sends his Spirit (or breath) and creates man (Ps. 104:10, 30 [LXX 103:10, 30]). Eliphaz says that it is God who sends water for the fields (Job 5:10). Job responds to Zophar that God does send water but it is a destroying flood (Job 12:15; LXX: *epaphiēmi*). Indeed, God overpowers man and changes his appearance (in old age) and then sends him away (to his death; Job 14:20). By implication, the book of Job shows that God sends lightning (38:35) and lets loose the wild donkey (39:5 [LXX: *aphiēmi*]). In all of these poetic passages, some of the very basic events of life are called God-sent.

More frequently than any other use, however, is the association between God's sending and the office of prophet. The outstanding example in the OT is Moses (sometimes listed with his brother, Aaron). Throughout the OT, Moses is described as the one sent by the LORD (Exod. 3:10-15; Deut. 34:11; 1 Sam. 12:8; Ps. 105:26 [LXX 104:26]). The LORD sends Nathan and Gad to David (2 Sam. 12:1; 24:13). He asks Isaiah whom he should send; Isaiah says, "Send me" (Isa. 6:8). God's Spirit on him is an anointing to bring good news (*euaggelizō*), and he is sent to bind up the brokenhearted (Isa. 61:1).[17] The LORD tells Jeremiah that he will go wherever he is sent (Jer. 1:7). In his career Jeremiah must assert that God has sent him (19:14; 26:12, 15 [LXX 33:12, 15]; 42:21 [LXX 49:21]; 43:1 [LXX 50:1]) and has not sent the false prophets (14:14, 15; 23:21, 32; 27:15 [LXX 34:15]; 28:15 [LXX 35:15]; 29:9 [LXX 36:9]). God sends Ezekiel (3:5-6) but once again not the false prophets (13:6). The people believe that the LORD has sent Haggai (1:12).

A recurring theme in the prophets is that God consistently sent his servants, the prophets, throughout the history of Israel (2 Kgs. 17:13; Jer. 7:25; 25:4; 26:5 [LXX 33:5]; 29:19; 35:15 [LXX 42:15]; 44:4 [LXX 51:4]; Zech. 7:12). The truly sent prophet was the one whose words would come to pass (Jer. 28:9 [LXX 35:9]). The LORD had said that he would raise up a prophet like Moses, whose pronouncements would come to pass (Deut. 18:18-22). This sending of prophets to tell of God's designs probably foreshadows the mission of proclaiming the good news through the prophetic scriptures (Rom. 16:25-26).

Through the prophet, the LORD promises those held captive that he will send a savior and champion to deliver them (Isa. 19:20). After the captivity God promises to send his messenger (Mal. 3:1), Elijah, before him (Mal. 3:23 [4:5; LXX 3:22]). He will send a surviving remnant from among the nations to declare the glory of God and to serve as priests (Isa. 66:19-21). These promises of salvation and worldwide benefit point directly to the New Testament doctrine of the salvation Christ secured and the sending of that message to the whole world.[18]

---

[17] Christ applies these words to his ministry in Luke 4:18. The degree to which this declaring of good news can be applied to the New Testament mission generally requires further study.

[18] Roger D. Aus ("Paul's Travel Plans to Spain and the 'Full Number of the Gentiles' of Rom. XI 25," *NovT* 21 [1979]: 237-42) argues that Paul understands Isaiah 66 as the theological foundation to his desire to preach the word to Spain, and, in part, of his entire mission to the Gentiles. He also draws parallels between the list of nations mentioned in Isaiah 66:19 and the missionary journeys of Paul.

## CONCLUSION

The Creator God, who sent humankind from paradise (Gen. 3) and scattered it across the face of the earth (Gen. 10:1-11:9), also promised that all nations would be blessed through the seed of one man, Abraham (Gen. 11:10-12:3). This Sovereign continued to involve himself with creation in order to accomplish his will. This involvement is often seen in the action of God's sending, especially his sending of the prophets. At times they proclaimed a message of judgment, but it is God's delight to send the message of salvation and hope leading to repentance and fellowship. Isaiah looks to a time when the LORD will send a remnant to the entire earth, and peoples from far nations will worship Israel's God (Isa. 66:19; cf. 19:18-25).[19] This will be fulfilled when Christians, sent by God, accomplish their mission.

---

[19] Significant in the Isaiah 66:19 passage is the mention of nations listed in the table of nations in Genesis 10. This suggests an undoing of Babel as the nations come together and with one voice praise their God (cf. Rev. 5:9-14).

# 2

# Mission in Intertestamental Judaism

## Clifford H. Bedell

Although the intertestamental period has been defined in various ways, this study marks the beginning of this era at the time of Malachi's prophecy in the middle of the fifth century B.C.E.[1] and its ending at 51 C.E. with the writing of Paul's Thessalonian letters.[2] A wide range of primary sources for this period of Jewish history is available, including ethnic and religious histories (principally Jewish and Roman), wisdom literature, stories, apocalypses, and so on; moreover, the New Testament should not be overlooked as a significant source for information concerning the intertestamental period. In addition to ancient sources there exists a growing body of modern literature that treats directly or indirectly the question of the Jewish mission during the intertestamental period.[3] The Jewish people faced a set of circumstances during this

---

[1] Gleason L. Archer Jr. (*A Survey of Old Testament Introduction*, 2d ed. [Chicago: Moody, 1974], 431) places the date at 435 B.C.E. Robert H. Pfeiffer (*Introduction to the Old Testament* [New York: Harper & Brothers, 1948], 614) locates the time of writing at about 460 B.C.E.

[2] See Merrill C. Tenney, *New Testament Survey*, 2d ed. (Grand Rapids: Eerdmans, 1985), 263-73, for the possibility that James and Galatians were written earlier than 51 C.E.

[3] Some of the most helpful of these are Paul Bowers, "Paul and Religious Propaganda in the First Century," *NovT* 22 (1980): 316-23; H. L. Ellison, *From Babylon to Bethlehem: The Jewish People from the Exile to the Messiah* (Exeter: Paternoster, 1976); Martin Goodman, *Mission and Conversion: Proselytizing in the Religious History of the Roman Empire* (Oxford: Clarendon Press, 1994); Ferdinand Hahn, *Mission in the New Testament*, trans. Frank Clarke, SBT, no. 47 (Naperville, Ill.: Alec R. Allenson, 1965), 21-25; Joachim Jeremias, *Jesus' Promise to the Nations* (reprint, Philadelphia: Fortress, 1982); Scot McKnight, *A Light among the Gentiles: Jewish*

time that differed from earlier periods in their history, with some of these circumstances affecting their attitudes toward Gentiles and mission. In addition, several recent studies have examined the extent and nature of a Jewish mission to Gentiles during the intertestamental period. Israel was to be "a light to the Gentiles" (Isa. 42:6; 49:6). Were Gentiles actually being enlightened? Were any Jews actually seeking to missionize Gentiles?

## THE IMPORTANCE OF A NEW SETTING

God had spoken regularly to his people by the prophets over the centuries (Jer. 7:25), but the prophetic voice seems to have been silenced during the intertestamental period. When Judas Maccabeus and his brothers were perplexed as to what they should do with the defiled altar-stones, no prophetic word was offered to provide direction (1 Macc. 4:46). Shortly after this, the Jewish people resolved to have Simon as their leader and high priest until the appearance of a trustworthy prophet (1 Macc. 14:41). Perhaps, the increasing reliance on oral tradition as well as the frequent use of pseudepigraphy during this time also assume a recognition of prophetic silence on the part of Jewish people. It is unsuitable, then, to look for a prophetic word in the intertestamental period in which God sends his people to fulfill a particular task. The Sender may still send, but the sending comes as a subjective, internal (and therefore ultimately unverifiable) conviction in response to "the word of the LORD" as it came to the Jewish people through the repeated reading of the scriptures in the synagogues.

During the United and Divided Kingdoms, Jews tended to relate to the surrounding peoples on the national level, and on this level relations were frequently hostile and militaristic. But with the Assyrian and the Babylonian captivities a new social situation prevailed; Jews now had to learn to live in alien social environments among the idolatrous pagans. Kuhn writes of "a different sociological structure."[4] The dynamics of social relationship had changed from an emphasis on the national level to a focus on personal relations. Formerly it had been the Gentile, as the resident alien, who had interacted with Jews on the personal level. The resident alien had been part of a minority and the Jews in the majority, but now the demographics were reversed. Social

---

*Missionary Activity in the Second Temple Period* (Minneapolis: Fortress Press, 1990); Emil Schürer, *The History of the Jewish People in the Age of Jesus Christ (175 B.C.—A.D. 135)*, ed. by Geza Vermes, Fergus Millar, and Martin Goodman (Edinburgh: T. & T. Clark, 1986), 3:150-76; J. Julius Scott, *Customs and Controversies: Intertestamental Jewish Backgrounds of the New Testament* (Grand Rapids: Baker, 1995), 335-52.

[4] Karl Georg Kuhn, "*prosēlytos*," *TDNT* 6:730.

pressures forced Jews to relate to Gentiles personally in the market and in the forum instead of on the battlefield or as a minority subject people. The resident alien had been under some benign social pressure to convert to Judaism; the pagan masses among which the Jewish Dispersion lived were under no such pressure. New forces must evolve if these were to convert to the God of Israel. The return to the land after the Babylonian captivity did little to reduce personal contact with Gentiles. A large Jewish Diaspora continued to live outside of the land of Israel during the intertestamental period. Jews within the land continued to have contact with Gentiles, since for much of this period they were a conquered people living in an occupied territory.

This increased personal contact with Gentiles led to a range of opinions toward them within intertestamental Judaism.[5] Some Jews took a dim view of Gentiles. For the writer of the Psalms of Solomon, the Gentiles were responsible for the repeated plunder and subjugation of Jerusalem (*Pss. Sol.* 2:1-2, 19-24; 17:1-25), and the desire of this writer was for God to destroy the sinful nations (*Pss. Sol.* 2:25; 8:23; 17:21-25). In the Book of Jubilees, all the uncircumcised are destined for destruction and annihilation (*Jub.* 15:26). The *War Scroll* of the Qumran community seems to take particular delight in the future judgment of God upon the nations.[6]

Nevertheless, this negative picture of the Gentiles is not the entire story. There was also a recognition that God created all people and cares for all. According to Philo, all created things are "brothers, since they have all one Father, the Maker of the universe" (Philo, *Decalogue*, 64; cf. Josephus, *Antiquities*, 2.152). Ben Sira taught that while people have compassion for their neighbor, "the compassion of the Lord is for all living beings" (Sir. 18:13). There was a continuing recognition that Israel was responsible to be a light to the Gentiles (cf. Rom. 2:19-20). In the Wisdom of Solomon, the Jewish people are God's sons "through whom the imperishable light of the law was to be given to the world" (Wis. 18:4). In the Testaments of the Twelve Patriarchs, the light of the law was given to Israel "for the enlightenment of every man" (*T. Levi* 14:4; cf. *T. Naph.* 8:4, 6). Finally, some look forward to the salvation of Gentiles in the last time, often in connection with the coming of the Messiah.[7] So, for example, the writer of the Testaments of the Twelve Patriarchs foresees the coming of a future high priest from Levi and a future king from Judah, which will result in the

---

[5] Scott, *Customs and Controversies*, 336.

[6] See, for example, 1QM 4:12; 6:5-6; 9:5-9; 11:13-17; 12:11-12; 14:5, 7-8; 15:1-2; 16:1; 17:1; 19:3-4.

[7] See *1 Enoch* 10:21; 48:4; 90:30-33; 91:14; *4 Ezra* 6:26; *2 Bar.* 72:1-5. It should be noted that in *2 Bar.* 72:1-5 only those nations that did not oppress Israel will be saved.

salvation of the Gentiles as well as the tribes of Israel (*T. Sim.* 7:2).[8] Also in the last time, Gentiles will come to Jerusalem to worship and to give gifts to Israel.[9] In light of this future inclusion of Gentiles in God's work of salvation, was there any effort on the part of Jews to bring Gentiles into obedience toward the God of Israel during the intertestamental period? That remains an open question among scholars.

## THE QUESTION OF AN INTERTESTAMENTAL JEWISH MISSION

Traditionally, scholars have assumed a great intentional missionary effort among Jews on behalf of their pagan neighbors near and far. For example: "The Maccabean victory appears to have given new stimulus to the Jewish missionary movement. Proudly faithful to the God who had wondrously rescued them from their enemies, the Jews were well fitted to propagandize for their religion."[10] Hahn declares in a similar vein: "Extensive and intensive recruiting for the Jewish faith was obviously undertaken by Hellenistic Jews."[11] At the beginning of his discussion of Jesus' view of mission, Jeremias states, "At the time of Jesus' appearance an unparalleled period of missionary activity was in progress in Israel."[12]

Some scholars, such as McKnight and Goodman, have recently drawn different conclusions.[13] McKnight, for example, uses a sharply intentional definition of a "missionary religion" as one that "self-consciously defines itself as a religion, one aspect of whose 'self-definition' is a mission to the rest of the world, or at least a large portion of that world."[14] He goes on to argue that such a religion must not be merely confessionally "missionary" but in practice actually "missionary." With this definition in mind, he asks questions of the data. Do we know the names of any Jewish missionaries of this period? Do we have records of individual missionaries being sent by synagogues? Do

---

[8] The future salvation of the Gentiles is a common theme in the Testaments of the Twelve Patriarchs (*T. Levi* 2:11; 4:4; *T. Jud.* 24:6; 25:5; *T. Zeb.* 9:8; *T. Ash.* 7:3; *T. Ben.* 10:5).

[9] Tob. 13:11; *1 Enoch* 53:1; *T. Ben.* 9:2; *2 Bar.* 68:5; *Sib. Or.* 3:702-31; 772-75.

[10] Bernard Bamberger, "Proselytes," in *The Universal Jewish Encyclopedia* (New York: Ktav, 1969), 9:1.

[11] Hahn, *Mission*, 22.

[12] Jeremias, *Promise*, 11.

[13] See McKnight, *Light among the Gentiles*, and Goodman, *Mission and Conversion*.

[14] McKnight, *Light among the Gentiles*, 4.

we have records of any strategies to bring the message of God's law and God's covenant to pagans? Do we have news of any well-known converts of such missionary effort? McKnight fails to find convincing evidence of intentionality, of "sending," in this vast mass of evidence, with perhaps the one exception of Jews in Rome, who seemed to have been intentionally busy in missionary activity among Roman pagans during the second century B.C.E.[15] McKnight treats this evidence as an aberration in the usual lack of hard evidence. Yet McKnight admits that there were pagans who were converting to Judaism. He writes, "It is safe to conclude, first of all, that Gentiles were converting to Judaism and that such conversion took place throughout the Roman Empire. The presence of 'proselytes/God-fearers' indicates quite clearly that conversions were taking place."[16] For McKnight, the missionary activity of Jews during this time appeared to be more along the lines of "instructing inquirers rather than evangelizing Gentiles."[17]

In spite of impressive research, rigorous thought, and a sound conclusion in light of his definition, there is a basic problem in McKnight's hypothesis. McKnight's definition of a missionary religion places too much emphasis on intentional effort rather than on results.[18] McKnight has also underestimated the dynamic of a "sacred magnetism"[19] in Judaism, a "Come!" mentality, an attractive, centripetal force, in contrast to the "Go!" dynamic, the centrifugal force of the New Testament.[20] This concept of "sacred magnetism" assists in maintaining the possibility of the Jewish mission during the intertestamental period even if it may be impossible to demonstrate the existence of Jewish

---

[15] Ibid., 74.

[16] Ibid., 115.

[17] Ibid.

[18] Analogous is the modern mission board that measures its effectiveness by its efforts rather than by its results. Donald McGavran (*Understanding Church Growth* [Grand Rapids: Eerdmans, 1970]) as well as the church-growth movement that arose during the 1960s emphasized results rather than process, since the success of a missionary movement, in the ultimate analysis, does not depend on effort expended but upon results effected.

[19] George W. Peters, *A Biblical Theology of Missions* (Chicago: Moody, 1972), 21. McKnight, of course, recognizes that Jews in this period were a light to the Gentiles. See, for example, McKnight, *Light among the Gentiles*, 48. Yet, for McKnight, this activity of attraction does not qualify as missionary activity. If, however, mission is defined more broadly as the accomplishing of the task to which one has been sent by God, then serving as God's light to the Gentiles could certainly be viewed as missionary activity.

[20] Peters, *Missions*, 21, 52, 300. However, the importance of attraction within the teaching of the New Testament should also not be missed. So, for example, Paul saw believers as lights who hold forth the word of life in the midst of a crooked and perverse generation (Phil. 2:14-16; cf. Matt. 5:14-16).

missionaries beyond the shadow of any reasonable doubt. A believing society may be "missionary" *in its effect*—and therefore participating in "mission"—without sending out missionaries! Accordingly, one may analyze the mission activity in intertestamental Judaism by looking at the actual growth accomplished and also the dynamic forces that attracted pagans to faith in Israel's God even without a program of missionaries actually being sent out to evangelize Gentiles.[21]

### Evidence of Conversions

The testimony of several sources shows that many Gentiles were drawn to Judaism during the intertestamental period. According to Josephus, multitudes of Greeks in the city of Antioch were attracted to Judaism (*Jewish Wars*, 7.45), many women in the city of Damascus became converts (*Jewish Wars*, 2.559-61), and there were adherents to the Jewish Law in every city in Syria (*Jewish Wars*, 2.463). In fact, Josephus could boast that every city, whether Greek or barbarian, and every single nation contained those who had taken on the observance of the Jewish Law (*Against Apion*, 2.282; cf. 2.123). Josephus also makes reference to conversion by force, which occurred during the Hasmonean dynasty under the authority of the priest-kings John Hyrcanus I, Aristobulus, and Alexander Jannaeus. Josephus details the military campaigns of John Hyrcanus I against the Idumaeans and the Samaritans,[22] as well as the incursions of his sons Aristobulus I and Alexander against the Ituraeans and Idumaeans. Each of these expeditions, Josephus notes, resulted in forced conversions to Judaism (*Antiquities*, 13.254-58, 318-19, 395-97). The principals were Hasmonean priest-kings intent on maintaining and enlarging their hegemony. To compel captives to become Jews was as much for them a matter of political expediency as religious fervor. Our consciences may be scandalized, but sizeable groups of people became Jews religiously as a result of these military conquests and forced conversions.

The book of Acts portrays a number of proselytes (Acts 2:11; 6:5; 13:43), Gentile God-fearers (Acts 10:2, 22; 13:16, 26, 43, 50; 17:4, 17), and Gentile participants in synagogue worship (Acts 13:44, 48; 14:1; 17:4, 12, 17; 18:4). One outstanding example is Cornelius, a certain officer in the Roman army, who was stationed in Caesarea. Luke informs us of his piety, his ability to encourage his family in faith, his generosity, and his prayerfulness (Acts 10:1-2). He assumes

---

[21] J. Herbert Kane (*Christian Missions in Biblical Perspective* [Grand Rapids: Baker, 1976], 30-33) saw these forces at work: the synagogue, the Jewish scriptures, the Sabbath, Jewish monotheism, Jewish morality, and the belief that a Messiah was to come who would bring about God's kingdom on earth.

[22] See also Ellison, *Babylon*, 66.

strategic importance that is hard to exaggerate as he becomes the first-known Gentile to believe formally and openly in Jesus and experience with his household the gift of the Holy Spirit (Acts 10:44-48).

One further piece of evidence is the document *Joseph and Aseneth*, which purports to tell the story of Aseneth's repentance of idolatry and conversion to the God of Israel prior to her marriage to Joseph. The whole story would have made little sense if conversions to Judaism were completely outside the experience of Jews in the intertestamental period.[23]

### Informal Jewish Missions

In social situations throughout the Dispersion, there is the strong possibility of missionary activity conducted informally in the intertestamental period as devout Jews, in the marketplace and in the synagogue, conversed with their pagan neighbors, encouraging them toward full personal commitment to God as he is revealed in the Jewish scriptures. As one might expect, records of conversion to Judaism by informal personal conversation are few and limited to the rich and the famous. One outstanding account is given by Josephus regarding the king of Adiabene, Izates by name (*Antiquities*, 20.34-48). A Jewish merchant named Ananias appears to have introduced him to the Jewish faith and assured him that compliance with the laws regarding circumcision were not required of him. Later, however, another Jew named Eleazar found king Izates reading the law and urged him to complete his obedience by being circumcised. He did so fearlessly and was protected from his own people, some of whom felt that he had given too much credence to foreign "superstitions." This sort of experience was probably replicated hundreds of times in the lives of ordinary folk of the intertestamental period as they encountered devout Jewish businessmen in their travels. Such events would tend to remain unrecorded.[24]

---

[23] It should also be remembered that conversions are not always instantaneous. Contemporary missiological theory contributes to understanding conversion as a process. James F. Engel (*Contemporary Christian Communications: Its Theory and Practice* [Nashville: Thomas Nelson, 1979], 225) developed a powerful tool in his "spiritual decision process," more popularly known as "the Engel's scale." When his scale is "contextualized" to the Jewish mission during the intertestamental period, one may look at Jewish missionary activity during this period and see the possibility that in addition to full conversions many pagans may have gained some knowledge of Judaism, while others may have grasped the personal implications of Judaism, and still others through synagogue attendance may have developed a positive attitude toward the act of becoming a Jew.

[24] Another convert from among the "rich and famous" recorded by Josephus was a high-ranking woman in Rome named Fulvia (*Antiquities*, 18.81-84).

The translation of the Hebrew scriptures into Greek also certainly furthered the Jewish message among the Gentiles. Philo felt that the Septuagint did have and would continue to have an effect on all the nations. For Philo, this translation was a source of wonder not only for the Jews but for all other nations (*Moses*, 2.25). It revealed the beauty of the Jewish laws to the rest of humankind (*Moses*, 2.26). God gave this translation so that the greater part, or even the whole, of the human race might profit and move toward a better life by observing the Law (*Moses*, 2.36; cf. *T. Levi* 14:4). Philo looked forward to the time when every nation would abandon its ways and throw overboard its ancestral customs in order to turn to the Law of Moses alone (*Moses*, 2.44). In fact, the scriptures may have found their way into the hands of many who, like the Ethiopian eunuch (Acts 8:27-35), sought to understand the meaning of these texts. Throughout the Jewish Dispersion, it was the ubiquitous synagogue that served as the chief social structure in mediating, through the reading and explanation of the Septuagint, the Jewish Law and faith.

The New Testament gives some evidence for actual Jewish missionaries during the intertestamental period. In Matthew 23:15 we have Jesus' most important statement about Jewish intertestamental missions: "Woe to you, scribes and Pharisees, hypocrites! For you traverse sea and land to make a single proselyte, and when he becomes a proselyte, you make him twice as much a child of hell as yourselves" (Matt. 23:15). The implications of this one statement are numerous! Assuming this to be a genuine utterance of Jesus, it is implied that he believed both the Pharisees (craftsmen and businessmen) and the scribes, their professional instructors, planned and practiced proselytization in their travels. Pleased with even meager results, the Pharisees, thought Jesus, also were successful in transferring their subtle vices to their converts.

Perhaps Saul of Tarsus was himself active as a Jewish missionary in the intertestamental era prior to his conversion to Christ. Such is the implication of his words, "If I still preach circumcision, why am I still persecuted?" (Gal. 5:11). There evidently was a period in his pre-Christian experience when Saul tried to persuade "God-fearing" Gentiles to complete their conversion to the Jewish faith by circumcision. Those who followed Paul throughout Galatia, instructing his converts to faith in Jesus that they must also be circumcised, also qualify as intertestamental Jewish missionaries. These are seen with particular clarity in Paul's remark, "Would that those who are troubling you would even mutilate themselves" (Gal. 5:12). McKnight styles such "Torah missionaries"[25] and says they have as an aim "the 'comple-

---

[25] McKnight, *Light among the Gentiles*, 104.

tion' (Gal. 3:3) of their conversion through the total submission to the Torah."[26]

## CONCLUSION

God's sending during the intertestamental period was indirect but powerful, the voice of God heard in the reading and explanation of scripture in the synagogue. McKnight is convincing in demonstrating that intertestamental Judaism was seldom formally intentional in its missionary activity. Yet there is a general body of evidence that pagans were being attracted into a covenantal relationship with Judaism and Judaism's God throughout the intertestamental period. This process by which Gentiles were drawn to the God of Israel tended to be informal, personal, relational, opportunistic, somewhat successful, and extremely strategic.

---

[26] Ibid.

# 3

## Mission in Jesus' Teaching

## John D. Harvey

Martin Hengel has called Jesus "the primal missionary."[1] In so doing, he places his finger on a key aspect of Jesus' self-understanding.[2] The record of Jesus' teaching found in the synoptic gospels reflects the fact that he had a clear understanding of his own mission.[3] He taught

---

[1] Martin Hengel, *Between Jesus and Paul: Studies in the Earliest History of Christianity*, trans. John Bowden (Philadelphia: Fortress, 1983), 62.

[2] This view of Jesus' self-understanding differs considerably from the views proposed by many scholars engaged in the current quest for the historical Jesus. Suggestions include Jesus as an itinerant social reformer (Crossan), a charismatic conduit of God's power (Borg), an advocate of restoration eschatology (Sanders), the leader of a peace party (Thiessen), the leader of a wisdom resistance party (Schüssler Fiorenza), and a marginal preacher and healer (Meier). For a survey of these and other proposals as well as critiques of each, see Ben Witherington III, *The Jesus Quest: The Third Search for the Jew of Nazareth* (Downers Grove, Ill.: InterVarsity, 1995).

[3] The present chapter will be limited to Jesus' teaching as found in the synoptic gospels, with material from John's gospel being included only incidentally. Although the scope of this chapter is inadequate to permit an extended discussion of various approaches to the study of the synoptic gospels, it may be noted that an evangelical approach to the historical documents of the NT uses a hermeneutic of "good will" rather than a hermeneutic of suspicion. In other words, the burden of proof is on those scholars who would argue that the Gospel record of Jesus' teachings is unreliable. An evenhanded use of the historical-critical method leads to the conclusion that "what can be checked is accurate, so that it is entirely proper to believe that what cannot be checked is probably accurate as well" (Craig L. Blomberg, *The Historical Reliability of the Gospels* [Downers Grove, Ill.: InterVarsity, 1987], 254). Such considerations permit the present chapter to proceed on the assumption that the words ascribed to Jesus by Matthew, Mark, and Luke may be taken at face value as an accurate record of his teachings.

that he was sent by the Father with the task of seeking and saving the lost and that—although he envisioned a future worldwide mission—his own mission was focused on the nation of Israel. Jesus' teaching on mission, however, encompassed more than his own task. It included the task entrusted to his disciples.[4] Prior to the resurrection, the disciples' mission was identical to and an extension of Jesus' mission. The resurrection, however, brought a significant change both to Jesus' role in mission and to the disciples' actual mission. As the risen Christ, he assumed the role of sender, who sent the disciples with the task of bearing witness to the forgiveness of sins that was now available in him. Their mission was now to be to "all the nations," and that universal mission was to be carried out by obedient disciples who would continue their mission until Jesus returns.

## JESUS' MISSION

Jesus' teaching on his own mission may be organized under four headings. The phrase "the one who sent me" provides a starting point for discussing both the *sender* and the *sent one*. Jesus' perspective on the *task* entrusted to him is introduced by the phrase "I came." His understanding of the *activity* and *scope* of his mission is seen in statements introduced by "I was sent." His *message* and the *results* of his mission are closely related to the idea of "the kingdom of God."

### *"The one who sent me . . ."*

Every mission involves a sender and a sent one. In a saying recorded in all three synoptic gospels, Jesus alluded to such a relationship in connection with his own mission: "He who receives you receives me, and he who receives me receives the one who sent *(ton aposteilanta)* me" (Matt. 10:40; Mark 9:37; Luke 9:48). With this statement, Jesus established three facts in regard to his mission: first, there was a sender; second, Jesus himself was the sent one; third, there was a close identification between the sender and the one who was sent.

---

[4] The topic also includes a number of aspects that can be summarized briefly. Prior to Jesus' coming, the prophets (Matt. 23:29-39; Luke 13:31-35) and John the Baptist (Matt. 11:7-19; Luke 7:24-28; 16:14-17) were sent as messengers to Israel. During Jesus' ministry, the disciples were sent on minor "missions" to perform a variety of preparatory functions, such as making arrangements for the Passover meal (Matt. 26:17-19; Mark 14:12-16; Luke 22:7-13). Finally, at Jesus' return, the angels will be sent to gather in the harvest (Matt. 24:29-31; Mark 13:24-27). Although each of these items fits the definition of "mission" as set forth for the present work, none of them is a major emphasis of Jesus' teaching.

That the *sender* is the Father may be determined from other passages in Jesus' teaching.[5] His first public statement, for example, was that he must be "among the things of my Father" (Luke 2:49).[6] At another time he made it clear that he viewed himself as a steward of those things "handed over" to him by the Father (Matt. 11:25-27; Luke 10:21-24). Jesus, therefore, saw the top priority of his mission to be the faithful discharge of those activities entrusted to him by the Father.

What characterizes this Father who sent Jesus? He is, above all, one who takes the initiative in mission.[7] This quality is pictured in several of Jesus' parables. In Luke 15 the Father is portrayed, first, as a shepherd who leaves ninety-nine sheep in order to find the one that is lost (Luke 15:3-7; cf. Matt. 18:12-14); then, as a woman who searches diligently for a lost coin (Luke 15:8-10); and finally, as a father who runs to meet the lost son who is returning home (Luke 15:11-32). In the parable of the marriage feast, he is pictured as a king who repeatedly sends his servants to invite to the banquet as many men and women as will come (Matt. 22:1-14; cf. Luke 14:16-24). In each instance the Father's initiative is plainly in view.

Because the Father took the initiative in mission, it was crucial that Jesus, the *sent one*, faithfully discharge the mission entrusted to him by the Father. Jesus' awareness of this fact was reflected in his commitment to doing the Father's will, a commitment most clearly evident at two crucial times in his life. Matthew's account of Jesus' baptism includes the cryptic statement, "Permit it at this time; for in this way it is fitting for us to fulfill all righteousness" (3:15). Matthew undoubtedly included this saying because of his special interest in "righteousness," but it also serves to highlight Jesus' understanding that obedience was

---

[5] The concept of the Father sending the Son into the world is a particularly Johannine theme (cf. John 5:19-24; 6:38-39; 8:38-42; 11:41-42; 12:44-50; 16:25-28; 17:1-6). Although the idea is less prominent in the synoptics, "Father" is Jesus' characteristic way of addressing and referring to God in those books as well (forty-five times in Matthew; five times in Mark; sixteen times in Luke).

[6] Literal translation. The phrase may be interpreted either as "in my Father's house" (NIV) or "about my Father's affairs" (NKJV). For a concise discussion see John Nolland, *Luke 1:1-9:20*, WBC (Dallas, Tex.: Word, 1989), 131-32. Either interpretation is possible, but the immediate context suggests the first. In either case, it is *his Father's* things with which Jesus was concerned.

[7] This initiative surely grows out of what might be termed "God's availability." See Donald Senior and Carroll Stuhlmueller, *The Biblical Foundations for Mission* (Maryknoll, N.Y.: Orbis Books, 1983), 151.

central to the accomplishment of his mission.[8] By submitting to John's baptism, Jesus affirmed his willingness to carry out his Father's will.[9] That same willing obedience was evident in Gethsemane when he prayed, "Thy will be done" (Matt. 26:42; Luke 22:42; cf. Matt. 26:39, 44; Mark 14:36). So, both at the beginning of his public ministry and at the beginning of his passion ministry, Jesus affirmed his commitment to carry out the mission entrusted to him by "the one who sent" him.

So closely was Jesus identified with the Father who sent him on mission that to receive one was to receive the other. In John's gospel, Jesus declared that he possessed the same knowledge, judgment, will, actions, and words as the Father.[10] In the synoptics, however, the primary point of continuity is that of authority. When the paralytic was brought to him, Jesus declared that he had the authority *(exousia)* to forgive sins (Matt. 9:6; Mark 2:10; Luke 5:24), a declaration that the scribes correctly understood as a claim to the exercise of divine authority. Elsewhere, he claimed lordship over the Sabbath (Matt. 12:9; Mark 2:28; Luke 6:5) and the ability to interpret the OT law authoritatively (Matt. 5:17-48), both of which were claims with connotations of deity. When questioned as to the source of his authority, Jesus implied, but left unspoken, his answer: the source was the Father (Matt. 21:23-27; Mark 11:27-33; Luke 20:1-8). It is clear from Jesus' teaching, therefore, that the one sent on mission possesses the same authority as the one who sends him or her. This continuity of authority has a direct parallel in the disciples' mission.

### *"I came . . . "*

Jesus' perspective on the *task* entrusted to him is revealed in his statements introduced by the phrase "I came" *(ēlthon)* or its equivalent.[11] These statements ascribe to Jesus "a special status as one who

---

[8] The noun *righteousness* occurs seven times in Matthew, as opposed to once in Luke and not at all in Mark. The adjective *righteous* occurs nineteen times in Matthew, two times in Mark, and eleven times in Luke. For a concise discussion, see Donald A. Hagner, *Matthew 1-13*, WBC (Dallas, Tex.: Word, 1993), 56. For an extended treatment, see Benno Przybylski, *Righteousness in Matthew and His World of Thought*, SNTSMS, no. 41 (Cambridge: University Press, 1980).

[9] Hagner (*Matthew 1-13*, 57) writes, "In his first words in the Gospel, Jesus refers to the fulfilling of God's will in nothing less than the establishing of the salvation he has promised . . . through what now begins to take shape."

[10] See John 5:19-24, 30; 6:38; 8:28-29; 12:49.

[11] For a concise discussion of these "programmatic-eschatological *ēlthon*-words," see John P. Meier, *Law and History in Matthew's Gospel: A Redactional Study of Mt. 5:17-48*, AnBib, no. 71 (Rome: Biblical Institute Press, 1976), 66-69.

comes with a particular mission."[12] They also relate Jesus' mission to past, present, and future periods of salvation history and make it clear that a proper understanding of that mission must reckon with its relation to the OT, its salvific purpose, and its potential for causing division.

With the declaration "Do not think that I came *(ēlthon)* to abolish the Law or the Prophets; I did not come *(ouk ēlthon)* to abolish, but to fulfill" (Matt. 5:17), Jesus related his mission to the immediately preceding period of salvation history and its most visible feature, the OT scriptures. Although there are several interpretations of this verse, the most likely is that Jesus came to realize the promises recorded in the OT.[13]

The discussion of Matthew 5:17 often revolves around Matthew's use of "fulfill" *(plēroō)* and neglects Jesus' use. In the synoptic gospels, Jesus uses *plēroō* thirteen times and its cognate, *anaplēroō*, once. Eight times it refers to the realization of OT promises.[14] Another four uses have the sense of bringing to complete measure.[15] The two remaining occurrences are in Matthew 3:15 and 5:17. Although John Meier argues for prophetic fulfillment in 3:15, the idea of bringing to complete measure seems more natural.[16] In 5:17, however, the conjunction of "prophets" and "fulfill" suggests that the realization of the OT promises is in view. Luke 24:44 may be cited in support of this interpretation: ". . . that all things which are written about me in the Law of Moses and the Prophets, and the Psalms must be fulfilled *(plērōthēnai)*." Elsewhere, Jesus uses "the Law and the Prophets" as a designation for the OT as a whole (Matt. 7:12; 22:40; Luke 16:16), and in Matthew 11:13 he stated, "all the prophets and the Law prophesied until John." Jesus' point seems to be that—contrary to appearances—his mission was in direct continuity with the immediately preceding period of salvation history.

A group of three "I came" statements reveals that Jesus understood the purpose of his task to be salvific. To Zacchaeus he affirmed, "The Son of Man came *(ēlthen)* to seek and to save that which was lost"

---

[12] David E. Garland, *Reading Matthew: A Literary and Theological Commentary on the First Gospel* (New York: Crossroad, 1993), 62.

[13] The three primary interpretations of this verse are: (1) Jesus came to obey perfectly the commandments of the OT law; (2) Jesus came to teach the OT law in such a way as to establish it; or (3) Jesus came to realize the promises recorded in the OT. See Hagner (*Matthew 1-13*, 105-6), who argues for the second interpretation.

[14] Matt. 13:14; 26:54, 56; Mark 14:49; Luke 4:21; 21:22; 22:16; 24:44.

[15] Matt. 13:48; 23:32; Mark 1:15; Luke 21:24.

[16] See Meier, *Law and History*, 76-80, and the discussion above.

(Luke 19:10).[17] This attitude of seeking what is lost is pictured elsewhere in the parables of the lost sheep (Matt. 18:12-14; Luke 15:3-7) and the lost coin (Luke 15:8-10). It required Jesus to spend time with those on the margins of society (e.g., Matt. 8:1-17) and drew criticism from the Pharisees. In response to that criticism Jesus declared, "I did not come *(ouk ēlthon)* to call the righteous, but sinners" (Mark 2:17; cf. Matt. 9:13). Luke clarifies the redemptive nature of this latter statement by including Jesus' final phrase, "to repentance" (Luke 5:32).[18]

Jesus not only came to seek the lost, he also came to save them. The third statement in this group makes that fact explicit: "The Son of Man did not come *(ouk ēlthen)* to be served, but to serve and to give his life as a ransom for many" (Matt. 20:28; Mark 10:45). Jesus' use of "ransom" fixes this saying firmly within the sphere of redemptive activity, for the OT background is one of obtaining deliverance by paying a price.[19] The phrase "for many" is echoed in his instructions during the Passover observance where the redemptive aspect of his mission is also made explicit: "This is my blood of the covenant, which is poured out for many for forgiveness of sins" (Matt. 26:28).[20]

From this group of sayings, Jesus' perspective on the purpose of his task becomes evident. He sought men and women with the explicit intent of calling them to repentance, and he gave his life as a means of obtaining deliverance for them. The OT allusions connected with the third saying link his mission closely with the Father's plan of redemption, which entered a new phase in the period of salvation

---

[17] This statement has a parallel in the variant reading of Matthew 18:11, which appears to be an assimilation to the saying in Luke (cf. Bruce M. Metzger, *A Textual Commentary on the Greek New Testament*, 2d ed. [Stuttgart: United Bible Societies, 1994], 36). A third, similar statement occurs in a textual variant earlier in Luke's gospel (9:56). For a summary of the issues surrounding this latter variant, see I. Howard Marshall, *The Gospel of Luke*, NIGTC (Grand Rapids: Eerdmans, 1978), 407-8.

[18] For similar comments, not introduced by "I came," see Matthew 21:31-32; Luke 7:37-50; 18:9-14.

[19] See, for example, Exod. 34:20; Lev. 19:20; 25:25. For a full discussion of the OT background, see C. Brown, *"lytron,"* in *The New International Dictionary of New Testament Theology*, ed. Colin Brown (Grand Rapids: Zondervan, 1978), 3:189-95. For an extended discussion of the saying itself, see S. Page, "Ransom Saying," in *DJG*, ed. Joel B. Green and Scot McKnight (Downers Grove, Ill.: InterVarsity, 1992), 660-62.

[20] For a more detailed discussion of this verse, see the chapter on Matthew below.

history following the ministry of John the Baptist (Matt. 11:12; Luke 16:16).[21]

Subsequent to his death, however, the redemptive purpose of Jesus' mission would not always be accepted or understood; it would, in fact, cause division and result in opposition. A final pair of "I came" statements addressed this idea. As part of his commissioning discourse, Jesus declared that he had come to cause division: "Do not think that I came *(ēlthon)* to bring peace on the earth; I did not come *(ouk ēlthon)* to bring peace, but a sword" (Matt. 10:34; cf. Luke 12:51). Because Jesus' mission called men and women to change direction (repent), it would inevitably separate God's people from the unrepentant. This separation would result in opposition and hostility—even within households (Matt. 10:35-36; Luke 12:52-53). Nevertheless, the loss of father, mother, son, or daughter pales when it is compared with the gain of eternal life (Matt. 10:37-39; cf. 19:29).

In Luke's gospel the preceding saying follows another "I came" statement placing the anticipated division after Jesus' suffering and death: "I came *(ēlthon)* to cast fire upon the earth; and how I wish it were kindled! But I have a baptism to undergo, and how distressed I am until it is accomplished" (Luke 12:49-50). Since Jesus always used "fire" to refer to judgment, this saying suggests that the division which occurs may be viewed as a form of judgment upon those who refuse to accept the redemptive purpose of his mission.[22] That division had not yet taken place, however, because Jesus longed for the fire to be "kindled." His mission would not be complete until he had been "baptized" with the baptism of his suffering and death (cf. Mark 10:38-39).

### *"I was sent . . . "*

Closely related to Jesus' *ēlthon* statements is a group of sayings introduced by the phrase "I was sent" *(apestalēn)*. These latter state-

---

[21] Luke 16:16 is the simpler verse: "The Law and the Prophets [were] until John; from then the gospel of the kingdom of God is being preached, and everyone *biazetai* into it." Matthew 11:12 may be divided into three phrases: (1) "And from the day of John the Baptist until now"; (2) "the kingdom of heaven *biazetai*"; (3) "and *biastai harpazousin* it." For summaries of the discussion that reach different conclusions on (2) and (3), see D. A. Carson, "Matthew," in *Expositor's Bible Commentary*, ed. Frank E. Gaebelein (Grand Rapids: Zondervan, 1984), 265-68, and Hagner, *Matthew 1-13*, 306-7. Carson's interpretation, which takes *biazetai* positively ("is forcefully advancing") but *biastai* ("violent men") and *harpazousin* ("are seizing/attacking") negatively, is probably to be preferred. In either case, the first phrase relates the beginning of a new stage in God's plan of redemption to the ministry of John the Baptist.

[22] Cf. Matt. 5:22; 7:19; 13:40, 42, 50; 18:8-9; 25:41; Mark 9:43-49; Luke 17:29.

ments provide insight, first, into the primary *activity* in which Jesus was engaged while on mission and, second, into the *scope* of that mission.

Luke 4:43 makes it clear that Jesus knew that he was sent to preach: "I must preach *(euangelisasthai)* the kingdom of God to the other cities also, for I was sent *(apestalēn)* for this purpose" (cf. Mark 1:38). Luke then adds his editorial comment that Jesus "kept on preaching *(ēn kērussōn)* in the synagogues of Judea" (Luke 4:44). These verses conclude the series of pericopae that began with Jesus' inaugural teaching in Nazareth, when he quoted Isaiah 61:1-2: "The Spirit of the Lord is upon me, because he anointed me to preach the gospel *(euangelisasthai)* to the poor. He has sent *(apestalken)* me to proclaim *(kēruxai)* release to the captives, and recovery of sight to the blind, to set free those who are downtrodden, to proclaim *(kēruxai)* the favorable year of the Lord" (Luke 4:18-19).

At the beginning of his ministry, therefore, Jesus twice declared that his primary activity would be preaching.[23] Particularly appropriate for picturing this activity was the image of "sowing," and his interpretation of the parable of the wheat and the weeds makes it clear that Jesus himself is the sower (Matt. 13:37).[24] The close connection between preaching and sowing is also seen in Luke's gospel, where the parable of the sower follows immediately upon an extended preaching tour and introduces a section devoted to the importance of hearing and doing God's word (Luke 8:1-21). As Jesus' listeners responded in faith to the message he preached, they would be "saved" (Luke 8:12), and Jesus' missionary task ("to seek and save that which was lost") would be accomplished.

Another statement introduced by "I was sent" raises the issue of the *scope* of Jesus' mission: when his disciples asked him to send away the Canaanite woman, he answered, "I was sent *(apestalēn)* only to the lost sheep of the house of Israel" (Matt. 15:24). This statement suggests that during his lifetime Jesus limited his mission to the Jewish people. Also supporting this idea are his instructions when he sent out the twelve. Initially, he gave them specific instructions to go only to "the lost sheep of the house of Israel" (Matt. 10:5-6). Later, when discussing the persecution that they would encounter, he declared, "You

---

[23] The gospel writers regularly describe Jesus as being engaged in preaching (Matt. 4:12-17, 23-25; 9:35; 11:1; Mark 1:14-15, 35-39; Luke 20:1). In fact, Lucian Legrand (*Unity and Plurality: Mission in the Bible,* trans. Robert R. Barr [Maryknoll, N.Y.: Orbis Books, 1990], 63) notes, "In the New Testament, the verb *kērussein* becomes the standard designation for Jesus' basic activity (9 times in Matthew, 14 in Mark, 9 in Luke)."

[24] Jesus used this image repeatedly in his parables (Matt. 13:3, 24, 31; Mark 4:3, 26, 31; Luke 8:5; 13:19).

shall not finish going through the cities of Israel until the Son of Man comes" (Matt. 10:23). These particularistic statements cannot be explained away as later additions.[25] Furthermore, the parable of the vineyard owner—which was directed at the chief priests and elders—and the comment that followed suggest that Jesus saw himself as sent, first of all, to Israel (Matt. 21:33-44). In light of this evidence, some have questioned whether Jesus ever intended his message to extend beyond the boundaries of the nation of Israel.[26]

Jesus' particularistic statements, however, must be weighed against aspects of his teaching and practice that suggest a more universal scope. Several times he taught that Israel would be replaced as the exclusive inheritors of the kingdom (Matt. 8:11-12; 22:1-14, 43; Luke 13:28-29; 14:16-24), and he used non-Jews as positive examples (Matt. 12:41-42; Luke 4:25-27; 10:25-37; 11:31-32).[27] References to "all nations" or "the world" occur repeatedly in his teaching (Matt. 5·13-14; 13:38; 25:31-32; Mark 11:17), and statements that the gospel would be preached "in the whole world" seem to anticipate a mission which would reach beyond the nation of Israel (Matt. 24:14; 26:13; Mark 13:10; 14:9). Although there is some discussion regarding whether or not Jesus actually spent extended periods of time in territory that was predominantly Gentile, the centurion (Matt. 8:5-13; Luke 7:1-10), the Gadarene demoniac (Matt. 8:28-34; Mark 5:1-20; Luke 8:26-39), and the Canaanite woman (Matt. 15:21-28; Mark 7:24-30) all requested

---

[25] See Joachim Jeremias, *Jesus' Promise to the Nations*, trans. S. H. Hooke (London: SCM, 1958), 26-28.

[26] This issue has generated considerable debate. Ferdinand Hahn identifies four approaches: (1) Jesus gave no instructions for a mission to the Gentiles; it was a product of the early church's theological reflection; (2) Jesus was the first missionary to the Gentiles and actually stayed several times in Gentile territory; (3) Jesus did not inaugurate a Gentile mission during his lifetime, but after his resurrection he instructed his disciples to undertake such a mission; and (4) Jesus did not inaugurate a mission to the Gentiles, but his resurrection convinced his disciples that the final age of salvation had dawned (*Mission in the New Testament*, trans. Frank Clarke, SBT, no. 47 [Naperville, Ill.: Alec R. Allenson, 1965], 26-28). Hahn is satisfied with none of these suggestions, but he rejects much of the available evidence as inauthentic (e.g., Matt. 10:5-6, 23; 15:24; 28:18-20). The same is true of Jeremias (approach #4) who lays out portions of the evidence well, but rejects numerous passages as additions of the early church (*Promise*, esp. 22-24, 33-34). If all of the evidence of scripture is taken at face value, the third understanding is the best.

[27] Jesus refers positively to the men of Nineveh, the Queen of Sheba, the widow of Zarephath, Naaman, and the "good Samaritan."

and were granted assistance.[28] It appears, therefore, that although Jesus intentionally limited the scope of his mission to Israel, he received any non-Jew who came to him and envisioned a mission that would reach beyond the nation of Israel.

### *"Thy kingdom come . . . "*

If Jesus' primary activity was preaching, the primary *message* he proclaimed while on mission was "the kingdom of God."[29] The fact that Jesus spoke sometimes of "the kingdom" (Matt. 4:17; Luke 4:43) and other times of "the gospel" (Matt. 11:5; 26:13; Mark 8:35; 10:29; 13:10; 14:9; Luke 4:18; 7:22) does not need to lead to confusion over his message. The two terms are combined once as "the gospel of the kingdom" (Matt. 24:14), a construction in which "the kingdom" should probably be understood as standing in apposition to and, therefore, clarifying "the gospel."[30] This construction suggests that gospel (good news) describes the character of the message, while kingdom defines its content. Although various interpretations of the kingdom have been proposed, the best understanding is that the term "signifies God's sovereign, dynamic, and eschatological rule."[31] Three seemingly paradoxical aspects of this divine rule should be noted: (1) it is both "now" and "not yet"; (2) it is both "good news" and "bad news"; and (3) it is both minuscule and mighty.

Jesus frequently affirmed the present dimension of the kingdom. When questioned by John's disciples as to whether or not he was "the coming one" (i.e., the Messiah), Jesus pointed to the events of his min-

---

[28] It is true that in each case the contact was initiated by the Gentiles, but in none of them did Jesus finally reject the petitioner because he or she was not a Jew. On the issue of Jesus' travel outside of predominantly Jewish areas, see the discussion in Legrand, *Unity and Plurality*, 49-53.

[29] For a concise discussion of the interchangeability of "the kingdom of God," "the kingdom of heaven," and "the kingdom," see C. C. Caragounis, "Kingdom of God/Kingdom of Heaven," *DJG*, 417. For more extensive bibliography, see George Eldon Ladd, *A Theology of the New Testament*, 2d ed. (Grand Rapids: Eerdmans, 1993), 54-55.

[30] Jesus also uses the two terms in close context once: "The time is fulfilled and the kingdom of God is at hand; repent and believe the gospel" (Mark 1:15).

[31] Caragounis, "Kingdom," 417. Suggested interpretations include: (1) the church (Augustine), (2) a wholly future event (Weiss), (3) the religion that Jesus taught (Harnack), (4) a twofold reality, including the eternal, spiritual kingdom of God and the earthly, millennial kingdom of Heaven (Chafer), and (5) a wholly present event (Dodd).

istry as those prophesied in connection with the coming of the kingdom: "the blind receive sight and the lame walk, the lepers are cleansed
and the deaf hear, the dead are raised up and the poor have the gospel
preached to them" (Matt. 11:4-5; Luke 7:22; cf. Isa. 29:17-19; 35:5-6;
42:6-7; 61:1-2). It was, in fact, the "favorable year of the Lord" (Luke
4:19).[32] This year of Jubilee was no longer future, for Jesus' mission
had brought it into the present (Matt. 4:17; Mark 1:15).[33]

Elsewhere, Jesus taught that the emancipating power at work in his
ministry showed that "the kingdom of God has come upon you" (Luke
11:20; Matt. 12:28).[34] His listeners should not look for further signs of
the kingdom's coming because "the kingdom of God is in your midst"
(Luke 17:20-21).[35] Those disciples who witnessed his ministry saw and
heard the things that "many prophets and kings wished to see . . . and
to hear" (Matt. 13:16-17; Luke 10:23-24)—to them "it has been
granted to know the mysteries of the kingdom" (Matt. 13:11; Mark
4:11-12). From these statements it is clear that Jesus viewed his mission as inaugurating the initial manifestation of the kingdom. As David
Bosch notes, "Something totally new is happening; the irruption of a
new era, of a new order of life. The hope of deliverance is not a distant
song about a far-away future. The future has invaded the present."[36]

Jesus' mission made it possible for men and women to experience
the present blessings of the kingdom. Yet a second series of teachings
makes it clear that, in some respects, the kingdom is still future and
will be fully consummated only when Jesus' disciples "see the Son of
Man coming in his kingdom" (Matt. 16:28; cf. Mark 9:1; Luke 9:27).
This future coming will make it possible for them to enjoy fellowship
with Jesus at the banquet of the kingdom (Matt. 8:11-12; 26:29; Mark
14:25; Luke 13:28-29; 22:18, 28-30). Until that coming, both the be-
atitudes (Matt. 5:3-12; Luke 6:20-23) and the disciples' prayer (Matt.

---

[32] For a two-thirds-world perspective on Luke 4:16-20, see Kwame Bediako,
*Christianity in Africa: The Renewal of a Non-Western Religion* (Maryknoll,
N.Y.: Orbis Books, 1995), 144-48. For an extended discussion of Luke 4:16-
20 that interacts with liberation theology, see the chapter on Luke below.

[33] For argumentation in support of the interpretation that the arrival has
already taken place, see Robert H. Gundry, *Mark: A Commentary on His
Apology for the Cross* (Grand Rapids: Eerdmans, 1993), 64-65.

[34] For linguistic evidence supporting the idea of arrival and actual presence,
see W. D. Davies and Dale C. Allison, *A Critical and Exegetical Commentary
on the Gospel according to Saint Matthew*, ICC (Edinburgh: T & T Clark,
1991), 2:340, n. 36.

[35] Alternatively, "within your reach." For a concise summary, see Marshall,
*Luke*, 655-56.

[36] David J. Bosch, *Transforming Mission: Paradigm Shifts in Theology of
Mission*, American Society of Missiology Series, no. 16 (Maryknoll, N.Y.:
Orbis Books, 1991), 32.

6:9-13; Luke 11:2-4) direct the gaze of Jesus' followers toward the future blessings that will arrive when the Son of Man returns. As Jesus' first coming brought the initial manifestation of the kingdom into the present, so his second coming will bring its ultimate manifestation in the future. Bosch concludes, "There remains . . . an unresolved tension between the present and future dimensions of God's reign. It has already arrived, and yet is still to come."[37]

Not only did Jesus teach a dual dimension to the time of the kingdom's coming, he also taught that its coming would have a two-fold impact. His mission brought a message that included both the good news of salvation and the bad news of judgment. It is true, as Senior notes, that Jesus minimized the motif of eschatological vengeance upon the Gentiles.[38] It is also true that he relativized race and status by emphasizing faith and obedience as the criteria for entry into the kingdom.[39] The Jews could not expect to be included simply because they were Jews (Matt. 8:10-12; cf. Luke 13:28-30). Nevertheless, it must not be concluded that the theme of judgment was entirely absent from Jesus' teaching on the kingdom.

The double-edged impact of the kingdom's consummation is most clearly seen in the parables Matthew recorded as part of Jesus' Olivet Discourse (Matt. 24:45-25:46). The faithful servant, the prudent virgins, the slaves who invest their talents wisely, and the sheep are all rewarded. The unfaithful servant, the foolish virgins, the slave who hides his talent in the ground, and the goats are all judged. This idea of a separation at the consummation of the kingdom appears elsewhere in Jesus' teaching. The parable of the wheat and the weeds (Matt. 13:24-30, 36-43) and the parable of the dragnet (Matt. 13:47-50) both picture such a separation. Failure to respond properly to the invitation to the Messianic banquet brings judgment (Matt. 22:1-8; cf. Luke 14:15-24), as does failure to prepare properly for it (Matt. 22:9-14). As noted above, Jesus came to cause division and to bring the fire of judgment upon earth (Luke 12:49-53). The accomplishment of his mission meant that the process of division could begin and the fire of judgment could be kindled.

Division and judgment might lie in the future, but there is no need to wait until the future to learn the *results* of Jesus' mission. Those results are also pictured in his teaching on the kingdom. In particular, three parables depict Jesus' expectation that the kingdom would have an impact far greater than its small beginnings might suggest.

In the parable of the mustard seed Jesus pictured the growth of the kingdom (Matt. 13:31-32; Mark 4:30-32; Luke 13:18-19). What be-

---

[37] Ibid.
[38] Senior and Stuhlmueller, *Biblical Foundations*, 154.
[39] Ibid.

gins as "smaller than all seeds" grows to become "larger than the garden plants."[40] So it will be with the kingdom: from insignificant beginnings, it will outgrow any similar enterprise. Coupled with the parable
of the mustard seed is the parable of the leaven, in which Jesus pictured the transformation brought about by the kingdom (Matt. 13:33;
Luke 13:20-21).[41] As a small amount of yeast eventually permeates
and transforms a large quantity of flour, so the kingdom will affect
everything that it touches. Mark alone records the parable of the seed
growing in secret, in which Jesus pictured the inevitable outcome of
the preaching of the kingdom (Mark 4:26-29).[42] The seed contains
within itself the potential to grow and produce a harvest. In the same
way that sowing seed leads to a harvest, the preaching of the kingdom
will produce men and women who are gathered into it. The process
might be mysterious, but the product is certain. From its insignificant
beginnings, the kingdom of God will grow—mysteriously, yet inevitably—until it dwarfs all other kingdoms and transforms all that it
touches.

## THE DISCIPLES' PRE-RESURRECTION MISSION

The insignificant beginnings from which the kingdom would grow
were the disciples Jesus had gathered around him during this three-
year public ministry. The twelve, in particular, had been called with
the explicit purpose of being prepared for mission (Matt. 4:18-22; Mark
1:16-20; Luke 5:1-11). As part of that preparation, Jesus sent them
out to practice the ministry he had modeled for them.

The synoptic gospels record two accounts of Jesus commissioning
his disciples for mission prior to his death and resurrection: the commissioning of the twelve (Matt. 9:35-10:42; Mark 3:13-19; 6:7-13;
Luke 9:1-6), and the commissioning of the seventy (Luke 10:1-20).[43]
Although the relationship between these two commissionings is hotly
debated, few scholars question the historicity of the commissioning of

---

[40] Robert H. Gundry (*Matthew: A Commentary on His Literary and Theological Art* [Grand Rapids: Eerdmans, 1982], 267) notes: "The mustard seed
was the smallest of the Palestinian seeds that could be seen with the naked eye
and had become proverbial for smallness. . . . On the other hand the mustard
plant grows to a height of 8-12 feet . . . and the rabbi Simeon b. Halafta is
reported to have said he had a mustard plant to the top of which he could
climb as to the top of a fig tree."

[41] For a discussion of the incongruity created by Jesus' use of both the leaven
and the mustard seed, see Carson, "Matthew," 318.

[42] For the close connection between sowing and preaching, see the discussion above.

[43] For a discussion of the textual variant at Luke 10:1 ("seventy" or "seventy-two"?), see Metzger, *Textual Commentary*, 126-27.

the twelve.[44] Fitzmyer and others have suggested that Luke created the mission of the seventy, yet, as Marshall writes, "it is unlikely that Luke simply invented the second mission . . . and more probable that he was following his sources."[45] Darrell Bock concurs, "The proclamation ministry extends beyond the Twelve and reflects roots in a real mission sent out by Jesus."[46] Because of the overlap in content of these two accounts, the instructions contained in them will be treated together.

Before examining the details of those instructions, it is important to note the context in which they were given. Both accounts are set in the context of addressing spiritual, not physical, need. Jesus' comment that "the harvest is plentiful, but the workers are few" occurs in different settings in Matthew and Luke (Matt. 9:37; Luke 10:2), but in both cases his concern was the spiritual need of the people to whom he sent the disciples. The twelve were sent to a leaderless flock whose pitiful state aroused Jesus' compassion (Matt. 9:36); the seventy were sent to those who would next hear Jesus' kingdom message (Luke 10:1). It was into the field of the spiritually needy that Jesus sent his disciples to reap the plentiful harvest.

The workers were, indeed, few. Initially they consisted solely of John the Baptist and Jesus—and Herod had imprisoned John. The need was greater than Jesus alone could meet. It was necessary, therefore, that others be commissioned to meet the need. In order to accomplish the task assigned to them, they were given the same *authority* as Jesus had exercised (Matt 10:1; Mark 3:15; 6:7; Luke 9:1). They carried out the same *activities* as he had: preaching and healing (Matt. 10:7-8; cf. Mark 3:14-15; 6:7; Luke 9:1-2). They preached the same *message* as he had: the kingdom of God (Matt. 10:7; cf. Luke 9:2). Their *target group* was the same as his had been: the nation of Israel (Matt. 10:5-6). Even the *results* were the same (Luke 10:17-20). Their task was, in short, identical to that of Jesus.

In order that they might carry out their task effectively, Jesus also gave them very specific guidelines regarding their *conduct*. They were to make no elaborate preparations before departing (Matt. 10:9-10; Luke 9:3; cf. Mark 6:8-9), and they were to focus on responsive hearers (Matt. 10:11-15; Mark 6:10-11; Luke 9:4-5; 10:5-11). In addition,

---

[44] For a concise summary of major views, see Robert H. Stein, *Luke*, NAC (Nashville: Broadman, 1992), 303, n.13.

[45] Marshall, *Luke*, 413. Contrast Joseph A. Fitzmyer, *The Gospel according to Luke X-XXIV*, AB, vol. 28A (Garden City, N.Y.: Doubleday, 1985), 843.

[46] Darrell L. Bock, *Luke—Volume 2: 9:51-24:53*, BECNT, no. 3B (Grand Rapids: Baker, 1996), 991. For a detailed discussion of the sources and historicity of Luke 10:1-24, see ibid., 986-91.

it was important that they understand the *circumstances* of their mission. Since opposition would be fierce, they were to be innocent but prudent (Matt. 10:16; Luke 10:3). Although they would encounter religious and civil persecution, they should view that opposition as an occasion for witness (Matt. 10:17-20). Indeed, opposition would provide an opportunity for expanded evangelism (Matt. 10:23). In light of these circumstances, it was important that they maintain the proper *perspective*: "Do not fear." They do not need to fear because the truth must emerge (Matt. 10:26-27), physical death pales beside eternal death (Matt. 10:28), and God is in control (Matt. 10:29-31). Their pre-resurrection mission might be divisive and costly (Matt. 10:34-39), but it had eternal implications (Matt. 10:32-33), and it brought eternal rewards (Matt. 10:40-42).

## THE TURNING POINT: JESUS' RESURRECTION

Jesus' resurrection marked a major turning point in his status. Prior to the resurrection, he was the itinerant Son of Man (Matt. 8:20; Luke 9:58), sent to do the Father's will (Matt. 26:39, 42; Mark 14:36; Luke 22:42). Subsequent to the resurrection, however, he is the Christ who suffered and rose from the dead on the third day (Luke 24:46), just as the OT prophesied (Luke 24:44). As Legrand notes, "The Resurrection has established Jesus as Lord and Christ. It has made him 'Son of God in power,' has revealed him as the triumphant sovereign of heaven and earth, Son of God exalted to the Father's right hand and sender of the Spirit."[47]

The resurrection also marked a turning point in Jesus' teaching on mission. His own mission was completed, and his role changed from sent one to *sender*. In this new role he assumed many of the prerogatives previously ascribed to the Father. His name is equal with the Father's (Matt. 28:19), and it is in his own name that forgiveness of sins is to be proclaimed (Luke 24:47). That name carries weight (Mark 16:17-18), for he has been given "all authority . . . in heaven and on earth" (Matt. 28:18). Just as he kept the Father's will, so his disciples are to teach others to keep that which he commanded (Matt. 28:20).[48] It is he who would send the promise of the Spirit to empower them for witness (Luke 24:48-49; Acts 1:4-5, 8), just as he was anointed by the Father in a similar way (Luke 4:18). As the Father was always present with him (John 8:29), so he would be present with his people (Matt. 28:20).

---

[47] Legrand, *Unity and Plurality*, 85.

[48] The verb Jesus uses in Matt. 28:20 (*entellomai*) is a cognate of the noun (*entolē*), which he regularly used to describe the OT Law (e.g., Matt. 5:19; 15:3, 6; 19:17; 23:36-40).

With the change in Jesus' role came another important change in the mission enterprise. The focus of mission shifted to Jesus' disciples. They were now the *sent ones*. They were the ones who would further the Father's purposes for judgment and redemption.

## THE DISCIPLES' POST-RESURRECTION MISSION

Although the disciples' post-resurrection mission was not a major element in Jesus' teaching prior to his death, it was an undertaking he anticipated and to which he alluded in advance. A future universalistic mission was presupposed by Jesus' references to the gospel of the kingdom being preached "in the whole world" (Matt. 24:14; 26:13; Mark 13:10; 14:9). The resurrection, however, brought that worldwide mission to the forefront.

An account of Jesus' final words to his disciples is included in each of the four gospels; a parallel incident is recorded in Acts.[49] Each passage is set in the immediate context of a post-resurrection appearance.[50] Table 3.1 compares the various passages.

Each account—except Mark's—includes a statement by Jesus which may be interpreted as a validation of his authority. In each passage, Jesus commanded an activity that was part of his pre-resurrection ministry, indicated the scope of the disciples' mission, and gave his disciples reassurance for the task at hand. The cumulative result is that the disciples received explicit instructions for continuing Jesus' mission, instructions spoken by the one who would authorize and accompany them as they carried out that mission.

The basic nature of their *task* continues to be that of extending Jesus' ministry. Jesus made disciples (Matt. 4:18-22; Mark 1:16-20; Luke 5:1-11). He proclaimed both the gospel (Luke 4:18) and repentance (Mark 1:15). He forgave sins (Matt. 9:1-8; Mark 2:1-12; Luke 5:17-26; 7:44-50), as well as retaining them (John 8:21-24; 9:41). He was a faithful witness of that which he saw and heard (John 3:11). Yet the primary *activity* in which the disciples were to be involved now shifts. Before the resurrection, Jesus authorized them both to preach and to heal (Matt. 10:7-8). Now the emphasis falls heavily on the

---

[49] As the discussion in the chapter on Mark suggests, the best evidence supports the ending at Mark 16:8 as original. Nevertheless, nothing in Mark 16:14-20 is unique in the NT, for even the attesting signs of Mark 16:17-18 have parallels (cf. Luke 10:17-20 and Acts 28:1-6). The material in this passage, therefore, is included in the present chapter for purposes of comparison.

[50] For a helpful analysis, see L. Legrand, "The Missionary Command of the Risen Christ: I. Mission and Resurrection," *Indian Theological Studies* 23 (1986): 296-302.

| | MATT. 28:18-20 | MARK 16:15-18 | LUKE 24:46-49 | JOHN 20:21-23 | ACTS 1:4-8 |
|---|---|---|---|---|---|
| **AUTHORITY** | all authority (v. 18) | — | it is written (v. 46) | as the Father sent me (v. 21) | Father . . . by his authority (v. 7) |
| **ACTIVITY** | make disciples (v. 19) | preach the gospel (v. 15) | repentance . . . be proclaimed (v. 47) | forgive . . . retain sins (v. 23) | be my witnesses (v. 8) |
| **SCOPE** | all the nations (v. 19) | all creation (v. 15) | all the nations (v. 47) | any (v. 23) | remotest part of the earth (v. 8) |
| **MEANS** | baptizing . . . teaching (vv. 19-20) | be baptized (vv. 15-16) | — | — | — |
| **REASSURANCE** | with you always (v. 20) | signs will accompany (vv. 17-18) | promise of my Father (v. 49) | receive the Holy Spirit (v. 22) | baptized with the Holy Spirit (v. 4, 8) |

*Table 3.1*

preaching/teaching dimension of their task. Their primary role is that of witnesses (Luke 24:48; Acts 1:8). Their task is one of proclamation (Mark 16:15; Luke 24:47) and teaching (Matt. 28:19-20). Miracles are simply signs that accompany them as they proclaim the good news (Mark 16:17-18).[51]

The emphasis of their *message* also shifts. Previously, their message was a simple one: "The kingdom of God is at hand" (Matt. 10:7). Now they are to proclaim "repentance for forgiveness of sins" (Luke 24:47), for they are to be witnesses of Jesus' death and resurrection (Luke 24:46). Both of these elements were implicit in Jesus' kingdom message, but now they are to be made explicit in the disciples' preaching. It is the risen Christ and the salvation blessings bestowed by him that take center stage. As well, Jesus' teachings are to be propagated (Matt. 28:20), an addition that expands considerably the message to be communicated.

With the recognition of Jesus' exalted status also comes a new *scope* for the disciples' mission. Now they are to carry their witness to "all the nations" (Matt. 28:19; Luke 24:47; cf. Mark 16:15). This universalistic scope is, in fact, the most consistent element running through the five commissioning accounts.[52] The scope of their mission is expressed in various ways, but in each account Jesus expanded the disciples' mission far beyond "the lost sheep of the house of Israel." It is no longer a particular mission, receiving non-Jews who seek assistance; it is now a universal mission, actively carrying the good news to Jew and Gentile alike. Again, what was implicit in Jesus' teaching and practice becomes explicit in the task entrusted by Jesus to his followers.

There is less than might be expected in Jesus' final words, which address the *results* of the disciples' mission. Two phrases, however, point the way. The first is found in Matthew 28:20: "teaching them to observe all that I commanded you." It is through obedient disciples that the mission will move forward. "All that I commanded you" includes, among other teachings, Jesus' instructions on mission. Jesus assumed that the eleven would pass on those instructions as part of

---

[51] Even in this deemphasis on miracles, however, there is a continuity with Jesus' mission, for he was willing to discontinue a "successful" healing ministry in order to get on with the task of preaching the kingdom (Luke 4:38-44). Healing was clearly secondary to his primary task of preaching.

[52] Contrast Benjamin Jerome Hubbard (*The Matthean Redaction of a Primitive Apostolic Commissioning: An Exegesis of Matthew 28:16-20*, SBLDS, no. 19 [Missoula, Mont.: Scholars Press, 1974], 122-28), who does not believe that the Gentile mission was originally part of the commissioning. Given the consistency with which the universalistic scope appears in the commissioning accounts, however, it seems more natural to attribute it to Jesus than to Hubbard's unknown redactor.

their message. As the eleven obeyed Jesus' final words and made disciples who, in turn, were taught to obey those same words, a chain reaction would begin that would continue his mission until he returns.

The ever-expanding impact of that chain reaction is clearly indicated by a second phrase, found in Acts 1:8: "both in Jerusalem, and in all Judea and Samaria, and even to the remotest part of the earth." That which began with Jesus in Palestine would ultimately—through his disciples—reach the entire world. In addition, Bediako notes that this phrase points to more than mere geographical progression,[53] since one of the key concepts developed in the book of Acts is the way in which the gospel crossed cultural—as well as geographical—thresholds.[54] It is through the preaching of Jesus' followers that the great expectations pictured in Jesus' parables would be realized. Through their obedience, the mustard seed would grow into a worldwide movement, the leaven would transform human society, and the seed growing in secret would produce a great harvest.

## CONCLUSION

A number of important principles related to mission emerge from Jesus' teaching. First, the primary impetus for mission is spiritual need. Both Jesus and his disciples were sent to men and women who were spiritually needy. Although physical needs are, at times, addressed during the course of mission, the focus is spiritual. Second, the primary purpose of mission is redemptive. This principle follows the first logically. Jesus came to seek and save the lost. After the resurrection, the disciples were sent to proclaim forgiveness of sins. In both cases the purpose was to further the divine plan of redemption. Third, mission has a worldwide scope. Jesus anticipated a universal mission, and the disciples' post-resurrection mission was explicitly universal. The redemptive purpose of mission extends to "all the nations." Fourth, the one sent on mission exercises the same authority as the sender. Just as the Father conferred his authority on the Son, so Jesus conferred his authority on the disciples. The continuity of authority is simply the most prominent example of the close identity between sender and sent one. Fifth, obedience should characterize the one sent on mission. Jesus was committed to doing the Father's will, and he expected his disciples to obey everything he had commanded them. If the divine intentions for mission are to be accomplished, then obedience is essential for the one who is sent. Sixth, preaching/teaching is the primary activity expected of the one sent on mission. Jesus was sent to preach. The disciples' pre-resurrection mission included preaching, and their post-

---

[53] Bediako, *Christianity in Africa*, 154.
[54] See the discussion in the chapter on Acts below.

resurrection mission emphasized preaching and teaching. Proclamation must remain central to the mission enterprise. Seventh, faithful communication of the mission message will bring positive results. Jesus envisioned mission resulting in extensive growth and intensive transformation. The mission message contains within itself the potential to produce those results. What is required, therefore, is the faithful communication of that message.

There are, of course, other principles that can—and should—be drawn from Jesus' teaching on mission. The preceding seven are simply a starting point. They serve to remind us, however, that Jesus had much to say on the topic and that his words point the way for the church's understanding of the task entrusted to it.

# 4

# Mission in the Early Church

## David P. Seemuth

The imperatives encountered in the New Testament surrounding mission explicitly express many of the actions that were already taking place in the early days of the church's experience.[1] The resurrection of Jesus Christ and the coming of the Spirit of God inaugurated a new era in the mission of God. These events also marked a change in the disciples' understanding of the role of Jesus, and their own subsequent roles then shifted dramatically with the revelation (to them at least) of the Son of God and Messiah. Strictly speaking, this revelation did not occur until the resurrection of Jesus Christ.[2] Until that time, as

---

[1] The commands to "go," whether given to the Eleven in Matthew 28:19 or to specific disciples in Acts (5:20; 8:26; 9:11; 28:26), indicated that active proclamation and involvement with the overall society, whether Jew or Greek, was essential. They were truly "sent ones."

[2] In the gospels, there is a remarkable "dullness" on the part of the disciples when it comes to recognizing the true identity of Jesus. They vacillate between amazement and doubt. They are amazed at the works of Jesus but then deeply troubled even to the point of abandonment at Jesus' crucifixion. The doubt vanishes, however, when Jesus is clearly revealed as the risen one. This is most profoundly seen in the way Luke treats the identity of Jesus in Luke-Acts. There is a pre-resurrection Christology and a post-resurrection Christology. Luke's use of christological titles of "Son," "Christ," "savior," and "Lord" gives evidence of this twofold distinction. See C. F. D. Moule, "The Christology of Acts," in *Studies in Luke-Acts*, ed. Leander E. Keck and J. Louis Martyn (Nashville: Abingdon, 1966), 159-85; Donald L. Jones, "The Title *kyrios* in Luke-Acts," in *Society of Biblical Literature 1974 Seminar Papers*, ed. George MacRae (Cambridge, Mass.: Society of Biblical Literature, 1974), 2:85-101; William Kurz, "The Function of Christological Proof from Prophecy for Luke and Justin" (Ph.D. diss., Yale University, 1976); idem, "Hellenistic Rhetoric in the Christological Proof of Luke-Acts," *CBQ* 42 (1980): 171-95.

the gospels record, confusion abounded regarding the identity of this teacher, miracle worker, and leader named Jesus.

The early church encountered the gospels and other New Testament writings as those who were "knowledgeable" of Jesus' true identity. Thus, they read the narrative of the gospels as those who understood what had already occurred in history. The text expounds on what, from the authors' points of view, were most important for the early church. As a result, we can see glimpses of the concern of the New Testament writers for their audiences and, therefore, the setting of the early church with reference to mission. Something new and amazing had begun, and the believers saw the overall historical situation as perfectly suited for this new revelation of God to humanity (Gal. 4:4).

The biblical text also gives the modern reader a taste of the broader historical and cultural trends of the period. The milieu, while certainly not monolithic, exhibited powerful characteristics that shaped the expectations and even the experiences of the people. The Greek and Jewish cultures, which provided the soil in which the church would initially grow, contained fertile elements to enhance such growth. After examining the cultural setting in which the mission of the early church took place, this chapter will also look at certain key issues that moved the first Christians toward mission.

## THE JEWISH CULTURE: EXPECTATION AND ANTICIPATION

Within the Jewish setting, religious/cultural distinctives that prepared the people well for the Christian gospel included the messianism and apocalypticism of the period.[3] One is hard-pressed to boil down Jewish expectation into a few general trends, but certain points are evident. Messianic expectation married social discontent. The result was the offspring of anticipation and action.[4] In the Essene community, for instance, the idea of a Messiah was linked to the purity and anointed authority of the leaders.[5] The future, however, was to include not only a predominantly priestly as opposed to a royal Messiah, but also a messianic kingdom with Messiah as judge.[6] The quest

---

[3] Donald Senior and Carroll Stuhlmueller, *The Biblical Foundations for Mission* (Maryknoll, N.Y.: Orbis Books, 1983), 28-31; James D. Newsome, *Greeks, Romans, Jews: Currents of Culture and Belief in the New Testament World* (Philadelphia: Trinity Press International, 1992), 66-101.

[4] Bo Reicke, *The New Testament Era: The World of the Bible from 500 B.C. to A.D. 100*, trans. David E. Green (Philadelphia: Fortress, 1968), 112-13.

[5] Alan F. Segal, *Rebecca's Children: Judaism and Christianity in the Roman World* (Cambridge, Mass.: Harvard University Press, 1986), 67.

[6] Newsome, *Greeks, Romans, Jews*, 144-45.

for ritualistic purity and proper interpretation of the Law was inseparably linked with the desire to be a part of the coming messianic kingdom. The pure would be judged as worthy by the Messiah-judge.

A messianic hope existed also in the broader Jewish society. The
Psalms of Solomon spoke of such a future expectation in reaction to
the events of the day. This messianic "Son of David" shall rise up and
overthrow the Gentiles and rule with power and justice (*Pss. Sol.* 17:21-
32).[7] Although messianism is not rampant in the literature of the period, the hope of such a dynamic, powerful, and just figure is clear.

Closely related to this messianism is the apocalypticism of the period.[8] The movement of human history, it seemed to some Jewish writers, was marching to its final and dramatic climax. God would soon
be victorious and bring forth the inauguration of God's kingdom on
earth. The Ethiopic Book of Enoch *(1 Enoch)*, written from as early as
the third century B.C.E. and as late as the first century C.E., contains
great expectation of such events.[9] In the first section of the book, the
writer noted that there would be ultimate judgment for the sinner by
the Son of Man (*1 Enoch* 48:2-3) and this apocalyptic judge would
rule in mighty fashion (*1 Enoch* 49:2-4). The writer of the Testament
of the Twelve Patriarchs also expected judgment for the wicked and
rest for the "righteous."

> The heavens shall greatly rejoice in his days and the earth shall
> be glad; The clouds shall be filled with joy and the knowledge of
> the Lord will be poured out on the earth like the water of the
> seas. . . . And the glory of the Most High shall burst forth upon
> him. And the spirit of sanctification shall rest upon him. . . . In
> his priesthood sin shall cease and lawless men shall rest from
> their evil deeds, and righteous men shall find rest in him.[10]

The *Book of Jubilees*, while not apocalyptic in the strict sense, contains the same expectation of a glorious future for the faithful and
judgment for the wicked. As Newsome states, "The future of humankind is described in which there is a return to the Torah, an event that
results in the restoration of peace and joy to human life and which
ushers in an age in which the human life span will again reach a millennium."[11] The third book of the *Sibylline Oracles* (completed before

---

[7] See Newsome, *Greeks, Romans, Jews*, 99.

[8] D. E. Aune, "Apocalypticism," in *DPHL*, ed. Gerald F. Hawthorne and
Ralph P. Martin (Downers Grove, Ill.: InterVarsity, 1993), 25-35.

[9] Newsome, *Greeks, Romans, Jews*, 81.

[10] *T. Levi* 18:1-11. The translation of this text is by H. C. Kee, in *The Old
Testament Pseudepigrapha*, ed. James H. Charlesworth (Garden City, N.Y.:
Doubleday, 1983-85), 1:794-95.

[11] Newsome, *Greeks, Romans, Jews*, 91. See *Jub.* 23:26-27.

the end of the first century C.E.) speaks of the coming wrath of the "Immortal" one (*Sib. Or.* 3:601-6) and the ushering in of a blessed existence for the faithful (*Sib. Or.* 3:767-802).

Such messianic and apocalyptic expectation provided fertile ground for the growth of the Christian gospel. The proclamation of Simeon in the Temple is obvious evidence that such expectation was part and parcel of proclamation and explanation of the role of Jesus (Luke 2:25-35). The frequent attestation of Jesus as the Christ (Messiah) and Son of David links the story of Jesus with this future hope of the Jews. However, this expectation was not the genesis of the designation of Jesus as the Messiah. Certainly themes were picked up that mirror the apocalyptic writings, but the concept of Jesus as Messiah was based upon the disciples' understanding of the radical change of Jesus from dead leader to risen Lord.

## THE HISTORICAL SETTING: THE GENTILE WORLD

The Gentile world also held expectations with reference to the spiritual realm. Certainly one finds the existence of the different philosophical schools. However, the Epicureans, Cynics, Stoics, and others never gained a great following in comparison with the vast numbers of people in the society who were unaffiliated with formal philosophical teachings. The highly educated identified themselves with those who adhered to various philosophical schools.[12] Paul showed he was acquainted with some of the teachings of the philosophers, but there is little evidence that many converts to the Christian gospel came from this "religious elite."[13]

Historically, the traditional Greek and Roman religion serves as a starting point for understanding the Gentile religious scene. While within the Greek culture some people remained loyal to the traditional religion with the pantheon of Roman or Greek gods, the majority of the populace ignored these religious rites. Even the emphasis on the role of the emperor as the high priest of the religion did not cause a great religious turning toward the traditional religion. Indeed, people burned incense to the emperor later in the post-apostolic period, but this was done more as a sign of political loyalty rather than of serious and deep religious commitment and devotion.

---

[12] Bruce Manning Metzger, *The New Testament: Its Background, Growth, and Content,* 2d ed. (Nashville: Abingdon, 1983), 61-70; Robert H. Gundry, *A Survey of the New Testament,* 3d ed. (Grand Rapids: Zondervan, 1994), 61-62.

[13] Acts 17:16-34 portrays Paul's awareness of the philosophical scene and his ability to converse with those involved in it. However, the Acts account indicates only a few believed (Acts 17:34). Paul also quoted an Epicurean-like saying in 1 Corinthians 15:32.

The "mystery religions" had more appeal to the first century C.E. mindset, but even these groups were not gaining great numbers of adherents. The cult of Cybele, devotion to Isis and Serapis, and Mithraism were forms of this broad category of the "mysteries." The existence of these different forms of ritualistic and personal religions presents a picture of people with a spiritual longing.[14] Apparently the state religion did not meet the spiritual need of the masses. Thus, the elaborate initiatory rites and ongoing rituals of these groups struck a chord among their adherents. The groups did have certain tenets that mirror the early Christian teachings and, perhaps, provided a touchstone for the proclamation of the gospel. These are: (1) teachings about a god who died but had then been resuscitated and now lives, (2) a promise of individual immortality, (3) a removal of class distinctions within the group as each person was now seen to be at the same level within the religion, and (4) a religious experience involving an outpouring of emotion and declarations of personal attachment to a supernatural deity.[15] The adherents of mystery religions who heard the Christian gospel would not be immediately repulsed by the teaching. On the contrary, they may have been drawn to the tenets of the gospel by their own experience and understanding, even though there were large distinctions between Christianity and these different groups. Again, these groups did not attract large masses of the population, but the thought contained within the group could provide a starting point for the spread of the gospel among such people.

It has been noted to this point that large numbers of people did not identify themselves with the philosophies, the traditional Greco-Roman religion, or the mystery religions. There was not one majority group that identified with one religion within the Greco-Roman world. However, a large group of Gentiles was inclined toward the superstitious and magical.[16] Indeed, this was perhaps the majority of the people. Monuments built and offerings given to spirits that inhabited the countryside were frequent among the masses. The average Roman was concerned to placate such animistic deities.

The spirit world, according to those inclined toward the magical, exercised enormous control over everyday life. If one could manipulate the spirits, through chantings, formulas, or other means, events would turn out as desired.[17] Such magical practice is defined by David

---

[14] Gundry, *Survey*, 58-60; Metzger, *New Testament*, 66-70.

[15] Newsome, *Greeks, Romans, Jews*, 27-30; Thomas D. Lea, *The New Testament: Its Background and Message* (Nashville: Broadman, 1996), 46-48.

[16] David Aune, "Magic in Early Christianity," *ANRW* II.23.2 (1980): 1521; Clinton E. Arnold, *Ephesians, Power and Magic: The Concept of Power in Ephesians in Light of Its Historical Setting* (Grand Rapids: Baker, 1992), 19-20; Gundry, *Survey*, 59.

[17] Arnold, *Ephesians*, 18-20.

Aune through two criteria: First, "magical practice" is a deviation from the sanctioned religious practice. Secondly, "goals sought within the context of religious deviance are magical when attained through the management of supernatural powers in such a way that results are virtually guaranteed."[18] The difference between the religious and the magical is that in religion one prays for help from the gods; in magic one coerces the gods to act in the desired fashion.

The following principles further define the "magical" world view.[19] First, there are good spirits and bad spirits, which requires that one distinguish between the two. Second, fear of the demons moves one to act in such a way as to be protected from them. Third, identification of specific spirits that oversee different aspects of life aid in finding individual help (or hurt, if directed to other people). Those who held to such principles tended to be the uneducated and the poor. Indeed, the style of writing found in the so-called magical papyri betrays the common language of the people. As such, many were attracted to these ideas and held to these principles. Hans Dieter Betz asserts, "Magical beliefs and practices can hardly be overestimated in their importance for the daily life of the people."[20] As the gospel entered this first-century society, where many held to this world view, there was both a negative reaction and a positive reaction toward this message of a superior figure who has control over life and death and nature. There was at times a negative reaction to assertions of an exclusive deity and positive reactions to the power of such a figure. However, any understanding of a local church situation of first-century Christians must take into account the power of this magical viewpoint.

It is interesting that the gospel texts as well as the book of Acts record instances of what might be interpreted as magical by those so inclined. The healings of Jesus, the casting out of demons, and the power of Jesus over nature were all very appealing to one concerned about being victimized by the evil spirit world. The apostles' actions, likewise, showed that this same power is now resident among the faithful believers in Jesus (Acts 14:8-18; 19:11-20; 2 Cor. 12:12). It is surely an accurate statement that Jews seek signs and Greeks seek wisdom, but the common Greek poor also seek signs that evidence victory over the demons. One traces the movement of the gospel in Acts by certain extraordinary signs, which validated the power of the Holy Spirit resident in the early Christian leaders. Such power resonated strongly in the lives of those who sought to become free of demonic influence in daily life.

---

[18] Aune, "Magic," 1515-16.

[19] Arnold, *Ephesians*, 18.

[20] Hans Dieter Betz, "Introduction to the Greek Magical Papyri," in *The Greek Magical Papyri in Translation*, ed. Hans Dieter Betz (Chicago: University of Chicago Press, 1986), xli.

## THE NEW PEOPLE OF GOD:
## TOWARD SELF-UNDERSTANDING

It is important to recognize that the admonishment toward mission in the New Testament had both an explanatory role and a motivational role. Mission was already occurring. What we then encounter in the New Testament is both a description of people embracing the gospel as it confronted them either in a Jewish or Gentile context and an urging of people toward spreading the work and message of God in Christ. The early church realized that God's own "missionary zeal" and merciful actions were evident in their midst. These believers also were well-acquainted with those men and women who exhibited "missionary zeal." Indeed, the early church owed its very existence to the combination of a God who desired to save and people who were willing to be the agents of God's redemptive work. The biblical texts that contain mission commands elucidate the impetus and understanding that caused men and women to go forth and have the impact they did. The reflection of the church upon these men and women, as well as upon the God of mission, required explanations for the powerful actions that did occur and must continue to occur.

In particular, three important issues rose to the forefront of the early church's concern. The first question addressed the boundaries of God's work. The second issue focused on the justice of God. The third point concerned the future of the mission. Clearly God acted without the people fully understanding these aspects of mission. Jesus acted first and explained later. Even Jesus' appearance to the disciples on the road to Emmaus in Luke 24 was not fully understood, although it was directly experienced by them. The disciples in Acts proclaimed a message, worked miracles, and witnessed many becoming followers of "the Way" before they completely understood what was happening. Only under the power of the Holy Spirit did Peter realize what was occurring on the day of Pentecost, for instance. Explanation often came after the actions of a God of mission and of the human agents cooperating in that mission.

### The Boundaries of Mission

God does not show favoritism (Acts 10:34). This basic statement, found here in reference to the universal scope of the message of the gospel but also in the context of judgment (Rom. 2:11) and with a view to interpersonal relationships (Eph. 6:9; Col. 3:25), forms an appropriate starting point in examining the background of mission within the early church. In many ways, the early church grappled with the boundaries that distinguished those acceptable to God from those who were not. The inclusion of material in the gospels that highlighted the destruction of commonly held boundaries within Israel (that is, the good Samaritan [Luke 10:33], the faithful centurion [Matt. 8:5-13], the Syrophoenician woman [Mark 7:24-30]) served to break down longstanding assumptions regarding the domain of God's gracious activity. God could work in the Samaritan to provide care for the needy. Jesus recognized the faith, and therefore approved, of one who, as a soldier in a nation under foreign rule, may have symbolized all that was seemingly wrong with the Jewish society. The early church came to recognize that God's grace could extend to all, because even the crumbs of God's mercy were sufficient to meet the needs of Gentile believers.

In the book of Acts the movement from a Judean-Jewish society to a Hellenistic-Jewish society and then to a Gentile world provided evidence and explanation that the previously held understanding of the boundaries of God's redemptive work was outmoded. Paul's understanding revealed in Galatians and Romans of his own calling (and God's calling to redemption through Paul) furthered the destruction of these fences. One might argue that Paul's appeal in Galatians 1 that his gospel was not from any human agent or the result of some theological seminar validated the destruction of old boundaries. Paul had these old boundaries embedded in his psyche until his Damascus road experience. He himself would have taken pride in his possession of the law and in his relationship with Yahweh through the covenant marked out by circumcision (Rom. 2:17-3:9). Indeed, that is what made Paul adept at using the diatribal style in Romans; he was the ideal Jewish interlocutor. Nevertheless, Paul's gospel, which destroyed the Jew-Gentile boundary, came directly from Christ himself. Under no circumstances could one argue that God favored any people, class, sex, or position. All such boundaries are gone; therefore, any mission must likewise cut across all such boundaries.

### The Justice of God

One of the paramount concerns of the early church revealed in the New Testament surrounds the need for the justice of God. This operates in three directions with reference to the mission of the church. First, there is a need to guarantee the justice of God in God's relationship with unbelievers. Second, one must secure an understanding of how justice relates to the salvation of the believer. Third, the church must respond in a just way to God's just actions. Paul's whole treatment of the "righteousness of God" is arguably the concern to show that God acts rightly. If God's actions are perfectly in line with righteousness, then an appropriate response to this just God is necessary. The approach that Paul took to explain the state and future of the

Gentiles in Romans 1:18-32 is more a commentary on God than on the Gentile. True, the Gentile acts abhorrently, but God acts honorably at every turn. God's response of "giving them over" to the consequences of their sinful acts is seen as perfectly justified as a judge's proper and necessary reaction. At no point can one say that God is not justified in the actions taken. Similarly, the Jew is condemned justly by God because of God's just stand based on the law the Jew so closely embraces. So the law (both written and unwritten) rightly shows all humanity as deserving judgment. Even Paul's treatment of the issue of the seeming abandonment of the Jews is seen as both a just and merciful act of God (Rom. 9-11). Also, the statements contained in the speeches of Acts about the culpability of the Jews and the need for repentance of all humanity are based upon the understanding that God is intrinsically just.

In response, then, believers must understand that their salvation is not only based on the mercy and grace of God but also on the justice of God. God's requirement that sin be atoned for must be upheld. So one constantly finds appeal to the actions of Jesus as atonement, redemption, reconciliation. These are equally justice terms as well as words rich in the concept of mercy. One cannot have atonement without the law structure that allows for substitution in place of the sinner. One cannot buy back the slave without the provision of law. One cannot find reconciliation until law demands equal standing of both offender and offended. The gospel fully meets the law's requirements for atonement, redemption, and reconciliation. The term "justification" is essentially a legal term, since God's justice must be upheld.

Finally, with reference to justice, even the church as the new people of God must act in just fashion. The concern of the apostles in Acts 6 and the subsequent appointing of "deacons" was a concern for justice. The actions of the apostles when accused of violating civil ordinance give the impression of absolute innocence. God's mighty, vindicating actions confirm that, indeed, they are justified in God's sight and should be considered as free from impurity in the eyes of the readers. The admonishment of James with reference to not playing favorites is essentially a concern for justice within the church. Even the expectation of Paul, Peter, and the other apostles and New Testament writers that believers live in a holy manner is based on the concern that believers act like the holy, just God. It is the God of justice who is the God of mission.

### The Future of Mission

The mission that God undertook and that the believers continued has an endpoint. This endpoint is either the death and subsequent reception of the believer by the Lord or it is the return of the risen Christ

(Phil. 1:20-26; 2 Cor. 5:8-10). Thus, there are time constraints upon the believers to complete the mission. This in itself is motivation for the believers to act. There is also an expectation that one's actions do count at the time of the Lord's evaluation in heaven (2 Cor. 5:10). So, whether believers follow the example and the imperatives in the commands of Jesus and the apostles will be measured by the Lord they serve. The return of the Lord, however, marks the definitive end-point in the mission of God to save humanity.

## CONCLUSION

Mission in the early church was unmistakably linked to a historical and cultural milieu, yet the milieu did not define the mission. Certainly expectations and understandings or misunderstandings existed in the New Testament era that either helped or hindered the movement of the Christian gospel. Yet these exist in all settings at all times. At times, the culture assists the proclaimers of the gospel message when themes and issues resonate with hearers, but at other times there is a consequent resistance by a culture with suspicions or abhorrence for specific ideas.

However, there was a remarkable confluence of expectations and anticipations among both Gentiles and Jews in the apostolic era, which were met by the gospel message. Though different in specifics, the general longing for a dramatic movement of God, either by sovereign act or through magical coercion, provided an answer to the longings of expectant people. God seemed to act powerfully in Christ, particularly in his death and resurrection. This provided ultimate fulfillment to messianic expectations and extraordinary hope that God is able to control the final realities of death, and, therefore, the issues surrounding life.

The church today, as those who are responding to the message of the gospel and following the Lord Jesus, must also, like the earliest believers, confront issues of boundaries, justice, and the future of mission. Each believer has specific boundary issues ingrained from family, society, and other experiences. Such perceptions of how God may work need to be confronted by the teachings of the New Testament message concerning the universal scope of mission and the universal need of the message. Identifying and changing such preconceived notions of how God works is a great challenge for the local context of convinced believers who struggle with their own prejudices surrounding the boundaries of God's grace.

It is these same convinced believers who must wrestle with the concept of the "righteousness of God" and begin to imitate the gracious giver of the gospel message. Such a struggle is always within a cultural context and brings the believer up against gender, racial, and class issues that must be addressed based on God's own standard of justice rather than on the prevailing wave of thought that happens to be in vogue. Such actions provide further evidence of the advance of mission, since God is seen through a struggle for justice as the Lord of the small, the unrecognized, and the disadvantaged, as well as the Lord of the great, the conspicuous, and the privileged.

Finally, the ultimate hope of the return of the risen one and the expectation of judgment and reward motivated the early church in its mission. A definitive point awaits on the horizon that marks an end to all earthly things and a new future for believers. Thus, they can carry on in hardship, difficulty, and oppression. For God will bring forth vindication.

# PART TWO

# PAUL'S WRITINGS

# 5

# Mission in Paul's Epistles: Genesis, Pattern, and Dynamics

## Don N. Howell Jr.

In the decade that spanned three missionary journeys, from his commissioning with Barnabas by the church in Antioch (Acts 13:1-3) to his arrest in Jerusalem (Acts 21:33), the former Pharisee Paul became the catalyst for the planting of the Christian church throughout the urban centers of the eastern Mediterranean. This intense period of missionary activity moved Christianity beyond its Judean confines to the teeming centers of population in the Greco-Roman world. With unparalleled abandon Paul devoted himself to the mission he believed the God of his fathers set him apart for. His success as a pioneer church-planting missionary is evidenced by his statements in Romans 15 that the foundation laying ministry has now been "fulfilled" from Jerusalem to Illyricum (v. 19) and that there remains no more room for him to work in that region (v. 23). Later he makes the rhetorical boast that the gospel "has been proclaimed to every creature under heaven" (Col. 1:23).

What was the mission of Paul, that specific task to which he felt called by divine authority, for which he was empowered, and toward which he focused an energized obedience? In this chapter, the following three dimensions of the Pauline mission will be examined: its genesis and definition, its pattern and aims, and the dynamics behind its success. An exploration of the mission's theological bearings appears in the next chapter.

In broader salvation historical terms Paul refers to the "sending" of the Son by the Father to accomplish the redemption of mankind (*exapostellō*, Gal. 4:4; *pempō*, Rom. 8:3). Christ is God's divine agent dispatched from heaven to be born in human likeness and to die as a

sin offering.[1] Though "sending" in scripture may at times simply denote prophetic commission with no thought of preexistence (cf. Isa.
48:16b; Jer. 7:25; Ezek. 3:4-5; Zech. 2:8, 9, 11), in Romans 8:3 and
Galatians 4:4 God's act of sending appears to predate not only the
redemptive mission but also Christ's assuming the "likeness of sinful
flesh" (Rom. 8:3) and his being born of a woman (Gal. 4:4). Nevertheless, the language of mission in Paul is largely focused on his own role
in God's redemptive program. The mission of the servant-Son—incar-
nate, crucified, and exalted—is made known in the mission of the ser-
vant-apostle.[2]

## THE GENESIS AND DEFINITION OF THE PAULINE MISSION

Even as the mission of Jesus is captured in his favorite self-designation, Son of Man, so Paul's mission finds summative expression in his
major self-designation, apostle (*apostolos*). This term provides the key
to Paul's self-understanding as an agent sent by God. Therefore, it is

---

[1] C. A. Wanamaker, "Christ as Divine Agent in Paul," *SJT* 39 (1986): 517-
28.

[2] The standard critical view in New Testament scholarship is that there are
seven letters alone which can be confidently assigned to Paul: Romans,
1 Corinthians, 2 Corinthians, Galatians, Philippians, 1 Thessalonians, and
Philemon. However, there are not a few scholars over a wide theological
spectrum who have dissented from the majority view and capably defended
the integrity of the six disputed letters. For Ephesians and Colossians: Markus
Barth, *Ephesians 1-3*, AB, vol. 34 (Garden City, N.Y.: Doubleday, 1974),
36-50; D. A. Carson, Douglas J. Moo, and Leon Morris, *An Introduction to
the New Testament* (Grand Rapids: Zondervan, 1992), 305-9, 331-34; Peter
T. O'Brien, *Colossians, Philemon*, WBC, vol. 44 (Waco, Tex.: Word, 1982),
xli-xlix; E. Percy, *Die Probleme der Kolosser und Epheserbriefe* (Kobenhavn:
Lund C. W. K. Gleerup, 1946). For 2 Thessalonians: F. F. Bruce, *1 and 2
Thessalonians*, WBC, vol. 45 (Waco, Tex.: Word, 1982), xxii-xlvii; Carson,
Moo, and Morris, *Introduction*, 344-46; B. Rigaux, *Saint Paul. Les Épîtres
aux Thessaloniciens* (Paris: J. Gabalda, 1956), 124-52. For the pastoral epistles:
Carson, Moo, and Morris, *Introduction*, 359-71; Donald Guthrie, *The Pastoral Epistles* (Grand Rapids: Eerdmans, 1957), 11-52; J. N. D. Kelly, *A Commentary on the Pastoral Epistles* (London: Adam and Charles Black, 1963),
3-36; Bruce M. Metzger, "A Reconsideration of Certain Arguments against
the Pauline Authorship of the Pastoral Epistles," *ExpTim* 70 (1958-59): 91-
94; C. F. D. Moule, "The Problem of the Pastoral Epistles," *BJRL* 47 (1964-
65): 430-52; E. K. Simpson, *The Pastoral Epistles* (London: Tyndale, 1954),
1-23; Ceslas Spicq, *Les Épîtres Pastorales* (Paris: J. Gabalda, 1947), xcv-
cxxx. The reconstruction of the mission of Paul in these chapters is drawn by
and large from the undisputed letters, but related texts are cited from the
entire Pauline corpus.

necessary to examine Paul's understanding of apostleship and the origin of his apostleship in his conversion and commission.

### The Apostle

In every letter ascribed to Paul, with the exceptions of Philippians, Philemon, and the Thessalonian correspondence (cf. 1 Thess. 2:7), Paul is identified from the outset as the "apostle" of Jesus Christ (Rom. 1:1; 1 Cor. 1:1; 2 Cor. 1:1; Gal. 1:1; Eph. 1:1; Col. 1:1; 1 Tim. 1:1; 2 Tim. 1:1; Titus 1:1). With this term Paul does not place himself in isolation from but in solidarity with the other commissioned apostles (plural *apostoloi*: 1 Cor. 4:9; 9:5; 12:28-29; 15:7, 9; Gal. 1:17, 19; Eph. 2:20; 3:5; 4:11; 1 Thess. 2:7). He is the last in the series of authorized representatives commissioned by the risen Christ (1 Cor. 15:5-8). His calling as one "abnormally born" (*ektrōma*, 1 Cor. 15:8) is a badge of honor, since his apostleship follows a cruciform pattern of weakness and dependence (1 Cor. 15:9-10), not self-promotion like the super apostles (2 Cor. 11:5; 12:11) who are also false apostles (2 Cor. 11:13).[3]

Paul employs the term *apostle* in two ways. First, in a solemn, official sense it refers to representative spokesmen commissioned by the risen Lord with responsibility to carry out the task of extending and establishing the church under authoritative tradition (1 Cor. 9:1, 5; 12:28; 15:5-11; Gal. 1:17; 1 Thess. 2:7; Eph. 2:20; 4:11). The essential qualifications of true apostles are: (1) direct commission from the risen Lord (Gal. 1:1), (2) eyewitness experience of the resurrection (1 Cor. 9:1; 15:8; cf. Acts 1:20-22), (3) authority (*exousia*, 2 Cor. 10:8; 13:10) to receive and transmit divinely revealed and universally normative tradition (*paradosis*, 1 Cor. 11:2; 2 Thess. 2:15; 3:6; cf. 1 Cor. 15:3), and (4) the authenticating miraculous "signs of an apostle" (2 Cor. 12:12; cf. Rom. 15:19; 1 Thess. 1:5). Second, Paul occasionally applies the term *apostle* in a nontechnical sense to those "sent ones" who engage in pioneer church-planting ministry, as Andronicus and Junia apparently did (Rom. 16:7), and to those who represent the churches in specific missions (2 Cor. 8:23; Phil. 2:25). Luke applies the term *apostle* in Acts in its technical sense exclusively to the twelve (28 times) and to Paul and Barnabas in Acts 14:4, 14 as missionaries of the church in Antioch.[4]

The importance of the term *apostle* for understanding the Pauline mission can be felt when its New Testament usage and meaning are

---

[3] Gordon D. Fee, *The First Epistle to the Corinthians*, NICNT (Grand Rapids: Eerdmans, 1986), 732-34.

[4] P. W. Barnett, "Apostle," in *DPHL*, ed. Gerald F. Hawthorne and Ralph P. Martin (Downers Grove, Ill.: InterVarsity, 1993), 47-48.

compared to its historical parameters. Because *apostolos* has such a meager history of pre-Christian usage,[5] scholars have posited a variety of backgrounds to explain its prominence in the New Testament.[6] Gradually, it seems, a consensus has developed, with refinements, around K. H. Rengstorf's thesis[7] that the *šālîaḥ* or "sent one" of rabbinical Judaism provides the most likely provenance for the New Testament concept of apostleship.[8] The rabbinic *šālîaḥ* was sent as the authorized representative of the commissioner as expressed in the Mishnaic statement, "the one whom a person sends is like the sender" (*m. Berakoth*, 5.5). Jesus expressed the same concept in John 13:16: "a messenger (*apostolos*) is not greater than the one who sent him (*pempō*)." Even if this thesis is correct, as it probably is, it is unable to account fully for the New Testament evidence. First, it was the relationship of the representative to the sender, not the content of the commission, that is primary in the *šālîaḥ* convention. Second, a Jewish missionary was never called *šālîaḥ* because it was primarily a secular or legal not religious convention. Yet in the commission of the apostles by Jesus (including Paul as "one abnormally born," 1 Cor. 15:8) the content of their message and the scope of their mission are inseparably bound up with the authority they receive as his representatives. In his earthly ministry Jesus commissions the twelve (Matt. 10:1-4; Mark 3:13-18; 6:30; Luke 6:12-16) to announce the dawning of the kingdom to the lost sheep of Israel (Matt. 10:6-7). The miraculous signs that they perform authenticate the message they proclaim, which is itself bound up with the identity of their Sender. Then, in his last charge to the apostles, the risen Lord commands that they preach the gospel to all the nations of the world (Matt. 28:16-20; Luke 24:45-49; Acts 1:8; John 20:21-23). His universal authority (Matt. 28:18) determines

---

[5] Most of the occurrences in LSJ (p. 220) are related to seafaring, whether a naval squadron or expedition, commander of a naval force, or more specialized meanings such as colony, cargo, packet, or order for dispatch. Twice in Herodotus the term refers to a messenger or envoy (1.21; 5.38). The LXX (I Kgs. 14:6) and Symmachus (Isa. 18:1) each have one occurrence in the sense of messenger. Josephus (*Antiquities*, 1.146; 17.30) uses it twice of emissaries. K. H. Rengstorf ("*apostolos*," *TDNT* 1:407-13) further shows that the conceptual link to various terms attested of religious messengers in Hellenism is also tenuous. This provides a stunning contrast to the NT use of *apostolos*, which occurs seventy-nine times in twenty-one books across the entire span of the NT.

[6] A fine survey of the major proposals is provided in Francis H. Agnew, "The Origin of the NT Apostle-Concept: A Review of Research," *JBL* 105 (1986): 75-96.

[7] Rengstorf, "*apostolos*," 1:414-20.

[8] Agnew, "Review of Research," 90-96; Barnett, "Apostle," 47-48; Joseph A. Fitzmyer, *Romans*, AB, vol. 33 (New York: Doubleday, 1993), 231-32.

the universal scope of the mission (Matt. 28:19-20), and the solidarity of Sender and sent one (John 20:21) underscores the gravity of the message of forgiveness or judgment with which they bind their listeners (John 20:23).

The same components—authority, proclamation, universality—are also integral to the commission of Paul as the last apostle (see below). It is the missionary element of Jesus' authoritative commission that sets the NT apostolate apart from any historical precedents. Further, it is the missionary element that provides the connection between the technical and nontechnical uses of the term *apostle*. Since the universal proclamation of the gospel of forgiveness through the crucified and exalted Son is central to the office of apostle, those who engage in pioneer church-planting ministry in unreached frontiers can be called functional apostles (Acts 14:4, 14; Rom. 16:7), even if they are not apostles in the official sense. The mission, not the office, is what possesses abiding validity even until the end of the age.[9]

### Conversion-Commission

In two major passages (Gal. 1:11-17; Rom. 1:1-5) Paul traces his own apostleship to the Damascus Christophany. Here is the genesis of his mission and its defining moment. Galatians 1:11-17 is one of the few autobiographical accounts of Paul's conversion-commission in the Pauline corpus (cf. Phil. 3:4-11; 1 Tim. 1:12-16).[10] In Galatians 1:10-2:14 Paul defends his apostolic standing and authority. He stands in independence from and yet agreement with the Jerusalem apostles. By condemning those who would pervert the gospel of justification by grace (1:6-9) before reviewing his conversion, Paul shows that the content of the message he proclaims flows directly out of the Damascus Christophany. Paul has been attacked for (1) being a man pleaser in the sense that his law-free gospel is a unique creation designed to gain the approval of his Gentile constituency (1:10); and (2) being inferior to the Jerusalem apostles in authority, since they received their commission directly from Jesus, unlike Paul, whose call was mediated

---

[9] Larry W. Caldwell's *Sent Out! Reclaiming the Spiritual Gift of Apostleship for Missionaries and Churches Today* (Pasadena, Calif.: William Carey Library, 1992) is a major attempt to establish the abiding validity of functional apostleship until the return of Christ. "Apostleship, indeed, is the gift of cross-cultural church planting that God is using, and will continue to use, in reaching the unreached billions in today's world" (154).

[10] I take Romans 7:7-25 as a representative account of "the person under the binding authority of the law" viewed from Paul's present Christian perspective rather than a purely autobiographical account. Luke's three biographical accounts are found in Acts 9:1-20; 22:1-21; 26:2-23.

through them.[11] Paul counters that the gospel of grace he received was by direct revelation from Jesus Christ, not through human mediation (1:11-12). The risen Christ and the gospel were revealed to Paul at the same moment: to preach the gospel (v. 11) is to preach Christ (v. 16).

As a background to his conversion Paul first reviews his pre-Christian career as a persecutor of the church of God (1:13-14; cf. Phil. 3:6; Acts 8:1, 3; 9:1-2). His persecuting activity arose from motives of zeal for the Law and for God. The acclamation by the early Christians of the crucified Jesus as Lord and Messiah was more than gross error, it was blasphemy and had to be stamped out at any cost.[12] Though God's gracious election of Paul predated his birth (cf. Isa. 49:1; Jer. 1:5) the historical turning point came with his effectual call as he neared Damascus (Gal. 1:15-16a). Everything originated in God's pleasure to reveal his Son to this object of grace. The mission to which he was set apart was to proclaim the gospel of God's Son to the Gentiles (cf. Rom. 1:5). The non-Jewish world would be the sphere of his mission; the proclamation of justification by faith in God's Son would be its task and content. Call and conversion were, then, inseparably woven into one transforming experience in which the apostle's Torahcentric values were radically reversed and Jesus Christ became the new gravitational center of his life (Phil. 3:4-11).[13]

Paul immediately obeyed this commission to preach Christ to the Gentiles both in Arabia and in the synagogues of Damascus (Gal. 1:16b-17). He had no direct contact with Jerusalem or the apostles until three years after his conversion (1:18ff.). Neither his first (1:18) nor second (2:1) post-conversion visit to Jerusalem involved extensive contact with the apostles or any conferral of authority. The pillar apostles, James, Peter, and John, confirmed the integrity of the Pauline mission and the distinct spheres of their respective missions to the Jewish and Gentile worlds (2:7-10).

The second major passage, Romans 1:1-5, focuses on the christological content of the gospel he is called to proclaim to the Gentiles. Paul's other favorite self-designation, servant or bond slave (*doulos*),

---

[11] Richard N. Longenecker, *Galatians*, WBC, vol. 41 (Dallas, Tex.: Word, 1990), 26-27.

[12] Martin Hengel (*The Pre-Christian Paul*, trans. John Bowden [Philadelphia: Trinity Press International, 1991], 79-86) explores the theological reasons behind the persecution and rules out any psychological interpretation of Paul's conversion.

[13] On the unity of conversion and commission in Paul's Damascus experience, see David J. Bosch, *Transforming Mission: Paradigm Shifts in Theology of Mission* (Maryknoll, N.Y.: Orbis Books, 1991), 125-29; W. P. Bowers, "Mission," *DPHL*, 613; J. N. Everts, "Conversion and Call of Paul," *DPHL*, 161-62.

forms a kind of a conceptual hendiadys with "apostle" (Rom. 1:1; 2 Cor. 4:5; Gal. 1:10; Phil. 1:1; Titus 1:1): his authoritative office is fulfilled with humble obedience under the lordship of Christ. His apostolic consecration is for the purpose of proclaiming a carefully prescribed message, the gospel (Rom. 1:1), which is the theme of Paul's magnum opus, the epistle to the Romans.[14] The impassioned defenses that Paul makes in his letters of his apostolic authority (1 Cor. 9; 2 Cor. 1-7, 10-13; Gal. 1:10-2:21; 1 Thess. 2-3) grow out of this inseparable bond that unites his message to his office. To attack the apostle is in essence not a criticism of the messenger alone but an assault on the gospel of salvation by faith in the merit of God's Son. To dethrone faith in place of the works of the Law is to undermine the message and to destroy the mission (cf. Rom. 10:3; Gal. 2:21; Phil. 3:9). So Paul begins his greatest written work by setting his apostolate within its defining context, the gospel.

The gospel he proclaims is given a fourfold qualification. First, it is the gospel of God (Rom. 1:1b), that is, God sovereignly purposed it from eternity and is now commanding its open proclamation through the apostles. The gospel both reveals how a person can stand righteous before God (1:17) and how God can remain righteous while justifying sinners (3:25-26). The gospel is theocentric with an anthropological thrust. Second, the gospel is the historical culmination of the promises of salvation recorded throughout prophetic scripture (1:2). Paul's mission is played out on the stage of salvation history, which began with Abraham and now comes to realization in Christ. This gospel is no innovative myth designed by a creative mind but stands in organic continuity with the Old Testament. Promise, shadow, and anticipation have now become fulfillment, substance, and realization. Third, the gospel is a message about God's Son (1:3-4). The preexistent, eternal Son is set forth in two phases of his redemptive mission: in the phase of weakness (incarnation) he is the Son of David (1:3), and in the phase of lordly power (exaltation) he is "appointed the Son of God in power according to the Spirit of holiness" (1:4). The latter concerns his investiture with kingly authority and lordly power after his death and resurrection (cf. Acts 2:31-36; 13:33; Heb. 1:5; 5:5). The phase of weakness and humiliation is now transcended by the phase of exaltation. Paul's mission, then, is profoundly christological. Fourth, the gospel is universal in scope, that is, it is a message of salvation to be proclaimed to all peoples everywhere. Specifically, his commission is to deliver the gospel to the "Gentiles" *(ethnē)*, the non-Jewish peoples of the world, in order to bring them to a faith issuing in obedience (Rom. 1:5; cf. 15:18). The theocentric, salvation historical, christo-

---

[14] Douglas Moo, *Romans 1-8*, WEC (Chicago: Moody, 1991), 22-28.

logical, and universal character of his message means that Paul is fundamentally driven by theological truths communicated to him in his initial encounter with the risen Jesus.

## THE PATTERN AND AIMS OF THE PAULINE MISSION

From the moment of his conversion Paul understood the proclamation of the gospel of Jesus Christ to be his mission in life. But he was more than an itinerant evangelist. His aim was to bring the Gentiles to the obedience of faith (Rom. 1:5) and to organize his converts into self-governing churches. Paul energetically labored not to gain large numbers of isolated converts but to present each person mature in Christ (Col. 1:28-29). Such maturity was nurtured in the corporate unity of the congregation of believers as each exercised his or her gifts to the edification of the whole (Eph. 4:11-16). In short, Paul was a pioneering, church-planting evangelist.

### Contextualized Proclamation Aimed at the Conversion of Individuals

Paul's letters attest that the verbal proclamation of the gospel was the starting point of his missionary task. Proclamation language permeates the Pauline corpus. The two major verbs Paul uses for preaching are *kērussō* (nineteen times in the Pauline corpus) and *euangelizomai* (twenty-one times).[15] What was the content and nature of Paul's proclamation?

The terminology Paul uses to identify his message provides an initial answer to this question. Paul refers to the *word (logos)* of God (1 Cor. 14:36; 2 Cor. 4:2; 1 Thess. 2:13) and the word of Christ (Col. 3:16) or of the Lord (1 Thess. 1:8; 4:15; 2 Thess. 3:1); the *utterance (rhēma)* of God (Eph. 6:17) and the utterance of Christ (Rom. 10:17); the *gospel (euangelion)* of God (Rom. 1:1; 15:16; 2 Cor. 11:7; 1 Thess. 2:2, 8, 9; 1 Tim. 1:11) and the gospel of his Son (Rom. 1:9), of Christ (Rom. 15:19; 1 Cor. 9:12; 2 Cor. 2:12; 9:13; 10:14; Gal. 1:7; Phil. 1:27; 1 Thess. 3:2), of the glory of Christ (2 Cor. 4:4), or of the Lord Jesus (2 Thess. 1:8); the *mystery (mustērion)* of God (1 Cor. 2:1; 4:1; Col. 2:2) and the mystery of Christ (Eph. 3:4; Col. 4:3). In each case *theou* is a genitive of origin or source, whereas *Christou* or its equivalent is an objective genitive: the message originates from God the Father and concerns or is about Jesus Christ. The Father planned the drama of redemption, which is carried out by the Son in his death and resurrection. One of the most consistent and pervasive themes of Paul's

---

[15] Other proclamation terms include: *martureō*, "to testify" (1 Cor. 15:15); *gnōrizō*, "to make known" (1 Cor. 15:1; Gal. 1:11; Eph. 6:19); *prographō*, "to portray" (Gal. 3:1); *diangellō*, "to proclaim" (Rom. 9:17); *katangellō*, "to proclaim widely" (Rom. 1:8; 1 Cor. 2:1; 9:14; Phil. 1:17-18; Col. 1:28).

letters is that the person and work of Jesus Christ, particularly his death and resurrection, are the content of the proclamation.[16]

Can we reconstruct with greater specificity the central lines of his preaching?[17] The central tenets of Paul's preaching when he first entered a city to evangelize can be drawn from 1 Thessalonians 1:9-10.[18] Paul's message included: (1) the essential difference between idols and the one true and living God (theology proper); (2) the death and resurrection of Jesus, the Son of God (Christology); (3) the return of Jesus to judge (God's wrath) unbelievers and rescue his people (soteriology/eschatology); (4) an appeal to "turn" (repentance) from idols and to "serve" (faith/obedience) the living God. This seems to be the irreducible core of the Pauline gospel.[19]

What must not be missed is that Paul's proclamation is aimed at the conversion of individuals.[20] This is not merely the imparting of factual

---

[16] See especially Rom. 10:14; 15:20; 16:25; 1 Cor. 1:18, 23; 2:2; 15:1-4, 11, 12, 14, 15; 2 Cor. 1:19; 2:14, 15; 4:5; 11:4; Gal. 1:8-9, 16; 3:1; 5:11; Eph. 3:8; Phil. 1:15-18; Col. 1:28; 4:3; 1 Tim. 2:5-7; 3:16; 2 Tim. 2:8.

[17] Others have attempted to isolate the content of Paul's preaching. C. H. Dodd (*The Apostolic Preaching and Its Developments* [New York: Harper & Row, 1936], 20-24) sought to uncover the early apostolic proclamation and show its continuity with Paul's preaching. Roland Allen (*Missionary Methods: St. Paul's or Ours?* [reprint, Grand Rapids: Eerdmans, 1962], 68-69) focused on Paul's missionary preaching as it was expressed in his letters to the Thessalonians. More recent attempts have been made by William Barclay ("A Comparison of Paul's Missionary Preaching and Preaching to the Church," in *Apostolic History and the Gospel*, ed. W. W. Gasque and R. P. Martin [Grand Rapids: Eerdmans, 1970], 165-75); and Dean S. Gilliland (*Pauline Theology and Mission Practice* [Grand Rapids: Eerdmans, 1983], 268-75). Both Barclay and Gilliland argue that a distinction between preaching and teaching is artificial. In a similar way, James I. H. McDonald (*Kerygma and Didache: The Articulation and Structure of the Earliest Christian Message*, SNTSMS, no. 37 [Cambridge: University Press, 1980]) demonstrates that the preaching-teaching distinction in Acts and Paul lies in their context (posture of the communicator and addressees) rather than in the content of the message.

[18] Charles A. Wanamaker (*Commentary on 1 and 2 Thessalonians*, NIGTC [Grand Rapids: Eerdmans, 1990], 84-89) defends the thesis that this is a record of Paul's own preaching in Thessalonica over against the common view that Paul merely takes over a pre-Pauline formula summarizing early missionary preaching to the Gentiles.

[19] Paul identifies this core message with a variety of expressions, but his favorite term is clearly "gospel" (*euangelion*), which is found sixty times in the Pauline corpus. For an excellent survey of Pauline usage, see B. Luter, "Gospel," *DPHL*, 369-72.

[20] In Gilliland's fine treatment of the subject of conversion (*Pauline Theology*, 97-117), he defines conversion as a realignment of one's loyalties and transfer of allegiance from self to God.

information but the reciting of salvation historical truth that accosts
the soul and demands a response. This is verdict theology. At the climax of the proclamation is an appeal to respond in faith and repentance.[21] The kerygmatic mission of Paul is to persuade his listeners to
appropriate personally God's offer of salvation (2 Cor. 5:11). He must
not only expound what God has done in Christ to provide for the
atonement of sins (2 Cor. 5:19, 21) but, as an ambassador of Christ,
urge them to be reconciled to God (2 Cor. 5:20).

Does this mean that Paul proclaimed the gospel in exactly the same
way regardless of the circumstances or the nature of the audience?
May God forbid!, as Paul himself would answer. Paul's speeches in
Acts attest to his creativity in adapting the message to fit his listeners'
world view, whether Jews and Gentile god-fearers in the synagogue of
Pisidian Antioch (Acts 13:16-43: the culmination of salvation history),
untutored rural pagans of Lystra (Acts 14:15-17: the Creator's blessings and the folly of idolatry), sophisticated and speculative philosophers in Athens (Acts 17:22-31: the unknown God of their own in-
scription), or animists in Ephesus (Acts 19:11-20: the gospel
authenticated through power encounter). Paul is caricatured in contemporary scholarship as an elusive and self-contradictory figure whose
thought processes are so elastic as to defy integration.[22] Nevertheless,
it is true that for interpreters to understand Paul properly they must
have a generous tolerance for creative tensions flowing from the same
mind. This is because the apostle, in line with his contextualization
policy outlined in 1 Corinthians 9:19-23, makes contingent applica-

---

[21] Admittedly, the language of repentance (Rom. 2:4; 2 Cor. 3:16; 7:9-10;
12:21; 2 Tim. 2:25) and forgiveness (Rom. 4:7; Eph. 1:7; 4:32; Col. 1:14;
2:13; 3:13) is not prominent in Paul. R. H. Gundry ("Grace, Works, and
Staying Saved," *Bib* 66 [1985]: 33-38) makes the plausible argument that
since Palestinian Judaism thought of repentance as a human work in the syn-
ergistic interplay of divine grace and human merit, Paul avoided using language that might imply anything other than absolute dependence on God's
grace in Jesus Christ.

[22] Hendrikus W. Boers, "The Foundations of Paul's Thought: A Methodological Investigation—The Problem of the Coherent Center of Paul's
Thought," *ST* 42 (1988): 55-68; Leander E. Keck, "Images of Paul in the
New Testament," *Int* 43 (1989): 341-51. Even with the more moderate development theorists such as Jürgen Becker (*Paul: Apostle to the Gentiles*,
trans. O. C. Dean Jr. [Louisville, Ky.: Westminster, 1993]), it is difficult if
not impossible to retain a coherent center of thought in the apostle's message.
Such development theories may testify more to the flexibility of Paul in
contextualizing his message to the diverse needs of the churches than to any
real substantial theological shifts.

tions while retaining the coherence of his core message.[23] The present author has elsewhere argued that Paul's employment of Greek terms, whereby he empties their pagan connotations and pours into them new semantic content, is the work of a master contextualizer.[24] Paul is the example par excellence for modern missionaries who wish not just to verbalize their message but to penetrate the minds of the listeners.

### The Pioneering and Pastoral Care of Emerging Churches

It is uniformly recognized by Pauline scholars as well as by missiologist-practitioners that the apostle was more than a soul-winning evangelist. His letters, which are pastoral communications that address the particular needs of churches, confirm that his aim was to establish self-governing congregations that would carry on the Christian mission after his departure. W. P. Bowers expresses it nicely:

> Paul did indeed engage in missionary preaching stage by stage in his journeys. And he actively sought individual conversion as part of his calling. But these evangelistic functions were pursued as necessary preliminary steps in a larger missionary objective to form communities of believers region by region throughout his part of the world. It is hardly accidental that Paul did not picture himself as a maker of bricks but as a builder of buildings (1 Cor. 3:10). His mission was focused on corporate achievement.[25]

Paul, then, assumed two roles in the corporate mission: pioneer and pastor. His task included both the founding of congregations as an itinerant evangelist-church planter and the continual nurture of those churches through follow-up visits, envoys, and letters.

---

[23] The language is drawn from the writings of J. C. Beker, especially the major work, *Paul the Apostle: The Triumph of God in Life and Thought* (Philadelphia: Fortress, 1980) and his more recent work, *The Triumph of God: The Essence of Paul's Thought*, trans. Loren T. Stuckenbruck (Minneapolis: Fortress, 1990). Beker argues for coherence only for the seven uncontested Pauline epistles.

[24] Don N. Howell Jr., "The Apostle Paul and First Century Religious Pluralism," in *Christianity and the Religions: A Biblical Theology of World Religions*, ed. Edward Rommen and Harold Netland, EMS Series, no. 2 (Pasadena, Calif.: William Carey Library, 1995), 95-99.

[25] Bowers, "Mission," 609.

## Paul the Pioneer

The strategic priorities of Paul's mission are nowhere set forth as clearly as in Romans 15:14-33. But we must place this passage in the wider context of the epistle. L. Legrand writes that Romans is *the* missionary charter of the apostle in which the careful exposition of his missionary theology (1:18-15:13) is bracketed by an inclusio of texts "that govern the construction of the Letter to the Romans and assign all of the theological developments of the letter their proper place in Paul's personal conception of mission."[26] In the epistolary opening (1:1-17) Paul introduces the gospel as the defining character of his apostleship and in the epistolary closing (15:14-33) he sets forth the priorities that govern the fulfillment of his mission.

The situation of the apostle Paul at the time of writing is critical. He views the eastern Mediterranean phase of his mission as coming to a close. The indefatigable pioneer is planning a new western phase, to the unevangelized province of Spain (15:23-24). He needs the personnel and prayer (and financial?) support of the church in Rome for the Spanish mission (15:24, 28b-29). But first he must go to Jerusalem and "seal" this phase of ministry by delivering the funds collected from the Gentile churches for the impoverished believers in Judea (15:25-28a, 30-31). As he composes his mission charter, then, he feels pulled in three directions: Jerusalem, Rome, and Spain.

The vision for Spain represents the *pioneer* character of his mission. Reflection on the past only deepens his excitement about the future. In reviewing what Christ has accomplished through him during the past decade of work in the eastern Mediterranean, Paul summarizes the governing principles of the mission. The *product* of his work is the faith-inspired obedience of the Gentiles (15:18b; cf. 1:5). The *activity* of the mission is the proclamation of the gospel in word (15:16, 19) and steadfast endurance as an example in deed (15:18c). The *attestation* of his missionary message is in accompanying miraculous signs (15:19a; cf. 2 Cor. 12:12), while the *power* of the mission comes from the Holy Spirit (15:19a). The *geographical range* of the mission to this point has been the major population centers from Jerusalem in the southeast to Illyricum in the northwest (15:19b). The *ambition* of the mission is to proclaim the gospel in the unreached, unevangelized areas (15:20-22). Paul purposefully avoids areas already pioneered by others. His vision is to bring the gospel to the "regions beyond" (2 Cor. 10:16), where Christ is not known. The priority of the unreached has conditioned his movements from Antioch to Galatia to Macedonia to Achaia to Asia and now drives him forward to Spain.

---

[26] Lucien Legrand, *Unity and Plurality: Mission in the Bible*, trans. Robert R. Barr (Maryknoll, N.Y.: Orbis Books, 1990), 115.

What, then, does Paul mean when he says he "has fulfilled"[27] the gospel from Jerusalem all the way around to Illyricum (15:19)? It must mean, at the least, that as far as his strategic priority of pioneer church planting is concerned, his mission has been accomplished in the eastern Mediterranean. As the trail-blazing pioneer, he has established churches in the major urban centers of five Roman provinces, Syria, Galatia, Asia, Macedonia, and Achaia. That Jerusalem, not Damascus or Antioch, is the starting point sets his pioneering mission within the wider framework of salvation history: the Christian mission itself began there with the gospel "to the Jew first."

### Paul the Pastor

The second concern that underlies the writing of Romans is Rome itself and the decentralized body of "saints" to whom the letter is addressed (1:7a).[28] Rome represents the *pastoral* character of the mission for, even while seeking to enlist the church's support for his Spanish mission (15:23-24, 28-29), he addresses a number of problems in the Roman church that have been reported to him in Corinth. Paul addresses a church that is primarily Gentile yet with a Jewish-Christian minority, a mixture that brought with it thorny relational problems. For example, Paul must enjoin mutual respect and acceptance between the "strong" (so-called liberated Gentile believers) and "weak" (scrupulous Jewish believers) groups in the church (14:1, 3; 15:7), even as he had to address the danger of disunity in most of the churches he established (cf. 1 Cor. 1:10-17; Gal. 5:15; Phil. 4:2-3; 1 Thess. 5:12-13). Thus Paul assumes a pastoral role even while reflecting on and defending the integrity of his mission and enlisting support for the new pioneer campaign.

The pastoral dimension of the mission, however, poses a problem. How can one who is a pioneer church planter, driven forward by a vision for the unreached, devote so much of his time and energy to the pastoral care and follow up of the churches he established (cf. 2 Cor. 11:28-29)? This tension is felt when comparing Paul's objectives in Romans 1:10b-15, where he is off to Rome to impart a spiritual gift to a church he did not found and to reap a harvest there as he has among other Gentiles, with his determination in Romans 15:20-22 not to build

---

[27] The perfect tense verb *peplērōkenai* indicates that as far as Paul's strategy is concerned the gospel mission "stands fulfilled" in this geographical area. The NIV translates by the paraphrastic "fully proclaimed."

[28] In Romans 16:3-15, where Paul greets twenty-six individuals he has met in his apostolic journeys who are now in Rome, he also salutes five groups of believers that, including the church in the home of Priscilla and Aquila, point to a series of decentralized house churches in Rome (16:5a, 10b, 11b, 14, 15).

on the foundation of others. The pioneering role Paul affirms and the pastoral role he assumes seem to remain in tension.[29]

W. P. Bowers addresses this tension and offers a satisfying synthesis of the data.[30] Bowers's thesis is that Paul's missionary vocation in the eastern Mediterranean found its "fulfillment" (15:19) not only in evangelistic preaching but in the firm establishment of churches grounded in the apostolic traditions. The holistic mission, as Paul conceived it, encompassed (1) initial evangelistic preaching aimed at conversions, (2) founding of congregations committed to Christ and to one another, and (3) nurturing of the emerging churches toward Christian maturity both individually and corporately, a goal clearly articulated in such passages as Colossians 1:24-2:7 and Philippians 1:19-27. This is why Paul maintained a pastoral commitment to the churches he founded, such as the troubled church at Corinth, to whom he dispatched at least four letters (cf. 1 Cor. 5:9; 2 Cor. 2:3, 4, 7, 9; 7:8, 12), sent two trusted envoys on sensitive missions (1 Cor. 4:17; 16:10-11; 2 Cor. 2:12-13; 7:5-16), and made at least two personal follow-up visits (2 Cor. 2:1; 12:14, 21; 13:1-2). This is why he undertakes extended residential missions, such as the eighteen months in Corinth (Acts 18:11) on the second missionary journey or the three-plus years in Ephesus (Acts 19:8, 10; 20:31) on the third journey. This is why Paul can wish to leave temporarily his pioneering work in Corinth to attend to the pressing needs of the embryonic church at Thessalonica (1 Thess. 2:17-3:13), why he does on occasion delay work in the "regions beyond" in order to strengthen an existing work, in this case the church at Corinth (2 Cor. 10:15-16), and why he can abandon a promising start in Troas to attend to the pressing needs of a troubled church, again the one at Corinth (2 Cor. 2:12-13). The immediate priorities can be shifted without compromising the long-range objective of the mission, namely, the establishment of spiritually healthy congregations in the unreached frontiers of the Roman world. The pioneer-pastor tension, then, becomes one of formal inconsistency rather than one of substantive contradiction, a characteristic feature of Paul's thought in many other areas as well.[31]

---

[29] Günther Bornkamm (*Paul*, trans. D. M. G. Stalker [New York: Harper & Row, 1971], 57) expresses well the cross-currents in Paul's activity.

[30] W. P. Bowers, "Fulfilling the Gospel: The Scope of the Pauline Mission," *JETS* 30 (1987): 185-98.

[31] N. T. Wright ("Putting Paul Together Again," in *Pauline Theology I: Thessalonians, Philippians, Galatians, Philemon*, ed. Jouette M. Bassler [Minneapolis: Fortress, 1991], 186-90) provides a brief but insightful criticism of the tendency of contemporary scholarship to assign contradictions and sloppiness of thought to Paul. Many of these so-called contradictions are antinomies or tensions one encounters in great thinkers.

## THE DYNAMICS BEHIND THE SUCCESS
## OF THE PAULINE MISSION

### Confidence in the Holy Spirit

More than eighty years have passed since the Anglican missionary-statesman Roland Allen wrote his classic work contrasting the mission methodology of his day with that of the apostle Paul.[32] Though many of his illustrations, drawn mainly from Anglican work in China, are dated, his criticism of paternalistic missionary approaches to the training of believers and the development of churches remains all too painfully true as we approach the twenty-first century. Running as a sub-theme throughout Allen's work is the centrality of the Holy Spirit in any effective missionary endeavor. Allen believed that the missionaries of his day lacked confidence in the Holy Spirit to build the church through Word and sacrament. This was in marked contrast with the apostle Paul, who demonstrated a deep-seated confidence in the Holy Spirit to guide, preserve, and pastor the church during his sustained absence. Allen called missionaries and mission agencies to recover the apostle's bedrock conviction that the Spirit dwells in the church to convict, correct, guide, and fortify her. This does not mean the missionary's abdication of prayerful concern for and ongoing pastoral communication to freshly planted churches. Such conviction, however, will translate into willing retirement and withdrawal accompanied by gradual and real hand-over of responsibility to the local leadership.

Does the available evidence bear the weight of this thesis that the governing ethos of Paul's church-planting mission was his confidence in the Spirit? The answer is yes. For Paul, it was the empowering presence of the Spirit of God that gave to the new covenant ministry its glorious character (2 Cor. 3:7-18). The corporate church was the temple of the Spirit (1 Cor. 3:16-17). From the following representative look at the evidence concerning the church in Thessalonica, it is clear that Paul's mission was carried out at every level in conscious dependence on the Spirit.

An early test of Paul's confidence in God to preserve the church came in Macedonia on the second missionary journey. After an encouraging start brought infant churches into being in Philippi,

---

[32] The first edition of Roland Allen's *Missionary Methods: St. Paul's or Ours?* was printed in 1912. Gilliland's *Pauline Theology and Mission Practice* is in many ways an updating and expansion of Allen's work, and in a similar way he stresses the centrality of the Holy Spirit in every dimension of the Pauline mission.

Thessalonica, and Berea, the apostle was prevented by persecution from continuing his discipling of young believers (Acts 16:40; 17:9-10, 13-15). Yet in Paul's extended absence the fledgling groups in Philippi and Thessalonica matured into exemplary churches marked respectively by sacrificial giving and missionary zeal (Phil. 1:5-6; 4:10-19; 1 Thess. 1:7-8). The results in Thessalonica are particularly impressive since Paul spent at most two to three months and possibly much less from the time he initially entered the city until he was driven out.[33] Paul later writes (from Corinth in early summer, perhaps four or five months after leaving Thessalonica) that he was "torn away" from them in person not in thought, and despite every effort he has been prevented by Satan from returning (1 Thess. 2:17-18). In fact, Paul would not make his way again to Macedonia until the latter part of his third missionary journey after leaving Ephesus and en route to Corinth (Acts 20:1-2). What was intended to be a "short time" (1 Thess. 2:17) turned into a five and one-half year separation. Yet God by his Spirit preserved the church so that Paul, on the eve of his visit to deliver the gifts of the Gentile churches to the impoverished brethren in Judea, could praise the churches of Macedonia as being willing and sacrificial participants in that offering (2 Cor. 8:1-5; cf. Acts 20:4).

How is it that such an effective church-planting work could be accomplished in such a short period of time with such limited direct missionary involvement and follow up? While it would not be wise to extrapolate a universal paradigm from first-century Thessalonica (the cultural obstacles and spiritual resistance to planting an indigenous church among the Buddhists of Central Thailand or the Uyghur Muslims of N.W. China, for example, are much greater), the fact remains that the apostle's dependence on and confidence in the work of the Holy Spirit at every level of the church-building endeavor was the essential factor that gave the work its dynamic staying power. Even in this so-called enlightened day of missiological depth and sophistication there often exists a hidden and subtle form of paternalism born out of an anemia of assurance that the Spirit is both able and committed to guide, preserve, and perfect the church that he indwells.

The following discussion begins by looking carefully at the explicit references Paul makes to the Spirit in the Thessalonian correspondence, drawing heavily on the exhaustive work on Pauline pneumatology by

---

[33] Acts 17:2 records Paul preaching in the synagogue on three consecutive Sabbaths. His total time in the city was probably longer since he developed such an intimate relationship with the believers (1 Thess. 2:7-11) and received repeated monetary gifts from Philippi to support his work there (Phil. 4:16). Still, the misunderstanding over his eschatological teaching (1 Thess. 4:13-5:11; 2 Thess. 2:1-12) is evidence that his stay was cut short while the church was still in an embryonic state.

Gordon Fee.[34] Paul employs the term *pneuma* only eight times in 1 Thessalonians and 2 Thessalonians (1 Thess. 1:5, 6; 4:8; 5:19, 23; 2 Thess. 2:2, 8, 13). Of these, once it is translated "breath" (2 Thess. 2:8), once it refers to the human spirit (1 Thess. 5:23), and once it refers to a prophetic utterance (2 Thess. 2:2). It would be grossly inaccurate to conclude, however, that the five remaining explicit references to the Spirit exhaust the Spirit-language of these letters. There is much more here than meets the eye.

### 1 Thessalonians 1:5-6

Two dimensions of the Spirit's centrality in the pioneer stages of this new church plant are identified. First, the effectiveness of the preaching as it penetrated the hearts of the listeners ("it came to you in . . . ") rather than the manner in which it was proclaimed is traced to the Spirit.[35] The Spirit powerfully drove home the truth of the message to the minds and consciences of the listeners, producing deep conviction or full assurance (1:5). Second, the ability of the believers to experience such joyful reception of the word even in much affliction originated in the work of the Spirit. In so doing they became imitators of the Lord Jesus and the apostles, who similarly experienced joy in suffering (1:6). Deep conviction and unrestrained joy, then, were the hallmarks of the Spirit's work in their lives at the initial proclamation of the gospel. The apostle's assurance in the positional reality of the Thessalonians' election by God (1:4) emerges from his firsthand observation of their personal, experiential appropriation of the word of God. The Spirit is everywhere in the genesis of this new community of God![36]

### 1 Thessalonians 4:8

Paul's belief in a new community endowed with the Spirit does not mean that its obedience to the Spirit is automatic. Ethical instruction

---

[34] Gordon D. Fee, *God's Empowering Presence: The Holy Spirit in the Letters of Paul* (Peabody, Mass.: Hendrickson, 1994).

[35] Fee (*Empowering Presence*, 44-45) cites this as the majority view among commentators. However, it is possible that we have here another all-too-familiar false dichotomy; perhaps the language refers to the powerful Spirit-produced conviction in which the apostles delivered their message *and* in which it was received by the listeners.

[36] This is true not only with respect to the exemplary Thessalonian church but also the troubled Galatian and Corinthian congregations where the apostle also reminds the believers of their vivid initial experience of the Spirit when they were converted under the proclamation of the gospel (Gal. 3:1-3; 1 Cor. 2:4-5).

(paraenesis) backed by apostolic authority was central to his ministry when among them, and is followed up with detail in his letters (1 Thess. 4:1-2). The low moral standards of first-century Greco-Roman culture, particularly with regards to sexual intercourse before and outside of marriage (*porneia*), exerted a powerful influence on the church.[37] It was not enough to call the church to the avoidance of all sexual activity outside of marriage and to honorable self-control over the body, both of which Paul did without compromise (4:3-4). The appeal must be supported by the requisite spiritual resources to enable obedience. It is for the maintenance of such purity, Paul says, that God gives to believers the Holy Spirit (4:7-8). The Spirit is holy and communicates God's holiness to God's people.[38] Sandwiched between the instruction (4:3-4) and the source of enablement (4:7-8) is a comparison and a warning of judgment (4:5-6): the pure church must stand in stark contrast to heathen society characterized by dishonorable passions that, acted out, injure and defraud the victims and in turn invite God's judgment. Those in Thessalonica yearning for relief from the downward spiral of sexual abuse and exploitation will be attracted to the honorable conduct of these Christians. Their self-control, faith, love, and hope will shine as lights in the community and roll back the darkness (5:4-11). Does Paul, then, not create a powerful fusion between Spirit and mission in his instruction?

## 1 Thessalonians 5:16-24

Couched in the middle of a series of eight rapid-fire imperatives (5:16-22) is the command "Do not quench the Spirit" (5:19). The three preceding imperatives relate to the spiritual character and lifestyle of believers—continual rejoicing, unceasing prayer, thanksgiving in all situations (5:16-18). The four commands that follow relate to the corporate worship of the church, particularly its posture toward prophetic utterances in the assembly (5:19-21). Most commentators relate the prohibition not to quench the Spirit exclusively to the commands that follow; that is, the Spirit is suppressed when the church proscribes for whatever reason "charismatic manifestations" in the church, such as prophecy. The connection of v. 19 with what follows is unmistakable. The spiritual energy created by the Spirit as believers exercise their spiritual gifts to the edification of the whole is a flame to be fanned not quenched. Further, the cautionary words that follow in vv. 21-22 bring balance to what precedes: openness to the charismatic manifestations of the Spirit must be combined with vigilance to test the genuineness of the utterance as to its conformity to apostolic tradition (2 Thess.

---

[37] F. Hauck and S. Schültz, "*pornē*," *TDNT* 6:579-84.

[38] For a helpful discussion of the implications of 1 Thessalonians 4:7-8 for Paul's understanding of the Spirit, see Fee, *Empowering Presence*, 51-53.

2:15) and the canon of edification (1 Cor. 14:3). Paul does not discourage the church's use of spiritual gifts even after ignorant or perhaps malicious individuals used the gift of prophecy to disturb the church with errant doctrine (2 Thess. 2:1-2). He continues to delegate to the church the task of weighing prophetic utterances according to the sound traditions he delivered to them (2 Thess. 2:15). Any prophetic utterance or other charismatic manifestation that does not conform to apostolic teaching or is divisive rather than edifying is an "evil kind" of expression that is not of the Spirit and must be avoided.

The apostle Paul's antidote to charismatic excesses in the church is not disuse of spiritual gifts but correction of abuse. Here we encounter Paul's characteristic respect for a very young congregation's ability to monitor its own life and worship. Fear of abuse does not drive Paul to legislating or "micromanaging" the conduct of the Thessalonians with a myriad of laws. He simply urges them to apply their Christian minds in testing all things, believing that they have both the capacity and will to do so. If anything, he is more concerned that the exercise of their spiritual gifts in an open and free atmosphere not be choked off by the timid and uncomfortable souls around them. A fire can be controlled, but the cold ashes of once flaming embers that were constantly doused with the waters of fear and suspicion can only be swept away. The apostle was not afraid of the principles of grace and liberty because he believed the indwelling Spirit, if allowed to govern without hindrance, would pastor and perfect the church.

The command not to quench the Spirit, however, may well condition the imperatives that precede it (1 Thess. 5:16-18) as much as it does those that follow. This is made probable by the fact that elsewhere in the New Testament the actions of rejoicing, prayer, and thanksgiving are attributed to the work of the indwelling Spirit. Joy translated into rejoicing is a mark of the Spirit's presence (Acts 13:52; 1 Thess. 1:6; Gal. 5:22; Rom. 14:17; 15:13). Prayer is an activity undergirded by the Spirit of God (1 Cor. 14:15; Rom. 8:26-27; Eph. 6:18), of which supplication and thanksgiving are integral parts (Phil. 4:6-7). Unhindered joy and unceasing prayer with thanksgiving are burning embers lit by the fire of the Spirit and must be fanned not quenched just as much as the exercise of charismata in corporate worship.

The commands are followed by a prayer for the God of peace to sanctify the church in preparation for the return of the Lord Jesus Christ (1 Thess. 5:23-24). Though the Spirit is not referred to explicitly, his work is implied in God the Father's sanctifying work. In 4:7-8 it is the Holy Spirit who is given by God to enable the believer to grow in holiness. Further, Paul speaks elsewhere of the human spirit as the locus of the Spirit's work in the personality (Rom. 8:16). The apostle prays with confident faith that God will by his Spirit continue to sanctify believers in preparation for the return of Christ. Such confidence reaches its zenith when Paul projects himself into the future and contemplates the joy he will experience when his spiritual children are ushered into the Lord's presence at his return (1 Thess. 2:19-20).

### 2 Thessalonians 1:11

Once again Paul contemplates the glorification of believers at the time of Christ's return (1:10). To this very end Paul prays that God will "by his power" make them worthy of his calling and bring to fulfillment every desire for goodness and every act of faith. Paul probably uses *en dunamei* as a shorthand expression for the power of God's Spirit (cf. 1 Thess. 1:5). In Galatians 5:22 both faith and goodness are part of the ninefold fruit of the Spirit. Here the Thessalonians' pursuit of goodness and faith-inspired action is grounded in the effective work of God by his Spirit.

### 2 Thessalonians 2:13

In 2 Thessalonians 2, Paul is anxious to correct the false teaching that had entered the church and actually been accepted by some that the day of the Lord has, in some sense, already arrived. What form this alien teaching took is uncertain but Paul counters that several antecedent events must take place before the day of the Lord—his final return to judge unbelievers and gather his elect—will arrive (2:3-12). The main antecedent event is the revelation of "the man of lawlessness" (2:3) or "the lawless one" (2:8). This individual will display miraculous signs and wonders that originate in Satan's effective working to counterfeit God's supernatural miracles (2:9). The same phenomena that accompanied the apostolic preaching to authenticate its truthfulness (Rom. 15:19; 2 Cor. 12:12), namely, "signs and wonders" wrought by the Spirit of God, here arise from the spirit of Satan and are intended to deceive. Fee comments that this may well explain why Paul is reluctant to bring forward his apostolic "signs and wonders and miracles" (2 Cor. 12:12) as the definitive mark of his authentication when he defends himself against the attacks of the false apostles in 2 Corinthians 10-13: "For him the evidence of apostleship lies ultimately not in the miraculous—in the sense of 'signs and wonders,' since Satan can also produce these—but in his own 'imitation of Christ' in his sufferings and in the fruit of such imitation, the conversion of the Corinthians themselves."[39]

Many will be led astray by the miraculous works of this evil personage (2 Thess. 2:9-11). But the apostle is confident that the Thessalonians are not among them, for God elected them to salvation, evidenced by

---

[39] Fee, *Empowering Presence*, 76-77.

their belief in the truth and the sanctifying work of the Spirit (2:13). Once again the Spirit is associated with holiness communicated to believers (cf. 1 Thess. 4:7-8; 5:23). This is positional sanctification or "setting apart" of believers as God's holy people, which takes place at conversion (cf. Rom. 15:16; 1 Cor. 1:2, 30; 6:11) and is designed to issue in personal and experiential holiness also produced by the indwelling Spirit (1 Thess. 4:8). God has inaugurated his good work of salvation in these believers by the effectual work of his Spirit and is continuing by the same Spirit to perfect them. This is the ground of Paul's thanksgiving for them even as he contemplates the ominous events that await fulfillment on the stage of human history (2 Thess. 2:1-12). Warning, command, prohibition, exhortation, prayer, and thanksgiving all find their place within an overall atmosphere of assurance that these are God's Spirit-created people, whose present and future are secure in his redemptive purposes.

### Summary of the Pneumatology of the Thessalonian Epistles

Though the explicit references to the Holy Spirit are few in number, they are comprehensive in scope. First, the power of the Holy Spirit, which accompanied the initial proclamation of the gospel by the apostolic team in Thessalonica, brought deep conviction (1 Thess. 1:5). Even though resistance was fierce, the Spirit made the apostolic visit result in a successful beginning (1 Thess. 2:1-2). Second, the conversion of these people was wrought by the same Spirit. He brought them first to deep conviction of sin, followed by a joyous response to the promise of forgiveness (1 Thess. 1:5-6). The Spirit set them apart as God's holy people when they believed the truth (2 Thess. 2:13). Third, their ongoing Christian experience and growth is everywhere seen as Spirit-led: holiness in personal morality (1 Thess. 4:8); joy, prayer, and thanksgiving (1 Thess. 5:16-18); the desire to do God's good will and actions that spring from faith (2 Thess. 1:11). Fourth, the wise exercise of spiritual gifts in the assembly, especially prophecy, is a manifestation of the Spirit flaming among them and must not be quenched (1 Thess. 5:19-22; 2 Thess. 2:1-2). Paul believes that the Spirit has been intimately involved on every level of the church-planting mission in the Macedonian capital, from initial evangelism to the gathering and nurturing of the congregation. He is certain that even in his forced and extended absence the same Spirit will preserve, strengthen, and perfect this young church.

This section has addressed what represents a major lacuna in Pauline mission studies, namely, constant reliance on the Holy Spirit as the governing ethos of that mission. The apostle Paul's dependence on and confidence in the empowering presence of the Spirit of God can be seen at every level of his Gentile mission. In his wide-ranging article on the Pauline concept of mission, W. P. Bowers looks at the apostle's missionary activity before exploring his missionary thought.[40] In an otherwise penetrating analysis there is one glaring omission—scarcely a reference is made to the Spirit as the generative force of the Gentile mission. Bowers's conclusion is that Paul's eschatological self-understanding is the theological matrix that conditions his concept of mission.[41] However, what signaled the inauguration of the eschatological age to the apostles was the outpouring of the Spirit upon the church of both Jew and Gentile. The promised age of the Spirit had begun now that Jesus had taken his lordly position at the right hand of the Father in fulfillment of Psalm 110:1. The exalted Lord Jesus was now mediating his presence to his new covenant people by the Spirit (Acts 2:16-21, 33, 38-39). The salvation of Gentiles apart from adherence to the Jewish law was confirmed by the baptism of the Spirit (Acts 10:44-48; 11:15-17). The decisive argument set forth by Peter at the Jerusalem Conference in support of the Pauline mission to the Gentiles was that God accepted the Gentiles "by giving the Holy Spirit to them just as he did to us" (Acts 15:8). Who, then, could stand in the way of believing Gentiles entering on equal terms with believing Jews if they were co-heirs of the same Spirit of promise? Both the universality of the mission (cf. Gal. 3:14; Eph. 1:13-14) and its eschatological character were authenticated by the definitive presence of the Spirit from the outset. Paul's post-Damascus life was dedicated to building the new community of God's people, who would by the leading of the Spirit declare God's salvation to the nations still in darkness.[42]

### Collaborative Ministry

R. W. Funk identified literary units in the undisputed Pauline letters on the basis of their form and content and labeled them "apostolic parousia" passages (Rom. 15:14-33; 1 Cor. 4:14-21; Phil. 2:19-24;

---

[40] Bowers, "Mission," 608-19.

[41] Bowers, "Mission," 618. This is essentially the same conclusion articulated in Bosch, *Transforming Mission*, 123-78.

[42] W. Paul Bowers ("Church and Mission in Paul," *JSNT* 44 [1991]: 89-111) questions the common view that Paul enjoined or expected his churches to replicate the aggressive, mobile church-planting mission that he himself was engaged in. Though individually called believers, like Paul, may launch into active missionary outreach (centrifugal mission) the role of churches "as churches" was to facilitate accession to themselves by an attractive Christian lifestyle and wise response to the inquiries of seekers (centripetal mission). While I cannot endorse Bowers's central thesis here, he deserves a hearing. It is both surprising and unfortunate that the published articles of W. Paul Bowers in this area are rarely if ever referred to in the major treatments of Pauline mission.

1 Thess. 2:17-3:13; Phlm. 21-22).[43] The apostle in these passages makes his presence and authority felt by expressing his pastoral concern for the church, his anxious plans to visit at the first opportunity, and the more immediate visit of an envoy in his place. "The letter and the envoy are anticipatory substitutes for Paul's own personal presence when he cannot travel, but both function as a means of conveying his apostolic presence."[44] This balances the thesis of R. Allen, cited earlier, that Paul practiced conscious retirement from his churches in order to allow them the freedom to develop their own patterns of life and worship under local leaders. In Thessalonica and elsewhere his withdrawal was sometimes necessitated by persecution and his letters are intended to be his pastoral voice to areas of the church still lacking. Even here, though, Paul is reluctant to rule by apostolic decree but rather challenges the church to direct its own affairs within the parameters of sound apostolic tradition. The trust he places in his emissaries once again reveals his deep confidence in the Spirit to guide the ongoing life of the church through members of his missionary team.

The central section of 1 Thessalonians (2:17-3:13) falls into this category of apostolic parousia. Paul writes of his "intense longing" to see these from whom he has been prematurely "torn away" (2:17). In his place he sent Timothy to strengthen and encourage their faith in the midst of trials and persecutions (3:2-3). In his heart is a mixture of assurance and anxiety: assurance that these believers will be gloriously perfected at the return of Christ (2:19-20) and anxiety that the tempter might undermine their faith and his efforts prove vain (3:5). But Timothy's mission to Thessalonica was a success, and he has now returned to Paul in Corinth with a thrilling report of their faith, love, and loyalty, which fills the apostle with prayerful thanksgiving (3:6-10).

Into the hands of young Timothy, Paul committed the pastoral aftercare of this vulnerable church. What an excellent choice it was and how clearly it demonstrates the wisdom of Paul's collaborative approach to ministry.[45] Timothy's pastoral ministry in both Thessalonica and Philippi (cf. Phil. 2:19-24) proved to be a rich source of blessing to those churches and must in large part be due to the training he re-

---

[43] R. W. Funk, "The Apostolic Parousia: Form and Significance," in *Christian History and Interpretation: Studies Presented to John Knox*, ed. W. R. Farmer, C. F. D. Moule, and R. R. Niebuhr (Cambridge: University Press, 1967), 249-68.

[44] P. Trebilco, "Itineraries, Travel Plans, Journeys, Apostolic Parousia," *DPHL*, 449.

[45] D. J. Harrington, "Paul and Collaborative Ministry," *New Theology Review* 3 (1990): 62-71.

ceived from his apostle-mentor. Converted on Paul's first visit to Lystra (Acts 14:6-20) and added to the missionary team on his second visit there (Acts 16:1-3), Timothy was young both in faith and in ministry experience when he represented Paul to the churches in Macedonia. Probably in his late teens at this time,[46] he was less than two years old in the Lord with only a few months experience in full-time missionary work. But Paul had seen the Spirit of God confirm God's call to Timothy and use the young man among the churches of Galatia. Less than a year after his conversion Timothy was commended by the brothers of Lystra and Iconium for his exemplary life and ministry among them (Acts 16:2). Then, at the time of his ordination to missionary work, the Spirit both gifted him for ministry and inspired several prophetic utterances that publicly confirmed his suitability for evangelistic and pastoral work (1 Tim. 1:18; 4:14). Paul would trust the Spirit of God to use this servant to strengthen the church during his absence.

In fact, Paul's deep commitment to team ministry is another expression of his confidence in the Spirit. One of the keys to the success of Paul's mission was his ability to attract capable and dedicated men and women to work alongside him both in itinerant evangelism and in settled discipleship and follow up. It was a very diverse team of four that evangelized Macedonia: the battle-scarred veteran and converted Pharisee, Paul; the maturing leader and Hellenistic Jewish believer from Jerusalem, Silas; the fresh recruit, half-Greek, half-Jew, Timothy; and the Greek layman, Luke, who joined the party at Troas (Acts 16:6-10). Here is solid biblical precedent for multicultural missionary teams demonstrating the unity of the Spirit in their proclamation of Jesus Christ whose gospel transcends all such sociological barriers (Gal. 3:28; Col. 3:11).

E. E. Ellis lists the names of thirty-six co-workers that are referred to in Paul's letters.[47] Of those who were long-term co-workers, some were clearly subordinates (Erastus, Mark, Timothy, Titus, Tychicus), others maintained a cooperative but independent relationship to the apostle (Apollos, Priscilla and Aquila), and still others joined him only on specific missions (Barnabas, Silas). Of greatest significance were those who had preaching and teaching gifts which Paul nurtured and utilized on behalf of the churches. In these Paul invested his energies, instructing them in apostolic doctrine and tradition and the christological interpretation of the Old Testament (Rom. 6:17; 16:17; 1 Cor.

---

[46] This is based on the fact that thirteen years later (approximate date for the writing of 1 Timothy, 62-63 C.E.) Timothy is urged to let no one despise his "youth" (*neotēs*, 1 Tim. 4:12).

[47] E. E. Ellis, "Paul and His Coworkers," *DPHL*, 183-89.

11:2; Gal. 1:14; Col. 2:8; 2 Thess. 2:15; 3:6). Though his trust was at times betrayed (Demas being the clearest example: Col. 4:14; Phlm. 24; 2 Tim. 4:10), he committed to these individuals the pastoral care of the young churches he had planted, believing that the Spirit would superintend the teaching of his co-workers and guide the church to maturity. Timothy (1 Thess. 3:6-10; Phil. 2:19-24) and Titus (2 Cor. 2:12-13; 7:5-16; 8:16-24; 12:18) were special instruments of the Spirit that Paul dispatched on difficult and sensitive missions. To the former he would commit the pastoral ministry of the strategic church in Ephesus (1 Tim. 1:3) and to the latter the leadership of the newly organized church in Crete (Titus 1:5).

The apostle commends the local administrators, teachers, and preachers who assumed leadership roles in the local congregations and urges the churches to submit to their oversight (1 Cor. 16:15-18; Gal. 6:6; Phil. 1:1; 4:2-3; 1 Thess. 5:12-13). Though Paul is famous (or infamous) for his statements about the subordination of women to male leadership in the church (1 Cor. 11:3-16; 14:33-35; 1 Tim. 2:11-15), he commends in his letters a remarkable number of women as highly valued co-workers. He identifies these women with the same designations as his male associates in ministry as they are similarly engaged in the ministries of teaching and preaching (Rom. 16:1-2, 3, 6, 7, 12, 13, 15; Phil. 4:2-3; Col. 4:15; Phlm. 2; cf. Acts 16:14-15, 40; 18:26).

F. F. Bruce captures the principal factor that drives the apostle to train others and delegate vital ministry concerns to them: "In all these things, discipline, administration and others, the presence and directive power of the Holy Spirit were so real to Paul that he implies them even where he does not explicitly mention them. If he did not trust his converts, corporately or individually, to advance along the lines he laid down for them, his 'ways in Christ' (1 Cor. 4:17), he trusted the Holy Spirit to work in his converts."[48]

### Intercessory Prayer

Behind the energetic and high-profile activity of Paul the missionary were the hidden springs of a prayer life born of a profound faith in a sovereign God and loving Father. His letters reveal Paul to be a man of prayer, engaged in continual intercession for the churches of his mission.[49] The following discussion looks at only the most explicit of the Pauline prayer material, in four categories: (1) reports of prayer

---

[48] F. F. Bruce, "Paul in Acts and Letters," *DPHL*, 689.
[49] Krister Stendahl, "Paul at Prayer," *Int* 34 (1980): 240-49.

for the churches and others; (2) intercessory wish prayers; (3) personal appeals for prayer for himself; and (4) instruction about prayer.[50]

Paul has a deep concern for the spiritual progress of the churches that his mission has spawned. He views himself, the commissioned apostle, and the churches he has established as bound to each other and to God the Father in a triangular relationship through the cords of intercessory prayer.[51] Paul's intercession, and that of believers, is grounded in the priestly intercession of the exalted Christ "for us" (Rom. 8:34). His intercession is empowered, even in the present condition of weakness where he is uncertain what to pray for, by the indwelling Spirit who intercedes with unuttered groanings in perfect harmony with the will of the Father (Rom. 8:26-27).[52] Paul's prayer reports reveal a pastor's concern first and foremost for the spiritual perfecting of the churches. For the *Thessalonians,* an infant church from which he was prematurely "torn away" (1 Thess. 2:17), he prays constantly (1 Thess. 1:2-3; 2 Thess. 1:11) that he might be able to see them and complete the parts of their faith that are still lacking (1 Thess. 3:10). He asks that God will bring to fulfillment their good purposes prompted by faith (2 Thess. 1:11). For the troubled *Corinthians,* Paul prays that they might respond rightly to his strong admonitions (2 Cor. 13:7) and be perfected in unity (2 Cor. 13:9). For the *Romans,* a church he has yet to visit, he prays that God will fulfill his long intention of coming to them so that he might impart a spiritual gift and exchange mutual encouragement (Rom. 1:9-12). For the *Ephesians,* he asks for spiritual wisdom and insight in the knowledge of God, the incomparable riches of their inheritance in Christ, and God's resurrection power on their behalf (Eph. 1:16-19a). He prays for their inner strengthening through the Spirit of Christ (Eph. 3:16-17a) and the ability to comprehend the full dimensions of Christ's love (3:17b-18) so that they will be filled with the full measure of God's presence (3:19). For the

---

[50] In all, there are forty-five explicit passages on prayer in the Pauline corpus, not including thanksgiving reports, berakot, and doxologies. Paul normally directs his prayers to the person of God the Father, who is designated, either explicitly or implicitly, as the object of Paul's prayer in 75 percent of the texts. The Lord Jesus Christ is sometimes addressed in prayer, but this is the exception rather than the pattern. There are a few passages in which the object of prayer is not mentioned.

[51] Gordon P. Wiles, *Paul's Intercessory Prayers: The Significance of Intercessory Prayer Passages in the Letters of Paul,* SNTSMS, no. 24 (Cambridge: University Press, 1974), 4-5. On the centrality of intercessory prayer for Paul's theology of mission, see David G. Peterson, "Prayer in Paul's Writings," in *Teach Us to Pray: Prayer in the Bible and the World,* ed. D. A. Carson (Grand Rapids: Baker, 1990), 100.

[52] Peter O'Brien, "Romans 8:26-27: A Revolutionary Approach to Prayer?" *Reformed Theological Review* 46 (1987): 65-73.

*Colossians*, the apostle requests a fuller knowledge and understanding of God's will, faithful and fruitful lives pleasing to him, growth in the knowledge of God, and inner strengthening (Col. 1:3, 9-11). For the *Philippians*, Paul prays for a love deepened with spiritual discernment, moral discernment, purity, and spiritual virtues that spring from their righteous standing in Christ (Phil. 1:3-4, 9-11). Only with the *Galatians*, whom he approaches with direct admonitory tones, is intercession not mentioned. Paul also intercedes for individuals such as Timothy, for whom he constantly prays (2 Tim. 1:3), and Philemon, asking that his friend will actively share his faith and fully understand all he has in Christ (Phlm. 4-6).

Seven times Paul breaks out into formal prayer, openly verbalizing his intercession for the churches (Rom. 15:5, 13; 1 Thess. 3:11-13; 5:23; 2 Thess. 2:16-17; 3:5, 16).[53] These model "wish prayers" similarly have as their primary concern the spiritual welfare of the recipients: spiritual unity (Rom. 15:5), overflowing hope (Rom. 15:13), abounding love and moral purity (1 Thess. 3:12-13), sanctification (1 Thess. 5:23), hearts encouraged and strengthened for witness in word and deed (2 Thess. 2:16-17), grounding in God's love and Christ's perseverance (2 Thess. 3:16), and continual peace (2 Thess. 3:12). As in the intercession reports, Paul's first priority in his wish prayers is the spiritual character and inner life of the church. It is stunning that in the prayer reports and wish prayers of Paul there is virtually no petition for physical healing, daily bread, better economic conditions, or physical comforts—concerns that dominate the minimalist prayer life of the twentieth-century Western church. He fully understands that the reputation of the church among outsiders and its witness to the wider community will rise or fall according to its moral purity and relational unity.[54]

Paul also appeals to the churches to pray for him and his ministry (1 Thess. 5:25). He asks the Thessalonians to pray that the message of the Lord will spread rapidly in Corinth even as it did in Thessalonica and that he might be delivered from the wicked designs of those who oppose his preaching (2 Thess. 3:1-2). The Corinthians can assist him in their prayers, in conjunction with many others, for deliverance from hostile opponents and mortal danger (2 Cor. 1:10-11). As he prepares to leave for Jerusalem, with the gifts collected from the Gentile churches

---

[53] In each of the "wish prayers" the main verb is an aorist active optative of obtainable wish (or voluntative optative).

[54] Though I question Bowers's thesis (see footnote 42) that Paul did not envision a centrifugal mission for his churches, I agree that the centripetal witness of attraction and response is repeatedly enjoined in his letters. See Bowers, "Church and Mission," 97-101, 105-6 (especially p. 106, n. 1) for the data on centripetal witness.

for the impoverished saints there, Paul implores the Roman church to participate in his prayer struggle that he will be rescued from the unbelievers in Judea and that the believers will joyfully receive the gifts and the churches' representatives (Rom. 15:30-32). While under house arrest in Rome, Paul urges the Ephesians to pray that he will fearlessly proclaim the gospel (Eph. 6:19-20) and the Colossians that God will provide fresh opportunities to make Christ known (Col. 4:3-4). He is confident (though not certain) that through the prayers of the Philippians he will be acquitted and released from incarceration in Rome (Phil. 1:19). Even as God himself is Paul's co-worker in the gospel mission (1 Cor. 3:9), the Gentile churches are active participants and helpers through their intercession for him. Paul directly links his own welfare and the ongoing success of his mission with the prayerful engagement of the churches on his behalf.[55]

Finally, the apostle provides instruction concerning prayer. The intercession of the indwelling Spirit sustains the inadequate prayers of believers (Rom. 8:26-27). In congregational prayer, men and women should not pray with head covered and uncovered respectively (1 Cor. 11:4-5, 13-16), nor speak to God without an interpreter (1 Cor. 14:2, 13-15, 28). Prayer should be at all times in the Spirit, keeping alert and persevering for all the saints (Eph. 6:18). Making all requests known to God replaces anxiety with peace (Phil. 4:6-7). Prayer is to be watchful and full of thanksgiving (Col. 4:2). Intercession should be for all people in civil authority so that tranquility will prevail (1 Tim. 2:1-2). All people should pray without anger and discord (1 Tim. 2:8). Material provisions are consecrated by the word of God and prayer (1 Tim. 4:5). The hallmarks of Pauline prayer are mental and spiritual alertness, boldness, specificity, perseverance, thanksgiving, and the guidance of the Holy Spirit.

Paul's dynamic prayer life flows out of a radically theocentric world view informed by a profound confidence in a sovereign God and loving heavenly Father who responds to believing prayer.[56] His mission of evangelism, church founding, and pastoral nurture gained its life and vitality from the wellspring of his prayers and that of the churches.

---

[55] Paul's profound belief in the power of intercessory prayer is also evidenced by the *examples of prayer* dispersed throughout his letters. Paul prays earnestly for the salvation of his fellow Israelites (Rom. 9:1-3; 10:1). Epaphras strives in prayer for the Colossians that they might stand fully assured in the will of God (Col. 4:12). The believing widow is known by the pattern of her continuous prayer ministry (1 Tim. 5:5). Paul's hope of seeing Philemon again rests in his friend's prayer to that end (Phlm. 22). The Jerusalem saints will overflow with praise and thanksgiving in their prayers for the Corinthians due to their generous gifts (2 Cor. 9:13-14).

[56] W. B. Hunter, "Prayer," *DPHL*, 730.

G. P. Wiles summarizes the results of his definitive study of Paul's intercessory ministry by stating, "Prayer buttressed all his mission work—in advance of his visits, during them, and after he departed. All his plans were conceived under the constant sense of the guidance and will of God."[57]

## CONCLUSION

The essential core of the Pauline mission, however, is not found in its genesis, strategic pattern, or underlying dynamics. Paul's self-understanding as God's apostle is as one "set apart for the gospel of God" (Rom. 1:1). It is the *message*—the gospel of God—that defines and determines the man and his mission. In one unsurpassed account of the conversion-commission, Paul describes his transformation in terms of a new personal relationship with Christ Jesus the Lord and the righteousness gained by faith alone, wholly apart from the law (Phil. 3:7-9). Such theological and experiential realignment brought with it a fresh purpose in life: to know more fully the Lord who apprehended him and to make him known to the Gentiles (Phil. 3:10-14). The next chapter focuses on the charter of Paul's mission, the epistle to the Romans, where the church's preeminent theologian-missionary expounds his defining convictions and driving commitments.

---

[57] Wiles, *Intercessory Prayers*, 296.

# 6

## Mission in Paul's Epistles:
## Theological Bearings

## Don N. Howell Jr.

If the Pauline letters could be compared to the Himalaya Mountains, then the epistle to the Romans is Mt. Everest. Undoubtedly chapter 8 of Romans would be the summit of the highest peak as Paul anticipates the cosmic triumph of God's lordship over his created and redeemed world (8:18-25) and celebrates the assurance of coming glory for its kingdom citizens (8:26-39). From here the grandeur of the entire range can be viewed. It is in this grand epistle, Romans, that we have the defining charter of Paul's mission.[1] Here we become acutely aware that fundamental to all Paul thought and did was his confidence in the sovereign, righteous, and gracious God and Father who in Jesus Christ had inaugurated and would one day consummate the redemption of his created world. The person and salvation-historical purposes of God the Father alone provide a field of integration broad enough to gather all dimensions of Pauline thought into a satisfying unity.[2] Theological convictions both created and energized the Pauline mission.

### THE EPISTLE TO THE ROMANS:
### A THEOCENTRIC MISSIOLOGY

The apostle Paul was a man whose thoughts were full of God. Nowhere is this more evident than in Romans. Morris demonstrates from

---

[1] Arland J. Hultgren, *Paul's Gospel and Mission: The Outlook from His Letter to the Romans* (Philadelphia: Fortress, 1985); Lucien Legrand, *Unity and Plurality: Mission in the Bible*, trans. Robert R. Barr (Maryknoll, N.Y.: Orbis Books, 1990), 115-24.

[2] This idea is well-expressed in Dean S. Gilliland, *Pauline Theology and Mission Practice* (Grand Rapids: Eerdmans, 1983), 20.

the use of the Greek term *theos* that Paul's God concept saturated his thinking.[3] Of 1,314 explicit references to God (*theos*) in the New Testament, 548 (or 40 percent) are by Paul. *Theos* occurs 153 times in Romans, which comes to once every 46 words (only 1 John has a greater concentration for *theos*, once every 34 words). In Romans *theos* occurs far more often than other major terms of theological significance: law (*nomos*, 72 times), Christ (*Christos*, 65), sin (*hamartia*, 48), Lord (*kyrios*, 43), faith (*pistis*, 40). Romans is first and foremost a written declaration of the self-revelation of God in the person and work of Jesus Christ. But Romans is no abstract theological treatise, for here Paul expounds his gospel in the greater context of his apostolic mission. The inclusio of texts that identify his missionary agenda (Rom. 1:1-15; 15:14-33) frame the articulation of the gospel, the constitution of his mission.[4] The doctrinal teaching of Romans, then, carries with it a missiological thrust and intent. This is the message Paul has proclaimed for over a decade in the eastern Mediterranean provinces and now must make known in the un-reached frontier of Spain.

### The Dual Nature of Romans

Much debate has focused on Paul's original intent and purpose in writing Romans. While the introductory section (1:1-15) and the closing chapters (15:14–16:27)[5] indicate several specific occasional purposes for the letter, the rest of Romans (1:16–11:36) reads like a doctrinal treatise or theological exposition. The wide variety of proposals[6] has developed into an unnecessary dichotomy: either Romans is a theological abstract or it is a wholly occasional letter just like the other Pauline writings.[7] Or to put it in another way, Romans is viewed ei-

---

[3] Leon Morris, "The Theme of Romans," in *Apostolic History and the Gospel: Biblical and Historical Essays Presented to F. F. Bruce on His 60th Birthday*, ed. W. Ward Gasque and Ralph P. Martin (Grand Rapids: Eerdmans, 1970), 249-63. See also Halvor Moxnes, *Theology in Conflict: Studies in Paul's Understanding of God in Romans* (Leiden: E. J. Brill, 1980), 16. Both Moxnes and Morris base their statistics on Robert Morgenthaler, *Statistik des neutestamentlichen Wortschatzes* (Zurich: Gotthelf, 1958).

[4] Legrand, *Unity and Plurality*, 121.

[5] See in particular the ministry review in 15:14-22, report on immediate and future plans in 15:23-29, request for prayer in 15:30-33, personal greetings in 16:1-16, and allusion to false teachers in 16:17-19.

[6] For a representative list of twelve major proposals for the purpose of Romans, see Leon Morris, *The Epistle to the Romans* (Grand Rapids: Eerdmans, 1988), 7-18.

[7] The major recent work on "the Romans problem" is Karl P. Donfried, ed., *The Romans Debate*, 2d ed. (Peabody, Mass.: Hendrickson, 1991).

ther as emerging from Paul's own situation—facing Jerusalem, climaxing his eastern Mediterranean ministry, and aspiring toward Spain (cf. 15:14-33)—or as the apostle's response to particular problems arising in the church in Rome. Actually both factors, Paul's own situation and the state of the Roman church, probably contributed to the composition of Romans, producing its dual occasional-expositional character.

Paul begins by addressing the saints in Rome (1:7), expressing some knowledge of their circumstances, though never having personally visited them (1:8-13). Though the origin of the church in Rome is shrouded in obscurity, there is enough data available both from the New Testament and secular sources to enable scholars to make a plausible reconstruction.[8] Christianity was probably introduced into the Jewish community in Rome by Hellenistic-Jewish-Christian missionaries within a few years of Stephen's martyrdom (35 C.E.; cf. Acts 8:1, 4; 11:19-22). The expulsion of Jews from Rome under Claudius in 49 C.E. (Acts 18:2) may have been due to the proclamation of the Christian gospel in those quarters.[9] When Jews began to filter back into Rome following Claudius's death (54 C.E.), a Gentile church was well established as in other major cities such as Ephesus, Corinth, Antioch, and Philippi. So, writing from Corinth in the winter of 57 C.E. (Acts 20:3), Paul addresses a church that is primarily Gentile yet with a Jewish Christian minority. To this heterogeneous community struggling with cultural tensions, Paul is keenly aware of the need to address such issues as the equality of Jew and Gentile through God's justifying grace (Rom. 1:16-17), the false inferences of antinomianism (3:8; 6:1), the goodness of the law (7:7-25), and the inviolate nature of God's promises to Israel (11:11-29). The argument of chapters 9–11 demands a definite historical situation, as Campbell's research has shown.[10] The problem of reconciling God's righteousness (1:17) with the nonfulfillment of

---

[8] Wolfgang Wiefel, "The Jewish Community in Ancient Rome and the Origins of Roman Christianity," in *The Romans Debate*, ed. Karl P. Donfried (Peabody, Mass.: Hendrickson, 1991), 85-101; F. F. Bruce, *Paul: Apostle of the Heart Set Free* (Grand Rapids: Eerdmans, 1977), 379-85; C. E. B. Cranfield, *A Critical and Exegetical Commentary on the Epistle to the Romans*, ICC (Edinburgh: T & T Clark, 1975-79), 1:16-22; James D. G. Dunn, *Romans 1–8*, WBC (Waco, Tex.: Word, 1988), xliv-liv; Joseph A. Fitzmyer, *Romans*, AB, vol. 33 (New York: Doubleday, 1993), 25-39.

[9] This hinges on interpreting Suetonius's statement, *impulsore Chresto* (*Life of the Emperor Claudius*, 25.4), as a mistaken inference by the historian that Christ was actually present in Rome at that time.

[10] W. S. Campbell, "The Freedom and Faithfulness of God in Relation to Israel," *JSNT* 13 (1981): 27-45; idem, "The Place of Romans IX-XI within the Structure and Thought of the Letter," in *Studia Evangelica VII: Texte und Untersuchungen zur Geshichte der altchristlichen Literatur* (Berlin: Akademie-Verlag, 1982), 121-31.

the patriarchal promises must have been a burning issue for Jewish Christians and probably a cause for relational tension with their Gentile brethren. Even the ethical instruction (paraenesis) of 14:1–15:13 can be interpreted along racial lines, the stronger brother being the Gentile believer and the weaker brother the more sensitive Jewish Christian.[11]

However, the situation of the apostle Paul at this critical time should not be overlooked. He explicitly states that his eastern Mediterranean ministry is coming to an end and that he has his sights set on Spain (15:17-24). The support of the church at Rome for the Spanish mission is imperative (15:28-29). His final task in the present phase of ministry is to deliver the voluntary offerings of his Gentile churches to the impoverished saints in Jerusalem, concerning which reception he is quite anxious (15:25-27, 30-31). As Paul winters in Corinth and composes his magnum opus, then, three factors converge in his mind: Rome, Spain, and Jerusalem. The critical juncture becomes the catalyst for deliberate reflection, and the apostle dictates to Tertius (16:22) a letter that *both* sets forth his gospel—perhaps to deepen the Romans' confidence in his message in light of his opponents' criticisms, so that they will without hesitation support his Spanish mission—*and* addresses concrete problems in the church.[12] Paul is here the concerned pastor *and* visionary pioneer.

### The Gospel of God's Righteousness

The apostle begins by identifying himself as one "set apart for the gospel of God" (1:1). The gospel originates in the purposes of God for redemptive history: it fulfills the promises God made in the prophetic scriptures (1:2) and concerns the Davidic-born Son of God (1:3). It is God whom Paul serves in the preaching of the gospel (1:9), a service fulfilled as a gracious stewardship (1:5), a binding obligation (1:14), and an eager ambition (1:15).

In the thematic statement for the entire epistle (1:16b-17), Paul sets his vocation and the message he proclaims in its theocentric parameters: it is God's almighty power directed to the salvation of those who believe (1:16b). Then, as further explanation and confirmation, the apostle adds that in this gospel the righteousness of God is revealed (1:17a). The gospel concerns the extension of God's power to humanity's salvation. In Paul, salvation (*sōtēria*; cf. also the cognate verb "save" [*sōzō*]) is a broad term encompassing the entire range of God's redemptive activity—past, present, and future. For the believer

---

[11] Peter Stuhlmacher, *Paul's Letter to the Romans: A Commentary*, trans. Scott J. Hafemann (Louisville, Ky.: Westminster, 1994), 219-21.

[12] John Ziesler, *Paul's Letter to the Romans* (Philadelphia: Trinity Press International, 1989), 15-16.

salvation has already been accomplished (Rom. 8:24; Eph. 2:5, 8; 2 Tim. 1:9; Titus 3:5), is in the process of being realized (1 Cor. 1:18; 2 Cor. 2:15), and awaits a final future manifestation (Rom. 5:9-10; 1 Cor. 3:15; 5:5; 2 Tim. 4:18). God's salvific power is for all who believe, "for the Jew first and then for the Gentile" (Rom. 1:16b). Though Paul's primary calling is the proclamation of this gospel to the Gentiles (1:5, 13; 11:13; 15:16, 18; 16:4), he never forgets the salvation-historical priority of Israel (1:2-3; 3:1-4; chaps. 9–11). This dual emphasis and resulting tension of the full and free inclusion of the Gentiles by faith into God's redemptive plan (2:14-15, 26-29; 3:22, 29, 30; 4:11, 16-18; 9:24-26, 30; 10:12-13, 20; 11:11-12, 25, 30; 15:9-12, 27; 16:26) *and* the undiminished priority of Israel (2:9-10; 3:1-2; 9:4-5; 11:1-2, 24, 28-29) form the horizon for Paul's defense of his law-free gospel and the inviolate nature of God's own righteousness. "It can be said with only some exaggeration the key to understanding Romans lies in the untangling of the perplexing interconnectedness of this universalism and particularism—'to *all* who believe'; 'to the Jew *first.*'"[13]

God's salvific power extended to believers is expressed par excellence as the revelation of his righteousness (1:17a, *dikaiosunē theou*). Since Luther's *simul justus et peccator* declaration, Reformed interpreters have taken *theou* as a genitive of relationship, thus denoting righteousness as that which counts "before God."[14] In recent decades this traditional view has been expanded to emphasize both the gift character of righteousness credited to man and its source (*theou* as a genitive of origin or author) in God's own righteous character and activity.[15] The fact that righteousness characterizes God's being and actions is made clear in Romans 3:5, 25-26; 9:14. God's inherent righteousness forms the basis of the demand for the justifying act. As J. Murray contends, the genitives of origin (source) and relationship are not mutually exclusive, and Paul's intended sense is perhaps richer than any of these modern grammatical categories.[16] As one "set apart"

---

[13] Douglas Moo, *Romans 1–8*, WEC (Chicago: Moody. 1991), 63. Dunn (*Romans 1–8*, 40) goes even further: "The need to explain and defend this double emphasis is the driving force behind the whole epistle."

[14] Herman N. Ridderbos, *Paul: An Outline of His Theology*, trans. John Richard De Witt (Grand Rapids: Eerdmans, 1975), 161-66.

[15] Rudolf Bultmann, *Theology of the New Testament*, trans. Kendrick Grobel (New York: Scribner's, 1951), 1:270-85; Hans Conzelmann, *An Outline of the Theology of the New Testament*, trans. John Bowden (London: SCM, 1969), 218-20; Cranfield, *Romans*, 1:97-100.

[16] John Murray, *The Epistle to the Romans*, NICNT (Grand Rapids: Eerdmans, 1959-65), 1:30-31. Moo (*Romans 1–8*, 65-70) similarly takes the comprehensive approach to *dikaiosunē theou* in 1:17: it is "the act by which God brings people into right relationship with Himself" (70), thus combin-

to proclaim the gospel (1:1), Paul views himself as an instrument of bringing the Gentiles into a right relationship with God through faith in his Son. This is a mission of extending God's saving power to all who believe.

### The Universal Need for God's Righteousness

Paul first demonstrates the absolute necessity for a God-given righteousness by painting in dark colors the spiritual condition of humankind (1:18–3:20). Only a righteousness appropriated by faith can avert the eschatological outpouring of God's wrath (1:18, cf. 2:5), even now revealed in God's abandonment (1:24, 26, 28) of the rebellious to their reprobation. The sin of the Gentile world (1:18-32) is a deliberate rejection of the knowledge of God gained from natural revelation (1:19-23). The Gentiles perceived God's omnipotence and divine nature (1:19-20), refused to acknowledge God's right to glory and thanks (1:21), and entered a downward spiral from idolatry to sexual perversion (1:22-32). Sin and corresponding guilt are thus defined theologically (vertically) rather than socially (horizontally). The result is that even Gentiles, ignorant of God's special revelation in the gospel, are without excuse (1:20). God's character is vindicated even in judgment: Gentiles indeed acknowledge the righteous decree of God in punishing sin (1:32). The outpouring of God's wrath, then, is not an irrational outburst of pent-up anger against innocent, unfortunate victims but the expression of his righteousness against those who violate his character.

What about the Jew, chosen by God and separated from the gross Gentile immorality catalogued in 1:24-32? By hypocritically judging

---

ing both God's saving activity and the gift of forensic righteousness. An even more synthetic approach is brilliantly developed for *dikaiosunē theou* in Ernst Käsemann, "The Righteousness of God," in *New Testament Questions of Today*, trans. W. J. Montague (London: SCM, 1969), 169-93. The original article forms the basis for the updated presentation in his *Commentary on Romans*, trans. and ed. Geoffrey W. Bromiley (Grand Rapids: Eerdmans, 1980), 21-32. Käsemann attempts to deal with Paul's theological breadth by fusing a variety of elements—"present and future eschatology, 'declare righteous' and 'make righteous,' gift and service, freedom and obedience, forensic, sacramental and ethical approaches" (Käsemann, "Righteousness," 171-72)—around a unitary center, *dikaiosunē theou*. Here we have synthesis in its purest form: "*dikaiosunē theou* is to Paul God's sovereignty over the world revealing itself eschatologically in Jesus" (Käsemann, "Righteousness," 182). For a brief but penetrating critique of Käsemann, see G. Klein, "Righteousness in the New Testament," in *IDBSup*, ed. Keith Crim (Nashville: Abingdon, 1976), 750-52. See also Moo, *Romans 1–8*, 81-82, 86, 403-4.

the ignorant, immoral Gentile (2:1, 3), the Jew undercuts any claim to leniency before the judgment of God (2:1). To prove the equal culpability of the Jew, Paul delineates the principles by which God judges: it is according to truth not profession (2:2), according to deeds not mere words (2:6-10), and according to the revelatory knowledge one has received, whether the enlightenment of the conscience (Gentiles) or the explicit standards of the law (Jews) (2:12-15). The revelation of God's wrath is ultimately an eschatological occurrence to be meted out on a fixed day (2:5, 16). Again, the focus is on God's action springing from his character; it is God's mercy that leads people to repentance (2:4); his judgment is truthful (2:2), righteous (2:5), and impartial (2:11).

When judged by these principles, which are the expression of God's own nature, the Jew is condemned (2:17-29). The intense dialogue format in 2:17-29 heightens the severity of the Jewish indictment.[17] Though blessed with inestimable salvation-historical privileges (2:17-20), the Jews make empty their boasting by violation of the law and consequent desecration of God's name (2:21-24). They nullify the meaning of circumcision, intended as a sign and seal for a people covenanted in obedience to Yahweh (2:25). In fact, a morally upright pagan who follows the dictates of his conscience will condemn the law-breaking Jew, who renders void the vastly superior revelation he has received (2:26-27). To enforce his indictment the apostle goes as far as redefining the term *Jew* as one circumcised in heart by the Spirit. Such a redefinition does not mean, however, the collapse of Israel into Christianity.[18] In such a case God's faithfulness (3:3) to his covenant people would be negated (3:1-4). Paul's point is rather that God's righteousness (3:5) and truthfulness (3:7) are vindicated in his judgment of sin, for his very nature demands such a reckoning.

The inescapable deduction of the preceding exposition in 1:18–3:8 is the universal guilt of all people, both Jews and Gentiles (3:9-20). In this conclusion, supported by a catena of six Old Testament quotations, the main point of emphasis is the universality of the condemnation ("all," 3:9, 12, 19, 20; "no one," 3:10, 11, 12). The culpability of the Jew is particularly pronounced since the Jews are the people of the law (3:19). This means that the law only serves God's

---

[17] J. Christiaan Beker (*Paul the Apostle: The Triumph of God in Life and Thought* [Philadelphia: Fortress, 1980], 78-83) stresses the Jewish, dialogical character of Paul's argument at this point but probably goes too far in viewing the entire section, 1:16–4:25, as a dialogue with Jews.

[18] Cranfield, *Romans*, 1:176, appropriately remarks how contrary that would be to the whole tenor of Romans.

salvation-historical purpose of revealing sin and underscoring guilt (3:20), so that people will seek a faith-based rather than law-based righteousness. Sin is against God, guilt and condemnation are before God, and judgment and wrath proceed from God. This dark, ominous portrayal of humanity's spiritual state enforces the reality that from God alone can the dilemma be solved. The problem and its solution are given their theocentric bearings. Paul's mission springs from theological convictions regarding the grave spiritual condition of the entire human race, both Jews and Gentiles. Paul possesses a profound conviction that God has commissioned him to proclaim to all people a message of deliverance from the inescapable outpouring of God's righteous judgment against their sin.

### The God Who Is Both Just and Justifier

The illuminating brilliance of God's solution, contrasted against the dark backdrop of universal guilt (1:18–3:20), is the revelation of his righteousness apart from the law (3:21; cf. 1:17). Romans 3:21-26, if not the key to the entire epistle,[19] is certainly the heart of the argument of 1:16b–4:25. In the work of Christ, God inaugurates his salvation-historical purpose of removing universal guilt and imputing righteousness, thus transforming the relationship between Jew and Gentile (3:21). The basis for the necessity of this righteousness is that all people have sinned and stand in need of God's glory (3:23). The means of receiving this righteousness is faith in Jesus Christ (3:22; also 3:25-26).[20] The manner of justification is God's free grace, irrespective of meritorious deeds (3:24a). The ground of justification is the redemptive (v. 24) and

---

[19] W. S. Campbell, "Romans III as a Key to the Structure and Thought of the Letter," *NovT* 23 (1981): 22-40. Cranfield (*Romans*, 1:199) calls this section "the centre and heart of the whole of Romans 1:16b–15:13."

[20] On this point, see Cranfield, *Romans*, 1:203; Fitzmyer, *Romans*, 345-46; Moo, *Romans 1–8*, 224-25. They each argue that *Christou* in *pistis Christou* is most certainly an objective genitive. This traditional objective genitive interpretation is ably defended by Arland J. Hultgren, "The *Pistis Christou* Formulation in Paul," *NovT* 22 (1980): 248-63. Modern scholars who challenge the traditional approach and take *Christou* as a subjective genitive include Richard B. Hays, *The Faith of Jesus Christ: An Investigation of the Narrative Substructure of Galatians 3:1-4:11*, SBLDS, no. 56 (Chico, Calif.: Scholars Press, 1983); Morna D. Hooker, "PISTIS CHRISTOU," *NTS* 35 (1989): 321-42; Karl Kertelge, *"Rechtfertigung" bei Paulus: Studien zur Struktur und zum Bedeutungsgehalt des paulinischen Rechtfertigungsbegriffs* (Münster: Aschendorff, 1967), 162-66; Richard N. Longenecker, *Galatians*, WBC (Dallas, Tex.: Word, 1990), 87-88; Sam K. Williams, "Again Pistis Christou," *CBQ* 49 (1987): 431-47.

propitiatory (v. 25) sacrifice of Christ, an event "purposed" (v. 25) by God the Father.[21]

It is the final purpose for the work of Christ, however, that climaxes this crucial section: the demonstration of the righteousness of God (3:26a). The need for the demonstration is due to God's forbearance in passing over sins committed before Christ's coming (3:25b-26a). Here *dikaiosunē* refers to the inherent justice of God rather than the act of justification. This is evident from the reason given in verse 25 for this demonstration, God's forbearance in passing over past sins, and from the subsequent clause, "that he might be just even while justifying the one who has faith in Jesus." The propitiatory work of Christ, which is the ground of the believer's justification, demonstrates the righteousness of God, for in that work God is shown to be both just and the justifier. At the cross the demands of God's justice were perfectly satisfied so that he can be the justifier of the one who simply believes in Jesus. The ultimate dilemma for Paul is, how can a righteous God remain so while justifying the unrighteous? The atoning work of Christ answers all of the exigencies introduced by this question, for in it the full measure of God's wrath is poured out on a perfect substitute, the Lord Jesus Christ, thereby satisfying the demands of divine justice while at the same time providing a basis upon which the ungodly can be justified.[22]

Paul is preeminently concerned in Romans with vindicating God's righteousness in his act of justification. It is the person and character of God around which the argument revolves. Not the justified man but the justifying God is on center stage. Soteriology is grounded in Christology, and Christology in Paul's doctrine of God.

### The One God of All People

If everyone, whether Jew or Gentile, is justified by faith (1:17; 3:22, 25-26), then a law-based righteousness is excluded (3:27-28). Since God is one, as every Jew confessed in the *Shema* (3:30a; cf. Deut. 6:14), he is God of both Jew and Gentile (Rom. 3:29). Therefore, both Jew and Gentile are declared righteous through the same principle of

---

[21] The verb *protithēmi* in verse 25 is used in the sense of "purpose" rather than "display." In its other NT occurrences (Rom. 1:13; Eph. 1:9) *protithēmi* means "purpose." In Romans 8:28 and 9:11 the cognate noun *prothesis* has the same meaning. God's "purposing" the sacrifice of Christ fits the context perfectly with its setting in salvation history (see Cranfield, *Romans*, 1:208-10). Moo (*Romans 1–8*, 232), however, opts for the meaning "set forth, display," which also has an adequate contextual fit.

[22] For a helpful statement of this point, see G. B. Caird, review of *Paul and Palestinian Judaism: A Comparison of Patterns of Religion*, by E. P. Sanders, in *JTS* 29 (1978): 541-42.

faith (3:30b). It is God's oneness and immutability that determine the means of justification. But does this not nullify the law and implicate God of acting arbitrarily, since he instituted the law and now has shifted his method of dealing with humankind (3:31a)? Not at all, Paul says (3:31b), for God has always justified men and women on the basis of faith (chap. 4).[23] Abraham was justified by believing in God's promise prior to his circumcision (4:1-3, 9-12; Gen. 15:6). David likewise testifies to the blessing of imputed righteousness apart from works (Rom. 4:6-8; Ps. 32:1-2). Abraham's faith was in God's person and promises (Rom. 4:3, 17-21). The believer in Christ walks in the same faith of Abraham, as his offspring, trusting in the promises and power of the same God (4:5, 11b-12, 16-18, 23-24). Abraham's and David's God is still the justifying God of today, declaring Jew and Gentile righteous on the basis of faith. Not only is the principle of imputed righteousness by faith established but the imputer's unchanging character is confirmed. As for the law, it serves another salvation-historical purpose: it reveals sin as transgression (4:15b), which provokes the wrath of God (4:15a). Ultimately, though, such a fearful revelation serves God's redemptive purpose as people flee to Jesus Christ alone for righteousness (4:25; cf. 3:20; 5:20-21; 7:7-13). God's oneness, then, demands a unified method in declaring people righteous—faith in Jesus Christ apart from the law—and this gives to the Pauline mission its universal and transcultural character.

### A New Life Lived for God

Paul's progression of thought in Romans 5–8, while not a rigidly structured logical argument, as Beker points out,[24] still reveals an inseparable linkage with the preceding exposition of God's justifying grace (1:18–4:25). Both major divisions are integrated into Paul's eschatological framework. N. A. Dahl perceptively establishes the con-

---

[23] This sketch of the argument of 3:27-4:25 adopts the second of the three major views of 3:31 discussed in Moo, *Romans 1–8*, 256-58. Moo's objection to this approach, namely, that *nomos* in the immediate context is used in its character of commanding obedience rather than convicting of sin, is cogent. However, it is the very commanding character of the law that precedes and creates conviction, due to humankind's inability to obey those commands (Rom 2:21-22; 7:7-12). Further, the convicting role of the law emerges twice in the near context (3:19-20; 4:15). Moo sees here an anticipation of the believer's fulfillment of the law as expressed in 8:4, but there is no such clear terminological anticipation (as with, for instance, *en pneumati* in 2:29) in 3:31.

[24] Beker, *Paul the Apostle*, 64-69. Moo (*Romans 1–8*, 299-304) argues impressively in support of a primary division at 5:1 and proposes a "ring composition" or chiastic structure to the paragraphs in 5:1–8:39.

nection: "It should be observed that the logic of Paul in these chapters is not that justification must have ethical consequences and therefore in the end will lead to salvation, but that the justifying grace guarantees and proleptically gives a share in the eschatological life, which must be lived and thus will have 'ethical consequences.'"[25]

The theocentric stream in chapters 5–8, though perhaps not as prominent as in chapters 1–4 and 9–11, still flows steadily as a moving force through the argument. The new eschatological life that the justified person enters is essentially a new relationship with God the Father mediated through the Lord Jesus Christ (5:1, 11). Former enmity with God (5:10) is replaced by an objective state of peace with God (5:1) because of the reconciliation effected through Christ's death (5:10). This already realized work of God in justification and reconciliation (5:9a, 10a, 11b) brings with it the assurance of future salvation from God's wrath (5:9-10). The believer is thus filled with joyous hope for the coming revelation of God's glory (5:2b, 11a), a hope undergirded by God's love objectively demonstrated in the death of Christ (5:8) and mediated internally by the Holy Spirit given by God (5:5).

The transfer from universal sin and guilt (1:18–3:20) to this new life (3:21-26; 5:1-11) is then presented in the context of an analogy concerning Adam and Christ. Adam sums up humanity's condemnation (1:18–3:20); Christ, the second Adam, sums up the justification of believers (3:21–5:11).[26] The dilemma of condemnation transcends transgression of the Mosaic Law because it springs from solidarity with Adam (5:12-14). Through the comparison and contrast of Christ and Adam, Paul underscores the surpassing extent of God's grace over the effects of Adam's sin (5:15, 17, 20b-21). God's grace (5:15, 17, 20, 21) and free gift (5:15, 16, 17) through Christ are out of all proportion to the consequences of Adam's transgression. There is not just replace-

---

[25] N. A. Dahl, "Two Notes on Romans 5," *ST* 5 (1952): 42. The "already-not yet" eschatological continuum of God the Father's redemptive program unites both juridical and participatory concepts into its broader framework. Any attempt to prioritize these two lines, whether Albert Schweitzer's "double-crater" theory (*The Mysticism of Paul the Apostle*, trans. William Montgomery [New York: Macmillan, 1956], 225) or E. P. Sanders's "solution to plight" deduction (*Paul and Palestinian Judaism* [Philadelphia: Fortress, 1977], 442-47, 474-502), must in the end render asunder what the apostle Paul has joined together. For a discussion of this point, see Don N. Howell Jr., "Pauline Eschatological Dualism and Its Resulting Tensions," *Trinity Journal* 14 (1993): 3-24.

[26] Thus both Christ and Adam embody the principle of federal headship. See S. Lewis Johnson Jr., "Romans 5:12: An Exercise in Exegesis and Theology," in *New Dimensions in New Testament Study*, ed. Richard N. Longenecker and Merrill C. Tenney (Grand Rapids: Zondervan, 1974), 298-316.

ment, but such super-abounding provision (5:15, 17, 20) that the recipients of this grace become reigning monarchs over the old dominion (5:14, 17, 21).

Paul then deals with the implications of these relationships with
Adam and Christ for his understanding of the Jewish law. If sin and
salvation emerge from two representative heads, what was the purpose of the law? The answer is that it was given to reveal, even stimulate, sin and provide the opportunity for God's grace to abound (5:20-
21). Underlying each of these expansions on the law (cf. 3:20; 4:15;
5:13-14; 7:7-8) is Paul's doctrine of God, in particular his firm convictions about God's holy character, immutability, and sovereignty. The
gracious, unchanging, carefully superintended redemptive plan of God
must be demonstrated in order to vindicate God's character from any
charges of arbitrariness or caprice.

These final verses (5:20-21) set the stage for what follows: if grace
abounded when sin increased (5:20), can we not further the supremacy
of grace by a life of sin (6:1)? Section 6:2–7:6 is a necessary excursus
to refute this false inference. Far from engendering a life of sin, Paul
says, the believer is placed in a new eschatological realm or redemptive order, "in Christ" (6:11, 23), where the dominion of sin is broken
(6:2, 6, 7, 10, 11-14, 15-22) and ethical righteousness (6:13, 16, 18,
19, 20) and holiness (6:19, 22) become the way of life. The new life is
predicated on the onetime event of Christ's death and resurrection
(6:4). United with Christ's death (6:3, 4a, 5a, 8a), mediated by water
baptism (6:3-4), the believer has died to sin as a dominating power
(6:6b, 7, 11, 14). United with Christ's resurrection (6:4, 8-10), the
believer rises to live a new life for God (6:4b,11-14), even as Christ's
risen life is lived for God (6:10b). This union also brings with it the
promise of the future resurrection of the body (6:5b, 8b).

The death and resurrection of Christ are the ground not only for the
new status of juridical righteousness (3:24-26; 4:24-25; 5:9-11) but
also for a new eschatological existence in Christ, characterized not by
sin but by ethical righteousness. The juridical is logically precedent to
the ethical, as 6:14 again underscores: release from the law's condemnatory sentence results in freedom from sin's domination. Both, however, are grounded in the death and resurrection of Christ. The resurrection, which underlies the new eschatological life and the new
obedience, is attributed to the work of the Father (6:4b). Behind the
resurrection, which is itself the foundation of the new life, is the glory
of the Father.[27] Believers base their new life of service to God (6:12) on

---

[27] "Glory" here refers to God's power as gloriously exercised. Power and
glory are often associated in both testaments (Exod. 15:6; 1 Chr. 16:28; Ps.
145:11; Col. 1:11; 1 Pet. 3:11; Rev. 1:6; 4:11; 5:12-13; 7:12; 19:1). Paul
uniformly attributes the resurrection of Christ to God's working (Rom. 4:24;
8:11; 10:9), which he does again in v. 9 by the divine passive *egertheis*.

the objective reality of their participation in Christ (6:11). Paul's pattern is to base his imperatives on the indicative of God's work in Christ.[28] One who has been placed in the new eschatological realm in Christ, where sin has been conquered and righteousness reigns, can only by utter incongruity and self-contradiction continue to participate in sin—thus the introductory rhetorical question, "We died to sin; how can we live in it any longer?" (6:2). Even as the work of the Father executes the event upon which new life is based (6:4b), so Paul, in characteristic fashion, orients the imperative of the new obedience toward the person of God: believers are alive to God (6:11b), offer their body to God (6:13), and are now enslaved to the lordship of God (6:22; cf. 12:1-2), the end of which is eternal life, the gift of God (6:22b-23).[29]

The imperative of the new obedience results from the believers' freedom from the condemnatory sentence of the law, which Paul simply asserted in 6:14-15. In 7:1-6 the apostle grounds that assertion in the believer's death to the law through participation in Christ's death.[30] The general principle of law releases its binding authority over a person at death (7:1), illustrated in the marriage relationship, which is dissolved at, and only at, the death of husband or wife (7:2-3). So, by dying to the law (7:4, 6) through participation in Christ's death (7:4), the believer is released to serve in the newness of the Spirit (7:6; cf. 6:4). In Christ's death, the believer died to both sin (6:2, 6, 7, 10, 11) and the law (7:4, 6), with the connection of sin to law again stated in 7:5. The result is a new life with a Godward direction: believers are released from the law to belong to Christ and bear fruit for God (7:4b; cf. 6:10, 11, 13, 22).

### The Goodness of the Law and the Immutability of the Law-Giver

Until this point Paul's references to the law have been either (1) to deny a law-based righteousness (2:12-27; 3:21, 27, 28; 4:13-16); (2) to indicate the law's purpose in furthering God's salvation-historical purpose: to reveal sin as transgression (3:20; 4:15b; 5:13), to stimulate sin (5:20; 7:5), and to declare humankind's status as condemned before (3:19) and subject to the wrath of a righteous God (4:15a); or (3) to assert believers' freedom from the law's indictment through Christ's death (6:14, 15; 7:4, 6). Such a view of the law, particularly the direct linkage among sin, the flesh, and the law as expressed in 7:5, would

---

[28] Ridderbos, *Paul*, 253-58.

[29] On this dual theocentric focus, see ibid., 264-65.

[30] Romans 7:1-6 is a continuation of the excursus begun in 6:1. There is no inferential marker here, as in 6:1,15; 7:7,13. Yet 7:1-6 is also transitional, since the subject shifts from freedom from sin to freedom from the law, preparing for the excursus of 7:7-25.

seem to implicate the law as itself inherently evil. Such a false inference about the law, and ultimately about God's character, the apostle now refutes in the excursus of 7:7-25.

"By no means" (7:7, 13) is the law to blame for sin (7:7) or for death, which results from sin (7:13). Rather, sin exploited human nature's propensity for committing that which is forbidden and produced a flagrant violation of the law's commands (7:7b-11). God's original design with his restrictive commands, as in the case of Adam (Gen. 2:15, 16; 3:23), was to promote and enhance life under his full blessing, thus the command was "unto life" (Rom. 7:10). Or in the case of his covenant people Israel, obedience to the law's command issued in life or covenant blessing (Lev. 18:5; Deut. 28:1-14; cf. Rom. 10:5; Gal. 3:12). God's positive redemptive purpose in giving the law is similarly reiterated. The law was given to reveal sin (Rom. 7:7), so that sin's exceedingly devastating effects, primarily death (7:10-11), would produce a desperate flight to the only source of salvation, God's grace in Jesus Christ (7:24-8:1; cf. 5:21b; 11:32; Gal. 3:22, 24).[31] Paul's entire exposition of the law in Romans emerges from the fact that it is God's law (Rom. 7:22, 25), originating in God's determinate purpose and righteous character. Behind the apostle's view of the law is his doctrine of God. Therefore the law itself is holy, righteous, good, and spiritual (7:12-13, 14, 16). The fault lies in humankind's Adamic nature, the flesh (7:5, 18, 25; cf. 8:3-9, 12, 13), and its operating principle, sin (7:5, 7, 8, 9, 11, 13, 14, 17, 20, 23, 25), which exploit the law for their evil purposes. God's law and therefore God's character, of which the law is the expression, are defended against all charges of caprice and defectiveness. Three central Pauline convictions—God's unchanging will, justification through faith in Christ apart from the law, and the divine origin of the law—are creatively integrated in the argument of Romans.[32]

---

[31] The *hina* purpose clauses in Galatians 3:22, 24 and Romans 5:21; 11:32 show that even in its negative preparatory role an ultimately positive, salvific program is served, and this unites the purpose statements of the law. See Ridderbos, *Paul*, 152.

[32] This is disputed by Heikki Räisänen (*Paul and the Law* [Philadelphia: Fortress, 1986], 140-53) and E. P. Sanders (*Paul, the Law and the Jewish People* [Philadelphia: Fortress, 1983], 70-81), who agree that Paul makes a valiant but unsuccessful attempt to synthesize and integrate these convictions. Räisänen charges the apostle with outright contradiction and thus failure logically to absolve God from the charge of defective foresight (152). For one defense of the apostle against the charges of being (1) generally coherent but inconsistent and at times contradictory (Sanders) or (2) so elastic in his thinking that tensions and contradictions are a constant feature of his theology (Räisänen), see Stephen Westerholm, *Israel's Law and the Church's Faith: Paul and His Recent Interpreters* (Grand Rapids: Eerdmans, 1988), 179-92.

### The Spirit of God

The positive counterpart to the cry of despair in 7:24 and dilemma of the divided self in 7:25b comes in chapter 8, particularly verses 1-17. The Holy Spirit, only briefly anticipated in earlier chapters (2:29; 5:5; 7:6), now fully emerges (nineteen times in chapter 8) as God's great eschatological gift who enables obedience to the law (8:4), guarantees the future resurrection of the body (8:11), leads and testifies to sonship (8:14-16), and helps in intercessory prayer (8:26-27). While the emphasis is on freedom from sin's domination in the believer's life, this new ethical triumph enabled by the Spirit is grounded in the juridical sentence against sin God effectively accomplished in Christ's death (8:1, 3b; cf. 6:14). There is no condemnation (*katakrima*) to those in Christ (8:1) because God himself, having sent his Son in the likeness of sinful flesh and as a sin offering, thereby condemned (*katakrinō*) sin in the flesh (8:3b).[33] Since God judicially condemned sin in his Son's death, the one in Christ faces no condemnation. The two clauses in 8:2-3a, then, present freedom from sin's lordship as a result or evidence of the new juridical status of the believer, even as the purpose clause of 8:4a makes obedience to the law the expressed, and now fulfillable, purpose of this status. There is an interchange of juridical (8:1, 3b) and ethical (8:2, 3a, 4) lines, both grounded in God the Father's accomplishment of his redemptive purpose (8:3b). The theocentric direction does not end there. What God did in his Son (8:3b) is now effectively implemented in the lives of believers through God's Spirit (8:9, 14), so that they overcome the force of the sinful

---

[33] The noun *katakrima* occurs elsewhere in Romans only in 5:16,18, where it refers to the juridical sentence of condemnation following Adam's sin. The verb *katakrinō* occurs in 8:3, where it is linked to Christ's being a sin offering (*peri hamartias*), and in 8:34, where Christ's death is also the explicit ground for the removal of condemnation. It seems clear, then, that a juridical meaning is demanded and should not be removed simply because the connection with the preceding verses (8:2 would be a perfect sequel to 7:25a) might seem forced. The weaker inferential particle *ara* occurs in 8:1 (cf. *oun* in 5:1; 6:1, 15; 7:7, 13; 8:12), so the connection with 7:24-25 is somewhat looser and probably picks up from earlier references to juridical righteousness (e.g., 5:1, 16, 18; 6:14b). The whole dilemma of interpreters at this point in the argument of Romans serves to highlight how Paul integrated ("distinction without divorce") the juridical and ethical lines. Cranfield (*Romans*, 1:382) argues unsuccessfully against rendering *peri hamartias* in v. 3 as "sin offering" (so NIV), though admitting that is its dominant sense in the LXX. For the apostle Paul, release from the guilt of sin is the precedent for freedom from sin's enslaving power. While the latter is the dominant motif of chapters 6–8, he does not hesitate to introduce the former at certain points in that argument as reminders of his earlier exposition in 1:18-4:25 and 5:12-21. See also Dunn, *Romans 1–8*, 415-22.

nature (8:7-8). As adopted sons of God (8:14, 16) and heirs of God (8:17), believers express the intimacy of this new relationship by crying "Abba Father" (8:15).

## The Cosmic Triumph of God's Lordship

The new status as God's children and heirs, because of union with Christ, guarantees a future share in the glory of God (8:17). This glorification, anticipated in 2:7, 10; 3:23; 5:2, is a full restoration of humankind's original participation in the radiance of the divine glory to be fully realized in the eschatological future. Redemption is here provided its universal dimensions as the children of God strain, along with all creation, toward the unveiling of their full liberty (8:18-25). The complete redemption of humankind with creation is the purpose of God, who subjected creation not to frustration alone but to a frustration that groans "in hope" toward its future transformation (8:20-21). The background is the fall of humankind and its effects on the natural world—the curse of Genesis 3:17-19 is prefaced by the promise of Genesis 3:15. As with the condemnatory sentencing of the law so with the curse upon the natural world, God's gracious and universal redemptive purposes are furthered in all he does.[34]

V. O. Eareckson sees Romans 8:18-25 as God's full response to the great damage of the fall and its cosmic effects documented in 1:18-32. There is a sense of finality in 8:18-25 to the argument of Romans at this point as the "horizon of Paul's vision is extended to its greatest limits" and "the totality of the redemptive work of Christ is seen to extend to the very farthest reaches of the cosmos."[35] Yet, while such a cosmic perspective is essential to vindicate the purposes of the Creator-Redeemer against any charge of deficiency, chapters 9-11 remain absolutely necessary for a comprehensive theodicy. For Paul is expounding not redemption for its own sake but redemption as the expression of God's character and will. How his character can be inviolate while Israel remains in unbelief and the covenantal promises remain unrealized constitutes a theological problem of major proportions and must carry the argument forward to its satisfying conclusion in chapter 11.

## God's Unbreakable Chain of Salvation

In the present tension of hope inaugurated but awaiting consummation, the believer is sustained by the support of the Spirit's intercession (8:26-27) and God's promised protection in all circumstances (8:28-

---

[34] On this point, see Cranfield, *Romans*, 1:413-14.

[35] Vincent O. Eareckson, "The Glory to Be Revealed Hereafter: The Interpretation of Romans 8:18-25" (Ph.D. diss., Princeton Theological Seminary, 1977), 163.

39). The theocentric reference point is particularly pronounced as the
argument begun in 5:1 now reaches its climax. The Spirit's intercession is read by God, who searches the heart and knows by intimate
familiarity the unuttered requests of his Spirit (8:27). The believer's
assurance of God's providential protection in every situation (8:28a)
is because God forges an unbreakable chain from calling to final glorification for the objects of his love (8:28b-30). Whether in verse 28 the
subject of the main verb "works together" (*sunergei*) is "all things,"
"God," or an understood "he" referring to God,[36] the sense is still
much the same: the omnipotent God directs all events in his children's
lives to conform them to the image of his Son (8:28-29a), because he
has bound himself in the entire salvation process to secure their glorious destiny (8:28-30). Such security is confirmed by a series of rhetorical questions all answered by the redemptive actions of God himself:
he is for us (8:31); he did not spare but delivered up his Son (8:32); he
elected and justified (8:33); he raised Christ to a position at his right
hand (8:34). The redemptive events on which the believer's security
rests spring from the love of Christ (8:35, 37) and the love of God in
Christ (8:39).[37] Paul weds two firm convictions about God that under-
lie his steadfast security: (1) God's unfailing love, and (2) God's sovereign control of the expansive sweep of the universe, whether life, death,
angels, rulers, things present, things to come, spiritual powers above
and below, or any created thing. What the apostle believes about God
conditions his view of everything else. Here is where the integrating
truth of Paul's missionary theology resides. In this central section of
the epistle (chaps. 5-8), Paul thus develops a comprehensive view of

---

[36] Bruce Metzger (*A Textual Commentary on the Greek Testament* [Stuttgart:
United Bible Societies, 1975], 518) comments that the external support for
*ho theos*, though "ancient and noteworthy," is far inferior to the diversified
support for the shorter reading. An Alexandrian editor perhaps made explicit
the subject he understood implied with the verb *sunergei*. Carroll D. Osburn
("The Interpretation of Romans 8:28," *WTJ* 44 [1982]: 99-109) discusses
the strengths and weaknesses of four alternative renderings. The fourth possibility, taking *to pneuma* of v. 26 as the understood subject, is unlikely since
the subject has already shifted from "Spirit" to "God" (implicitly) in v. 27a.
Cranfield (*Romans*, 1:428-29) takes *panta* as the subject, which he feels actually heightens the emphasis on God's transcendent power and control. This
seems the best approach.

[37] Such interchange of God-Christ language is characteristic of Paul and
should prevent any interpreter from rigidly setting theocentrism against
christocentrism as competing rivals. See Kazimierz Romaniuk, *L 'amour du
pére et du Fils dans la sotériologie de S.Paul* (Rome: Biblical Institute Press,
1974), 253-55. For a full exploration of the God-Christ interchange in Paul's
letters, see Don N. Howell Jr., "God-Christ Interchange in Paul: Impressive
Testimony to the Deity of Jesus," *JETS* 36 (1993): 467-79.

Christian salvation. The past (justification through Christ's death) has secured the future (eschatological glory) that now conditions the present (Spirit-led sanctification). This understanding of salvation demands that he assume both a pioneering and pastoral role to fulfill his mission. As God's co-worker (1 Cor. 3:9a), he is committed to bringing the people of God, individually and collectively, to maturity "in Christ" (Col. 1:28-29).

### Israel and the Gentile Mission

Does Paul's special consecration to Gentile evangelism, a bedrock conviction to which he constantly returns (Rom. 1:5, 13; 11:13; 15:16-19; Gal. 1:16; 2:2, 8, 9; Eph. 3:1, 6, 8; Col. 1:27; 1 Thess. 2:16; 1 Tim. 2:7; 3:16; 2 Tim. 4:17), mean that Israel as an ethnic people has no place in his mission? It is clear that the agreement between Paul and the pillar apostles that he go to the Gentiles and they to the Jews (Gal. 2:7-9) was not a rigid arrangement that sealed Paul off from Jewish evangelism or, for that matter, prevented the Jerusalem apostles from engaging in the universal mission to which they were commanded (Matt. 28:19; Acts 1:8).[38] For Paul's ongoing strategy was to enter the synagogues of Gentile cities and to evangelize both Jews and Gentile god-fearers who would become the nucleus of new congregations (Acts 9:20; 13:5, 14, 43; 14:1; 17:1, 10, 17; 18:4, 7, 19, 26; 19:8). Barrett perceptively comments: "The constant repetition of this practice is Luke's version of Paul's 'to the Jew first but also to the Greek' (Rom. 1:16), but what was to Luke little more than a missionary technique is to Paul a theological principle."[39]

Gradually, however, there was a shift of focus away from Jewish evangelism due to the stubborn resistance of his racial kinsmen to the gospel (Acts 13:46-48; 18:6; 22:21; 26:20; 28:28). But though Paul devoted himself to the special task of evangelizing Gentiles, the salvation of Israel was never far from his heart.[40] Like Moses (Exod. 32:31-32), Paul could wish to stand under the curse of God, if possible, for the benefit of his fellow Jews (Rom. 9:1-3). He earnestly prays for their salvation (10:1). Paul is deeply troubled by the present apostate state of his racial kinsmen. For if Israel is permanently cast off, God's covenantal pledge of a redeemed nation ushering in universal king-

---

[38] F. F. Bruce, *The Epistle to the Galatians*, NIGTC (Grand Rapids: Eerdmans, 1982), 124-25.

[39] C. K. Barrett, *A Critical and Exegetical Commentary on the Acts of the Apostles*, ICC (Edinburgh: T & T Clark, 1994), 1:611.

[40] Barrett (*Acts*, 1:656-57) points out that what we have in Acts 13:46 (cf. 18:6; 28:28) is a strategic shift of ministry priorities not a rigid abandonment of the evangelization of Jews, even as Galatians 2:7-9 is not a separation of Jewish and Gentile evangelism into two mutually exclusive missions.

dom blessing (cf. Gen. 12:1-3; 13:14-16; 15:1, 4, 7, 18, 19; 17:1-8) must remain unfulfilled, implying either unfaithfulness to his word or inability to accomplish what he has promised. Paul takes up the problem of Israel in Romans 9–11, not only to relate his mission to her future but to vindicate God's faithfulness to his declared purposes for this people.[41]

The apostle sets forth a threefold argument in chapter 11 to the dilemma of Israel's standing rejection of her Messiah. First, Israel's present state of apostasy, though real, is not total, for God has preserved a remnant according to his gracious election, a pattern that can be seen in Israel's history (Rom. 11:1-10). This remnant chosen by grace (11:6) is a harbinger of hope for the restoration of the nation as a whole.

Second, Paul categorically denies that Israel's stumbling is beyond recovery, that is, without further positive implications for herself and the world (11:11a). Israel's present rejection is providentially superintended by God to serve his wider salvation-historical purposes for the Gentiles as well as for Israel (11:11b-24). Her stumbling triggers a fourfold redemptive chain with expanding effects in each progressive stage: (1) the transgression (11:11-12), loss (11:12), and rejection (11:15) of Israel lead to the salvation (11:11), reconciliation (11:15), and spiritual wealth (11:12) of the Gentile world; (2) the salvation of the Gentile world then provokes Israel to jealousy (11:11b, 14; cf. 10:19); (3) when the full number (11:25b) of the Gentiles is reached, Israel, provoked to jealousy by the Gentiles' inclusion, is saved (11:26-27) and thus attains her own fullness (11:12b); (4) this fullness (11:12b) or acceptance (11:15b) of Israel ushers in even greater spiritual wealth (11:12b) or life from the dead (11:15b) for the entire world. This fourth and final stage in the salvific progression is surely the long-awaited cosmic redemption earlier described in Romans 8:18-25, where the horizon of Paul's vision of God's redemptive plan is extended to its farthest limits!

Third, Israel's rejection can be neither final nor permanent because of God's immutable covenant promises (11:25-32). Her election, traced to the patriarchs, must stand, because God's calling and gifts are irrevocable (11:28-29). His purposes are ultimately bathed in mercy for both Jew and Gentile (11:30-32). Disobedience, whether of Jew or Gentile (11:30-31), becomes God's tool for demonstrating his mercy to both. The outcome is that "all Israel will be saved" (11:26a). Ethnic Israel will in the future come to faith in her Messiah (11:26-27).[42] Paul

---

[41] J. C. Beker, "Romans 9-11 in the Context of the Early Church," *Princeton Seminary Bulletin Supplementary Issue* 1 (1990): 40-55; Bruce W. Longenecker, "Different Answers to Different Issues: Israel, the Gentiles and Salvation History in Romans 9-11," *JSNT* 36 (1989): 95-123.

[42] Longenecker ("Salvation History in Romans 9–11," 96-98) demonstrates that *Israēl* has an exclusively ethnic sense in chapters 9–11.

does not collapse the promises of Israel into the church but views the culmination of salvation history as the fulfillment of the patriarchal promises to the nation springing from Abraham.

This is why Paul can "magnify" (15:17, *doxazō*) his own ministry as apostle to the Gentiles, because under divine providence he is not only bringing salvation to the Gentiles but also thereby initiating the chain of events that will ultimately lead to Israel's deliverance. In other words, Paul's solution to Israel's rejection of the Messiah is the final restoration of Israel by means of the Gentile mission. "What emerges from all this is that Paul's mission cannot be viewed in isolation from Israel's restoration. The apostle views his Gentile mission both as a catalyst to the present salvation of a remnant from within Israel and as an essential precursor to the eventual salvation of all Israel; it is only when the 'full measure' of the Gentiles comes in that all Israel will be saved (Rom. 11:25-26)."[43]

This conclusion proves once again that this missionary charter of Paul's is primarily an exposition of God's character and purposes in salvation history rather than a soteriological excursus. The dualism of salvation by faith apart from ethnicity *and* the certainty of Israel's future redemption fit perfectly into Paul's "already-not yet" eschatological framework. The new community of justified believers consisting of Jew and Gentile possesses soteriological discontinuity with the law-based righteousness of first-century Palestinian Judaism[44] but salvation-historical continuity with the covenant promises of the Old Testament. There is both a universalism and an ethnocentrism in Paul's presentation of salvation history. The God of the new community, to which righteousness is imputed apart from the law, is the God of

---

[43] W. S. Campbell, "Israel," in *DPHL*, ed. Gerald F. Hawthorne and Ralph P. Martin (Downers Grove, Ill.: InterVarsity, 1993), 445. Both Longenecker ("Salvation History in Romans 9–11," 98-101) and Fitzmyer (*Romans*, 618-20) adequately refute the Sonderweg thesis of F. Mussner ("'Ganz Israel wird gerettet werden' [Röm 11,26]: Versuch einer Auslegung," *Kairos* 18 [1976]: 241-55) that Israel will be saved at the parousia of Christ in a "special way" other than explicit faith in his person.

[44] The "new perspective" on Paul (summarized in Daniel G. Reid, "The Misunderstood Apostle," *Christianity Today* [16 July 1990], 25-27), represented preeminently by E. P. Sanders and J. D. G. Dunn, has demonstrated that Paul was not combating pure legalistic righteousness or merit theology, which is a caricature of first-century rabbinic Judaism. Still, the apostle was significantly more pessimistic (or better, realistic) about human sinfulness and thus insistent on *sola gratia* than was Palestinian Judaism. Three helpful critiques of the "new perspective" are Stephen Westerholm, *Israel's Law and the Church's Faith*, 143-50, 165-69, 172-73; Moo, *Romans 1–8*, 213-18; Donald A. Hagner, "Paul and Judaism. The Jewish Matrix of Early Christianity: Issues in the Current Debate," *Bulletin for Biblical Research* 3 (1993): 111-30.

Abraham, who covenanted with a historical people their redemptive future. As J. C. Beker puts it: "The priority of Israel and the universality of the gospel can be maintained simultaneously because they both have a theocentric foundation."[45] The doxology of 11:33-36 brings the attention on God in these eleven chapters to a fitting culmination. The apostle can only extol the profound wisdom and knowledge of the God who designed, superintends, and will one day consummate this great blueprint for the salvation of all people, both Jew and Gentile.

### Living Sacrifices, Holy and Pleasing to God

The Pauline ethical instruction (12:1-15:13), far from being an applicational postscript, is the logical and necessary inference (12:1, *oun*) of the entire preceding theological exposition of 1:16-11:36. In chapters 6-8 Paul underlined the necessity of obedient and righteous living by the enabling of the Holy Spirit. Now Paul provides the concrete parameters for this new life. The exposition of the divine redemptive purpose in chapters 1-11 can be summarized as "the compassions of God" (12:1). The appeal to present oneself as a living sacrifice to God (12:1) and to discern the will of God (12:2) is predicated on God's character and compassionate activity. Both the ground and goal of the new life, then, are fundamentally theocentric.[46]

In the injunctions that follow, God is repeatedly set forth as the source, arbiter, and object of Christian ethical conduct. Believers are to avoid revenge for that is God's domain (12:19) and to submit to the secular authorities because they are God's ordained servants (13:1, 2, 4, 6). The church should allow for diversity in the nonessentials, for thanksgiving in such differences is offered to God (14:6), and all alike will give an account of their behavior at God's judgment seat (14:10-12). Convictions about such nonessentials are best kept between oneself and God (14:22). One should seek the edification of the church, for it is God's work (14:20). The Christian's service is in the kingdom of God (14:17) and is aimed at pleasing God (14:18). It is God who gives the endurance and encouragement necessary to preserve unity so that the united church can glorify the God and Father (15:5-7). Christ became a servant "for the sake of God's truthfulness" (15:8); that is, to vindicate God's character as faithful by fulfilling the patriarchal promises. The result of such vindication is that the Gentiles come to glorify God (15:9-12). God is the source of hope and peace and the object of trust (15:13). The ethical instruction thus builds to a doxological crescendo (15:6, 9: *doxazō*) as did the theological exposition in the outpouring of praise in 11:33-36.

---

[45] Beker, *Paul the Apostle*, 335.
[46] Cranfield, *Romans*, 2:595.

### The Offering of the Gentiles to God

As Paul brings the epistle to a close, he sets his own mission as apostle to the Gentiles in its theocentric parameters (15:14-33). The basis of his mission is the grace of God (15:15-16a). The task of his mission is the proclamation of the gospel of God (15:16b; cf. 1:1). The nature of his mission is service (or worship) to God (15:17). More specifically, his goal is to make a priestly offering of the Gentiles to God (15:16c) and lead the Gentiles to obey God (15:18). Perhaps the most concentrated attestation of the language of sacrifice in the Pauline corpus is in Romans 15:16, where Paul employs three cultic terms to describe his ministry: he is a priest-servant (*leitourgos*) of Christ Jesus, serving as a priest (*hierourgeō*) the gospel of God, making as an acceptable, holy sacrificial offering (*prosphora*) to God the Gentile believers.[47] As Paul approaches Jerusalem with the funds collected from the Gentile churches as their sacrificial offerings on behalf of the impoverished saints there, he perceives the gift as a token and seal of his own greater and more far-reaching sacrifice to God.[48]

In the final chapter Paul greets twenty-six individuals whom he has met in his apostolic journeys that have now made their way to Rome (16:1-16).[49] Then follows a warning against factious teachers (16:17-

---

[47] *Prosphora* can be literal (Eph. 5:2) or figurative as here. The cognate verb *prospherō*, so frequent in Hebrews (twenty times), never occurs in Paul. The verb *leitourgeō* occurs only in Romans 15:27 (cf. Acts 13:2; Heb. 10:11), while *leitourgia* is found in 2 Corinthians 9:12; Philippians 2:17, 30, and *leitourgos* in Romans 13:6 (clearly non-cultic); 15:16; Philippians 2:25. *Hierourgeō* is a hapax legomenon. Comparing these texts it is clear that the material gifts of the Philippians, whether to Paul (Phil. 2:17) or to the saints in Jerusalem (Rom. 15:27; 2 Cor. 9:12), and of Epaphroditus's ministry on Paul's behalf (Phil. 2:25, 30), are spiritual sacrifices offered to God just like Paul's offering of the Gentiles (Rom. 15:16).

[48] Bruce, *Paul*, 323.

[49] The integrity of chapter 16 has been questioned in the history of interpretation due to its actual contents and/or the complex textual history, which indicates there were longer and shorter rescensions of our extant epistle. Metzger (*Textual Commentary*, 533-35) summarizes the textual evidence: the doxology of 16:24-27 occurs at six different locations, but 15:1-12 is attested at every level of the tradition. Metzger allows for the "possibility" that Paul himself dispatched a shorter form of Romans without chapter 16, but assigns "probability" to the responsibility of Marcion for the shorter rescension (i.e., without chapters 15–16). The integrity of 16:1-23 (or 24) is ably defended by the following, who each admits probability in tracing the shorter rescensions to Marcion: Cranfield, *Romans*, 1:5-11; Karl Paul Donfried, "A Short Note on Romans 16," *JBL* 89 (1970): 441-49; Harry Gamble Jr., *The Textual History of the Letter to the Romans* (Grand Rapids: Eerdmans, 1977); Donald Guthrie, *New Testament Introduction*, 3d ed. (Downers Grove, Ill.: InterVarsity, 1970), 400-13; Ziesler, *Romans*, 19-26.

19), an expression of confidence in the triumph of the God of peace (16:20a; cf. 15:33), the closing benediction (16:20b), and personal greetings from his companions (16:21-24). Romans ends fittingly with a doxology to the only wise God; this sets the gospel in its salvation-historical context (16:25-27), just as the epistle began (cf. 1:1-5).[50] The proclamation of Jesus Christ to the Gentile world is the present revelation of an eternally planned redemptive program. What we have in the gospel is the divinely decreed manifestation of redemptive purposes originating in eternity past in the heart of God the Father. Romans has thus come full circle. Every aspect of Paul's thought finds its sphere of integration in the person and purposes of God the Father. As S. K. Williams expresses it:

> Ultimately in fulfilling his promises to Abraham, in making all peoples his children through Christ, he is doing nothing more or less than being true to himself—that is, to his own nature as creator and saviour. He is engaging in the work of being God: the source, the means, the goal of all that is.[51]

---

[50] Cranfield (*Romans*, 2:808-9), while maintaining the doxology of 16:25-27 is post-Pauline, judges its origin as an orthodox attempt to round off what seemed an incomplete ending. "In any case, placed where it now is, it seems to us to form a not unworthy, even if non-Pauline, doxological appendix to Paul's most weighty epistle" (2:809). William Sanday and Arthur C. Headlam (*A Critical and Exegetical Commentary on the Epistle to the Romans*, 5th ed., ICC [Edinburgh: T & T Clark, 1901], xcv, xcvi, 432-36), however, demonstrate (as did Hort before them) impressive parallels between the language of this doxology and passages in the Hauptbriefe. Consequently, they view 16:25-27 as Paul's own summary of the whole argument of the epistle. Larry W. Hurtado ("The Doxology at the End of Romans," in *New Testament Textual Criticism: Essays in Honour of Bruce M. Metzger*, ed. Eldon J. Epp and Gordon D. Fee [Oxford: Clarendon, 1981], 185-99) effectively disputes several traditional arguments against Pauline authorship and argues that the apostle's composition of the doxology remains a viable option. In a recent article K. H. Walkenhorst ("The Concluding Doxology of the Letter to the Romans and Its Theology," *Katorikku Kenkyuu* [Tokyo] 27 [1988]: 99-132) defends the integrity of the doxology on the basis of its connection with the exhortation in chapters 14–15. Internally, then, a good case can be made for its genuineness. External manuscript evidence is also impressive in support of its authenticity and location at the end of the epistle (p61, Aleph, B, C, D, 81, 1739, vg, eth, Clement).

[51] Sam K. Williams, "The 'Righteousness of God' in Romans," *JBL* 99 (1980): 290. Williams interprets *dikaiosunē theou* in 1:17 and throughout Romans as referring to God's nature, that is, the attribute of righteousness in the sense of faithfulness to his covenant promises. However, this interpretation is not necessary in order to preserve the theocentrism of Romans.

That is why at critical junctures the epistle rises to a crescendo of adoration for who God is (3:25-26; 8:38-39; 11:33-36; 15:5-13; 16:25-27). Romans, the charter of the Pauline mission, is first and last a book about God's redemptive self-revelation in the person and work of his Son.

## CONCLUSION

In recent years New Testament scholars have renewed a vigorous search for the "center" of Pauline thought.[52] It is this writer's belief that one must move beyond soteriology or even Christology to posit a center that can adequately integrate *all* aspects of Paul's missionary theology.[53] Christ's person and work have as their reference point the person and purposes of God the Father. The Son of God comes to fulfill the redemptive mission of the Father (Rom. 8:3; Gal. 4:4). Even his acclamation as King and Lord is ultimately intended for the Father's glory (1 Cor. 15:28; Phil. 2:11). Creation, judgment, and salvation in all aspects—past, present, and future—are defined in relation to God the Father. God alone is the source of all things (Rom. 11:36; 1 Cor. 8:6a). It is God from whom humankind is alienated and by whom it is finally judged. The Father plans (foreknowledge and election), superintends (salvation history), and both inaugurates and consummates (eschatological dualism) the salvation of his created and inhabited universe.

Through a personal encounter with the risen Lord Jesus on the road to Damascus, Paul's understanding of salvation was transformed simultaneously with his call to the apostolic mission (Rom. 1:5; Gal. 1:15-16). What God has done in the person and work of his Son must be proclaimed, believed, and lived out among the nations of the world. Pauline theology is thus the generative spring of the Pauline mission. The redemptive self-revelation of God in Christ is no abstract truth to be pondered but God's good news of saving power to be believed and obeyed (Rom. 1:5; 16:26). This gospel meets the human dilemma of universal guilt; it vindicates God as the just Justifier, who in the cross

---

[52] Helpful recent surveys of the "center" debate include T. Deidun, "Some Recent Attempts at Explaining Paul's Theology," *The Way* 26 (1986): 230-42; C. J. A. Hickling, "Center and Periphery in Paul's Thought," in *Studia Biblica 1978: Papers on Paul and Other New Testament Authors*, ed. E. A. Livingstone (Sheffield: JSOT, 1980), 199-214; R. P. Martin, "Center of Paul's Theology," *DPHL*, 92-95; Joseph Plevnik, "The Center of Pauline Theology," *CBQ* 51 (1989): 461-78; John Reumann, *"Righteousness" in the New Testament* (Philadelphia: Fortress, 1982), 105-21.

[53] Don N. Howell Jr., "The Center of Pauline Theology," *BSac* 151 (1994): 50-70.

satisfied his righteous wrath toward sin; it offers a righteousness before God to all people through faith alone; it provides the justified
person a new life of conquest over all the powers of the old order—sin,
death, and the flesh—through the empowering presence of the Spirit;
it guarantees a harvest among the Gentiles and ultimately the salvation of all Israel. It is no wonder, then, that Paul "magnifies" his own
ministry (Rom. 15:17), since by God's grace he has been divinely posi-
tioned on the culminative stage of salvation history, where the fulfillment of the ages has provisionally arrived (1 Cor. 10:11b), and has
been called to proclaim what God has done in Christ to reconcile the
world to himself (2 Cor. 5:19-21). It is in Romans, the missionary
charter of the apostle, that Paul expounds his theological convictions
in the context of his mission.

   S. Westerholm has real insight when he writes: "Paul could raise
no practical issue without resolving its place in a theological framework. His contribution to first-century Christianity was that of a pioneer missionary, coping with concrete problems as they arose in his
assemblies. On the other hand, the Church of the centuries is indebted
to his persistence in relating ephemeral issues to the themes of eternity."[54] Those who throughout the history of the church have captured the dynamic of Paul the missionary—whether Augustine, Luther,
Wesley, or Barth—have discovered more than a man but, through him,
have encountered his God, the sovereign and loving Planner, Adminis-
trator, and Consummator of redemption.

---

[54] Westerholm, *Israel's Law and the Church's Faith*, 222.

# PART THREE

# SYNOPTIC GOSPELS AND ACTS

# 7

## *Mission in Matthew*

## John D. Harvey

Chapter 3 addressed the topic of mission in Jesus' teaching and, in so doing, examined many passages in the synoptic gospels. Matthew, Mark, and Luke, however, did more than simply provide three "sayings" documents. Each author sought to tell the story of Jesus in the way he believed would be most helpful to those who would read the completed work. Each set Jesus' words and works within a narrative framework and wove them into a unified account of Jesus' life and ministry. In considering the theme of mission in the NT, therefore, it is necessary to examine each of the synoptic gospels to discover the way in which the individual authors understood the concept.

### INTRODUCTORY MATTERS

The unanimous witness of the early church fathers is that the gospel "according to Matthew" was written by the apostle Matthew.[1] Those same church fathers also provide evidence on the date of composition and the primary audience.[2] The first statement is that of Papias, as recorded in Eusebius's *Ecclesiastical History*, 3.9.1: "Matthew com-

---

[1] Donald A. Hagner: "It is difficult to believe that the Gospel would have been attributed to Matthew without good reason, since, so far as we can tell from the available data, Matthew was not otherwise a leading figure among the apostles or in the early Church" (*Matthew 1–13*, WBC [Dallas, Tex.: Word, 1993], lxxvi).

[2] Curiously, scholars frequently dismiss the clear testimony of the church fathers when discussing introductory matters. Given the sketchy nature of the internal evidence, external testimony holds more promise for deciding these issues. The burden of proof regarding the external evidence is on those scholars who seek to discount it.

posed the logia in the Hebrew dialect and everyone interpreted them as he was able."[3] Papias is followed by Irenaeus, who adds information on the date of the work: "Now Matthew published also a book of the Gospel among the Hebrews in their own dialect, while Peter and Paul were preaching the gospel in Rome and founding the Church" (*Eccles. Hist.*, 5.8.2).[4] These two witnesses are followed by Pantaenus, who also notes that Matthew wrote "in Hebrew letters" (*Eccles. Hist.*, 5.10.3) and by Origen, who notes that Matthew "was once a tax-collector but afterwards an apostle of Jesus Christ," and that he published his gospel "for those who from Judaism came to believe, composed as it was in Hebrew letters" (*Eccles. Hist.*, 6.25.4).[5]

The consistent testimony of the early church fathers, then, is that the gospel was written by the apostle.[6] It was written "in Hebrew" (or "in the Hebrew dialect") and was intended for Jewish-Christian readers.[7] If Irenaeus's words are taken at face value, the date of composition was in the early 60s C.E.[8] The place of composition and the desti-

---

[3] Papias lived from 60 C.E. until 130 C.E. and served as the Bishop of Hierapolis. Although nearly every word of his statement has been disputed, none of the arguments against his testimony is insurmountable. For extended discussions, see Robert H. Gundry, *Matthew: A Commentary on His Literary and Theological Art* (Grand Rapids: Eerdmans, 1982), 609-22; John Wenham, *Redating Matthew, Mark and Luke* (Downers Grove, Ill.: InterVarsity, 1992), 121-33.

[4] Irenaeus lived from 130 C.E. until 202 C.E. and served as Bishop of Lyons.

[5] Pantaenus died c. 200 C.E. Origen lived in Alexandria between 185 C.E. and 255 C.E.

[6] Other suggestions include: (1) an unidentified Jewish Christian (W. D. Davies and Dale C. Allison, *A Critical and Exegetical Commentary on the Gospel according to Saint Matthew*, ICC [Edinburgh: T & T Clark, 1988], 1:7-58), (2) an unidentified Gentile Christian (Kenneth W. Clark, "The Gentile Bias in Matthew," *JBL* 66 [1947]: 165-72), and (3) a Matthean "school" (Krister Stendahl, *The School of St. Matthew*, 2d ed. [Philadelphia: Fortress, 1968]).

[7] There is general agreement on this conclusion concerning the audience, and Hagner (*Matthew 1–13*, lxiv) lists five items that support it: (1) a concern with the fulfillment of OT prophecy, (2) Jesus' fidelity to the Mosaic Law, (3) the omission of any explanation of Jewish customs, (4) the formulation of discussions in typical rabbinic patterns, and (5) apologetic motifs that address explicitly Jewish charges.

[8] Suggestions as to the date of composition span at least sixty years, with the majority of scholars holding to a date between 80 C.E. and 100 C.E. For a helpful table, see Davies and Allison, *Matthew*, 1:127-28. Increasingly, however, other scholars are arguing for a date before 70 C.E. For example, John A. T. Robinson (*Redating the New Testament* [Philadelphia: Westminster, 1976], 92-117) suggests 50-60 C.E.; Gundry (*Matthew*, 599-602) suggests a date before 63 C.E.; Bo Reicke (*The Roots of the Synoptic Gospels* [Philadelphia: Fortress, 1986], 157-80) suggests 60 C.E.; Wenham (*Redating*, 238-44) suggests 40 C.E.

nation are not specified, but "among the Hebrews" suggests a locale somewhere in the eastern Mediterranean.[9]

The preceding external evidence does not address the occasion and purpose of Matthew's gospel. Suggestions on those matters must be based on internal evidence, and since Matthew (unlike Luke and John) does not provide a purpose statement, conclusions drawn from that evidence are somewhat subjective. The task is complicated by the diverse material found in the gospel:

> On the one hand, we have the particularism that limits Jesus' and his disciples' ministry to Israel. Together with this exclusivism . . . is the generally Jewish tone of the Gospel with, among other things, its stress on the abiding validity of the law, the necessity of righteousness, and the fulfillment of messianic prophecy. On the other hand, however, standing in sharp contrast to the preceding, are the universalism of the Gospel, its striking transference of the kingdom motif to a new community, and the particularly harsh sayings against the Jews.[10]

Given these apparently contradictory pieces of evidence, suggestions regarding occasion and purpose have frequently been poles apart. It is probably best, given the complexity of the book, to acknowledge the possibility of multiple purposes for Matthew's gospel.[11] The particularism and universalism noted above, however, suggest that prominent among those purposes must have been (1) providing material to evangelize fellow Jews (cf. Matt. 10:23), and (2) explaining the origins of the Gentile mission (cf. Matt. 28:18-20).

---

[9] A variety of specific locations have been suggested, including Antioch, Alexandria, Caesarea, and Transjordan. For an extended discussion, see Davies and Allison, *Matthew*, 1:138-47. It is impossible, however, to know for certain either the place of composition or the destination. Although most scholars believe that the author wrote to believers in his own geographical area, D. A. Carson ("Matthew," in *Expositor's Bible Commentary*, ed. Frank E. Gaebelein [Grand Rapids: Zondervan, 1984], 8:22) suggests that he might have been more itinerant than is usually assumed.

[10] Hagner, *Matthew 1–13*, lxvii.

[11] Carson ("Matthew," 22-25) suggests four aims: (1) to instruct and catechize, (2) to provide apologetic and evangelistic material, especially in winning the Jews, (3) to encourage believers in their witness before a hostile world, and (4) to inspire deeper faith in Jesus the Messiah. David E. Garland (*Reading Matthew: A Literary and Theological Commentary on the First Gospel* [New York: Crossroad, 1993], 6-9) suggests six aims: (1) to tell the story of Jesus, (2) to bolster the readers' faith, (3) to refute Jewish charges, (4) to explain present circumstances, especially Jewish rejection of the gospel, (5) to encourage steadfast obedience to Jesus' commands, and (6) to arm Jesus' disciples for mission.

## THE FRAMEWORK OF SALVATION HISTORY

A careful analysis of Matthew's gospel suggests that he viewed history in four periods: (1) the time of the law and the prophets, (2) the time of Jesus' kingdom proclamation, (3) the time of the messianic travail, and (4) the time of the consummation of the kingdom.[12] This salvation history framework is important for an analysis of the theme of mission in Matthew.

Matthew draws his readers' attention to the period of the law and the prophets by emphasizing the way in which the events of Jesus' birth and early years fulfill specific OT prophecies (1:22-23; 2:5-6, 15, 17-18, 23). Nevertheless, it is clear that the ministry of John the Baptist marks the end of that period (11:12-13). Matthew's description of John's ministry confirms its transitional character (3:1-12). His appearance (3:4) and call to repentance (3:7-10) are fully prophetic and connect him to the preceding era. Yet his message (3:2) is the same as that of Jesus (4:17), and he is able to announce that judgment has already begun (3:10).

The second period, inaugurated by Jesus' preaching about the kingdom (4:17), also fulfills prophecy (4:14-16). That preaching and the miracles associated with it demonstrate beyond any doubt that the kingdom is present (11:2-6; 12:28). In fact, Matthew has been careful to group the accounts of ten healing miracles in such a way as to portray Jesus as fulfilling the prophesied messianic mission, for all of the signs mentioned in 11:4-5 have been reported in 8:1-9:34. The end of this time period is marked by the eschatological signs that accompany Jesus' crucifixion and resurrection (27:50-53; 28:2). The earthquake in particular is a sign of God's judgment in the last days (Joel 3:16; Amos 8:9; Nah. 1:5-6), while the resurrection of the OT saints is a foretaste of the eschatological resurrection of the new age (Ezek. 37:11-14; cf. Isa. 26:19; Dan. 12:2).

Yet these eschatological signs do not mean that the end has come. The end will come when the Son of Man returns in glory (Matt. 16:27-28; 25:31; 27:64). In the interim, there will be a period characterized by false Christs (24:5), wars and rumors of wars (24:6), famines and earthquakes (24:7), persecution, false prophets, and apostasy (24:9-12). This period of "messianic travail" will end with another set of eschatological signs, including the sign of the Son of Man (24:29-

---

[12] For a helpful summary of the ways in which scholars have analyzed Matthew's understanding of salvation history, see S. McKnight, "Matthew, Gospel of," in *DJG*, ed. Joel B. Green and Scot McKnight (Downers Grove, Ill.: InterVarsity, 1992), 536-38.

30).[13] The return of the Son of Man will inaugurate the gathering of the elect at the consummation of the kingdom (24:31). Matthew alone includes in his gospel four parables that address this period of consummation: the wheat and weeds (13:24-30, 37-43), the dragnet (13:47-40), the wise and foolish virgins (25:1-13), and the sheep and goats (25:31-46).

The theme of mission in Matthew's gospel corresponds precisely with this four-part salvation history framework. To anticipate the discussion of the remainder of this chapter, it may be said that (1) during the period of the law and the prophets, mission was carried out by the prophets and was directed primarily toward Israel, (2) during the time of Jesus' kingdom proclamation, mission was carried out by Jesus and was directed primarily toward Israel, (3) during the time of the messianic travail, mission is carried out by Jesus' disciples and is directed toward all nations, and (4) at the time of the consummation of the kingdom, mission will be carried out by the angels and will be directed toward all nations.

## THE PROPHETS' MISSION

Matthew uses the word *prophet* (*prophētēs*) thirty-seven times— far more frequently than Mark's six times and marginally more frequently than Luke's thirty times. Although he notes that the people held both John the Baptist (14:5) and Jesus (21:11, 46) to be prophets, Matthew's primary focus is on the OT prophets, mentioning Jeremiah (2:17; 27:9) and Isaiah (3:3; 4:14; 8:17; 12:17) by name and quoting Hosea (2:15) and Zechariah (21:4) without naming them. He also identifies Asaph, the author of Psalm 78, as a prophet (13:35).

The fact that the prophets were "sent" on mission is clearly stated by Jesus (23:37), as well as being pictured in his parables of the vineyard owner (21:34-37) and the marriage feast (22:2-14). These passages suggest that the mission on which the prophets were sent was one of calling Israel to respond properly to God (cf. 10:41). Somewhat more prominent, however, is the eschatological component of the prophets' mission. Eleven times Matthew introduces OT quotations

---

[13] The term *messianic travail* is sometimes used to describe the period immediately preceding the messianic age. Cf. Donald A. Hagner: "The imagery of 'birth pangs' (1 Enoch 62:4; 2 Esdr 4:42) points to the commonly expected period of suffering (the 'woes of the Messiah'; cf. Mek Exod 16:29; b. Sabb 118a; b. Sanh 96b-97a) that would immediately precede the birth of the messianic age (cf. the imagery of Isa. 26:17; 66:7-8; Jer. 22:23; Mic. 4:9; and in the NT, 1 Thess. 5:3). Only such an extended period of travail in birth could bring forth the 'new birth' of the created order" (*Matthew 14–28*, WBC [Dallas, Tex.: Word, 1995], 691).

with "fulfillment formulae" (1:22; 2:5, 15, 17, 23; 4:14; 8:17; 12:17; 13:35; 21:4; 27:9). None of these quotations has any parallel in either Mark or Luke. In Jesus' words as well Matthew is careful to call attention to OT prophets in two places not noted by Mark or Luke. In 12:39, he identifies Jonah as "the prophet," and in 24:15 he specifically names Daniel "the prophet." This special attention to the way in which Jesus' life and teaching relate to the OT suggests that Matthew saw the prophets' primary mission as one of proclaiming the promised Messiah.

John the Baptist should also be included in this section, for he is the last and greatest of the prophets (11:9-13). The prophetic aspects of John's ministry have been noted above; it remains here to mention his "forerunner" status. In agreement with Mark and Luke, Matthew quotes Isaiah and Malachi to explain John's status (3:3; 11:10; cf. Mark 1:2-3; Luke 3:4-6; 7:27). He goes further, however, to make it clear that John is the Elijah who was to come (Matt. 11:14) and that the disciples understood this fact (17:13). John's special mission was to "make ready the way of the Lord." He both proclaimed the promise of Messiah and functioned as part of the fulfillment of that promise.

## JESUS' MISSION

As might be expected, the *sender* in Jesus' mission is the Father, most frequently the "heavenly" Father.[14] Regarding mission in general, the Father supplies laborers (9:37-38) and sends those laborers to engage in mission (for example, John the Baptist in 11:10, Jesus in 10:40, and the prophets in 23:37). Regarding Jesus' mission, the Father performs several specific functions. First, he superintends the preparations for mission by sending his angel to instruct Joseph (1:20; 2:13, 19)[15] and by sending John the Baptist to "make ready the way of the Lord" (3:3). Second, he commissions Jesus for mission by sending the Holy Spirit (3:16) and by speaking audibly (3:17). Third, he confirms Jesus' mission, again by speaking audibly (17:5).

The *sent one* is, of course, Jesus. Matthew's gospel is rich with titles for Jesus. The heading of Matthew 1:1 contains a cluster of three such titles: (1) Jesus Christ, (2) the son of David, and (3) the son of Abraham. Each of these titles introduces a major theme in Matthew's

---

[14] Although falling well short of John's 118 uses of "Father" to refer to God, Matthew's uses (forty-five) far outdistance Mark's (five) and Luke's (seventeen). "Heavenly Father" or its equivalent occurs twenty-one times.

[15] Although Matthew does not make the fact explicit, it is logical to assume that an angel also warned the magi to avoid Herod (2:12) and Joseph to avoid Archelaus (2:22).

gospel. Furthermore, each has a significant connection to Jesus' mission.[16]

Matthew's Jewish-Christian audience certainly would have taken note of the Greek translation of two important Hebrew words: *yĕšû'āh*—meaning "Yahweh is salvation"—and *māšîaḥ*—meaning "anointed one" or "Messiah."[17] Both names point to aspects of Jesus' mission: "Jesus" to the redemptive aspect (cf. 1:21) and "Christ" to the eschatological aspect (cf. 11:2-3). The redemptive aspect of his mission will be discussed below; the eschatological aspect has been touched on above in the discussion of the way in which Matthew portrays Jesus as fulfilling the messianic mission (8:1-9:34; 11:4-6; 12:28). It is sufficient here to note that Matthew's strategic use of this title reminds his readers that Jesus is the "anointed one," sent on mission as the fulfillment of the OT promises.[18]

Matthew is also intent on portraying Jesus as the promised Davidic king.[19] Two pairs of verses highlight Jesus' status as king. First, both Jesus (1:1) and Joseph (1:20) are connected to the Davidic dynasty by the title "son of David." Second, on the day of Jesus' entry into Jerusalem, he is twice hailed as "the son of David" (21:9, 15). The latter pair of verses is closely connected with Matthew's quotation of Isaiah 62:11 and Zechariah 9:9, which explicitly describe the one riding on the donkey as "your king." As the son of David, Jesus is the king who brings the kingdom and its benefits (cf. Matt. 12:28).

---

[16] Titles such as "Immanuel" (1:23; cf. Isa. 7:14) and "servant" (Matt. 12:15-21; cf. Isa. 42:1-4) also point to his mission. Other titles reveal the speaker's understanding of who Jesus is. "Lord," for example, is only used by those men and women who acknowledge Jesus' authority to heal, save, and admit to heaven (Matt. 7:21-22; 8:21, 25; 9:28; 14:28, 30; 15:22, 25, 27; 17:15; 18:21; 20:31, 33; 26:22). "Teacher" is used by those who demonstrate an inadequate understanding of who he is (8:19; 12:38; 19:16; 22:16, 24, 36). "Rabbi" is used only twice, both times by Judas in the context of betrayal (26:25, 29).

[17] Cf. Davies and Allison, *Matthew*, 1:155-56.

[18] Matthew includes the title "Christ" at several key points, none of which has parallels in either Mark or Luke: (1) at the end of the genealogy (1:16-17), (2) in connection with the visit of the magi (2:4), (3) in connection with John the Baptist's question (11:2), (4) in connection with Peter's confession (16:16, 20), (5) in Jesus' first passion prediction (16:21), (6) in Jesus' woes against the scribes and Pharisees (23:10), (7) in the Sanhedrin's mocking (26:68), and (8) in Pilate's questions to the crowd (27:17, 22).

[19] Matthew includes the title "son of David" eleven times (1:1, 20; 9:27; 12:23; 15:22; 20:30, 31; 21:9, 15; 22:42, 45) as compared to four times each in Mark (10:47, 48; 12:35, 37) and Luke (18:38-39; 20:41, 44). An additional piece of evidence is the question posed by the magi: "Where is he who has been born King of the Jews?" (Matt. 2:2).

Matthew's use of "son of Abraham" is the only time in the NT when the title is applied to Jesus. Its use in the heading points the reader back to Genesis 12:1-3, where Abraham is called to become the father of Israel (cf. Matt. 3:8-9). That call included a number of promises, but it is the promise of universal blessing that Matthew probably has in view: "In you all the families of the earth shall be blessed." This particular theme will be discussed below. It is sufficient here to note that the amount of space Matthew gives to Gentiles highlights the universal blessing as a significant feature of his thinking on mission.

A final aspect of Jesus' sonship is that of "Son of God." Although the Father-Son relationship between God and Jesus is strongest in John's gospel, it is also a significant concept for Matthew.[20] As the Son, Jesus demonstrates special concern for doing the Father's will (3:15; 6:10; 7:21; 12:50; 26:36-44). By highlighting this attitude in Jesus, Matthew reflects his understanding that obedience is crucial in carrying out mission.

The *task* of Jesus' mission is announced in the first pericope after the genealogy: "It is he who will save his people from their sins" (1:21). The redemptive nature of that mission is a significant concept for Matthew. Along with Mark and Luke, he records Jesus' confrontation with the scribes over his authority to forgive sins (9:1-9), notes that Jesus came to call sinners (9:13), and includes Jesus' three passion predictions (16:21; 17:22-23; 20:17-19). Matthew goes further, however, in developing the theme. By including Jesus' comment that submitting to John's baptism was "fitting . . . to fulfill all righteousness" (3:15), Matthew underlines the juridical importance of Jesus' mission. Later, his explicit identification of Jesus with the suffering servant of the OT (8:16-17; 12:15-21; cf. Isa. 53:4; 42:1-4) highlights the substitutionary nature of that mission. The inclusion of a fourth passion prediction (Matt. 26:1-2) emphasizes Jesus' impending death, and the statement at the Passover that the wine represents Jesus' blood "poured out for many for the forgiveness of sins" (26:28) points to the sacrificial nature of that death.

The phrase "his people" in 1:21 indicates the *scope* of Jesus' mission. The natural question, of course, is Who are his people? Since this OT prophecy was spoken to Israel, it is logical to conclude that the primary application is to Israel, and Jesus' statements in 10:5-6 and 15:24 support this conclusion. There are contextual considerations, however, which suggest that a broader definition should be adopted.

---

[20] In fact, Matthew includes the full title nine times, the same number of uses as appear in John's gospel (Matt. 3:17; 4:3, 6; 9:29; 14:33; 16:16; 17:5; 26:63-64; 27:54). Three additional passages, none of which has parallels in Mark or Luke, connect Jesus closely with the Father (2:15; 11:25-27; 17:24-27).

Two of these considerations come from the immediate context of 1:21. First, the mention of the four women in Jesus' genealogy (1:3-6) points out that Jesus' "people" included non-Jews who were sinful and helpless.[21] Second, Matthew's account of the visit of the magi (2:1-12) sharply contrasts the worship of the non-Jewish magi with the hostility of the Jewish leaders.

Additional considerations come from the broader context of the entire gospel. In particular, an examination of the people to whom Jesus ministers in 8:1-9:34 sheds light on the scope of his mission. In these chapters Jesus demonstrates compassion for the outcasts and delivers the helpless. Each of the individuals with whom Jesus deals in 8:1-17 is a member of a marginalized group. The Gadarene demoniac (8:28-34), the paralytic (9:1-8), and the individuals to whom Jesus ministers in 9:18-34 were unable to help themselves. Furthermore, it is interesting to note that, ethnically, these individuals include both Jews (8:1-4, 14-17; 9:1-8, 18-34) and non-Jews (8:5-13, 28-34). Taken together, these considerations suggest that—although the focus of Jesus' ministry is Israel (10:5-6; 15:24)—"his people" are the marginalized and hopeless members of society, both Jew and Gentile.

Matthew summarizes the *activity* of Jesus' mission as "going about . . . teaching in their synagogues, and proclaiming the gospel of the kingdom, and healing every kind of disease and every kind of sickness" (4:23; 9:35). Although Matthew uses these and other summary statements (cf. 11:1; 14:34-36; 15:29-31; 19:1-2) to keep Jesus' ministry in balance, his inclusion of five major discourses portrays Jesus as, above all, a teacher.[22] This theme will be discussed below; it is sufficient here to note that the aspect of Jesus' mission activity included in his final charge to his disciples is not preaching or healing but teaching (28:20).

The *message* Jesus preached and taught as part of his mission was "the gospel of the kingdom" (4:23; 9:35; 24:14), a phrase which is

---

[21] Although the details of each woman's situation have been debated at length, it may be said with certainty that (1) *at least* Rahab and Ruth were non-Jews, (2) *at least* Bathsheba committed sin in sleeping with David, and (3) *at least* Tamar and Ruth were helpless to advance their own causes. For more detailed discussions, see David R. Bauer, "The Literary Function of the Genealogy in Matthew's Gospel," in *Society of Biblical Literature 1990 Seminar Papers*, ed. David J. Lull (Atlanta: Scholars Press, 1990), 461-63; John Paul Heil, "The Narrative Roles of the Women in Matthew's Genealogy," *Bib* 72 (1991): 538-45.

[22] The verb "to teach" (*didaskō*) occurs fourteen times; the verb "to preach" (*kērussō*) occurs nine times; the verb "to heal" (*therapeuō*) occurs sixteen times. Cf. Ferdinand Hahn's comments on the distinction between *didaskō* and *kērussō* in Matthew's gospel (*Mission in the New Testament*, trans. Frank Clarke, SBT, no. 47 [Naperville, Ill.: Alec R. Allenson, 1965], 121).

unique to Matthew's gospel. Particularly characteristic of Jesus' teaching in Matthew are the kingdom parables.[23] The six kingdom parables collected in 13:24-50 may be grouped into three pairs that picture (1) the separation which will occur at the consummation of the kingdom (13:24-30, 37-43, 47-50), (2) the unexpected results of the preaching of the kingdom (13:31-33), and (3) the supreme worth of the kingdom (13:44-45).[24] The remaining kingdom parables picture the forgiveness and generosity of the God of the kingdom (18:23-35; 20:1-16), the importance of responding properly to God's gracious invitation (22:1-14), and the significance of prudence in waiting for the kingdom's consummation (25:1-13).

The *result* of Jesus' redemptive mission is the inauguration of the new covenant with its promised forgiveness of sins. Matthew's account of the Last Supper is the only one that includes the phrase "for forgiveness of sins" (26:28).[25] Carson is probably correct when he labels as "reductionistic" attempts to narrow the OT background of this verse to one passage.[26] "Blood of the covenant" most reasonably refers to Exodus 24:8 and "forgiveness of sins" to Jeremiah 31:34. In addition, the phrase "which is poured out for many" is probably an allusion to Isaiah 53:12.[27] "My blood" explicitly connects Jesus' death with the promised forgiveness of sins. Later, the eschatological signs that accompany his death (Matt. 27:50-53) signify that the mission announced in 1:21 has been completed.

## THE DISCIPLES' MISSION

The way in which the final pericope of Matthew's gospel (28:16-20) pulls together many of the themes from the rest of the work has been noted by a number of scholars.[28] David Bosch observes that "as

---

[23] Of the ten parables in Matthew's gospel that begin with the phrase "the kingdom is like," only two have parallels in Mark and Luke: the mustard seed (13:31-32; cf. Mark 4:30-32; Luke 13:18-19) and the leaven (Matt. 13:33; cf. Luke 13:20-21).

[24] For a discussion of the structure of the discourse, see Hagner, *Matthew 1–13*, 362-64.

[25] Gundry (*Matthew*, 528) suggests that the phrase has been suppressed at 3:2 and included here to connect it exclusively with Jesus' death. Carson ("Matthew," 538) admits that this suggestion is a possibility, but he adds an appropriate cautionary note.

[26] Carson, "Matthew," 537.

[27] Cf. Douglas J. Moo, *The Old Testament in the Gospel Passion Narratives* (Sheffield: Almond, 1983), 301-11.

[28] For example, Oscar S. Brooks, "Matthew xxviii 16-20 and the Design of the First Gospel," *JSNT* 10 (1981): 2-18; Gundry, *Matthew*, 593; David P. Scaer, "The Relation of Matthew 28:16-20 to the Rest of the Gospel," *Concordia Theological Quarterly* 55 (1991): 245-66.

far as use of language is concerned, the 'Great Commission' is perhaps the most Matthean [pericope] in the entire gospel: virtually every word or expression used in these verses is peculiar to the author of the first gospel."[29] As such—and given the mission focus of the passage—Matthew 28:16-20 serves as a lens through which Matthew's understanding of the disciples' mission may be viewed.

Jesus, the one who was sent on mission and who has accomplished his mission, now becomes the *sender*. Matthew's account of the meeting on the mountain (28:16-20) makes it clear that the disciples are sent on mission by the one who has all authority and who is worthy of worship.[30] Jesus had designated the mountain prior to his death (26:32; 28:16), and after the resurrection he had instructed the women to remind the disciples of the promised meeting (28:10). The disciples' arrival at the mountain highlights both his authority and their obedience. When Jesus appears on the mountain, he claims "all authority" (*exousia*, 28:18), and the disciples "worship" him (*proskuneō*, 28:17).[31]

The eleven disciples are the *sent ones*.[32] Jesus had called them with a view to mission (4:19). He had taught them about kingdom living (5:3-7:27), kingdom mission (10:5-42), the mysteries of the kingdom (13:3-52), relationships within the kingdom (18:1-35), and the future consummation of the kingdom (24:3-25:46)—all in order to prepare them more effectively for their mission. In anticipation of that mis-

---

[29] David J. Bosch, *Transforming Mission: Paradigm Shifts in Theology of Mission*, American Society of Missiology Series, no. 16 (Maryknoll, N.Y.: Orbis Books, 1991): 57. This concentration of vocabulary has led some scholars to suggest that the pericope is a purely Matthean creation. See, for example, Jack Dean Kingsbury, "The Composition and Christology of Matt. 28:16-20," *JBL* 93 (1974): 573-84. Hagner, however, notes that the Matthean style and vocabulary of the passage "does not amount to a demonstration that Matthew composed the passage ex nihilo" (*Matthew 14-28*, 883).

[30] Elsewhere in the gospel, mountains are places of revelation (5:1; 8:1; 15:29; 24:3) and of communion with God (14:23; 17:1; 26:30). For an extended study, see Terence L. Donaldson, *Jesus on the Mountain: A Study in Matthean Theology*, JSNTSup, no. 8 (Sheffield: JSOT Press, 1985).

[31] The themes of authority (7:29; 9:6, 8; 10:1; 11:27; 21:23-27; 22:43-44) and worship (2:2, 8, 11; 8:2; 9:18; 14:33; 15:25; 20:20) are both prominent ones in Matthew's gospel. Brooks ("Design," 5-14) has traced the former theme in some detail.

[32] It seems logical to take Matthew at his word and limit the audience to "the eleven disciples." For arguments as to whether more than the eleven disciples were present, see pro: D. Edmond Hiebert, "An Expository Study of Matthew 28:16-20," *BSac* 149 (1992): 341-42; con: Scaer, "Relation," 249-50.

sion, they had been given the keys to the kingdom with the expectation that they would storm the gates of Hades (16:17-19).[33]

Matthew's gospel has much to say about discipleship, but space permits a discussion of only three passages.[34] From the call of the first disciples (4:18-22; cf. 9:9-13) come three important truths. First, discipleship results in mission: not only will they have a passive role as followers, they will have an active role as "fishers of men" (4:19).[35] Second, discipleship demands obedience: when Jesus calls, both sets of brothers follow him "immediately" (4:19, 22). Third, discipleship involves sacrifice: Peter and Andrew leave their livelihood (4:20); James and John leave their livelihood *and* their father (4:22).

In sharp contrast to the response of these four disciples are the attitudes expressed by two other potential disciples (8:18-23). Jesus' response to a scribe who expresses his willingness to follow Jesus "wherever" he goes suggests that this person did not *understand* the full implications of discipleship (8:20). Similarly, his response to a son who asks permission to bury his father before following Jesus suggests that this person did not *accept* the full implications of discipleship (8:22).[36] Jesus' disciples follow him with their eyes open (knowing the demands of discipleship) and their mouths shut (not placing conditions on discipleship).

Between these two incidents, the conclusion of the Sermon on the Mount provides four tests of true disciples: (1) they enter by the narrow gate (7:13-14), (2) they produce good fruit (7:15-20), (3) they obey the Father's will (7:21-23), and (4) they act on Jesus' words (7:24-27).[37] The latter two tests connect especially closely with Jesus' final command, both in the call to obedience and in the expectation that the disciples will act on his words. Together these three passages sketch

---

[33] For a concise summary of this idea, see Mark Allan Powell, *God with Us: A Pastoral Theology of Matthew's Gospel* (Minneapolis: Fortress, 1995), 17-18.

[34] For a full-scale treatment, see Michael J. Wilkins, *Discipleship in the Ancient World and Matthew's Gospel*, 2d ed. (Grand Rapids: Baker, 1995).

[35] Rudolf Pesch ("Voraussetzungen und Anfänge der urchristlichen Mission," in *Mission im Neuen Testament*, ed. Karl Kertelge [Freiburg: Herder, 1982], 14-16) has noted the fact that "fisherman" (*halieus*) is part of the NT missionary terminology.

[36] The debate over whether or not the father was still alive (for example, Kenneth E. Bailey, *Through Peasant Eyes* [Grand Rapids: Eerdmans, 1980], 26-27) contributes nothing to the basic point of the encounter.

[37] A number of scholars have developed the theme of bearing fruit in Matthew's gospel. See, for example, Donald Senior and Carroll Stuhlmueller, *The Biblical Foundations for Mission* (Maryknoll, N.Y.: Orbis Books, 1983), 248; Bosch, *Transforming Mission*, 67-68; Powell, *God with Us*, 20-21. The importance for Jesus of doing the Father's will has been noted above.

the type of people who follow Jesus: (1) they recognize that being a disciple involves mission, (2) they understand the importance of obedience, (3) they accept the sacrifice involved, and (4) they bear good fruit.

Even for the eleven disciples, however, the *act of sending* involved overcoming an obstacle, for "some were doubtful" (*distazō*). Regardless of the precise nature of their doubt, it created an obstacle to their involvement in the mission Jesus had in mind for them.[38] Jesus responded to their doubt by "approaching" them (28:18). The verb used (*proserchomai*) is one of Matthew's favorites, but only in one other place is it Jesus who "approaches"—on the mountain of transfiguration (17:7).[39] The parallel is clear in that both times it is the glorified Christ who approaches and speaks to the disciples, once to comfort and once to challenge. Lucien Legrand writes, "Jesus enters [appears on] the scene. He takes matters in hand. He had been only the object of the account; now he becomes its subject. From the eleven disciples, the initiative passes to Jesus. The disciples had come and had offered only a wavering faith. Jesus comes, and the irresistible might of his word prevails."[40]

The mission *task* assigned to the eleven is one of "making disciples" (28:19). This task differs considerably from that assigned in the other synoptics, where the emphasis is on the proclamation of the gospel (cf. Mark 16:15; Luke 24:47). The verb Matthew uses (*mathēteuō*) occurs only four times in the NT, and three of those times are in his gospel (13:52; 27:57; 28:19).[41] Especially to be noted is the use in the parable of 13:52, where Jesus explains that "every scribe that has become a disciple of the kingdom" has a special responsibility: to "bring forth" (that is, teach) "his treasure."[42] For Matthew, the focus of the dis-

---

[38] For a summary of interpretive options as well as an analysis of the verb used, see Hagner, *Matthew 14-28*, 884-85. Perhaps the best understanding is the one he proposes: that they were "in a state of hesitation and indecision." Cf. David R. Bauer: "This doubt expresses a wavering, which hinders disciples from appropriating the full possibilities of endurance, power, and mission which are offered through Christ" (*The Structure of Matthew's Gospel: A Study in Literary Design*, JSNTSup, no. 31 [Sheffield: Almond, 1988], 110).

[39] Matthew uses the verb fifty-three times, as compared to Mark's six and Luke's eleven. Thirty-nine times other people approach Jesus; thirteen of those times it is his disciples who draw near.

[40] Lucien Legrand, *Unity and Plurality: Mission in the Bible*, trans. Robert R. Barr (Maryknoll, N.Y.: Orbis Books, 1990), 80.

[41] The fourth occurrence is in Acts 14:21. For background on the verb and further discussion, see Wilkins, *Discipleship*, 160-63. Cf. also Bosch, *Transforming Mission*, 73-74.

[42] See Carson ("Matthew," 331-33) for a summary of the issues and a similar conclusion.

ciples' mission is less one of public proclamation than one of intensive instruction.[43] This perspective, of course, is in accord with Matthew's portrait of Jesus as a teacher who repeatedly instructs his disciples at length and in depth. Such intensive instruction would be viewed by Matthew's Jewish readers as natural for any disciple, but as especially necessary for Gentiles coming into the church.

The task of making disciples involves three *activities*: going (28:19), baptizing (28:19), and teaching (28:20). Jesus had already instructed the disciples on various aspects of "going." Much of the commissioning discourse (10:1-42), for example, dealt with precisely that topic. At that time they learned about making preparations, targeting receptive hearers, facing persecution and opposition, relying on divine resources, and enduring to the end.

References to the activity of "baptizing" in Matthew's gospel are limited to John's ministry.[44] The baptism Jesus envisions here, however, is not John's baptism, for it is to be into (*eis*) "the name of the Father and the Son and the Holy Spirit." This phrase suggests that those who become disciples will be incorporated into the group that will form the church.[45] As Donald Senior notes, "Such ecclesial interest harmonizes with the whole tone of Matthew's Gospel."[46]

As mentioned above, the disciples' activity of teaching (*didaskō*) connects directly to the mission activity—at least for Matthew—in which Jesus was primarily involved (4:23; 5:2; 7:28-29; 9:35; 11:1; 13:54; 21:23; 22:16, 33; 26:55).[47] The content of the teaching makes the connection even closer: they are to teach "all that I commanded

---

[43] Legrand: "'Making disciples' conjures up the image of a master initiating his disciples through an organized process in the rabbinical style, progressively communicating a teaching and a lifestyle corresponding to this 'tradition.' This kind of activity suggests more the instructor's podium than the 'feet of those who announce good news'" (*Unity and Plurality*, 78).

[44] The verb appears six times in 3:6-16; the noun appears in 3:7 and in 21:25. Matthew excludes Jesus' reference to "the baptism with which I am baptized" in the discussion with James and John, for the textual variant in Matthew 20:22-23 is probably an assimilation to Mark's reading (cf. Mark 10:38-39). He uses a different word to refer to ritual washings (Matt. 15:2; cf. Mark 7:4; Luke 11:38). He does not record that Jesus or his disciples baptized anyone (cf. John 3:22; 4:1-2).

[45] Powell: "Baptism, for Matthew, signifies incorporation into the eschatological community created by Jesus" (*God with Us*, 24). Cf. Carson, "Matthew," 597; Legrand, *Unity and Plurality*, 78. Gundry (*Matthew*, 596) emphasizes the discontinuity between John's baptism and that commanded by Jesus. Scaer ("Relation," 254-55) highlights the continuity.

[46] Senior and Stuhlmueller, *Biblical Foundations*, 252.

[47] Brooks ("Design," 5-14) has traced the theme of teaching in some detail.

you."[48] This injunction is not surprising given Jesus' earlier statement (also in the context of mission): "A disciple is not above his teacher, nor a slave above his master. It is enough for the disciple that he become as his teacher, and the slave as his master" (10:24-25). If the eleven are to engage in mission, it is to be expected that they, like Jesus, will be involved in teaching others how to live as citizens of the kingdom.

The *result* of this process would be obedient disciples (28:20). For Matthew, obedience is the key quality in a disciple who is on mission. This theme may be seen throughout Matthew's gospel. Joseph "did as the angel of the Lord commanded him" (1:24; cf. 2:14, 21). Peter, Andrew, James, and John immediately obeyed Jesus' summons to follow him (4:18-22); Matthew responded in the same way (9:9). When Jesus commanded Peter to come to him on the water, Peter did so without question (14:25-29). Twice, Matthew notes that disciples "did just as Jesus had directed them" (21:6; 26:19). When the angel instructed the women to tell the news of the resurrection, they "ran to report it to his disciples" (28:8). Finally, after Jesus' resurrection the eleven "proceeded . . . to the mountain which Jesus had designated" (28:16).

The *scope* of their mission includes "all nations."[49] This phrase brings to a close the universal blessing theme that began in Matthew 1 and 2, where Jesus is called the son of Abraham (1:1), non-Jews are included in the genealogy (1:3-6), and the visit of the magi is recorded (2:1-12). As well, Matthew calls the place where Jesus began his ministry "Galilee of the Gentiles" (4:15) and quotes Isaiah 42:1-4 from the LXX, which translates the last line as "and in his name the Gentiles will hope" (Matt. 12:15-21).[50] Furthermore, Matthew repeatedly includes

---

[48] Bosch (*Transforming Mission*, 69) thinks that this phrase refers primarily to the Sermon on the Mount. Such an understanding, however, seems overly restrictive.

[49] Recently, David C. Sims ("The Gospel of Matthew and the Gentiles," *JSNT* 57 [1995]: 19-48) has argued at some length that the natural understanding of this phrase is more than counterbalanced (1) by negative Gentile characters, (2) by evidence of Gentile persecution, and (3) by anti-Gentile statements. His conclusion is that Matthew's community had no intention of embarking on a concentrated mission to the Gentiles. Sims's analysis, however, rests on the presupposition that Matthew's gospel was written c. 80 C.E. and engages in a selective reading of the evidence. Perhaps the most helpful aspect of Sims's article is that it highlights the fact that Matthew stereotypes *neither* all Jewish figures as bad *nor* all Gentile figures as good. Jesus is rejected by unbelieving Jews *and* by unbelieving Gentiles (cf. 20:18-19); conversely, he is accepted by believing Jews (9:19-22) *and* by believing Gentiles (8:5-13).

[50] The MT reading is: "And the coastlands will wait expectantly for his law."

unique universalistic elements in Jesus' teaching.[51] This accumulated evidence points to Matthew's concern that mission be extended to the Gentiles.

The *time frame* of the disciples' mission is found in the concluding promise, "I am with you always, even to the end of the age." The phrase "the end of the age" occurs four other times in Matthew's gospel (13:39, 40, 49; 24:3), and each time it "refers to the end of the present age through the parousia of the Son of Man and the experience of the final judgment of the wicked and the reward of the righteous."[52] As noted above, the eschatological signs accompanying the return of the Son of Man mark the transition to the final period of salvation history as Matthew understands it. The disciples' mission, therefore, will continue throughout the period of "messianic travail" (cf. 24:14).[53] The phrase "with you" echoes the explanation of the name Immanuel as "God with us" in 1:23 (cf. 26:29). Jesus' mission has been completed, but he is present with his disciples as they carry out their mission.

## THE ANGELS' MISSION

Matthew uses "angel, messenger" (*angelos*) twenty times.[54] He uses it once in an OT quotation to refer to John the Baptist (11:10). Once it refers to fallen angels (25:41). He uses it twice (once an OT quotation) in the narrative of Jesus' testing to depict angels as caring for Jesus

---

[51] Those elements are (1) his teaching on salt and light (5:13-16), (2) his commendation of the centurion's faith (8:10-12), (3) his response to the Pharisees' desire for a sign (12:41-42), (4) his interpretation of the parable of the wheat and weeds (13:38), (5) his commendation of the Canaanite woman's faith (15:28), and (6) his comment following the parable of the vineyard owner (21:43).

[52] Hagner, *Matthew 14-28*, 889.

[53] Contrast Joachim Jeremias, who argues that the preaching of 24:14 refers to "the angelic proclamation of God's final act" (*Jesus' Promise to the Nations*, trans. S. H. Hooke [London: SCM, 1958], 23). Given the uses of "the end" in 24:6 and 24:13 and the sequence implied in 24:14 by the words "and then," the more natural understanding of the verse is that the preaching "in the whole world for a witness to all the nations" refers to that carried out by the disciples. Furthermore, as the discussion below points out, the angels' mission will be one of reaping for judgment rather than one of proclamation.

[54] Thirteen of those uses have no parallel in either Mark or Luke (1:20, 24; 2:13, 19; 13:39, 41, 49; 18:10; 25:31, 41; 26:53; 28:2, 5). Mark uses the term six times, all of which have parallels in Matthew (Mark 1:2, 13; 8:38; 12:25; 13:27, 32). Luke uses the term twenty-six times, but only four of his uses have parallels in Matthew (Luke 4:10; 7:27; 9:26; 20:36).

(4:6, 11). Three times he uses it in a purely descriptive way (18:10; 22:30; 26:53).

The remaining thirteen uses fall into two groups, with the first group consisting of six references. At the beginning of Matthew's gospel an "angel of the Lord" carries special information to Joseph (1:20, 24; 2:13, 19), and at the end of the book, an "angel of the Lord" rolls the stone away from the empty tomb (28:2) and gives the women instructions for the disciples (28:5). In these passages angels are God's messengers; they convey special information about the birth and resurrection of Jesus. This aspect of their mission has strong parallels to Luke's gospel, where angels play a prominent role in announcing the birth of both Jesus and John the Baptist.[55]

The second group consists of seven references, all of which look to the return of the Son of Man. Three of them have parallels elsewhere in the synoptics (Matt. 16:27; 24:31, 36; cf. Mark 8:30; 13:27, 32; Luke 9:26), but Matthew also includes three parables that have no parallel in either Mark or Luke and which highlight the angels' connection with the judgment at the consummation of the kingdom. First, Jesus' interpretation of the parable of the wheat and the weeds makes it clear that "at the end of the age" the Son of Man will send out his angels as reapers (Matt. 13:39) who "will gather out of his kingdom all stumbling blocks and those who commit lawlessness, and will cast them into the furnace of fire" (13:41-42). Second, the parable of the dragnet pictures the same separation at the end of the age, when "the angels shall come forth, and take out the wicked from among the righteous, and will cast them into the furnace of fire" (13:49-50). Finally, the angels appear in a context of judgment in the parable of the sheep and goats (25:31). The prominence given to them in this collection of parables suggests that an important aspect of Matthew's understanding of mission is the reaping task entrusted to the angels at the consummation of the kingdom.

One final note on the angels' mission relates to the scope of that mission. Four pieces of evidence make it clear that their reaping will extend to all nations. First, the angels will reap the wheat and the weeds from the field that is "the world" (13:38). Second, "every man" will be repaid when the Son of Man comes in glory with his angels (16:27). Third, the angels will gather the elect "from the four winds" (24:31). Fourth, "all nations" will be gathered for judgment when the angels come in glory with the Son of Man (25:32).

---

[55] Fifteen of Luke's twenty-six uses of "angel" appear in the first two chapters of his gospel. Matthew's angel at the resurrection also has a parallel in Luke, for the "two men . . . in dazzling apparel" who appear at the tomb (Luke 24:4) are later described as "angels" (24:23).

## CONCLUSION

The theme of mission in Matthew's gospel corresponds to the four periods of his understanding of salvation history. Prior to the time of John the Baptist, the prophets engaged in a mission of proclaiming the promise to be fulfilled in the Messiah. Jesus' redemptive mission fulfilled that promise and resulted in the forgiveness of sins. The eleven were entrusted with the mission of making disciples of all the nations—disciples who understand and act on all of Jesus' words, including those at the end of Matthew's gospel. This self-perpetuating mission of the church will end at the return of the Son of Man. At that time the angels will be charged with the mission of reaping the harvest of earth and of separating the righteous, who will receive salvation, from the wicked, who will receive judgment. Matthew thus presents a comprehensive picture of the way in which God's purposes for salvation and judgment are carried out.

The church today stands squarely within the third period of Matthew's salvation history framework. Its mission, therefore, is clear: Sent by the one who has all authority, who enables them to overcome any obstacle, and who is always present with them, Jesus' followers are to make disciples of all the nations, disciples who are obedient in carrying out the task entrusted to them.

# 8

## *Mission in Mark*

## Joel F. Williams

Persecution and suffering are characteristic themes that run through-out Mark's gospel and his teaching on mission. Because Jesus has set his mind on God's interests (Mark 8:31-33) and does the will of God (14:35-36), he suffers at the hands of the religious and political leaders. Jesus also foresees similar difficulties for his followers. Anyone who follows Jesus must walk the path of self-denial, taking up the cross, preparing to suffer (8:34). Believers should expect persecution and pressure from family members, religious leaders, and government officials as they proclaim the gospel during the period between the resurrection and the second coming of Jesus (13:9-13). Mark's gospel makes it clear that Jesus faced difficulty and so will his followers; everyone will be salted with fire (9:49). It is unlikely that Mark's discussion of suffering was merely theoretical in nature, especially since an examination of the setting for Mark's gospel uncovers a set of circumstances in which persecution was a very real possibility. The next section looks at the historical situation surrounding Mark's gospel and Mark's purpose for writing, because this material serves as a significant background to the subject of mission in Mark. Mark wrote in a setting characterized by persecution to people who were suffering. While Mark's gospel includes several emphases on the topic of mission, the most dominant motif is that mission takes place in the context of a hostile world.

### THE SETTING AND PURPOSE FOR MARK'S GOSPEL

Early church tradition consistently attributes the authorship of the second gospel to Mark, an associate of the apostle Peter.[1] In addition,

---

[1] See especially the comments of Papias, which are recorded in Eusebius, *Ecclesiastical History*, 3.39.15. See also Irenaeus, *Against Heresies*, 3.1.1;

early evidence locates the place of writing for the gospel of Mark in or around Rome,[2] a setting that is important because Christians in the city of Rome faced a variety of difficult circumstances during the apostolic period.[3] The gospel probably did not reach this region through targeted missionary effort. A large Jewish population resided in the city of Rome, estimated at fifty thousand,[4] and apparently Christianity spread to Rome through the normal travel plans and business dealings of diaspora Jews.[5] By the time Paul wrote his epistle to the Romans in approximately 57 C.E., the Christian community in that city was well-established and must have included both Jews and Gentiles, since Paul finds occasion to address directly both Jewish (Rom. 2:17-

---

Tertullian, *Against Marcion*, 4.5; Clement of Alexandria and Origen as quoted in Eusebius, *Eccl. Hist.*, 2.15.1-2; 6.14.5-7; 6.25.5; as well as the anti-Marcionite prologue to the gospel of Mark. For recent studies that support the traditional view on the authorship of Mark's gospel, see Donald Guthrie, *New Testament Introduction*, 3d ed. (Downers Grove, Ill.: InterVarsity, 1970), 69-72; Martin Hengel, *Studies in the Gospel of Mark* (Philadelphia: Fortress, 1985), 45-53; D. A. Carson, Douglas J. Moo, and Leon Morris, *An Introduction to the New Testament* (Grand Rapids: Zondervan, 1992), 92-95. For an extensive discussion of the patristic evidence concerning Mark, see the work of C. Clifton Black (*Mark: Images of an Apostolic Interpreter* [Columbia, S.C.: University of South Carolina Press, 1994]), who does not regard the testimony of the early church fathers on the question of authorship to be inconceivable or implausible, but rather simply impossible to verify historically.

[2] Irenaeus, *Against Heresies*, 3.1.1; Clement of Alexandria, as quoted in Eusebius, *Eccl. Hist.*, 6.14.5-7; as well as the anti-Marcionite prologue to Mark. For arguments supporting a Roman origin for Mark's gospel, see Guthrie, *Introduction*, 61-63; Hengel, *Studies*, 28-30; Carson, Moo, and Morris, *Introduction*, 95-96. See also C. Clifton Black ("Was Mark a Roman Gospel?" *ExpTim* 105 [1993]: 36-40), who considers the matter not proven but also not improbable.

[3] On the early history of the church in Rome, see Black, *Apostolic Interpreter*, 225-31; Raymond E. Brown and John P. Meier, *Antioch and Rome: New Testament Cradles of Catholic Christianity* (New York: Paulist, 1983), 87-216; F. F. Bruce, *Paul: Apostle of the Heart Set Free* (Grand Rapids: Eerdmans, 1977), 379-92; John R. Donahue, "Windows and Mirrors: The Setting of Mark's Gospel," *CBQ* 57 (1995): 19-23; James S. Jeffers, "Pluralism in Early Roman Christianity," *Fides et Historia* 22 (Winter/Spring 1990): 4-17.

[4] George La Piana, "Foreign Groups in Rome during the First Centuries of the Empire," *HTR* 20 (1927): 346.

[5] See the comment of Ambrosiaster, the fourth-century commentator, who stated that the Romans embraced the faith of Christ even though they saw no sign of mighty works nor any of the apostles (in *Patrologia Latina*, 17, col. 46).

3:9, 7:1) and Gentile believers (Rom. 11:13). The book of Romans also hints that the Christian community was decentralized, meeting in various house churches. In his list of greetings in chapter 16, Paul seems to make reference to three separate house churches (Rom. 16:5, 14-15), and perhaps to two others (Rom. 16:10-11).

The first hint of difficulty for Roman believers is found in the writing of the Roman historian Suetonius.[6] According to Suetonius, Emperor Claudius expelled the Jews from Rome because of the constant disturbances created by "Chrestus." Apparently, Suetonius confused the name "Christus" with "Chrestus," and thus his report indicates that the coming of Christianity to Rome caused significant turmoil in the Jewish community, perhaps similar to the types of problems Luke records in Acts.[7] The book of Acts also shows that this banishment, which took place in 49 C.E. and lasted for five years, affected Christian Jews, since Luke reports that Priscilla and Aquila were in Corinth on account of Claudius's edict (Acts 18:1-2). The writer of the book of Hebrews, a work written to a Jewish Christian community in Rome, seems to reflect on this period of difficulty when he reminds his readers about their suffering in the former days, a time when they were reproached, their property was seized, and some were imprisoned (Heb. 10:32-34).

The next chapter in this story of suffering is recorded by Tacitus.[8] According to Tacitus's account, Nero blamed the Christians for the fire that ravaged Rome in 64 C.E. Vast numbers of Christians were arrested and convicted not so much for the charge of arson but simply for hatred of the human race (cf. Mark 13:13). Severe executions awaited these believers, in that they were torn apart by dogs, nailed to crosses, or set afire to serve as lamps for Nero's gardens at night.[9] In his account Tacitus seemed to reflect the attitude of many pagans in that he regarded Christians with disdain. For Tacitus, Christianity was a pernicious superstition, which he loathed for its abominations and considered worthy of extreme punishment. Nevertheless, Tacitus reported that many came to pity the Christians because of the excessive cruelty of Nero. The suicide of Nero in 68 C.E. did not bring immediate relief for Christians. The Roman believers could not help but be affected by the political and military turmoil caused by the rapid succession of four emperors in less than a year, by the constant rumors of

---

[6] Suetonius, *Life of the Emperor Claudius*, 25.4.

[7] Cf. Acts 13:50; 14:2-6, 19; 17:5-9, 13; 18:12-17.

[8] Tacitus, *Annals*, 15:44. See also the reference to this persecution in *1 Clem.* 5:1–6:2.

[9] Additional sources locate the martyrdom of the apostles Peter and Paul in Rome during the period of Nero's persecution. See *1 Clem.* 5.3-7; Ignatius, *Letter to the Romans*, 4.2-3; Irenaeus, *Against Heresies*, 3.3.1.

Nero's return, and by the Roman suppression of the Jewish revolt, climaxing in the destruction of Jerusalem and its Temple in 70 C.E.[10] All in all, the apostolic period provided dark days for Christians in the city of Rome.

A variety of dates has been suggested for the time at which Mark wrote his gospel.[11] On the basis of the evidence within Mark's gospel, it would be difficult to determine whether Mark was preparing his readers for a time of persecution, encouraging them in the midst of it, or reflecting back on it. Mark portrays a spectrum of potential responses to persecution. At one end of the spectrum is the reaction of Jesus, who bows in submission to the will of God (Mark 14:35-36) and gives his life as a ransom for many (10:45). At the other end of the spectrum is the picture of the seed in the rocky soil, which exemplifies those who fall away during persecution (4:16-17). One further response that Mark highlights is that of failure. Mark portrays the disciples as unable to understand (8:14-21) and unwilling to accept the necessity of suffering (8:31-33), with the result that they are unprepared for their hour of testing. They fail to follow Jesus by fleeing at his arrest (14:50), and they fail to identify themselves with him as exemplified by the denials of Peter (14:66-72). Jesus, however, does not give up on the disciples, since he predicts a time of restoration (14:27-28) and of faithful witness (10:39; 13:9-13) for the disciples after the resurrection. The disciples do not completely fall away. They are fallible followers of Jesus, but followers nonetheless. Undoubtedly, Mark wrote his gospel for a number of reasons, but perhaps Mark's primary purpose for writing his gospel was to encourage and to warn other fallible followers of Jesus who were facing difficult circumstances.[12] God is able to restore and use those who are fearful and prone to failure. Those who follow Jesus looking for recognition and comfort need to beware, because they will be ill-prepared for the suffering that will inevitably come their way (9:49; 10:30).

The remaining portion of the chapter will deal directly with Mark's teaching concerning mission, first by summarizing the material that

---

[10] For a brief discussion of the turmoil after Nero's death and of the Jewish revolt, see Helmut Koester, *Introduction to the New Testament*, vol. 1: *History, Culture, and Religion of the Hellenistic Age* (Philadelphia: Fortress, 1982), 313-15, 401-3. On the rumors concerning Nero's return, see Suetonius, *Nero*, 57.2; Tacitus, *Histories*, 2.8-9.

[11] For a brief summary of the possibilities, see Carson, Moo, and Morris, *Introduction*, 96-99; Hengel, *Studies*, 1-2.

[12] For the terminology of "fallible followers," see Elizabeth Struthers Malbon, "Fallible Followers: Women and Men in the Gospel of Mark," *Semeia* 28 (1983): 29-48; idem, "Disciples/Crowd/Whoever: Markan Characters and Readers," *NovT* 62 (1986): 123-24.

Mark shares with the other gospel writers and then by examining some of the distinctive emphases and unique features of Mark's approach to the subject of mission. In each case the theme of suffering or persecution casts a shadow on Mark's distinctive contributions to the topic of mission.

## THE MISSION TEACHING OF MARK'S GOSPEL

Too often, interpreters have passed over the subject of mission in Mark's gospel. As Senior states, "In contemporary Synoptic studies the role of mission is more neglected in the case of Mark than it is in Matthew or Luke-Acts."[13] Senior goes on to point out that even in the case of Matthew and Luke-Acts mission is not a central focus of study. Recent scholarly approaches to Mark's gospel have interpreted it either as a polemical document, attacking false teachers in the community, or a pastoral work, moving believers toward a greater devotion to Jesus.[14] However, Mark and his audience were not simply interested in inner-community debates and problems. It would be easy to overlook important aspects of Mark's gospel, unless there is a recognition that both Mark and his community cared about the universal proclamation of the gospel.[15]

Much of the material in Mark's gospel on mission has parallels to the teaching found in the other gospels.[16] Mark makes reference to different agents who are sent by God. In Jesus' parable of the vineyard, the prophets are pictured as servants who were sent by God but mistreated by the tenants (12:2-5). John the Baptist fits this pattern, since he is a prophet (11:32) who has been sent by God to prepare for the coming of the Messiah (1:2-3). Yet John is rejected by the religious leaders (11:30-33) and beheaded by Herod (6:27-29; 9:13). According to the parable of the vineyard, God also sends his beloved Son in a final effort to deal with the tenants (12:6-11). Jesus presents himself as an agent sent by God (9:37), who has come in order to preach (1:38), call sinners (2:17), and give his life as a ransom for many (10:45).

---

[13] Donald Senior, "The Struggle to Be Universal: Mission as Vantage Point for New Testament Investigation," *CBQ* 46 (1984): 66.

[14] On this distinction between polemical and pastoral approaches, see W. R. Telford, "Introduction," in *The Interpretation of Mark*, 2d ed., ed. William Telford (Edinburgh: T & T Clark, 1995), 36-37.

[15] On the importance of the mission theme in Mark's gospel, see also Klemens Stock, "Theologie der Mission bei Markus," in *Mission im Neuen Testament*, ed. Karl Kertelge (Freiburg: Herder, 1982), 131-32.

[16] There is also a continuity between the teaching of Jesus and the gospel of Mark on the subject of mission, a point that is made in Donald Senior and Carroll Stuhlmueller, *The Biblical Foundations for Mission* (Maryknoll, N.Y.: Orbis Books, 1983), 213-14.

Jesus calls disciples to follow him and be with him, but he also sends them out as his apostles (3:14; 6:7, 30). Jesus commissions them to preach repentance and to have authority over sickness and demonic power (3:14-15; 6:7-13), or, in other words, to be fishers of men (1:17). Last of all, angels serve as divine agents, since they are sent at the time of the second coming of Christ to gather the elect from the ends of the earth (13:27; cf. 4:29). This material on the subject of mission is familiar territory, but Mark also includes unique features. Three topics are of particular importance: the preaching of the good news throughout the world, the suffering of Jesus as a paradigm for his followers, and the lack of a post-resurrection commission by Jesus.

## The Proclamation of the Gospel to the Nations

In Mark 13 Jesus warns a select group of disciples about the difficulties of the future. This eschatological discourse of Jesus serves as the most extensive description in Mark of the time between the death and resurrection of Jesus and his second coming, a period described as birth pangs (13:8). The present age contains political turmoil (13:7-8), natural disasters (13:8), false teaching (13:5-6, 21-23), and persecution for Jesus' followers (13:9-13), leading up to a great tribulation such as the world has never seen (13:14-20). In the midst of his warning about the future, Jesus identifies the unavoidable task for believers during the period between the first and second advent. In the context of turmoil and persecution, the gospel must be proclaimed to all the nations (13:10). Actions and events identified as necessary in Mark's gospel must take place because they are part of the will and plan of God (*dei*, "it is necessary," 8:31; 9:11-13; 13:7, 10).

Both *proclamation* and *gospel* serve as prominent themes in Mark.[17] John the Baptist proclaims the message of repentance (1:4) and the impending appearance of a greater one (1:7). One of the purposes for which Jesus came was in order to preach (1:38-39) concerning the necessity of repentance and faith in light of the coming kingdom of God (1:14-15). Jesus also sends out his disciples to proclaim repentance (3:14; 6:7-12), and it follows from this commission that the responsibility for the worldwide proclamation of the good news (13:10; 14:9) falls to Jesus' followers. This is especially clear from the immedi-

---

[17] S. J. Anthonysamy, "The Gospel of Mark and the Universal Mission," *Biblebhashyam* 6 (1980): 87; Lucien Legrand, *Unity and Plurality: Mission in the Bible*, trans. Robert R. Barr (Maryknoll, N.Y.: Orbis Books, 1990), 63, 65. The verb *kērussō* is used twelve times in Mark's gospel (not including the two occurrences in 16:9-20), more often than any other book in the New Testament. The noun *euangelion* is used seven times in Mark (not including the use in 16:15) as compared to four times in Matthew and not at all in Luke or John.

ate context of Mark 13:10, in which the preaching of the gospel takes place with reference to the persecution of believers and their faithful testimony.[18]

The content of the Christian proclamation is the gospel. Mark uses the term *gospel* in two different but overlapping ways, as may be seen in a comparison of Mark 1:1 with 1:14-15. At the start of his narrative, Mark refers to his book as the gospel of Jesus Christ (1:1). In this instance, Jesus is the content of the gospel, or, in other words, the good news is a message about Jesus' life, ministry, death, and resurrection. However, in Mark 1:14-15, Jesus is not so much the content of the gospel as the proclaimer of the gospel.[19] Jesus preaches a message of good news that the time has been fulfilled and the kingdom of God has drawn near, so that everyone should repent and believe. Here the message of the gospel concerns the kingdom of God, but even in this instance the gospel points to Jesus, since he is the one who brings in the kingdom.[20] Therefore, an important aspect of the mission task is to proclaim Jesus. The proclamation of the good news is so valuable that Jesus is able to promise life to those who lose themselves for the gospel (8:35) and great reward to those who sacrifice possessions and family ties for it (10:29-30).

According to Mark 13:10, the scope of the mission extends to all the nations, and therefore to Gentiles (cf. 14:9).[21] Mark's gospel gives a significant place to Gentiles in a number of different ways. Jesus himself does not target an outreach to non-Jews, since his ministry is directed toward the people of Israel, who deserve to be satisfied first

---

[18] In Mark, the preaching of the gospel is not the responsibility of angels, and therefore it is problematic to use Mark as a witness for the idea that Jesus taught the universal proclamation of the gospel by God's angel at the end of the age, as is done in Joachim Jeremias, *Jesus' Promise to the Nations* (reprint, Philadelphia: Fortress, 1982), 22-23.

[19] In his chapter on "Euangelion," Willi Marxsen (*Mark the Evangelist: Studies on the Redaction History of the Gospel,* trans. James Boyce and others [Nashville: Abingdon, 1969], 117-50) emphasizes that in Mark's theology Jesus is both the content and bringer of the gospel, although Marxsen puts greater emphasis on Jesus as the content of the gospel.

[20] Robert H. Gundry, *Mark: A Commentary on His Apology for the Cross* (Grand Rapids: Eerdmans, 1993), 32.

[21] G. D. Kilpatrick ("The Gentile Mission in Mark and Mark 13:9-11," in *Studies in the Gospels: Essays in Memory of R. H. Lightfoot,* ed. D. E. Nineham [Oxford: Basil Blackwell, 1967], 145-58) stands alone in rejecting the idea that Mark 13:10 refers to a universal mission to Gentiles. Kilpatrick seeks to avoid this conclusion by changing the punctuation and by arguing that Mark 13:10 refers to a mission among diaspora Jews. For a response to Kilpatrick's position, see Stephen G. Wilson, *The Gentiles and the Gentile Mission in Luke-Acts,* SNTSMS, no. 23 (Cambridge: Cambridge University Press, 1973), 23-24.

(7:27). Nevertheless, Jesus does travel outside of Galilee into predominately Gentile territory, and while there he responds positively toward those who come to him for help (5:1-20; 7:24-8:9, 22-26; cf. 3:7-12).[22] He also foresees a future mission that goes beyond the limits of the people of Israel (7:27; 12:9; 13:10; 14:9).[23] In addition, Mark anticipates the true worship of God among the Gentiles through a unique feature in his account concerning the cleansing of the Temple. Only in Mark's gospel does Jesus justify his actions by stating that the Temple was intended "for all the nations" (11:17). Mark also shows his own openness to the Gentiles through his positive presentation of the Roman centurion. It is the centurion who recognizes the identity of Jesus through the manner of his death and confesses him to be the Son of God (15:39). Of course, none of this means that the Gentiles as a whole will be receptive to the gospel. The rulers of the world selfishly seek their own authority (10:42), and just as Jesus suffered at the hands of the political authorities (10:33-34; 15:1-26), so also his followers can expect to be persecuted by governors and kings (13:9-12). In fact, believers should anticipate that they will be hated by all on account of their devotion to Jesus (13:13).

The time frame for the worldwide proclamation of the gospel extends from the death and resurrection of Jesus until his second coming. In Mark 14:27-28, Jesus predicts that he will meet with his disciples in Galilee after the resurrection (cf. 16:7). The purpose for the meeting is to gather together the scattered sheep, that is, to restore the failed disciples. The location in Galilee seems to indicate that Jesus will once again send the disciples out on their mission, since Galilee has been the previous location for their commissioning (3:13-15; 6:7-13).[24] In other words, Jesus' prediction of a post-resurrection meeting

---

[22] Werner H. Kelber, *The Kingdom in Mark: A New Place and a New Time* (Philadelphia: Fortress, 1974), 45-65; idem, *Mark's Story of Jesus* (Philadelphia: Fortress, 1979), 30-42; Legrand, *Unity and Plurality*, 49-52; Senior, "Struggle to Be Universal," 77; Senior and Stuhlmueller, *Biblical Foundations*, 218-20. On the openness of Jesus to Gentiles in Mark's gospel, see also Stock, "Mission bei Markus," 141-43.

[23] Ferdinand Hahn (*Mission in the New Testament*, trans. Frank Clarke, SBT, no. 47 [Naperville, Ill.: Alec R. Allenson, 1965], 111-20) believes that Mark emphasizes the mission to the Gentiles, but Hahn overstates his case when he concludes that, for Mark, the time for the mission to the Jews was already past. A major problem for Hahn's view is that the primary reference to the universal proclamation of the gospel (13:10) occurs in a context in which it is assumed that believers will stand as witnesses before Jewish courts and in synagogues (13:9). Mark still holds open hope that there are scribes who are not far from the kingdom (12:28-34).

[24] Andrew T. Lincoln, "The Promise and the Failure: Mark 16:7, 8," *JBL* 108 (1989): 289.

supports the idea of a post-resurrection mission. Along similar lines, Jesus expects a future mission to Gentiles (7:27) after his crucifixion (12:6-9; cf. 15:39), a mission that takes place on the basis of his death on behalf of many (10:45; 14:24).[25] Mark 13:10 helps to indicate the end point for the universal mission, stating that the message of the gospel must first go out to all the nations. The use of the word *first* indicates a temporal relationship in which the mission task will be completed prior to some other event. That event appears to be the second coming of Jesus (13:26), since at that time the angels will gather the elect from throughout the world (13:27).

### The Example of Jesus and His Suffering

In Mark's gospel, the nature of Jesus' mission has implications for the mission task of his followers.[26] The activities of Jesus' followers— preaching the gospel (3:14; 6:12; 13:10; 14:9), casting out demons (3:15; 6:7, 13), healing (6:13), teaching (6:30), and serving (15:41)— all have a precedent in the prior work of Jesus. However, in Mark's gospel God's purposes for Jesus' ministry cannot be understood apart from Jesus' destiny in the cross. Mark emphasizes that Jesus' willingness to go the way of the cross serves as a paradigm for the path the disciples of Jesus must walk, if they are to fulfill God's purposes in the world. Those who follow Jesus must be prepared to follow in his sufferings.[27]

In Mark 14:36 Jesus calls to his Father in prayer, asking that the cup of suffering might be removed, but he bows in submission to his Father's will. It was the will of the Father that Jesus should suffer. The mission of Jesus included the cross. Mark highlights this aspect of Jesus' mission through his narration of three passion predictions in the central section of the gospel. The first passion prediction (8:31) takes place after Peter's confession of Jesus as the Messiah. Jesus then teaches the disciples that, as the Son of Man, he must suffer many things, including rejection by the religious authorities and death, after which his resurrection will take place. When Peter rejects this teaching, Jesus rebukes him for setting his mind on human interests rather than on God's concerns. The suffering of the Messiah, which was so objectionable to Peter, serves the interests of God. After the second prediction of his coming death (9:30-31), Jesus must correct the misunderstand-

---

[25] For a similar point, see Wilson, *Gentiles*, 30.

[26] David J. Bosch, *Transforming Mission: Paradigm Shifts in Theology of Mission*, American Society of Missiology Series, no. 16 (Maryknoll, N.Y.: Orbis Books, 1991), 38-39; Senior and Stuhlmueller, *Biblical Foundations*, 216-17, 225-28; Stock, "Mission bei Markus," 136-37.

[27] This is also a key emphasis in the book of 1 Peter, as may be seen in the discussion in chapter 11 below.

ing of the disciples by pointing out the importance of humble service. In this context, Jesus reminds the disciples that he has been sent by God (9:37). After the lengthy description of his future suffering in the third passion prediction (10:33-34), Jesus must once again teach the disciples on the necessity of service. Jesus concludes this teaching with a statement concerning why God sent him: "For also the Son of Man did not come to be served, but to serve and to give his life as a ransom for many" (10:45).

Following a Messiah who came to die on a cross involves sacrifice, suffering, and service. In Mark's gospel the individuals who follow Jesus leave something behind; they respond with sacrifice to answer Jesus' call. Peter and Andrew leave their nets (1:18), James and John their father (1:20), Levi his tax office (2:14), and Bartimaeus his mantle (10:50-52). In fact, the disciples, as Peter pointed out, left everything in order to follow Jesus (10:28), a sacrifice that the rich man was unwilling to make (10:21-22). Those who pay the price, however, receive abundant reward (10:29-30), since all who lose their lives for the sake of Jesus and the gospel will find true life (8:35). Followers of Jesus must also be prepared to suffer. Jesus' call to take up the cross must be fulfilled through a willingness and readiness to suffer and die for his sake (8:34). Suffering and death are not simply theoretical possibilities, however, since some believers will indeed face hatred, imprisonment, brutality, and the loss of life because of their devotion to Christ (10:39; 13:9-13). In addition, true greatness for believers comes from following Jesus' example of service (9:35; 10:43-44). Whoever wants to be first must be last, and whoever wants to be great must be a slave. Of course, nothing is automatic or easy about following a suffering Messiah, and Mark is well aware of human frailty. Particularly through his presentation of the disciples, Mark shows that living up to the demands of Jesus is difficult and that the prospect of persecution often produces fear and failure. Nevertheless, there is hope because Jesus is able to restore those who follow him and make them fishers of men (1:17).

### The Missing Post-Resurrection Commission

The end of Mark's gospel presents interpreters with a variety of problems, not the least of which is a major text-critical problem.[28] Manuscripts of Mark's gospel end in several different ways. A few manuscripts end the gospel at 16:8, a large number include the so-called longer ending of 16:9-20, one continues after 16:8 simply with

---

[28] A detailed presentation of the manuscript and linguistic evidence concerning this textual problem may be found in James Keith Elliott, "The Text and Language of the Endings to Mark's Gospel," *TZ* 27 (1971): 255-62.

the so-called shorter ending,[29] and finally several include both the shorter and longer endings. Although most English translations of the New Testament print the longer ending of 16:9-20, it is very unlikely that these verses were originally part of Mark's gospel. Based on external and internal evidence, the general consensus among New Testament scholars is that both the longer ending and the shorter ending are secondary, later additions to Mark's gospel.[30] Several different explanations have been offered for why Mark's gospel ends abruptly at 16:8, but a growing number of interpreters conclude that Mark's gospel ends at 16:8 because that is where Mark intended to finish. So, for example, Kümmel states, "There is an increasingly strong inclination to the view that 16:8 is the intended ending of Mk."[31] If Mark's gospel ends at 16:8, then Mark balanced the conclusion of his gospel with a message of encouragement and a warning. Mark shows that there is hope because Jesus is alive and has promised to meet with his disciples (16:7), but Mark also gives a reminder that failure is a continuing hazard by reporting the disobedience of the women at the tomb (16:8).[32]

The point at which the gospel of Mark ends has implications for a study of Mark's perspective on mission. If Mark intended to conclude his gospel at 16:8, which I believe he did, then he chose to finish his narrative without reporting a commission of the disciples by the resurrected Jesus. Each of the other gospels includes a commissioning scene after the resurrection in which Jesus sends out his disciples on their mission with his power and authority (Matt. 28:18-20; Luke 24:46-49; John 20:21-23; cf. Acts 1:8). Mark's gospel, by way of contrast, ends without a resurrection appearance and without a great commis-

---

[29] The shorter ending reads, "And they promptly reported to Peter and those with him all the things which had been commanded. And after these things also Jesus himself sent out through them, from east to west, the sacred and imperishable proclamation of eternal salvation. Amen." In light of the lack of manuscript evidence for this shorter ending, there is no reason to argue for its authenticity.

[30] As Metzger states, "Almost all textual studies and critical commentaries on the Gospel according to Mark agree that the last twelve verses cannot be regarded as Marcan" (Bruce M. Metzger, *The Text of the New Testament: Its Transmission, Corruption, and Restoration*, 3d ed. [New York: Oxford University Press, 1992], 228).

[31] Werner Georg Kümmel, *Introduction to the New Testament*, trans. Howard Clark Kee (Nashville: Abingdon, 1975), 100. For the same assessment, see Telford, "Introduction," 38; John Christopher Thomas, "A Reconsideration of the Ending of Mark," *JETS* 26 (1983): 415; Paul L. Danove, *The End of Mark's Story: A Methodological Study*, Biblical Interpretation Series, vol. 3 (Leiden: E. J. Brill, 1993), 1.

[32] Lincoln, "Mark 16:7, 8," 283-300.

sion.[33] Of course, Mark does not reject the idea that such an encounter between Jesus and his disciples took place. According to Mark, Jesus promised that he would meet with the disciples in Galilee after the resurrection (14:27-28), and the young man at the tomb repeats this promise (16:7). However, since Mark apparently decided not to record a description of this meeting, it is worth exploring the ramifications of this omission. How can Mark's view of mission be better understood in light of the missing post-resurrection commission at the end of his gospel?

Mark's deemphasis on the great commission allows him to stress other aspects of his understanding of the Christian mission. For example, without a post-resurrection commission, the continuing significance of Jesus' pre-resurrection commissions is highlighted. Jesus initially calls his disciples in order that he might make them fishers of men (1:17). When Jesus appoints the twelve, he does so with the intention of sending them out to preach and to have authority over demonic powers (3:13-15), and early in his ministry Jesus moves them out to begin their mission (6:7-13). When Jesus predicts a meeting with the disciples after the resurrection, he seems to indicate that he will gather together the scattered sheep at that time (14:27-28). In other words, Jesus will restore his failed disciples. The purpose for such a restoration is not so that they might take on new responsibilities, but so that they might accomplish what they were originally called to do, primarily to proclaim the message of repentance and draw people to Jesus. In addition, the lack of a great commission not only underlines the significance of the earlier commissions to the disciples but also highlights the demands that Jesus places on "anyone" or "whoever." In Mark's gospel Jesus explains prior to his death and resurrection what he wants his followers to do. Anyone who seeks to follow Jesus must live with self-denial and a willingness to suffer and serve, always standing unashamed of Jesus and his words (8:34-38; 9:35; 10:42-45).

In Matthew's record of the great commission, Jesus promises that he will be with his people always, even to the end of the age (Matt.

---

[33] Some have argued that the negative example of the women in 16:8 itself serves as an apostolic commission. Mark calls on his audience to obey God and "go and tell" by narrating the disobedience of the women and their refusal to "go and tell." For this view, see especially Thomas E. Boomershine, "Mark 16:8 and the Apostolic Commission," *JBL* 100 (1981): 225-39. See also Mary Ann Tolbert, *Sowing the Gospel: Mark's World in Literary-Historical Perspective* (Minneapolis: Fortress, 1989), 288-99; Danove, *End of Mark's Story*, 220-28; David Rhoads, "Mission in the Gospel of Mark," *CurTM* 22 (1995): 353. Objections to this view may be found in Lincoln, "Mark 16:7, 8," 297; Joel F. Williams, *Other Followers of Jesus: Minor Characters as Major Figures in Mark's Gospel*, JSNTSup, no. 102 (Sheffield: Sheffield Academic Press, 1994), 202.

28:20). There is nothing in Mark that corresponds to this promise of the continuing presence of Jesus with his people. Instead, Mark chooses to focus on Jesus' absence during the present age. Now is the time when the bridegroom is absent, when fasting is appropriate (Mark 2:20). The false prophets and false Christs claim to embody the presence of the Messiah, and believers should be careful not to be misled by them (13:5-6, 21-22). The coming of the Son of Man will not be missed, since he will come with great power and glory and will send his angels to gather up the elect from throughout the world (13:24-27). In this way, the recognition of Jesus' absence during the present time serves to increase the significance of Jesus' second coming.[34] During this age of turmoil and persecution, believers must endure suffering when carrying out their mission (13:9-13) and remain alert (13:33-37) as they wait for their deliverance and vindication at the second coming of Christ.[35] Believers should, therefore, follow the example of Christ, who chose during his trial to suffer for the truth, while looking forward to the second coming as the time of vindication (14:61-62).

In Luke's description of the post-resurrection commission, Jesus promises empowerment from the Holy Spirit to the disciples in order that they might fulfill their responsibilities as his witnesses (Luke 24:46-49; Acts 1:8). By way of contrast, Mark's gospel seems to deemphasize any post-resurrection power from the Spirit that enables Jesus' followers to validate their message to the world. John the Baptist predicts that Jesus will baptize his people with the Holy Spirit (Mark 1:8), but this Spirit baptism is neither narrated nor emphasized. Mark's gospel includes just one reference to the work of the Holy Spirit in the period between the first and second advent of Christ. The Holy Spirit will give believers an appropriate message to say as they stand in trial before their persecutors (13:11). Of course, Mark is not opposed to the idea of the miraculous, since he records numerous wonders performed by Jesus. In addition, he points out that Jesus' disciples healed the sick and delivered the demon-possessed (3:15; 6:7, 13), although they were not always able to produce such works (9:14-29). Moreover, Jesus teaches his disciples not to hinder those who perform miracles in his name (9:38-40). Nevertheless, Jesus does not perform miracles in Mark's gospel in order to validate the truth of his message.[36] Jesus repeatedly commands people to remain silent concerning his miracu-

---

[34] Lincoln, "Mark 16:7, 8," 298.

[35] Bosch, *Transforming Mission*, 39.

[36] The only exception to this statement seems to be the healing of the paralytic (2:1-12), which Jesus uses to show that he has authority to forgive sins. Even here, Jesus does not use the miracle to move those who object to a response of faith. The unbelieving scribes do not seem to react positively to the miracle since the opposition of the religious leaders continues to build in the following context (2:13-3:6).

lous deeds (1:43-44; 5:43; 7:36; 8:26; cf. 5:19; 7:24), and he stead-
fastly refuses to give miraculous signs to unbelieving people looking
for proof of his authority (8:11-13; 11:27-33; cf. 6:1-6). In Mark's
gospel Jesus performs miracles primarily because he has compassion
on those who need his help (1:41; 6:34). When Jesus predicts the conditions of his followers during the present age in his eschatological
discourse, he mentions their difficulties but makes no reference to miraculous deeds on their part. Instead, it is the false Christs and false
prophets who display signs and wonders in order to bolster their claims
and to lead others astray (13:22). Jesus' followers are weak, powerless
people who are dragged into court, beaten, and put to death (13:9-
12). When Mark deals with the circumstances of believers in the present
age, he does not turn his attention to their power but rather to their
persecution.[37] The display of great power and glory that vindicates the
proclamation of the gospel is the second coming of Jesus (13:24-26),
and believers must endure until this end (13:13).

This stress on the persecution of weak believers should not be taken
to mean that Mark thought of the Christian mission as ineffective.
Jesus teaches in striking terms about the growth of God's work in his
parables of the kingdom. The word of God encounters people who are
like good soil, in that they hear God's word and bear abundant fruit
(4:20). The kingdom of God is like a seed that grows without human
effort or involvement (4:26-29). In a similar way, God's kingdom is
like a mustard seed that starts small and then grows beyond all expectations (4:30-32). In Mark's gospel the result of the mission is the supernatural and ever-expanding growth of the kingdom of God.

## CONCLUSION

In our own time the mission of the church is presented on occasion
in triumphant terms, in which Christian soldiers march ever onward
and God's kingdom swiftly spreads from shore to shore. Without resistance, the light of God's Word transforms the darkness of the world
to dawn and then to the brightness of the noon-day sun. The teaching
of Mark's gospel on mission can serve as a corrective to an unrealistic
optimism. The witness of believers may occur in a world that is indif-
ferent or even openly hostile, and the proclamation of the gospel may
take place in the context of difficulty and persecution. Instead of offering more effective or successful methods, Mark points to the way of
the cross, the path of self-sacrifice and humble service. Believers do
not have miraculous powers that take away their potential for suffering or all resistance to the gospel. In fact, the world may become so
harsh that the faithful simply hang on in hope of their final deliverance

---

[37] Lincoln, "Mark 16:7, 8," 298.

at the coming of the Son of Man. The baffling miracle is, however, that in this hostile world the scattered seed finds good soil and grows. The gospel meets receptive hearts, and, in ways that cannot be explained by reference to human ingenuity or effort, the work of God moves forward.

# 9

## *Mission in Luke*

### William J. Larkin Jr.

Do Luke and Acts record, encourage, and model mission for the edification of Christians or are they actual instruments of mission? Is there justification for following Joseph Fitzmyer's contention that Luke's works are "preaching" and his theology kerygmatic? May we agree with him that "they proclaim the Christ-event and the kingdom of God and demand from those who are addressed the response of Christian faith as much as the writings of Mark or Paul—albeit in a different way"?[1] What interpreters decide about setting—especially date, occasion, audience, and purpose—has an important impact on their understanding of the teaching on mission contained in these works.

### HISTORICAL SETTING

The author of Luke-Acts is Luke, the physician and traveling companion of Paul, the missionary. This is a conclusion, not only supported unanimously by the early church[2] but congruent with the "we passages" of Acts (Acts 16:10-17; 20:5-15; 21:1-18; 27:1-28:16), which point to the author's participation in the events described. Critical scholars often have taken the predictive detail concerning the siege of Jerusalem in Luke 21:20-24 as a mark of post-70 C.E. composition. However, such a conclusion is unnecessary if one allows for the possibility that Jesus had truly prophetic powers and if one keeps in mind that the

---

[1] Joseph A. Fitzmyer, *The Gospel according to Luke I–IX*, AB, vol. 28 (Garden City, N.Y.: Doubleday, 1981), 152.

[2] D. A. Carson, Douglas J. Moo, and Leon Morris, *An Introduction to the New Testament* (Grand Rapids: Zondervan, 1992), 186.

detail describes no more than common practice in ancient warfare.[3] Instead, a date for the writing of Luke-Acts in the early sixties C.E. is preferable. The space devoted at the end of Acts to the events of 58-60 C.E. (Acts 20-28), along with the accuracy of its geographical, political, and socio-cultural detail, points to a work produced close to the time of these events. An early sixties date also makes the apparently abrupt ending of Acts understandable. Luke reports the course of early church history only as far as he knows it.

Theophilus, a high Roman official and the patron of Luke-Acts (Luke 1:3), is representative of Luke's audience: an intelligent Roman upper-middle-class reading public among whom Paul's case had sparked interest (Acts 28:30; Phil. 1:13).[4] He and the rest of Luke's audience have been informed about the gospel amid a cacophony of strongly dissenting voices. In addition to Luke-Acts, Romans and Philippians let us hear echoes of these voices, as Christianity responds to their challenge. Theophilus's Roman contemporaries despise the Christian faith as an eastern cult (Acts 16:20-21; 25:18-20; Rom. 1:13-17; cf. Tacitus, *Annals*, 15.44). Unbelieving Jews brand Christianity as a disorderly sect, hardly innocent before the state and unworthy of the attention of law-abiding Romans (Luke 23:4, 13-16, 22, 47; Acts 17:5-9; 18:13; 24:4-5; Rom. 13:1-8). Judaizers attack the legitimacy of a salvation by grace for the Gentiles (Luke 18:9; Acts 15:1-2; 21:20-21; Rom. 10:1-21; Phil. 3:1-16).[5]

If this is the occasion, what is Luke's purpose in writing Luke-Acts? Is it edification or evangelism? The soundest way to answer this problem is to examine Luke's preface (Luke 1:1-4) and also the central themes and literary genre of Luke-Acts.[6] Luke explicitly gives us his

---

[3] Ibid., 116-17. This chapter will pursue an analysis of Luke's teaching with the assumption that Luke knew and used the gospel of Mark and that Luke knew a combination of oral and written tradition of the sayings of Jesus, commonly designated "Q." The analysis, however, will always be congruent with the conviction that Luke provides an accurate and reliable account of Jesus' life and teaching.

[4] F. F. Bruce, *The Book of Acts* (Grand Rapids: Eerdmans, 1954), 31.

[5] Robert J. Karris ("Missionary Communities: A New Paradigm for the Study of Luke-Acts," *CBQ* 41 [1979]: 85-86) also sees opposition to Christianity as a key component in the situation of Luke's readers, but this is because they are Christian missionary communities bearing witness in the late seventies C.E. David J. Bosch (*Transforming Mission: Paradigm Shifts in Theology of Mission* [Maryknoll, N.Y.: Orbis Books, 1991], 85) proposes a setting in the eighties C.E. in which again, under Jewish and Gentile opposition from without and flagging enthusiasm from within, the church questions its identity and mission. To account for the intensity of Luke's concern with Judaism and Judaizing influences, a pre-70 C.E. situation is still to be preferred.

[6] W. Ward Gasque, "A Fruitful Field: Recent Study of the Acts of the Apostles," *Int* 42 (1988): 119.

purpose in the clause "so that you may know the certainty of the things you have been taught" (Luke 1:4). The kind of knowledge (*epiginōskō*) Luke desires for his readers includes both recognition of the truth about facts and Spirit-aided insight (Luke 7:37; 23:7; 24:16, 31; Acts 4:13; 12:14; 19:34; 22:24, 29; 23:28; 24:8, 11; 25:10). Luke wants his readers "to know the certainty (*asphaleia*)" of the things they have been taught. This certainty is the exact truth based on a clear understanding of the evidence (Acts 21:34; 22:30) and also the firm assurance that such truth has personal significance for the reader (2:36). The interpretation of the last phrase of Luke's purpose statement helps to determine whether this certainty of knowledge is for the edification of Christians or the evangelism of non-Christians. The NIV rendering—"so that you may know the certainty of the things you have been taught (*katēchēthēs*)"—suggests the edification purpose, since Theophilus is represented as having already made a decision and been catechized. Although *katēcheō* eventually became a technical term in the church for the instruction of new believers, in biblical usage it can also refer simply to informing someone about something. Luke uses it both ways in Acts (instructing, Acts 18:25; informing, 21:21, 24). The phrasing of Luke 1:4 parallels that of Acts 21:21, 24 where *katēcheō* means "to inform." From the content of Luke-Acts, the "things" of Luke 1:4 seem to be historical accounts and mission preaching, as opposed to doctrinal instruction. Theophilus is, therefore, the object of evangelism, not catechesis.

The distinctive theological themes of Luke and Acts are Jesus' saving mission divinely ordained in fulfillment of scripture; Jesus' constant concern for the poor and social outcast; Jesus' call to repentance and radical discipleship together with the promise of salvation blessings of forgiveness of sins; and the universal scope of the salvation offer (cf. Luke 24:46-48). These themes definitely advance an evangelistic purpose. Another characteristic feature that supports an evangelistic purpose is the frequent highlighting of non-Jews—and particularly in Acts, of non-Christian Romans—as individual characters. They often respond positively to Jesus' mission and the early church's missionary message (the Capernaum centurion, Luke 7:1-10; the Gerasene demoniac, 8:26-39; the Samaritan leper, 17:12-19; Cornelius, Acts 10:1–11:18; Sergius Paulus, 13:4-12; the Philippian jailer, 16:25-34; Felix and Festus, 24:10-26; 26:1-29).[7]

On the matter of literary genre, David Aune classifies Luke-Acts as "general history," analogous to general and antiquarian histories that "focused on the history of a particular people (typically the Greeks or

---

[7] Stephen G. Wilson, *The Gentiles and the Gentile Mission in Luke-Acts* SNTSMS, no. 23 (Cambridge: Cambridge University Press, 1973), 31, chap. 7; David H. Gill, "Observations on the Lukan Travel Narrative and Some Related Passages," *HTR* 63 (1970): 208-9.

Romans) mythical beginnings to a point in the recent past, including contacts (usually conflicts) with other national groups."[8] Such a genre serves well an evangelistic purpose that seeks to persuade Romans that this Christian gospel is true and for them.

Luke's summary of the gospel message displays how central the theme of mission is to his evangelistic purpose. This summary may be divided into two parts: salvation accomplished—"This is what is written: The Christ will suffer and rise from the dead on the third day"; and salvation applied—"and repentance and forgiveness of sins will be preached in his name to all nations, beginning at Jerusalem. You are witnesses of these things" (Luke 24:46-48). The reference to scripture indicates that Jesus comes on divine mission to fulfill what God has promised through the prophets. In addition, in the central portion of the gospel (9:51-19:44), mission is present, for Luke structures it as a travel narrative with a Jerusalem destination: a Jerusalem mission born of divine necessity (9:51; 13:32-35; 18:31-35).

*Salvation accomplished* is Luke's main focus in his gospel, while the focus of Acts is *salvation applied*. In light of this focus in his first volume, Luke highlights the subject of Jesus as the sent one in his gospel, but he also addresses the idea of Jesus as the sending one. Luke allegedly omits from Jesus' pre-resurrection teaching any reference to the universal scope of salvation and the Gentile mission (cf. Mark 11:17; 13:10; 14:9; cf. 10:45; 14:24), and this contention requires an answer.[9] The perspective of this chapter is that it would be an unnecessary limitation to look only to Luke 24:46-48 for information on this gospel's presentation of the church's mission.[10] Nevertheless, this passage does provide a valuable template for viewing Luke's distinctive contributions to the biblical teaching on mission. Indeed, it serves as an important source for isolating the Lukan emphases against the backdrop of the teaching of Jesus.[11]

---

[8] David E. Aune, *The New Testament in Its Literary Environment* (Philadelphia: Westminster Press, 1987), 139.

[9] Ferdinand Hahn, *Mission in the New Testament*, SBT, no. 47 (Naperville, Ill.: Alec R. Allenson, 1965), 128; Wilson, *Gentiles*, 49-51.

[10] Wilson, *Gentiles*, 31-58. For example, Gill ("Observations on the Travel Narrative," 221) finds the Gentile mission to be a consistent theme throughout the travel narrative.

[11] I do not share Wilson's critical conclusion that Jesus taught about a future apocalyptic proclamation to the Gentiles mission, not a Gentile mission in history, and that the post-resurrection great commission was probably a transposed Mark 13:10 accommodated to church practice (*The Gentiles*, 26-27, 47-48). Other explanations of the Mark 13:10 "omission," which take into account additional factors in Luke 21, show how Jesus' expectation of a historical Gentile mission is indeed present. The most satisfying explanation of the early church's prosecution of a Gentile mission is that the risen Lord did command it during a post-resurrection experience.

## JESUS AS THE SENT ONE

Luke deals with the subject of Jesus' mission by showing that God, in fulfillment of his covenant promises, sent Jesus to proclaim the good news of release. This teaching of Luke's gospel on Jesus' mission is covered in the following sections through an examination of the nature of God as the sender, the identity of Jesus as the sent one, and the empowerment of the Spirit as the commissioning event. A discussion of the duties and scope of Jesus' task is also included.

### The Sender: God, Fulfiller of Prophetic Promise through Divinely Ordained Salvation History

The thread of explicit witness to Jesus' divine sender begins in Zechariah's song. God has visited his people with redemption by raising up a horn of salvation in the house of David (Luke 1:68-69). It continues in Simeon's song, which says Jesus is the salvation God has prepared (2:30-32). The boy Jesus picks up the refrain with his question to his parents: "Didn't you know I had to be in my Father's house (or about his business)?" (2:49). It climaxes in the text of the Nazareth synagogue sermon that inaugurates his ministry. "The Spirit of the Lord is upon me, because the Lord has anointed me to preach good news to the poor. He has sent me to proclaim freedom to the prisoners" (4:18). Themes of fulfillment of covenant promises, salvation, even its universal scope, accompany many of the references. Yet in Jesus' teaching, except for the phraseology "him who sent me" (9:48; 10:16), the references to divine commissioning are much more oblique. It is expressed by the passive ("I must preach the good news of the kingdom of God . . . because that is why I was sent," 4:43) or in terms of a salvation history necessity (*dei*, "it is necessary," 9:22; 13:33; 17:25; 19:5; 24:7, 26, 44) or in expressions of scriptural fulfillment (22:37; 24:44). Luke highlights God's saving activity as a sending activity by stressing that Jesus is just the last in a long line of prophets and apostles who have been sent by God to his people and have been badly treated, rejected, even killed (11:49-51; 13:34; 19:14; 20:10).[12] Jesus' mission is to end in death as well, but that death will complete the pattern and mean decisive judgment on this generation.

### The Sent One: A Savior, Christ the Lord

The gospel summary says that it is the Christ who will suffer and rise from the dead (24:46). Luke's presentation of this Christ is well

---

[12] See David P. Moessner, "The 'Leaven of the Pharisees' and 'This Generation': Israel's Rejection of Jesus according to Luke," *JSNT* 34 (1988): 21-46.

expressed in the complex of terms the angel used on that first Christmas eve, "a Savior has been born to you; he is Christ the Lord" (2:11). The birth narratives of Luke 1-2 declare the truth that Jesus is the Messiah and that he has come to save (1:32-33, 68-69). That the salvation would occur through his suffering is hinted at by Simeon (2:34-35), but only after the resurrection does Luke communicate in the clearest possible terms that the Messiah had to suffer (24:26, 46).

The other surprise, the deity of the Christ, is stated openly from the beginning, usually by the use of the title Son of God and sometimes by the term *Lord*. Gabriel's explanation to Mary is most clear (1:32-35). The son she will bear will be called "Son of the Most High" and "Son of God." The juxtaposing of "Christ" and "Lord" in the angel's messianic birth announcement (2:11) is prepared for in Zechariah's song (1:76-79). This Spirit-filled hymn declares with the flexible term *Lord* (note its use in the immediate context to refer to God the Father, 1:77-78) that Christ and God are one and the same.[13] Luke's other editorializing makes the equation between Christ and God clear by paralleling Son of God and Christ (4:41/Mark 1:34; cf. Luke 9:20; 20:41). In addition, it is the alleged blasphemy of claiming to be the Christ, who is the Son of God, that leads to the Messiah's death (22:67-70). While "Son" does not appear any more frequently in Luke than the other synoptics, the gospel writer does have the consistent practice of using "the Lord" editorially in the narrative to refer to Jesus (e.g., 7:13; 7:19, cf. Matt. 11:2; Luke 10:1, 39; 11:39; 12:41-42; 13:15; 17:5-6; 18:6).

Luke's use of "Son of Man" does not differ significantly from the other synoptic gospels. Of all the titles, it is employed to refer to Jesus when his mission is being described in one of its three aspects: earthly ministry, death and resurrection, and parousia. The term occurs at the climax of Jesus' earthly mission in the summary statement: "The Son of Man came to seek and to save what was lost" (19:10). Luke seems to stress in two of his three passion predictions concerning the Son of Man that there is a spiritual hiddenness, a lack of understanding of these facts before the cross (9:44-45/Mark 9:31-32; Luke 18:31-34/ Mark 10:32-34). Luke emphasizes that the Son of Man's imminent and decisive return calls for perseverance and watchfulness (17:22-26, 30; 18:8; 21:27).

At the beginning of his mission, Jesus takes to himself the title prophet (Luke 4:24). It indicates his positive mission: the proclamation of the arrival of God's salvation and the miraculous work of displaying salvation blessings (4:23; cf. the allusions to Elijah and Elisha, 4:25-26; 9:8, 19; cf. 7:16; 24:19). At the same time there is

---

[13] Contrast Darrell L. Bock, *Luke—Volume 1: 1:1-9:50*, BECNT, no. 3A (Grand Rapids: Baker, 1994), 191-92.

the dark theme of the prophet experiencing rejection, even death (13:33; cf. 11:49-51; 19:14; 20:10). At Peter's confession, however, Luke shows that Jesus sees his basic identity not as a prophet, but as the Messiah (9:19-20).[14]

### The Commissioning: Spirit Empowerment at Jesus' Baptism

With regard to Jesus' commission, Luke's main emphasis is on Jesus' reception of the Spirit (3:22; 4:1, 14). Indeed, through the Isaiah 61 text in the inaugural sermon at Nazareth (4:18-19), Luke explicitly states the Spirit's role as both enabler ("the Spirit of the Lord is upon me") and commissioner ("He has sent me"). Jesus models a pattern that will be repeated by his followers. They too will be sent out in mission only after they have waited for Spirit empowerment (Luke 3:16; 24:49; Acts 1:4-8).

### The Task: Proclaiming the Good News of Release

Luke provides a key programmatic narrative, the sermon at Nazareth with its text Isaiah 61:1-2 (Luke 4:16-30), that describes Jesus' understanding of the purpose for which he was sent.[15] Interestingly, of the four infinitives from Isaiah that show the purpose of the Spirit's anointing and sending of Jesus, three involve preaching. The poor are evangelized (*euangelizomai*); the prisoners have release and the blind have recovery of sight proclaimed (*kērussō*) to them; the year of the Lord's favor, the Jubilee year, is proclaimed (*kērussō*). The other purpose is to send the oppressed away in freedom. Luke, then, regards the primary activity of Jesus' ministry as preaching. Other tasks are present, such as Jesus' healing and exorcism ministry or his sacrificial death and mighty resurrection, but these either validate or become the content of the gospel message. Luke's report of Jesus' ministry activity, especially in summary statements, keeps Jesus' preaching ministry before his readers (4:43-44; 8:1; cf. 7:22). In Luke's gospel Jesus' description of his ministry in salvation history framework also emphasizes the centrality of preaching and the necessity of commitment. "The law and the prophets were until John; from then the kingdom of God is being evangelized, the good news about it is

---

[14] Joseph G. Kelly's pursuit of a Lukan Christology with Jesus as the prophet Elijah at its center in hopes of being less offensive to Jews and promoting Jewish-Christian dialogue results in a wrongly focused view of Luke's Christology, which does have Jesus' messiahship and more, his deity, at its center ("Lucan Christology and the Jewish-Christian Dialogue," *JES* 21 [1984]: 688-708).

[15] For other passages in which Jesus points to his task by expressing the purpose for which he came, see Luke 5:32; 12:49-53; 19:10.

being told and everyone is being urgently invited into it" (16:16, cf. Matt. 11:12).[16]

Although Luke consistently summarizes the content of Jesus' preaching as the kingdom of God (4:43; 8:1; 9:11; 16:16), Luke's teaching on this theme reveals no marked emphases. It is the Nazareth sermon and the Isaiah quotation that again are the best starting points for expounding Luke's understanding of the nature and purpose of Jesus' preaching ministry.[17] When the quotation is taken quite literally or concretely, there are three contexts to which Jesus is sent to bring relief from suffering. In the economic context, he preaches good news to the poor and proclaims the "acceptable year of the Lord." In the political context, he proclaims release to the prisoners and sends the oppressed away in freedom. In the physical context, he proclaims recovery of sight to the blind.

A liberation theology hermeneutic has often found such an understanding of Luke's view of Jesus' and the church's mission in these verses.[18] There is also a strong tradition in Western Christianity for understanding many if not all of the phrases metaphorically and taking them as symbols for the spiritual salvation Jesus brings.[19] Two-thirds-world biblical scholars and theologians have protested against this polarization in interpretation, claiming that it reveals the "uneasy Western conscience about the 'spiritualization' or 'secularization' of the Gospel."[20] They call for "integral, holistic evangelism." They claim the meaning of the passage, especially the identity of the poor and of the good news addressed to them, must be understood in the interpreter's own context. For two-thirds-world Christians this is the context of "poverty, powerlessness, and religious pluralism."[21] In the

---

[16] Juan B. Cortes and Florence M. Gatti make a strong case for the positive meaning of *biazō* (neutrally, "to enter by force"; "On the Meaning of Luke 16:16," *JBL* 106 [1987]: 247-59).

[17] For a thorough discussion of the source of the wording of the quotation through a comparison of Luke with the Septuagint and Masoretic texts, see I. Howard Marshall, *The Gospel of Luke*, NIGTC (Grand Rapids: Eerdmans, 1978), 182-84.

[18] See the literature cited by Eben H. Scheffler ("Reading Luke from the Perspective of Liberation Theology," in *Text and Interpretation: New Approaches in the Criticism of the New Testament*, ed. Patrick J. Hartin and Jacobus H. Petzer [Leiden: E. J. Brill, 1991], 281); cf. Craig L. Nessan, "The Gospel of Luke and Liberation Theology: On Not Domesticating the Dangerous Memory of Jesus," *CurTM* 22 (1995): 130-38.

[19] See, for example, Marshall's handling of the passage (*Luke*, 182-84).

[20] Kwame Bediako, *Christianity in Africa: The Renewal of a Non-Western Religion* (Maryknoll, N.Y.: Orbis Books, 1995), 144.

[21] Vinay Samuel and Chris Sugden, *Evangelism and the Poor: A Third World Study Guide* (Oxford: Regnum Books, 1983), 22.

final analysis, however, such a procedure does not, in a completely satisfactory manner, move beyond the polarization. These interpreters normally opt for the concrete, physical, socio-economic understanding of Jesus' liberating mission. Or, if the spiritual is recognized, it is often as part of a "plurality of meanings" approach. Such an approach usually identifies the spiritual with or subsumes it under the concrete understanding.[22] At the most, spiritual salvation becomes just another type alongside the physical and the socio-economic.

What does Luke intend to say about Jesus' ministry? The following discussion will take up these verses according to a threefold organization: good news to the poor/Jubilee Year proclaimed, release to the prisoners and the oppressed, and recovery of the sight to the blind. In addition, it will be necessary to ask how Luke unfolds these themes in the rest of his gospel. This analysis will lead to an understanding of how Luke sees the concrete and the spiritual interacting in God's saving purposes. For Luke, the spiritual is primary, yet the liberation it brings is holistic. Jesus' sermon at Nazareth in Luke 4 includes references to God's provision for Gentiles, and therefore it is also important for understanding Luke's view of the scope of Jesus' mission.

### Good News to the Poor: Jubilee Proclaimed

The last phrase of the quotation, "to proclaim the year of the Lord's favor," when understood as a Jubilee Year, does involve the economic. J. Massynbaerde Ford explains,

> Jesus may have been inaugurating or proclaiming a jubilee year, in which, according to Jewish law, debts were cancelled, slaves (and prisoners) were released, and people returned to their own land and the land lay fallow but the poor were allowed to glean the fields and orchards of the crops or fruits which grew naturally.[23]

Among Jesus' contemporaries there were messianic pretenders who used the Jubilee Year concept and the Isaiah passage, especially the phrase "the day of vengeance of our God," to call their fellow countrymen to fight against the Gentiles for political and religious freedom

---

[22] See, for example, David Bosch's exposition of the themes of WCC's CWME conference in San Antonio, Texas, in which the topic Mission in Jesus' Way was articulated as "1. empowering the weak and lowly; 2. healing the sick; 3. saving the lost" ("Mission in Jesus' Way: A Perspective from Luke's Gospel," *Missionalia* 17 [1989]: 3-21).

[23] J. Massynbaerde Ford, "Reconciliation and Forgiveness in Luke's Gospel," in *Political Issues in Luke-Acts*, ed. Richard J. Cassidy and Philip J. Scharper (Maryknoll, N.Y.: Orbis Books, 1983), 82.

(e.g., Simon Bar Giora reported in Josephus, *Jewish Wars*, 4.508; cf. 11QMelch). However, as Luke presents it, Jesus consciously concluded his quotation of Isaiah 61 before the declaration of coming judgment. When we combine this fact with the rest of Jesus' sermon, in which he uses as illustrations God's saving initiatives to Israel's traditional enemies, we begin to see that the kind of "favorable year" Jesus declares is one of reconciliation, healing, and forgiveness.[24] Spiritual salvation has necessary implications for the economic sphere but should not be collapsed into a program of political-economic liberation.

The matter may be pressed further with additional study of Luke's use of "poor" (*ptōkos*, the Greek term for a person who is destitute, without any visible means of support). In that way we can discover more precisely what good news Jesus has for them. Three themes, then, become apparent. First, there is the promise of an eschatological reversal of one's present economic fortunes (Luke 1:53-55; 6:20-26 [cf. especially 6:20 and Matt. 5:3]; Luke 16:25). Because Luke emphasizes the presence of the kingdom in Jesus' ministry and the presence of salvation today (4:21; 11:20; 19:9; 23:43), those who follow a liberation hermeneutic claim that Jesus intended this eschatological reversal of fortunes to start in his ministry and to continue in the church through its support of struggles for economic justice. At the least, Christians are "to live already in the present according to the standards of the kingdom."[25] But the eschatological future is still truly future—that is, beyond history—for Luke. The promised eschatological reversal should not be transformed into immediate good news to the poor: you will receive physical alleviation in this life. Instead, there is a second theme, which gives the poor some immediate hope, namely economic repentance. For the rich, knowledge of the coming eschatological reversal means, if they would see the kingdom, they must repent of all behaviors and values that are incompatible with the kingdom. If riches are an idol, they must sell them, give to the poor, and follow Jesus (18:22). If they have gained riches wrongfully, they must make restitution (19:8). They must make involvement with the poor a part of their lifestyle in terms of their social relations (14:13-14). This is part of a larger theme: Luke's distinctive emphasis on Jesus' identification with the poor, powerless, and outcasts of society (Samaritans, 9:51-56; 10:30-37; 17:11-19; women, 13:10-17; cf. 8:1-3; tax collectors and sinners 5:27-32; 15:1-32; 19:1-10). The rich must also use their financial resources for the benefit of the poor (19:8). In these ways the poor will find themselves empowered and their conditions alleviated, as they participate, with the rich, as valued and cared-for members in the kingdom. This

---

[24] Ibid. Bosch (*Transforming Mission*, 110-11) says this "non-vengeance" understanding is further validated by the crowd's negative response.

[25] Nessan, "Gospel of Luke and Liberation Theology," 133.

economic repentance is just as revolutionary in its way as any call for a program for economic justice, which redistributes wealth through governmental or military coercion. Zacchaeus, at the climax of Jesus' teaching and healing ministry, declares he will give half of his possessions to the poor. According to Ford,[26] the rabbis saw twenty percent as an appropriate act of charitable piety. Zacchaeus will make fourfold restitution. The rabbis saw twofold as proper for tax collectors.

The poor are given hope of relief in the future and even now by means of the themes of eschatological reversal and economic repentance. But the final theme, economic discipleship, points to the priority that even the poor must give to the spiritual good news. The last poor person we meet in Luke is the destitute widow who gives to God through the Temple treasury "all that she had" (21:3). Jesus, by approval of her act, relativizes the physical-economic need in favor of the spiritual. In Luke's gospel the final word about the poor is not the good news of what they will receive to alleviate their need, but the challenge of what they must give as part of the life of radical discipleship in devotion to Jesus (9:23-25; 14:33).

### Release to the Prisoners and the Oppressed

Because neither the term *prisoner* nor *oppressed* is used again in Luke, there is not much direct guidance on choosing between a concrete political understanding and a spiritual meaning. Scheffler is correct that the rest of Luke's gospel does not support the concept of political oppression here.[27] Luke portrays Jesus most frequently bringing relief from demonic oppression (4:33-37; 6:18-19; 7:21; 8:2, 26-39; 9:37-43; 11:14-23; 13:10-17, 32), which immediately places this second task into the realm of the spiritual. Luke's use of the term "release" (*aphesis*), which occurs twice in the Nazareth sermon quotation (4:18-19), confirms this. In his hymn Zechariah promises that John the Baptist as Jesus' forerunner will give knowledge of salvation through the forgiveness of sins (1:77), and indeed John proclaims a preparatory baptism of repentance for the forgiveness of sins (3:3/Mark 1:4). In the healing of the paralytic Jesus claims authority on earth to forgive sins (Luke 5:21, 23-24). Luke alone records the encounter with the sinful woman at supper, in which Jesus declares her sins forgiven (7:47-49). The last time "forgiveness of sins" appears is in Jesus' post-resurrection commission, where it expresses the salvation blessings of the good news that the disciples are to proclaim to the ends of the

---

[26] Ford, "Reconciliation," 88.
[27] Scheffler, "Reading Luke," 289.

earth (24:47). Forgiveness of sins is the release Jesus and the church are sent to proclaim.[28]

### Recovery of Sight to the Blind

A case could be made for a metaphorical/spiritual understanding of "recovery of sight to the blind." The phrase speaks of a declaration of that recovery. Luke does use the imagery of darkness and light, blindness and sight to describe humankind's spiritual ignorance and the spiritual illumination that the Messiah will bring (1:78-79; 2:32; 3:6; 6:39; 22:53). Jesus' sermon, however, and its illustrations deal with the healing ministry of a prophet (4:23-27). In addition, Jesus includes healing as a significant feature in his ministry when he sends messages both to John the Baptist (7:21-23) and to Herod (13:32). Therefore, part of Jesus' mission is the miraculous deeds of mercy, restoring the whole person, as a sign of the completeness of salvation the arrival of the kingdom brings.

### Scope of Jesus' Mission

The omission in Luke of both Jesus' movement in Gentile territory during his ministry and his particularist statements about only going to "the lost sheep of the house of Israel" creates an interesting puzzle for anyone seeking to understand Luke's view of the scope of Jesus' mission and the salvation he came to bring. It is true that Luke does not use those passages in Mark that report Jesus' ministry in Gentile territory (Mark 7:24-30, 31-37). The setting of Peter's confession omits reference to Caesarea Philippi and leaves the impression, according to Fitzmyer, that Jesus is still in Galilee.[29] These omissions may be better understood when we combine them with the two accounts when Jesus does go or attempt to go into non-Jewish territory: Gadara or Gersera (Luke 8:26-39) and Samaria (9:51-56). On the first occasion he heals a demon-possessed person, and the work evokes such fear that all the multitude "of the region" ask him to leave (8:37; cf. Mark 5:17). In the second instance, the Samaritan villages will not receive him because he has set his face to go to Jerusalem. This pattern of movement and rejection probably should be understood according to Luke's "promise and fulfillment" salvation history framework. The Messiah must offer himself first to the Jews, for it is right that the people who

---

[28] Richard J. Dillon, "Easter Revelation and Mission Program in Luke 24:46-48," in *Sin, Salvation, and the Spirit: Commemorating the Fiftieth Year of the Liturgical Press*, ed. Daniel Durken (Collegeville, Minn.: Liturgical Press, 1979), 253.

[29] Fitzmyer, *Luke I–IX*, 773-74.

received the promise should be first to hear of its fulfillment (Acts 3:26; 13:46). Further, the climax of Jesus' mission is death in Jerusalem. This will offend the Samaritans with their competing place of worship. Therefore, Luke's omissions highlight the Jewish center of Jesus' saving mission.

Nevertheless, Jesus shows by his actions that the extent of his mission is not particularist; it is not to the Jew only but implicitly universal, to Jew and Gentile alike. He receives positively Gentiles who come to him (Capernaum centurion, Luke 7:1-10, cf. Matt. 8:5-13; the Gerasene demoniac, Luke 8:26-39/Mark 5:1-20; the thankful Samaritan leper, Luke 17:11-19). Jesus' declarations support the universal scope of the salvation offer. First, particularist statements are not present (Matt. 15:24; cf. Matt. 10:5b-6).[30] Second, universalist statements, either explicit or implicit, are consistently present throughout (Luke 4:25-27; 13:27-29; 14:21-24; 21:24). At the cleansing of the Temple, Luke omits the phrase "for all people" from Jesus' quotation "My house shall be a house of prayer" (19:46/Mark 11:17; Isa. 56:7). He did not do this to save Jesus the embarrassment of an incorrect prophecy, under the assumption that Luke wrote after the Temple's destruction, which occurred before all nations had been gathered to worship in it.[31] Rather, the Temple, which the Jews had coopted as a concrete symbol of ethnic pride, became, in Luke's presentation, an obstacle to God's saving purposes, especially in reaching the Gentiles. Hence, the Jewish Temple in Acts, while still a place for pious Jewish Christians to worship (for example, Acts 2:46; 3:1; 21:26; 22:17), comes under critique and judgment (7:1-53; 21:30).[32]

Luke himself highlights the universal scope of Jesus' saving work through the prophetic word that Jesus is "a light for revelation to the Gentiles" (2:32), through the quotation of scripture that "all flesh will see the salvation of God" (3:6/Isa. 40:5), and possibly through the tracing of genealogy to Adam not Abraham (Luke 3:38).[33] From the very beginning, Luke consistently presents from Jesus' teaching the commendation of Gentile receptivity to his mission, often in contrast to Jewish rejection (4:25-27; 7:1-10; 10:12-16, 33; 11:30-32; 17:11-19). Luke holds together the Jewish focus of Jesus' mission and the

---

[30] Wilson's (*Gentiles*, 50) explanation that Luke could not reconcile the particularist statements with his universalism should be replaced with a view that Luke wished to avoid needless offense to his non-Christian Roman reading public.

[31] Contrast Marshall, *Luke*, 721.

[32] See William J. Larkin Jr., *Acts*, IVP New Testament Commentary Series (Downers Grove, Ill.: InterVarsity, 1995), 313.

[33] Donald Senior and Carroll Stuhlmueller (*The Biblical Foundations for Mission* [Maryknoll, N.Y.: Orbis Books, 1983], 260) label this Luke's signalling of the "universal potential of the Jesus-event."

universal extent (Jew and Gentile) through a salvation history pattern of displacement of Jew by Gentile in terms of degree of receptivity of the gospel. This displacement is not at the same time a replacement. Luke speaks of unbelieving Jews being shut out while those from the ends of the earth enter the kingdom to eat the messianic banquet (13:28-29, cf. Matt. 8:12). Luke alone has a second call to the uninvited, this time presumably to the Gentiles, so that God's house may be full and no room left for the initially called, that is, Israel (Luke 14:23-24, cf. Matt. 22:10). Luke alone of the synoptic writers presents the time between Christ's first and second coming as "the times of the Gentiles" (Luke 21:24).

According to Luke, the results of Jesus' mission involve a number of surprises. First, Luke delights in bringing the good news that the salvation begins "Today!" (4:21; 19:9; 23:43). The two parables of the kingdom he does include point to the surprisingly large result of the mission when compared with small beginnings (13:18-21). Yet, once again surprisingly, Jews who are expecting the kingdom miss it and are displaced by Gentiles who are not initially seeking it (13:22-30). So fewer of those who were waiting for the kingdom (Jews) actually find it, while those who were originally not invited (Gentiles) actually enter it.

## JESUS THE SENDING ONE

Although the emphasis in Luke's gospel is on the mission of Jesus, Luke also presents Jesus sending out his disciples. The disciples take part in two missions during Jesus' earthly ministry, and they are sent out to the ends of the earth for a worldwide mission after the resurrection of Jesus.

### The Disciples' Mission during Jesus' Earthly Ministry: Centered on Israel

Luke points out that during his earthly ministry Jesus called disciples to be "fishers of men," that is, sent on mission to bear witness to the kingdom and call others into it (5:10-11; 8:39/Mark 5:19-20; Luke 9:60; cf. Matt. 8:22; cf. disciples when called are "named apostles" in Luke 6:13/Mark 3:16).[34] The gospel writer has two mission events for Jesus' disciples during his earthly ministry (Luke 9:1-6; 10:1-16). Luke presents these less as training missions than as an integral part of Jesus' own ministry. The first is a multiplication of Jesus' ministry, in which the disciples, with the same power and authority to cast out demons and heal, go "everywhere telling the good news and healing" (9:2, cf.

---

[34] Gill, "Observations," 212.

Mark 6:7; Luke 9:6/Mark 6:12-13). Luke goes on immediately and explicitly to identify this ministry as the cause of Herod's anxiety about Jesus (Luke 9:7-8). Luke also tells us that Jesus sent out the seventy-two as an advance team to villages he was about to enter (10:1). Since these seem to be Jewish villages, the seventy-two, as messianic fore-runners, are to heal the sick and declare that "the kingdom of God has drawn near" (10:9, cf. Matt. 10:7-8). What Luke emphasizes about this mission is its urgency (Luke 10:4) and its personal eschatological significance for those who receive or reject the messenger (10:6, 11-12, 16). At the same time Jesus relativizes the importance of the imme-diate results of the mission, that is, Satan's defeat in the mighty deeds of the disciples. For the messenger as well as the recipient, what is of utmost blessing is the personal embracing of the kingdom, the knowl-edge of a future place in heaven (10:17-20).

### The Disciples' Post-Resurrection Mission: "To the Ends of the Earth"

Any discussion of Jesus' command in Luke's gospel concerning a mission to the ends of the earth must wrestle with a curious combina-tion of evidence. On the one hand, Luke presents Jesus' saving work and mission as having an intended scope of universal application (2:30-32; 3:6; 4:16-30). Yet Mark's two references in Jesus' pre-cross teach-ing to the post-resurrection universal mission of his disciples are miss-ing from Luke (Mark 13:10; 14:9). The latter omission may be because Luke has chosen to report a similar story of a woman's care for Jesus at an earlier point in his gospel, and that story does not include Jesus' allusion to the gospel being preached and the woman remembered (Luke 7:36-50). In Jesus' eschatological discourse the former reference to the necessity of the gospel proclamation to all the nations is omitted, but not because Luke is adjusting Mark's eschatological understanding of the role of the Gentile mission in determining the end.[35] Rather, fur-ther probing of Luke's eschatology by scholars who tested Conzelmann's famous contention that Luke transformed Jesus' apoca-lyptic perspective into a salvation history one has led to the suggestion "that Luke recognized the eschatological content of such texts as Luke 1:32-33; 2:38; and Acts 2:17-21 and equated the church age with the inaugurated messianic kingdom."[36] Why, then, did Luke not use Mark 13:10? The question should be divided into two. Is there evidence else-where in Luke 21 for a post-resurrection Gentile mission? How does its expression differ from the Markan declaration and why? The evi-dence for a predicted Gentile mission is in Luke 21:13 and 21:24. The first verse is in a setting equivalent to the immediate context of Mark

---

[35] Contrast Wilson (*Gentiles*, 47, 54), who follows Conzelmann.

[36] D. C. Allison Jr., "Eschatology," in *DJG*, ed. Joel B. Green and Scot McKnight (Downers Grove, Ill.: InterVarsity, 1992), 208.

13:10. The thrust of Jesus' statements at this point are that there will be persecution, even official opposition involving law court appearances. Luke reports that Jesus says that "this will turn out for a witness." Given Luke's consistent use of witness terminology to describe the disciples' mission (Luke 24:48; Acts 1:8, 22; 5:32), there could well be an allusion to the disciples' post-resurrection mission here. The other verse speaks of Jerusalem trodden down by the Gentiles until "the times of the Gentiles (*kairoi ethnōn*) are fulfilled." The Acts rendering of the great commission also occurs within the context of discussing "the times and seasons (*kairous*)" that lead up to the end (Acts 1:6-8). Luke 21:24, then, seems to give a slightly more explicit reference to the Gentile mission. How are these times, *kairoi*, opportune times, if not as the period during which the nations are evangelized?[37] Admittedly, the coupling of Gentile mission with the end does not seem to be as strong as Mark 13:10, but it is still present through this sequential presentation. The idea of completeness indicates that the times of the Gentiles will be concluded. A simple "and" links these completed times to the eschatological signs that immediately precede the return of the Son of Man (Luke 21:25, 27). Luke's presentation, then, at least hints at the determinative role the Gentile mission has in the arrival of the end. It portrays the "between the times" according to his salvation history perspective by labeling it "times" that are completed. Mark describes the period in terms of an activity: world evangelization.

Luke alone of the synoptic writers has a possible allusion to the disciples' post-resurrection mission in his Last Supper discourse (22:35-38). Jesus' command about taking provisions—including, ironically, defensive weaponry—is built on a conscious contrast with his commissioning the disciples for a mission during his earthly ministry. "When I sent you out without purse, bag, and shoes, did you lack for anything?" When they answer, "No," Jesus responds with new commands on what to take, and the assumption seems to be that they will again be on mission. The hostility will increase so the preparations must be more thorough. The reason Jesus gives is his own impending suffering as an innocent, righteous one numbered with the transgressors in fulfillment of scripture (22:37/Isa. 53:12).

The one explicit great "commission" for the worldwide mission is in a post-resurrection appearance of Jesus. It is contained in the gospel summary that has framed much of our discussion (Luke 24:46-48).[38] What are the Lukan distinctives? The sender is the resurrected prophet,

---

[37] Vittorio Fusco, "Problems of Structure in Luke's Eschatological Discourse (Luke 21:7-36)," in *Luke and Acts*, ed. Gerald O'Collins and Gilberto Marconi (New York, N.Y.: Paulist Press, 1993), 87.

[38] Bosch (*Transforming Mission*, 91) notes that in form Luke 24:46-48 is not so much a mandate or commission as a statement of fact or a promise.

who can open the disciples' eyes to understand the scriptures, especially that they predicted the Messiah's death and resurrection (24:27,
32, 45). Moreover, they also predicted the universal mission of proclaiming repentance and forgiveness of sins in his name (24:46-47). So
participation in this mission fulfills scripture in the same way that
Christ's death and resurrection did. This sender promises an endow-
ment with power from the Holy Spirit, which is a pre-condition for
engagement in the mission (24:49; Acts 1:4, 8). For Luke, the promise
of the Spirit's presence is the reassurance Jesus gives that those sent are
not abandoned in their mission. The sent ones are more than the apostles
(Luke 24:33). From the way the commission is folded into the gospel
message, each succeeding evangelized generation becomes sent ones.
When individuals embrace the truth of a gospel, which proclaims that
"salvation applied" involves taking the message to all nations, they
naturally become proclaimers of the message.[39]

The task or activity of the mission focuses on preaching (kērussō).
There is no mention of healing, exorcism, or "signs and wonders"
ministries. What is proclaimed is summed up in two areas: the necessary response and the promised salvation blessings. This announcement of salvation applied, of course, is based on the foundation of
salvation accomplished in the death and resurrection of the Messiah.
The response called for is repentance, the turning away from a life of
sin and rebellion against God. Jesus' comments concerning repentance
in his parable of the rich man and Lazarus clarify why the command is
only to preach, not to preach and do the miraculous (16:30). The rich
man asks for the miraculous, for the return of Lazarus from the dead
to warn his brothers to repent so that they might avoid the place of
torment. Jesus contends that Moses and the prophets are enough. The
problem is not with the lack of evidence but with a calloused lack of
faith (16:29-31). So in the proclamation of salvation in the present
era, a witness to the fulfillment of the scriptures in the atoning death

---

[39] Guiseppe Betori ("Luke 24:47: Jerusalem and the Beginning of the Preaching to the Pagans in the Acts of the Apostles," in O'Collins and Marconi,
Luke and Acts, 120) brings this out most eloquently.

   It is an essential element of the identity of every church in every age
   that it carries to all nations the message which calls human beings to
   conversion. The church born as it is of the call which the risen Lord
   issues through his witnesses, experiences this finality "beginning from
   Jerusalem," that is, as already at work in the Christian community
   that comes into being in the city and is at the same time a model for
   every church.

   Dillon ("Easter Revelation," 244) says that those who view Christ's mission from the perspective of the resurrection will be "inevitably committed to
the mission of an Easter witness."

and victorious resurrection of Jesus Messiah is sufficient to evoke repentance and bring salvation blessings. Those salvation blessings are summed up in the phrase "forgiveness of sins." This liberation of all liberations means salvation as Zechariah foretold and Jesus announced and ministered (1:77; 4:18; 5:21, 23-24; 7:47-49; 23:34). The proclamation of repentance is to be made "in his name." The immediate and dynamic legitimation of the message comes from the authority of Jesus. The scope of the mission is clearly spelled out: "to all nations" (*panta ta ethnē*). Taken literally, it points to a target audience of all cultures, ethnic groups including the Jews, a truly comprehensive universal mission.[40]

## CONCLUSION

Luke proclaims the "salvation accomplished" portion of the gospel message in his gospel. Within a salvation history framework of promise and fulfillment, Jesus the Christ is sent by the Father to proclaim the good news of release and to accomplish a holistic but spiritually focused salvation. Even in this salvation history stage Luke forcefully portrays the scope of Jesus' mission: a Jewish focus during his earthly ministry but a universal extent (to both Jew and Gentile) in its "salvation applied" stage. Luke also presents Jesus as the sending one, as he sets in motion the key element in the "salvation applied" stage: commissioned heralds of the good news to the ends of the earth. With this gospel portrayal of Jesus' ministry Luke accomplishes the evangelistic purpose of his two-volume work. He not only expounds the gospel, but he gives persuasive warrant for it in the life and ministry of its central character, Jesus the Christ. Those who read the third gospel as Luke intended it to be read find themselves either evangelized or in possession of a document by which they may evangelize others. The gospel of Luke does mission.

---

[40] Wilson, *Gentiles*, 36, n. 4. Contrast Betori ("Luke 24:47," 111), who presents what is surely a minority opinion that the phrase in Luke-Acts never includes the Jews.

# 10

# *Mission in Acts*

## William J. Larkin Jr.

If the gospel of Luke manifests the traits of a "mission document" (see chapter 9), in what way does its companion volume Acts fulfill the same role? The third gospel evangelizes the Roman Theophilus by giving him assurance concerning the information he has received, that is, the accomplishment of salvation in the Messiah's divinely promised suffering and resurrection (Luke 1:1-4; 24:46). Acts finishes the task by granting assurance of the second half of the gospel message: salvation applied. It shows that repentance unto the forgiveness of sins has indeed been proclaimed in Jesus' name among all the ethnic groups (Luke 24:47).[1] In the process it addresses three important questions for a biblical theology of mission[2]: (1) What is the relation between the church and mission? (2) What is the relation between the worldwide mission of the church and the unique role the scriptures assign to Israel in God's saving purposes? (3) What is the relation between the Christian claims to a unique and exclusive salvation and the presence of such claims in non-Christian religions?

---

[1] According to Jacques Dupont ("The Salvation of the Gentiles and the Theological Significance of Acts," in *The Salvation of the Gentiles: Essays on the Acts of the Apostles*, trans. John R. Keating [New York: Paulist Press, 1979], 13), Luke's purpose for adding a second volume to his gospel was to demonstrate that the evangelization of the Gentiles is the fulfillment of messianic prophecy; cf. Lucien Legrand, *Unity and Plurality: Mission in the Bible*, trans. Robert Barr (Maryknoll, N.Y.: Orbis Books, 1990), 92.

[2] These questions are treated as part of the unfinished business of a biblical theology of mission in the following works: Ferdinand Hahn, *Mission in the New Testament*, trans. Frank Clarke, SBT, no. 47 (Naperville, Ill.: Alec R. Allenson, 1965), 170; Donald Senior and Carroll Stuhlmueller, *The Biblical Foundations for Mission* (Maryknoll, N.Y.: Orbis Books, 1983), 344-47.

## HISTORICAL SETTING

Among scholars who have dealt with the theological theme of mission in Acts there is unanimity that mission is very important, if not central, to Luke's purpose for the writing of Acts. They are equally unanimous in seeing Luke's use of mission as an edifying theme for the church of his generation.[3] Yet all of the scenarios concerning such an edifying occasion involve factors that may also be explained as circumstances for an evangelistic setting. Would not Acts' response to the theo-political rhetoric of Roman cultural supremacy also encourage an inquiring Roman to disregard the disdain of fellow Romans for this eastern cult and to embrace the gospel message concerning the reign of the true Lord of all (Acts 10:36)?[4] Would not any doubts Gentiles might have about the legitimacy of appropriating salvation blessings with Jewish roots make more sense if they came at the point of evangelism?[5]

The contention that Luke wrote Acts, in general, with an evangelistic purpose and, in particular, with a desire to confirm the truth of salvation's effective application to Gentiles is further supported by the rhetoric of characterization found in Acts. Whether the conversion account is of a group or an individual, of Jewish, mixed, or Gentile ethnicity, each highlights the desired response to the gospel and in that way fulfills an evangelistic purpose. For example, through Old Testament promise (2:21/Joel 2:32), through a description of the crowd's internal and external reactions (Acts 2:37, 41), and through Peter's explanation of the correct response to the salvation offer (2:38-40),

---

[3] Stephen G. Wilson, *The Gentiles and the Gentile Mission in Luke-Acts*, SNTSMS, no. 23 (Cambridge: Cambridge University Press, 1973), 95; Robert J. Karris, "Missionary Communities: A New Paradigm for the Study of Luke-Acts," *CBQ* 41 (1979): 93; David Tiede, "Acts 1:6-8 and the Theo-Political Claims of Christian Witness," *WW* 1 (1981): 41-51; Beverly Roberts Gaventa, "'You Will Be My Witnesses': Aspects of Mission in Acts of the Apostles," *Missiology* 10 (1982): 413-25; Senior and Stuhlmueller, *Biblical Foundations*, 276-77; Darrell L. Bock, "The Use of the Old Testament in Luke-Acts: Christology and Mission," in *Society of Biblical Literature 1990 Seminar Papers*, ed. David J. Lull (Atlanta: Scholars Press, 1990), 510; Legrand, *Unity and Plurality*, 92.

[4] Contrast Tiede, "Acts 1:6-8."

[5] Contrast Wilson, *Gentiles*, 248; Karris, "Missionary Communities," 80; Bock, "Use of the Old Testament," 510. Note that Bock begins his point with the phrase, "Theophilus as a Gentile either considering or more likely has responded to the Christian faith" needs reassurance he belongs in the movement. Bock does not explain why it is more likely Theophilus is already a Christian.

the Pentecost account serves not simply as a model to edify Christian witnesses but as an evangelistic call to non-Christians, in this case a Jewish group. Paul's conversion experience, reported three times throughout Acts (chaps. 9, 22, 26), includes a commissioning to missionary service. This might lead us to place Paul in the category of missionary model and to regard these accounts as oriented to the church's edification.[6] However, each succeeding account, while not abandoning the theme of Paul's commissioning, does bring out progressively more and more aspects of the gospel's "salvation applied" content (22:14-16; 26:16-18, cf. 26:22-23). By the time Luke arrives at Acts 26:29, Paul stands as a very explicit model of conversion.[7]

The other conversion experience reported multiple times concerns Cornelius, his household, and friends (10:1-11:18; cf. 10:7, 24; 11:14). Through commands in angelic visions and the Spirit's speaking, God takes the initiative in gathering the Cornelius group and bringing the messenger Peter to them (10:4-6, 22, 32; 11:14). Each successive telling of the vision gives more of the "salvation applied" content, including the values and responses worth emulating. The climax of Peter's speech links the Cornelius group to Acts' evangelistic purpose (10:42-43). The Holy Spirit affirms their saving hearing of the message by coming upon them while Peter is still speaking (10:44). Peter's spirited defense of his witness at Caesarea and his use of it to settle the dispute over circumcision also leave in the reader's mind a positive impression of this audience and its response to the gospel (11:1-18; 15:7-11). When these case studies are combined with a survey of the other conversion and witness accounts, particularly of individual Romans in Acts 16 and during the trial scenes (chaps. 24-26), it becomes increasingly apparent that Luke recounts these events in order to evangelize his reader. What is highlighted in each is not the example of the witness but its reception. In other words, each scene provides more detail about Lydia, the Philippian jailer, Felix, Festus, and Agrippa in their responses to the gospel message than about Paul in his method of witness. Luke, then, evangelizes his audience by giving an account that demonstrates the truth of the "salvation applied" portion of the gospel. Repentance and forgiveness of sins have been proclaimed effectively in Christ's name among all the nations. In the process, Luke also presents a model of mission Christians should learn to emulate.

---

[6] William S. Kurz, "Narrative Models for Imitation in Luke-Acts," in *Greeks, Romans, and Christians*, ed. David L. Balch, Everett Ferguson, and Wayne A. Meeks (Minneapolis: Fortress, 1990), 171-89.

[7] Robert L. Brawley, "Paul in Acts: Aspects of Structure and Characterization," in *Society of Biblical Literature 1988 Seminar Papers*, ed. David J. Lull (Atlanta: Scholars Press, 1988), 90-105.

## THE COMPLETED MISSION OF THE SON

Luke does not neglect the first half of the gospel: salvation accomplished. It is present in the speeches and summary statements about evangelistic work (for example, 2:23-32; 3:13-26; 4:1, 10-11; 10:36-41; 13:23, 27-37; 17:2-3; 18:5, 28; 24:15-21). However, it recedes somewhat into the background. What is to the fore is *mission*—salvation applied. Nevertheless, it is worth noting some of what Acts repeats and contributes concerning Luke's understanding of salvation accomplished.

### The Sender: God, Active Fulfiller of Prophetic Promise

In Acts, as in his gospel, Luke highlights the divine necessity of Jesus' mission according to the scriptures (his whole ministry, 13:23, 33; his death, 2:23; 3:18; 4:25; 13:27-29; 17:3; 26:23; his resurrection, 2:31; 13:34-37). He emphasizes God's active fulfillment of prophetic promises in these events (13:33). The ignorant yet culpable Jewish rejection of the Messiah through their crucifixion of him stands in contrast with God's determinant plan that his servant should suffer (2:23; 3:17-18; 13:27-29). Luke presents Old Testament prophetic proof of messianic resurrection as part of God's plan (2:25-32; 13:34-37) and lays out messianic suffering and resurrection as discussion points for Jews and God-fearers who would search the scriptures (17:3; 26:22-23). These emphases are possible only because of the resurrection, exaltation, and ascension of Christ and the outpouring of the Holy Spirit. The Easter revelation from the risen Lord in Luke 24 and the Spirit-filled preaching in Acts 2 and thereafter indeed lifted "the veil of mystery that hung over the teaching of the earthly Jesus concerning his destiny."[8]

What is further unveiled about the relation of the sender, God the Father, and the sent one, Jesus, is how active God was in Jesus' ministry. The Father "raises up" Jesus by bringing him onto the stage of human history, just as in the Old Testament he raised up prophets and kings to do his will (3:26, cf. 3:22/Deut. 18:15; Acts 5:30; 13:23, 33; cf. v. 22/1 Sam. 16:12-13).[9] Further, Luke characterizes Jesus' arrival

---

[8] Richard J. Dillon, "Easter Revelation and Mission Program in Luke 24:46-48," in *Sin, Salvation and the Spirit: Commemorating the Fiftieth Year of the Liturgical Press*, ed. Daniel Durken (Collegeville, Minn.: Liturgical Press, 1979), 244.

[9] Because of the use of terminology normally associated with Jesus' resurrection, it is common for commentators to take Acts 5:30 and 13:33 as references to that event. See, for example, I. Howard Marshall, *The Acts of the Apostles: An Introduction and Commentary* (Grand Rapids: Eerdmans, 1980), 119, 226. Contextual considerations, however, point in the direction of a general reference to Jesus' arrival in human history.

as God sending a "word" concerning the good news of peace and a "word" concerning salvation (Acts 10:36; 13:26). God works through Jesus during his earthly ministry in miraculous power as a foretaste of salvation blessings (2:22; 3:26; 10:38). No longer using the circumlocution of a "divine passive," Luke directly declares with reference to the resurrection that God, in contrast to humankind's death-dealing rejection, decisively and powerfully acts to raise Jesus from the dead (2:24, 32; 3:15; 4:10; 10:40; 13:30, 34, 37). In addition, God will send Jesus at his second coming to restore all things (3:20-21).

### The Sent One: Jesus, Lord and Christ

Luke describes Jesus' earthly mission—public ministry, death, resurrection, and his second coming—only within the confines of speech material, which are at the least in brief precis or summary form.[10] Therefore, there is little opportunity to develop much more about Jesus' mission beyond what is present in the third gospel. At the climax of the first speech, Peter speaking at Pentecost, Luke clearly trumpets Jesus' identity as "Lord and Christ" (2:36). By way of a new emphasis, Luke's use of christological titles in Acts presents more variety in describing Jesus' messianic role, especially with reference to his suffering and exaltation. He introduces "servant" (*pais*, 3:13, 26; 4:25, 27, 30), "holy and righteous one" (*hagios kai dikaios*, 3:14), and "prince" (*archēgos*, 3:15; 5:31). Though often obscured by its connection with other titles, Luke's use of "Lord" to designate Jesus as divine is consistently present in Acts (for example, 2:21, 36, 47; 4:33; 5:14; 8:25; 10:36; 11:17; 16:31, 32; 20:19, 21, 24, 28, 32, 35; 28:31). As in the gospel of Luke, the speeches of Acts present Jesus' earthly ministry as one of proclamation and miracle working (2:22; 10:36, 38) and its scope as including a Jewish focus but a universal extent (3:25; 5:31; 10:36; 13:23, 32-33; 26:23). But these components of Jesus' mission are clearly overshadowed by his suffering and resurrection, the heart of his saving work.

## THE CURRENT MISSION OF THE TRIUNE GOD

It is common to recognize that Luke's presentation of mission in Acts is less about the "Acts of the Apostles" than about the "Acts of the Holy Spirit," less about the mission of the church than about the mission of God.[11] Detailed study reveals how true these characterizations are. For Luke's narrative portrays each person of the Godhead as

---

[10] F. F. Bruce, "The Speeches in Acts—Thirty Years After," in *Reconciliation and Hope*, ed. Robert Banks (Grand Rapids: Eerdmans, 1974), 53-68.

[11] Wilson, *Gentiles*, 242; Gaventa, "You Will Be My Witnesses," 414-16.

a "sending one," both in commissioning and promoting mission. Each person of the Trinity is also a "sent one," a direct agent of mission, as well as a participant working through human agents. Finally, Luke does not hesitate to emphasize that the results of mission are divine results.

### Jesus and the Father and the Spirit as the Sending Ones

Luke does not limit commissioning to the direct report of the words of the risen Lord (Luke 24:46-48; Acts 1:8). In fact, neither of these statements is necessarily formulated as a command. The first is a statement of gospel content as the fulfillment of scripture, which includes the declaration: "Beginning from Jerusalem, you are witnesses of these things" (Luke 24:48). The latter, with its future tense formulation ("You shall be my witnesses"), could just as well be a prophetic promise.[12] Later, Peter tells Cornelius that divinely chosen eyewitnesses of the resurrection were commanded by the risen Jesus to warn about coming judgment (Acts 10:42; cf. Luke 24:47). Paul and Barnabas boldly announce to the hostile Jews at Antioch that "the Lord has commanded us" to declare good news to the Gentiles and indeed to the ends of the earth (Acts 13:47; cf. Luke 24:47; Acts 1:8). Paul, that "untimely born" apostle, is constantly aware of his divine commission (20:24; 26:16, 18). Indeed, the Father and the Spirit were involved in it (13:2, 4; 22:14-15). Peter, too, is aware of a divine commissioning at a key point during his ministry. God had chosen that through his mouth the Gentiles might hear the word of the gospel and believe (15:7). As Luke recounts the divine commissioning, it is the Spirit who tells Peter to go with the emissaries from Cornelius, not asking any questions for he has sent them (10:19-20). The book of Acts climaxes with Paul's declaration through a "divine passive" that "to the Gentiles this word of salvation is sent" (28:28).

The Triune God is the sending one par excellence, enabling and guiding faithful witnesses through adversity, the crossing of cultural thresholds, and any other impediment to the progress of the gospel to the ends of the earth. The Lord Jesus appears to Ananias and sends him to Paul in order to confirm and empower him in his conversion and calling (9:10, 17). By his angel the Lord leads Peter out of prison, so that he may "go to another place," presumably to continue his witness (12:17). Twice when facing adversity Jesus appears to Paul and encourages him to "keep on witnessing" (18:9; 23:11). God the Father declares the ritual purity distinctions null and void and from this Peter learns that God desires to remove any ethnic barrier to the hearing of the gospel (10:15, 28). God also guides in mission onto a

---

[12] C. K. Barrett, *A Critical and Exegetical Commentary on the Acts of the Apostles*, ICC (Edinburgh: T & T Clark, 1994), 1:79.

new continent, as Paul and his party interpret the vision of the Macedonians' call for help as "God summoning us to evangelize them" (16:10). Indeed, God the Holy Spirit is most active in guiding the church across cultural and geographical boundaries (8:29, 39; 16:6-7; 19:21).[13] The Spirit also promotes "unstoppable mission" in the face of impending adversity by preparatory testing of the witness's resolve (20:22-24; 21:4, 11, 13-14). Divine messengers also promote mission through guidance and comfort (8:26; 10:3; 27:23-25) and liberation for further witness (5:19-20; cf. 12:7, 11).

### Divine and Human Sent Ones

Luke lets his readers know from the very first verses of Acts that the agents of mission will be both divine and human. Describing the gospel of Luke as the first work about "all that Jesus began to do and to teach" (1:1) creates the expectation that he will continue to be on mission in this second volume. Luke almost immediately introduces human agents (1:2) and often describes a divine-human synergism in the prosecution of mission (for example, 2:4; 4:8, 29-31; 13:9; 19:11). Yet as the narrator unfolds the advance of the church in mission, the Triune God is consistently present, directly applying salvation blessings.

It is the exalted Lord who grants repentance and forgiveness to Israel (5:31) and pours out the Spirit (2:33). Luke describes conversion as the Lord opening an individual's heart (16:14), as the Lord's hand being with his witnesses (11:21), and as the Lord adding daily those being saved (2:47). The "divine passive" occurs in descriptions concerning large numbers of people "being added to the Lord" (5:14; 11:24). Jesus validates the "word of his grace" with miracles (14:3). So directly is he involved with these salvation blessings that the human agent will say to the sick: "Jesus Christ heals you!" (9:43). Moreover, Jesus is there in judgment, as the hand of the Lord is against those who oppose the progress of the mission (13:11).

The apostolic preaching sees the Father in mission as he "commands all men everywhere to repent" (17:30) and "calls" Jew and Gentile to himself (2:39). Salvation blessings come directly from him, whether repentance or the Holy Spirit or the miraculous (3:13; 11:17-18; 15:8; 19:11). Of particular interest to Luke is the Father's involvement in the Gentile mission. Using Old Testament salvific terminology, James tells how God first "visited" to take a people from among the Gentiles (15:14). Luke never tires of celebrating what God had done for the

---

[13] On the ambiguity of the reference to "spirit" (Paul's spirit or the Holy Spirit) in Acts 19:21, see William J. Larkin Jr., *Acts*, IVP New Testament Commentary Series (Downers Grove, Ill.: InterVarsity, 1995), 279.

"apostles" on the first missionary journey and beyond, opening a door of faith for the Gentiles (14:27; 15:4, 12; 21:19).

The work of the Holy Spirit is normally presented synergistically as witnesses filled with the Spirit speak the saving message and the response, whether positive or negative, manifests that God is at work (2:4, 37-41; 4:8, 13; 6:5, 10; 7:54, 57). One time, however, through Peter's proclamation, the claim is made that when the gospel is preached the Spirit is bearing direct parallel witness (5:32). Though angels often promote mission through supernatural guidance, there is only one instance when they are directly involved in mission. In that case it is a mission of judgment: Herod's death (12:23).

A final divine agent of mission is "the word of the Lord." Luke characterizes the advance of mission as the word of the Lord growing, especially in the context of human opposition (6:7; 12:24; 13:48-49; 19:20). This image does not simply describe the spread of the Word. It points to the life-giving power of the Word of the gospel. Legrand notes, "The church is animated by this Word living within it. The latter impels it to the fore. It finds its identity and cohesion in this Word, and this continual new beginning to the point that Luke unconsciously interchanges the terms . . . church . . . and . . . the Word."[14]

In his commission/promise, Jesus identifies the human agents by the second person ("You are witnesses," Luke 24:48; "You shall be my witnesses," Acts 1:8). The immediate context identifies the audience addressed as the apostles but also those with them who were witnesses of appearances of the risen Christ and therefore eyewitnesses of the resurrection (Luke 24:33; Acts 1:2, 6). In the book of Acts these two groups, but especially the apostles, are featured as on mission, bearing witness to salvation accomplished and applied in the suffering, risen, and exalted Christ (2:32, 37; 3:15; 4:2, 33; 5:20-21, 32, 42; 8:25; 10:42-43; 13:31). Yet this does not circumscribe the circle of witnesses, since Luke's very wording of the gospel message transforms all who embrace that message into witnesses (Luke 24:46-48). For it stands written that the way salvation is to be applied is that repentance and the forgiveness of sins are to be preached in Christ's name among all the nations. After receiving this message, each believer is compelled to ask, How may I be a part of this promise becoming true? The answer is by becoming a witness. Acts bears out this perspective, since the human agents of mission also include evangelists and missionaries (Philip, Acts 8:5, 12, 35, 40; Barnabas and Paul, 13:2; 14:4, 14; but quintessentially Paul, 9:20; 20:25; 28:31). Beyond this, ordinary Christians are on mission, even when scattered by persecution (8:4; 11:20).

Scholars often point to the anomalies that Luke seems to have created concerning the human agents of mission. With reference to their

---

[14] Legrand, *Unity and Plurality*, 92.

seeming lack of prompt obedience to the risen Lord's last commission/
promise, Peter's "conversion" to a direct Gentile mission points up the
strongly ingrained Jewish antagonism to the Gentiles, which probably
caused the delay in the Gentile mission.[15] Another difficulty concerns
Paul's apparent role as a mainly "non-apostolic" missionary, which is
anomalous with his apostolic self-understanding in his epistles. It would
be wrong to conclude with Hahn that Paul has been transformed into
a prototype for the post-apostolic church's missionary activity.[16] Rather,
Luke does present Paul's unique position as an apostle who was distinct from the twelve but who indeed received his commission from
the risen Lord, albeit from heaven (9:1-19; 22:6-16; 26:12-18).

### The Task of Mission

As might be expected in a work that focuses on "salvation applied,"
Acts presents a constellation of themes which expound the activity of
mission. Again, they derive their distinctive emphases from Luke's expression of the risen Lord's commission/promise (Luke 24:47; Acts
1:8). The preaching of the gospel in the power of the Spirit is the primary activity and character of the missionary task.

#### Activity

Luke 24:47-48 gives the twin themes of proclamation and witness.
Whether presented as "proclamation" (*kērussō*) or "announcement of
good news" (*euangelizomai*, cf. *katangellō*) or "witness" (*martureō*
and cognates), the missionary's primary activity is to tell "the truth to
the world about God's action in Christ."[17] This includes a declaration
of the Messiah and the saving events of his mission, especially his death
and victorious resurrection (2:32; 3:15; 4:2, 33; 5:32, 42; 10:41; 13:34).
Also present is the announcement of proffered salvation blessings, sometimes summed up in the phrase "kingdom of God" (8:12; 20:25; 28:31),
sometimes identified as "forgiveness of sins" (10:43; 13:38; 26:18).
Some would see Luke's understanding of salvation blessings as encompassing the total person (*aphesis* as both forgiveness and release

---

[15] Harold Dollar, *St. Luke's Missiology: A Cross-Cultural Challenge* (Pasadena, Calif.: William Carey Library, 1996), 170. The suggestion of Legrand
(*Unity and Plurality*, 99-101) that there was a priority commanded for a
Jewish mission in Jerusalem and Judea and Samaria, which explains the "delay," has merit. The solution of Wilson (*Gentiles*, 93) that the problem arises
because Acts 1:8 is a Lukan creation seems to rest on the assumption that the
apostles would have immediately obeyed the command if it had been given.
Dollar and Legrand give sufficient explanations for why they did not.

[16] Hahn, *Mission*, 134; cf. Senior and Stuhlmueller's more nuanced statement in *Biblical Foundations*, 271.

[17] Gaventa, "You Will Be My Witnesses," 417.

or liberation).[18] However, it is spiritual salvation that is Luke's consistent focus throughout Acts. Certainly there are miracles of "release" or healing, and indeed they point to the fullness of final salvation, which Jesus' death and resurrection assure (2:43; 3:1-10; 5:12-16; 9:32-42; 14:3, 8-10; 16:16-19; 19:11-12). Yet it is an "over-realized eschatology" that goes beyond Luke's understanding of the role of the miraculous in mission to insist that Acts teaches a type of "power evangelism" in which signs and wonders and healings are an essential component of the missionary's activity in effective witness.[19] For Luke, salvation may be applied with (9:35, 42; 14:3) or without (11:21; 13:43) extraordinary miraculous manifestations, and miracles may result in positive (8:5-8; 9:35, 42) or negative (14:8-20; 16:16-24) responses on the part of those who observe them. The miraculous is all at God's initiative according to his purposes, whether as a sign of his superior power (19:11-20) or a validation of the verbal witness (14:3) or a glorification of Jesus (3:13) or an evidence of the wholeness of salvation received by faith (3:16). Luke records the miraculous in cultural, especially animistic religious contexts, often where the gospel is entering for the first time (Samaria, 8:5-8; Lystra, 14:8-20; Philippi, 16:16-18; Ephesus, 19:11-20).

The preaching of Acts lacks an equal focus on salvation as liberation in socio-economic circumstances. For Luke, socio-economic liberation is a consequence of conversion. Those who enter the kingdom of God, the church, know its unity in the Spirit, which issues in the proper care of each other in all aspects of life (2:42-47; 4:32-37; 11:27-30; 16:15, 33-34; 20:34-35; 24:17).

When witness is born, not only to the facts of the saving events, but to their saving consequences and to the "prophetic argument" that elucidates the facts (2:32; 3:15; 10:42-43),[20] then believers other than the first apostles and eyewitnesses of those saving events may properly qualify as witnesses. Indeed, as Bosch points out, Luke's description of the church's mission activity in terms of witness is crucial for his "paradigm for mission."[21] For Luke, a call to witness is not a call to accomplish anything but simply to give testimony to what God has already done and is doing (salvation accomplished and applied). Furthermore, since Luke specifies that this can only be undertaken in the power of

---

[18] See, for example, David J. Bosch, *Transforming Mission: Paradigm Shifts in Theology of Mission*, American Society of Missiology Series, no. 16 (Maryknoll, N.Y.: Orbis Books, 1991), 107.

[19] Contrast C. Peter Wagner, *Lighting the World: A New Look at Acts, God's Handbook for World Evangelism* (Ventura, Calif.: Regal Books, 1995), 2:177-78.

[20] Dillon, "Easter Revelation," 254.

[21] Bosch, *Transforming Mission*, 116.

the Spirit, each succeeding generation of Christians can give witness with the same validity and power.

Two other descriptions of mission activity take into account the non-Christian audience's stance toward the gospel. First, complementing the bright motif of announcing "good news" is the dark theme of warning concerning the judgment to come or the cost of discipleship (*diamarturomai*, 2:40; 10:42; 20:21, 24; cf. 17:30). This is often given in contexts where opposition to the good news has arisen. Second, for Luke, the process of verbal witness also includes reasoning, discussion, dialogue, persuasion (for example, 17:2-4, 17; 18:4; 24:25). For the Jews, it is a matter of reasoning from the scriptures about the saving role of the Messiah in his death and resurrection (17:1-4); for the Gentiles, it may be matters foundational to that saving work: the reality of resurrection, morality, the coming judgment (17:17-18, 30-31; 24:25). The presence of this aspect of witness, together with the diverse examples of missionary preaching each adapted to its audience's level of understanding and needs,[22] manifests that Luke sees mission as a witness adaptable to culture with the message taking on different forms in different contexts.[23] This does not mean that Luke is assigning positive value to the audience's religious past so that Paul becomes the "pioneer of enculturation."[24] Rather, dialogue is always supportive of a proclamation function, which has at its heart a call to repentance from the ignorance and rebellion against the truth of God that non-Christian religions embody (14:15; 17:23, 29-30). Luke does not simply present the sharing of religious opinions in dialogue. Instead, the book of Acts shows respectful contact with integrity and the "give and take" of constructive and corrective engagement with non-Christian religions or world views, in which Christian witnesses reason in order to persuade others that their proclamation is true and should be embraced.[25]

---

[22] Contrast, for example, the proof from the Old Testament scriptures approach to Jews and God-fearers in chapters 2, 10, 13 with the argument from creation addressed to pagan Gentiles in chapters 14, 17.

[23] Gaventa, "You Will Be My Witnesses," 422.

[24] Contrast Legrand, *Unity and Plurality*, 111. Nor is this an indication of a liberal and magnanimous assessment of Gentiles pre-Christian religiosity. Contrast Wilson, *Gentiles*, 217.

[25] William J. Larkin Jr., "The Contribution of the Gospels and Acts to a Biblical Theology of Religions," in *Christianity and the Religions: A Biblical Theology of World Religions*, ed. Edward Rommen and Harold Netland, EMS Series, no. 2 (Pasadena, Calif.: William Carey, 1995), 84-87; Cf. I. Howard Marshall, "Dialogue with Non-Christians in the New Testament," *Evangelical Review of Theology* 16 (1992): 28-47.

*Character*

It is not an overstatement to say, "The intimate linking of pneumatology and mission is Luke's distinctive contribution to the early church's missionary paradigm."[26] This occurs not only as the risen Lord consistently makes the coming of the Spirit a necessary precondition for the engagement in mission (Luke 24:49; Acts 1:4), but it is also explicit (1:8) or implied (Luke 24:47) in the commission/promise.

Luke highlights three aspects of the role of the Holy Spirit in mission: initiator, guide, and empowerer. The discussion of the divine sender in mission has dealt with the first two roles. With reference to empowerment, Acts is the occasion for much interpretational debate over the purpose of the Spirit's coming at Pentecost. Is it for empowerment for witness only?[27] Is it for the bestowal of salvation blessings indiscriminately now that Jesus is ascended to God's right hand? Is it some combination of the two?[28] Luke consistently ties together conversion, baptism, and the coming of the Spirit (Acts 2:38; 9:17-18; 10:44-48; 19:2-6). The separation of conversion and the Spirit's coming (8:12, 15-18; 9:6, 17-19; 19:2-6) does not point to a necessary second experience of empowerment for witness. The accounts in Acts have no set pattern (cf. 8:12, 15-18 and 10:44-48) and manifest different purposes. Paul, called to faith directly from heaven without human agency, needs Ananias to address him (9:1-19). Ethnically prejudiced believers (Jews) may need to know that regeneration has actually happened to the "out group" (Samaritans, 8:4-17). Believers with partial gospel understanding (disciples of John the Baptist knowing only his baptism) need to understand the Holy Spirit has actually come (19:1-7). The coming of the Spirit, according to Luke, was an all-embracing gift of salvation. Special empowerment for witness, often described as "being filled with the Spirit," is a part of the blessings of salvation and Luke sees it as normative for the church (2:4; 4:8, 31; 6:3, 10; 7:55; 13:9). What he points out about the empowerment is its

---

[26] Bosch, *Transforming Mission*, 114.

[27] This is the main Pentecostal and charismatic view. See, for example, Roger Stronstad, *The Charismatic Theology of St. Luke* (Peabody, Mass.: Hendricksen, 1984), 63-68.

[28] Max Turner ("'Empowerment for Mission'? Pneumatology of Luke-Acts: An Appreciation and Critique of James B. Shelton's *Mighty in Word and Deed*," *Vox Evangelica* 24 [1994]: 113) gives a helpful taxonomy of the options: (1) a charismatic gift exclusively for empowerment for mission, (2) a charismatic gift to mature the Christian, edify the church, as well as empower for mission, (3) an all-embracing gift of salvation and special empowerment for mission, both are normative for the church, (4) primarily the gift of salvation with special empowering as a more occasional and specific charisma within the more general saving gift.

universality in the church. Regardless of gender, age, or socio-economic status, those who call upon the name of the Lord for salvation can have, in fulfillment of Joel 2, the Spirit poured out on them to speak God's message (Acts 2:16-21). The empowerment manifests itself in effectiveness in witness, which brings positive results (2:37-41), though not always. God can be so at work through Stephen, who is full of the Spirit, that his hearers are not able to counter his wisdom (6:5, 10). Yet instead of embracing the message they eliminate the messenger (7:54, 57).

The witness context is often a context of opposition and adversity (4:1-7, 29; 9:23-25; 13:45; 14:2; 19:9). Indeed, the gospel's call to repentance assumes potential opposition. Hence, Luke often describes the manifestation of the power of the Holy Spirit in witness as a boldness (4:13, 29, 31; 9:27, 28; 13:46; 14:3; 19:8; 28:31). Heedless of the consequences, the witness speaks with candor the plain and whole truth of the gospel (20:20-21, 26-27).

### The Scope of Mission

For Luke, the gospel's most crucial component for his evangelistic purpose is its scope. He writes Acts to prove to Theophilus that the salvation the gospel offers is really for him. No wonder Hahn calls it Luke's "dominating theme" and Dupont traces through what Wilson calls programmatic texts about the Gentile mission and consistently finds them to be the fulfillment of messianic prophecy (1:8; 2:39; 3:25-26; 13:46-47; 15:14-17; 18:6; 28:25-28).[29] From Jesus' final promise (1:8), which sets the structure for Acts, to the last words of Paul (28:25-28), the momentum for mission is consistently directed outward toward all nations (for example, 10:1-11:18; 13:2-3; 14:27; 16:9-10). Even when the church deals with internal matters, often the issue is the Gentile mission and its effects on its Jewish-Christian component (11:1-18; 15:1-35; 21:17-26).

Luke's presentation of the universal scope of the mission, however, also raises questions about Luke's views concerning the finality of Jewish rejection and its relation to the Gentile mission and the proper treatment of Judaism in any generation. Some say that the rejection is final and that Luke sees no continuing mission to the Jews.[30] Others argue that Luke declares the mission a success according to God's purposes and views the church of Jewish remnant and Gentiles according

---

[29] Hahn, *Mission*, 136; Wilson, *Gentiles*, chap. 9; Dupont, "Salvation of the Gentiles," 33.

[30] See, for example, Joseph B. Tyson, "The Problem of Jewish Rejection in Acts," in *Luke-Acts and the Jewish People: Eight Critical Perspectives*, ed. Joseph B. Tyson (Minneapolis: Augsburg, 1988), 137.

to a "restoration-exclusion" model.[31] Others would say that Luke in a qualified way does see a Jewish final rejection by distinguishing between the official or corporate Jewish rejection of the gospel and the continuing possibility of reception of the good news by individual Jews.[32] Given the way Luke presents Paul, after Jewish rejection, repeatedly beginning his witness in a new place with the Jews, and given the open-ended nature of Luke's description of Paul's stance at the very last rejection (28:30, "receiving all who came to him"), interpreters should probably conclude that, for Luke, though the rejection of Jewish "officialdom" is final, the mission to Jews is not. This "rejection" is not the trigger for the Gentile mission. Rather, Luke seems to see them as two parallel missions in fulfilling the design of God's saving purposes to apply salvation to all the nations.[33]

With reference to the scope of mission, Acts also addresses the issue of religious pluralism. As previously noted, Acts presents the cultural adaptability of the Christian witness through respectful contact, yet with integrity, and through constructive and corrective engagement with non-Christian religions (14:8-20; 17:16-31; 19:23-40).[34] Luke's assessment of non-Christian religions, however, is negative. God has left a witness to humans in every culture that a beneficent creator God exists, one upon whom humans are dependent for their physical life (14:15-17; 17:24-28). Yet, the beliefs and practices of non-Christian religions reveal that they are the product of blind ignorance (17:23, 27) and foolish rebellion (14:14-15; 17:25-29). As Acts assesses it, "religion represents a rebellious response to God whose glory is arrayed before them in nature, history and conscience."[35] Humans are culpable for this wrong response to God's witness and need to repent now (14:16-17; 17:30). It should also be noted that Luke links, though tangentially, the demonic and non-Christian religions (26:18; cf. 8:7, 9-13; 13:6-12; 16:16-18; 19:13-16). Whether by coopting the Spirit's power (8:18-20; 19:13-16), discrediting the Christian witness (16:16-

---

[31] See, for example, Jacob Jervell, "The Divided People of God: The Restoration of Israel and Salvation for the Gentiles," in *Luke and the People of God: A New Look at Luke-Acts* (Minneapolis: Augsburg, 1972), 41-74.

[32] John B. Polhill, *Acts*, NAC (Nashville: Broadman, 1992), 544-45; cf. David P. Moessner, "Paul in Acts: Preacher of Eschatological Repentance to Israel," *NTS* 34 (1988): 101-3.

[33] In support of this point, note the past tense of Acts 28:28: "this salvation has been sent to the Gentiles."

[34] As Lucien Legrand ("The Unknown God of Athens: Acts 17 and the Religion of the Gentiles," *Indian Journal of Theology* 30 [1981]: 166) observes, Acts avoids two extremes: initial direct critical confrontation with the particulars of a religion, and treating the religion as fulfilled in Christianity.

[35] Mark Shaw, "Is There Salvation outside the Christian Faith?" *East Africa Journal of Evangelical Theology* 2, no. 2 (1983): 55.

17), or promoting direct opposition (13:8, 10; 16:19-22; 19:23-27), the demonically inspired and the practitioners of non-Christian religions resist the advance of the gospel.

## The Results of Mission

Luke portrays the advance of the church's mission both in terms of quantitative and qualitative results. There is quantitative response, growth in numbers, which is consistently noted throughout Acts (2:41, 47; 4:4; 5:14; 6:1, 7; 9:31; 13:43; 14:1; 17:4, 12; 18:10; 19:26; 21:20). Though the response is never 100 percent, there is a continuing positive response, so that what Luke says of the Jerusalem church in the early days, he deems a true description of the church in any day: "and the Lord was adding to their number daily, those who were being saved" (2:47).

Equally important was the qualitative growth. Not only was there a solid response to the gospel of faith and endurance (2:47; 4:4; 8:12; 9:42; 14:27; 16:34; 18:8; cf. 11:23; 13:43; 14:23), but there was also a fruitfulness in the lives of the repentant leading to holiness (11:18; 19:18-19; 26:20), joy (8:8, 39; 13:48; 16:34), unity (2:46; 4:24, 32; 5:12), and mutual care (2:42-47; 4:32-37; 11:27-30; 16:15, 33-34). As is often pointed out, though conversion may be personal, a convert is enfolded into the Christian community, which results in consequences that are corporate as well.[36]

## Salvation History Framework

Luke sets salvation accomplished and applied within a "promise and fulfillment" salvation history framework as he introduces the gospel message with the simple phrase: "Thus it is written" (Luke 24:46). Proof from prophecy that substantiates the Gentile mission is such a widespread phenomena in Acts that Luke's readers can hardly miss the point. This offer of salvation to them is according to God's plan (Acts 2:16; 3:25; 13:47; 15:17; cf. also the allusions at 1:8; 2:39; 10:34; 15:14; 26:17; 28:28).[37]

If the salvation history framework can bring assurance concerning the desire of God for the salvation of people from all nations by linking past and present, it can bring a sense of urgency by linking the present time of proclamation to the future. Sometimes the urgency and decisiveness of the present moment of proclamation spring from

---

[36] Bosch, *Transforming Mission*, 117.

[37] Wilson, *Gentiles*, 243; cf. Bock's ("Use of the Old Testament," 506-9) analysis of the way Christology is made the foundation for mission in the "proof from prophecy" portions.

the good news that God is now pouring out his Spirit on all flesh in this time of refreshing (2:17; 3:20). Most often, the future end of history is portrayed as a time of reckoning, the last judgment. This message is especially addressed to Gentiles, whom God has let go their own way and overlooked their past sinful ignorance (14:16; 17:30). Now, however, the risen Christ has commanded his eyewitnesses to warn others about this coming judgment and to call those in all cultures to repent (10:42). In fact, his resurrection is the proof that he will return as judge (17:31). Thus, the missionary will speak to the resistant pagan of "sin, righteousness, and coming judgment" in the hope that fear might issue in faith and repentance (24:25).

Finally, for the Christian on mission the salvation history framework gives significance to a life of witness. For scripture prophesied this mission in the same way that it foretold the Messiah's death and resurrection (Luke 24:44-47). Thus, a person on mission is "making history," as the immediate context of Acts 1:8 also implies (1:6-7).

## CONCLUSION

In writing Acts Luke evangelizes Roman Theophilus concerning the truth of the "salvation applied" portion of his gospel message. In the process of demonstrating that the proclamation of repentance and forgiveness in Jesus' name among all the nations is according to God's prophetic plan and has indeed occurred, Luke also teaches about God's desires for the church concerning mission. Luke does not neglect the "salvation accomplished" portion of the gospel: the Messiah must suffer and rise from the dead. However, the main focus is on "salvation applied"—the church in mission taking the gospel to the ends of the earth. Luke constantly reminds us that this is the mission of the Triune God. Not only does he send and guide his missionaries (apostles, witnesses to the resurrection, evangelists, believers), but he is directly calling people to himself as his word grows and the number of his people increases. The activity of mission is bold proclamation and witness by the power of the Spirit to salvation accomplished and offered. The scope of mission will take the witnesses to all nations. This includes the Jews and adherents of non-Christian religions. The Jewish mission continues. Non-Christian religions evidence sinful humanity's blind ignorance and foolish rebellion. The result of mission will be the quantitative increase of the people of God manifesting a quality of life by the power of the Spirit, a life in community, a life of faith, endurance, joy, unity, and mutual care. Since all this is according to God's plan, those who hear the message must embrace it urgently, since it is decisive for their eternal destiny, and those who proclaim it know they are engaged in the most significant work in history.

What is the application of Luke's teaching on mission in Acts to today? Many of the distinctive features of his teaching are relevant to the prosecution of witness in the present time: the necessary empowerment with the Spirit, the appropriate qualities of a witness, the importance of boldness in the midst of adversity, and the contextualized preaching of the gospel to non-Christian philosophies and religions. One theme particularly stands out: the theocentric nature of the mission in its commissioning, agency, and results. Luke would remind us when our attention is so focused on human stratagems for what we are going to do for God in mission, that, first to last, Christian mission is the mission of God. God calls and sends his servants on mission. He himself is on mission, opening individual hearts and the door of faith to various ethnic groups. If Luke can help the late-twentieth-century church to recapture that understanding, then he will have enabled the church to engage in mission authentically. In this way the truth will once again be demonstrated that it is "in Christ's name," by his power, that repentance and forgiveness of sins are proclaimed and salvation is effectively applied to all the nations.

*PART FOUR*

# THE GENERAL EPISTLES AND JOHN'S WRITINGS

# 11

## *Mission in the General Epistles*

## Andreas J. Köstenberger[1]

The General Epistles do not contain the Great Commission, glowing accounts of the early church's missionary successes, or elaborate strategies of Christians' gospel proclamation. At first glance some may therefore conclude that the documents grouped together rather amorphously under the heading "General Epistles" contribute little, if anything, to our understanding of mission.[2] This conclusion, however, is

---

[1] This essay is adapted from the present author's "The Contribution of the General Epistles and Revelation to a Biblical Theology of Religions," in *Christianity and the Religions: A Biblical Theology of World Religions*, ed. Edward Rommen and Harold Netland, EMS Series, no. 2 (Pasadena, Calif.: William Carey Library, 1995). A fuller version will appear in Andreas J. Köstenberger and Peter T. O'Brien, *Mission in the New Testament*, NSBT (Grand Rapids: Eerdmans, forthcoming).

[2] This appears to be the view of David J. Bosch, *Transforming Mission: Paradigm Shifts in Theology of Mission*, American Society of Missiology Series, no. 16 (Maryknoll, N.Y.: Orbis Books, 1991), who focuses on the contributions by Matthew, Luke, and Paul, arguing that these three NT authors are "representative of first-century missionary thinking and practice" (55). The scripture index to Bosch's work includes references to only three passages in 1 Peter while there is not a single reference to the book of Hebrews in the over five hundred pages of Bosch's work. This exclusive focus on the Matthean-Lucan-Pauline axis of mission in the NT, with its resulting marginalization of the contributions of books such as 1 Peter, is, despite Bosch's assertion to the contrary, clearly reductionistic and may lead to serious distortions of the message of the entire scriptures regarding the church's mission. Cf. also Bosch's otherwise fine article, "Reflections on Biblical Models of Mission," in *Toward the 21st Century in Christian Mission*, ed. James M. Phillips and Robert T. Coote (Grand Rapids: Eerdmans, 1993), 175-92, which does not contain a single reference to any of the General Epistles.

premature, since, as will be seen, some of these documents make important contributions to the biblical theology of mission. Indeed, the failure by some to find mission represented in the General Epistles may be the result of an unduly narrow definition of this term.[3] Even if mission may not be the primary focus, one can still draw helpful implications for mission from a few of these books.

The following essay will focus on the writings whose contribution to the subject at hand is judged the most substantial, Hebrews and 1 Peter.[4] James emphasizes internal congregational matters; 2 Peter and Jude are concerned for the most part with combating false teachers; 1 John primarily seeks to refute a proto-gnostic heresy; 2 John and 3 John are brief personal letters.[5] Although these epistles may make a minor contribution to our understanding of mission, Hebrews and 1 Peter are more directly concerned with Christians' role in their world, so it is profitable to examine the teaching on mission in these works.

---

[3] Cf. Donald Senior and Carroll Stuhlmueller, *The Biblical Foundations for Mission* (Maryknoll, N.Y.: Orbis Books, 1983), 311, n. 10, who argue, against Ferdinand Hahn, *Mission in the New Testament*, trans. Frank Clarke, SBT, no. 47 (Naperville, Ill.: Alec R. Allenson, 1965), 142, that mission should not be defined exclusively in terms of verbal proclamation.

[4] This procedure is confirmed by a careful reading of the documents themselves and by a bibliographical survey, which reveals that there is virtually no literature on mission in any of the General Epistles except the books considered here. On mission in Hebrews, see Edwin A. Schick, "Priestly Pilgrims: Mission outside the Camp in Hebrews," *CurTM* 16 (1989): 372-76. On mission in 1 Peter, see Werner Bieder, *Grund und Kraft der Mission nach dem 1. Petrusbrief* (Zollikon-Zürich: Evangelischer Verlag, 1950); M. Chin, "A Heavenly Home for the Homeless: Aliens and Strangers in 1 Peter," *TynBul* 42 (1991): 96-112; Reinhard Feldmeier, *Die Christen als Fremde: Die Metapher der Fremde in der antiken Welt, im Urchristentum und im 1. Petrusbrief*, WUNT, no. 64 (Tübingen: J. C. B. Mohr [Paul Siebeck], 1992), and the review by William L. Schutter, *JBL* 113 (1994): 743-45; M. E. Kohler, "La communauté des chrétiens selon la première épître de Pierre," *RTP* 114 (1982): 1-21; Dan O'Connor, "Holiness of Life as a Way of Christian Witness," *International Review of Missions* 80 (1991): 17-26; Birger Olsson, "Mission la Lukas, Johannes och Petrus," *SEÅ* 51 (1986): 188-89; Ralph W. Quere, "The AIDS Crisis: A Call to Mission Based on 1 Peter," *CurTM* 14 (1987): 361-69; P. J. Robinson, "Some Missiological Perspectives from I Peter 2:4-10," *Missionalia* 17 (1989): 176-87; V. R. Steuernagel, "An Exiled Community as a Missionary Community: A Study based on 1 Peter 2:9, 10," *Evangelical Review of Theology* 10 (1986): 8-18. Senior and Stuhlmueller (*Biblical Foundations*, 297-302) focus on 1 Peter while devoting a mere page to Hebrews, James, Jude, and 2 Peter combined, commenting that "the remaining books of the New Testament offer little material that bears directly on the issue of mission" (309-10). Ferdinand Hahn (*Mission*, 137-43) virtually neglects the General Epistles apart from a few cursory references to 1 Peter.

[5] The Johannine epistles are treated elsewhere in this volume.

It seems appropriate to begin by tracing the concept of mission as it is presented in the writings considered here. Some may fear that such a procedure could prejudge the actual investigation undertaken below. This objection may be met by responding that, first, this preliminary sketch will be based on the terminology and theology drawn from an initial reading of the respective works; second, that allowances will be made for specific mission emphases of different writers; and third, that the resulting basic description will be revisited at the end of the study to see whether it should be corrected or expanded in the light of the detailed analysis below.[6]

What is God's will for his people in the interim between Christ's first and second comings? What is to be Christians' mission? Generally, mission relates to believers' relationship to the world, specifically in terms of believers' proclamation of the Christian gospel message. This, of course, may be accomplished by verbal preaching or by more indirect means, such as the witness of a holy life or of God-honoring relationships. A reading of the two books under consideration here with a view toward locating mission emphases yields the following insights:

1. Mission involves relevant aspects of the church's identity in Christ that are crystallized by its location in a certain historical, cultural, and theological context (for example, the acknowledgment of the supremacy of Christ in Hebrews or believers' holiness in 1 Peter).

2. The mission of God's people in the world may take on the form of either direct outreach or life witness or be a combination of both (Heb. 12:14; 1 Pet. 2:12; 3:15).

---

[6] This study will therefore proceed inductively from the mission terminology and theology found in the General Epistles (excluding the Johannine epistles). It is, of course, impossible to approach the study of a subject without a clear understanding of what one sets out to explore. The general definition of mission provided at the outset of the present volume may serve as an overall frame of reference, but it is also necessary to locate the concrete, specific concept of mission used by the respective writers of the New Testament. Senior and Stuhlmueller (*Biblical Foundations*, 3) provide an example of a definition that is unduly broad, if not ambiguous, when they define mission as "the God-given call to appreciate and share one's religious experience and insights, first within one's own community and tradition, and then with people and communities of other cultural, social, and religious traditions." Bosch (*Transforming Mission*, 8-11) somewhat misleadingly entitles an early section in his book "Mission: An Interim Definition." What this author provides, however, is not a definition of mission but a kaleidoscope of thirteen assertions regarding mission. When returning to definitional matters, Bosch is even more skeptical about the possibility of defining mission, contending that this may be possible merely by "imaginative creation or representation of evocative images." At another place, Bosch simply quotes a definition provided by Hahn (*Mission*, 54).

3. Believers' response to suffering and persecution at the hands of individual unbelievers or by political authorities is a significant statement to the world of believers' identity in Christ (Heb. 10:23-25, 32-39; 12:1-13; 13:12-13; 1 Pet. 1:6-7; 2:13-17; 3:13-18; 4:12-19; 5:1, 7-10).

The remaining part of this chapter will analyze the aspects of the theology of mission common to both Hebrews and 1 Peter, as well as the distinctive contribution of each book. An attempt will be made to explore possible implications of this teaching for a biblical theology of mission.

## MISSION IN HEBREWS AND 1 PETER: COMMON ELEMENTS

At the outset, a few commonalities between mission in Hebrews and 1 Peter may be noted in order to substantiate the appropriateness of providing a common general description of mission in these books. To begin with, both books deal with the issue of how the church and individual believers should respond to sufferings and persecutions toward the close of the first century, whether in the empire's capital or in the provinces of Asia Minor. According to the respective authors, believers work out their Christian faith in adverse circumstances through submission to authority; nonretaliation; love of enemies; harmonious, loving, and unified relationships within the church; recognition of the heavenly calling of believers; and perseverance. In light of the challenges at hand, one finds little *direct* exhortation to the verbal proclamation of the gospel. These writings do, however, reflect a concern for believers' witness by way of a godly life in the midst of a largely hostile environment, in the hope that thus some may be won to the faith. The NT church, like OT Israel, is to fulfill a mediatorial function between God and larger humanity (1 Pet. 2:5, 9; cf. Exod. 19:6; Isa. 43:21).

Both books also accentuate the temporary nature and essential foreignness of the believer's life in this world. The followers of Christ are sojourners, aliens, and pilgrims, pursuing the path toward their permanent home, heaven (Heb. 11:9, 13; 1 Pet. 1:1, 17; 2:11). Christian living in general, and the suffering of persecution for one's faith in particular, are thus set into a pointedly eschatological perspective. In the light of Christ's imminent return, the transitory nature of believers' afflictions is made visible. This comfort renders hardships more bearable, while focusing attention also on the rewards of eternal fellowship with Christ, promised to those who persevere. Moreover, both writings evidence an increased emphasis on God's final judgment.[7] This

---

[7] The terms "judge" (verb: *krinō*; noun: *kritēs*) and "judgment" (*krisis*) are found in Hebrews 9:17; 10:27,30; 12:23; 13:4; 1 Peter 1:17; 2:23; 4:5,6. To this should be added references to the "last day(s)" (Heb. 1:2; 10:25; 1 Pet. 1:20; 2:12), "the end of all things" (1 Pet. 4:7), and the return of Christ (1 Pet. 1:7,13; 4:13). Cf. Hahn, *Mission*, 142.

eschatological perspective determines the framework for the church's ordering of its external relationships. In the midst of their suffering, believers are reminded of their enduring heavenly inheritance, which puts their ordeal in proper perspective: it is merely temporary, and it should be seen as an opportunity for witness. This encompasses a variety of earthly relationships; as slaves of unbelieving masters, as wives of unbelieving husbands, as citizens of an anti-Christian state, believers are called to "submit" while testifying courageously to their Lord.

Finally, both authors accentuate the supremacy and uniqueness of Christ. According to the writer of Hebrews, Jesus is the captain of our salvation, the once-for-all sacrifice, the great high priest. For Peter, Jesus is the suffering servant of Isaiah who, in fulfillment of Old Testament typology, "bore our sins in his body on the cross" (1 Pet. 2:24).[8]

## MISSION IN HEBREWS

The book of Hebrews is an unlikely candidate to be consulted regarding its teaching on mission. Most would think of this epistle as solely concerned not with the church's relationship to the world but with internal matters. However, it was precisely because of external pressures and persecution for Christ's sake that some apparently were tempted to revert back to Judaism in order to escape such affliction. After setting the scene, I will highlight some of the major themes of the book that have a direct bearing on the book of Hebrews' contribution to a biblical theology of mission.

Hebrews is a homily, a word of exhortation (13:22), presented in the form of an artistically crafted epistle. As mentioned, the book appears to be directed toward a congregation in danger of drifting from its Christian faith back to Judaism. Probably written in Rome (13:14), the epistle was composed by an unknown second-generation believer (2:3), perhaps shortly before the destruction of the Jerusalem Temple in 70 C.E. In the face of this temptation to apostatize from the faith, probably due to the threat of imminent suffering, the author sets out to convince his readers of the superiority of Jesus and of the priesthood he instituted.[9] The letter thus serves to confirm the commitments

---

[8] On Christological emphases in Hebrews and 1 Peter, see especially Harald Hegermann, "Christologie im Hebräerbrief," 337-52, and Eduard Schweizer, "Zur Christologie des ersten Petrusbriefs," 369-82, both in *Anfänge der Christologie: Festschrift für Ferdinand Hahn zum 65. Geburtstag,* ed. Cilliers Breytenbach and Henning Paulsen (Göttingen: Vandenhoeck & Ruprecht, 1991).

[9] For a defense of these ideas concerning the date and setting of Hebrews, see Donald Guthrie, *New Testament Introduction,* 4th ed. (Downers Grove, Ill.: InterVarsity, 1990), 682-705; D. A. Carson, Douglas J. Moo, and Leon Morris, *An Introduction to the New Testament* (Grand Rapids: Zondervan, 1992), 397-404.

of a community that may have suffered religious and social ostracism, while insisting that those values require engagement in, not separation from, an antagonistic society.

The following discussion will center on the following relevant themes for mission: the speaking God, Father and Son, the supremacy of Jesus, "witness" and "race" terminology, and Christians' identity in this world as "pilgrims." Especially in the opening chapters the author of Hebrews presents God as a God who speaks and is active in mission "today." Mission takes place within the framework of God's salvation history, and for the writer of Hebrews the supremacy of Jesus is central to the proper understanding of God's work of salvation. The writer of Hebrews uses "witness" terminology and the metaphor of a "race" to clarify the nature of the mission task and the expression "pilgrim" to explain the status of believers in the world around them.

### The Speaking God[10]

The author of Hebrews portrays God as the God who speaks. Long ago he spoke to the fathers through the prophets at various times and in many ways; in these last days he has spoken by a Son (1:1-2). If disobedience to the word spoken through angels (that is, the Law) carried serious consequences, the recipients of Hebrews must pay even closer attention to what they have heard: the message at first spoken through the Lord, which was subsequently confirmed by those who heard and by God through signs and wonders and gifts of the Holy Spirit (2:1-4).

God is also speaking to the epistle's readers through scripture, particularly regarding the Son's superiority over angels (1:5-13; 2:5-8). Moreover, God, through the Holy Spirit, is speaking to the audience of Hebrews regarding Israel's experience in the wilderness (3:7-4:11): "Today, if you hear his voice, do not harden your hearts" (3:7-8). Since the psalmist reiterates God's call for "today," the author of Hebrews concludes that the original word addressed to Israel's wilderness generation had not yet exhausted its relevance in the psalmist's day. Moreover, God's message has continuing relevance even for the epistle's readers in their day: "For if Joshua had given them rest, he would not have spoken of another day after that. So there remains a Sabbath rest for the people of God. . . . Therefore let us be diligent to enter that rest, so that no one will fall, through following the same example of disobedience" (4:8-9, 11). As Paul commented in a similar passage, "these things happened as example for us" (1 Cor. 10:6).

---

[10] For some of the insights in the following two sections I am indebted to my student Raymond Bouchoc, "Mission in the Book of Hebrews," Seminar Paper at Southeastern Baptist Theological Seminary, Wake Forest, N.C., 1997.

The Hebrews' exhortation culminates in the statement that "the word of God is living and active and sharper than any two-edged sword" (4:12), once again drawing attention to the fact that the word of God is not antiquated or powerless but up-to-date and relevant. A later chapter chronicles in great detail the experiences of persons in the history of Israel, such as Abel, who through faith, though he is dead, "still speaks" (11:4).

To sum up: God has spoken to us in these last days through his Son, and he speaks to us through the experiences of God's people recorded in scripture. Indeed, God is alive (3:12; 9:14; 10:31; 12:22). This speaking, living, and active God is the one who sent Jesus and sustains a vital relationship with him.

### Father and Son

It is a well-known fact that John's gospel speaks of Jesus' relationship with God primarily in terms of a Father-Son relationship. It is not as widely known that the book of Hebrews likewise casts Jesus' relationship with God in those terms (see especially 1:5, quoting 2 Sam. 7:14). According to the author of Hebrews, Jesus, as the Son, came to do the will of his Father (10:7, 9; cf. Ps. 40:6-8). Jesus trusted his Father, serving as a model for all believers (Heb. 2:13; cf. 2:10; 12:4-13). As an expression of his sense of dependence, Jesus prayed to the Father, and, as the Son, he learned obedience through what he suffered (5:7-8). As far as his ministry is concerned, Jesus served the Father faithfully as a Son, including service as a priest in the Father's house (2:12, 17; 3:6). Thus the author of Hebrews consistently portrays Jesus as the Son of the Father, even the Son of God (4:14; 6:6; 7:3; 10:29).

However, the most striking aspect of the way in which the book of Hebrews portrays Jesus' relationship with God is not how the Son relates to the Father but how the Father relates to the Son. It is the Father who begot the Son (1:5; 5:5; cf. Ps. 2:7). The Father not only gave the Son dominion over the whole earth (Heb. 1:8) but also gave him authority over the angels (1:4), creation (1:10-12), and even the world to come (2:5-8). In that day, all of Jesus' enemies will be subdued (1:3; 10:13; cf. Ps. 110:1), so that what began with the incarnation of the Son culminates in the Son's everlasting dominion, in which all things are his as God the Father's rightful heir (Heb. 1:2). The Father crowned the Son with glory and honor (2:7); he raised him from the dead (13:20) and exalted him to his right hand (1:13; 8:1). All of this is the Father's doing. The writer of Hebrews exalts Christ and his work, but even in the exaltation of Christ the underlying truth is that all Christ is and does proceeds from the Father.

God is a speaking God, and it is he who, as the Father of Jesus, stands behind his entire mission, both in word and work. For the author of Hebrews, mission is conceived theocentrically, as rooted in God, carried out in complete dependence on him, even and especially in the midst of suffering. This is one of the major lessons regarding mission that the author of Hebrews seeks to impart to his readers.

### *The Supremacy of Jesus*

The author of Hebrews demonstrates Jesus' unique role in God's plan of salvation in no uncertain terms. The book opens with a number of startling claims regarding the supremacy of the revelation brought by Jesus and regarding the superior work and nature of Jesus. God's revelation in Jesus is superior, since God in ancient days spoke through prophets, while, in the last days, he spoke to us in revelation involving "a son" (1:1-2). Jesus' work is superior, since, through Jesus, God made the ages (1:2). Jesus also made purification from sin and sat down at the right hand of the majesty on high (1:2-3). Jesus' nature, too, is superior; he is the radiant splendor of God's glory and the exact representation of his nature (1:3). Finally, Jesus is superior to other spirit beings in nature, calling, and authority (1:4-2:18).

Jesus is presented as the great high priest (5:1-10:39; cf. 2:17), who was given an eternal priesthood according to the order of Melchizedek (5:1-7:28) and who instituted a new, superior covenant (8:1-10:39). The writer of Hebrews draws the implication that when Jesus "sat down" (1:3; 8:1; 10:12; 12:2), this indicated that there remained no further need for sacrifice. Complete atonement had been rendered (9:23-28). The question of how to deal effectively with sin is crucial, and Hebrews provides a powerful answer: Jesus has dealt once and for all decisively with sin. He has overcome the power of Satan. Regarding Israel, the extensive quotation of Jeremiah 31:31-34 with reference to Jesus (cf. Heb. 8:8-12; 10:16-17) implies that, now that a "new" covenant has been made and the "old" covenant is obsolete and no longer effective, Jews should find the fulfillment of God's promise of an eschatological covenant in Jesus.

### *"Witness" Terminology and the Metaphor of the "Race"*

Usually, one thinks of the term "witness" in the NT as something the church is enjoined to do with regard to Jesus Christ. In Hebrews, however, "witness" terminology is never applied to believers in the active sense of the term, that is, as a call for them to bear witness. Rather, it is God who bears witness to the faith of previous believers (11:2, 4, 5, 39; 12:1). The many verbal and allusive parallels to the intertestamental book of 2 Maccabees in 12:1-3 indicate, together with the exhortation of 12:4, that the author conceives of the Christian witness as one who is prepared to "resist to the point of shedding blood." This certainly was true for many of the believers mentioned in 11:32-38, as well as for martyrs of the Maccabean period. When facing the prospect of persecution, the Hebrew believers should therefore be inspired by the "great cloud of witnesses" who had gone—and suffered—before them (12:1), with Jesus, "the pioneer and perfecter of our faith . . . who endured such hostility from sinners against himself," as the supreme forerunner (12:1-3; cf. also 2:10; 6:20). Followers of Christ are to "hold fast to their confession" (4:14; 10:23) according to the example of "the Apostle and High Priest" of their faith (3:1).

By using the metaphor of a "race," even that of a marathon, the author urges his audience to view suffering as a form of divine discipline designed to perfect them as sons (12:5-11), just as Jesus himself learned obedience through suffering (2:10, 17-18; 5:7-9). This mindset would help believers persevere in their struggle as they "ran the race" by fixing their eyes on Jesus, just as he had fixed his eyes on God. Christians' primary focus, therefore, should not be on the world but, in Jesus, on God. The community's and the individual Christian's faithful practice of obedience is an essential prerequisite for mission.

On the heels of evoking the powerful image of the Christian life as a race run in front of spectators (thus highlighting the solidarity between all who ever ran the race), the author of Hebrews details a series of instructions that clarify the nature of the Christian's race. He exhorts his readers, "Pursue peace with all people, and the sanctification without which no one will see the Lord" (12:14; cf. Matt. 5:8, 9). External relationships and internal holiness thus belong together. Christians are to live lives of love, including the love of strangers, and, of course, marital love, in all purity (Heb. 13:1-2, 4). They are to remember prisoners as well as their leaders, imitating the latter's faith (13:3, 7). Also, believers are to bring "sacrifices" of praise and fellowship, offerings that are pleasing to God (13:16). For Jesus, God prepared "not sacrifices, but a body" (10:5-9). Jesus lived a life of total obedience to God; believers' entire lives, too, are to be consecrated to God and given wholly to God's service.

### Christians as "Pilgrims"

What is the identity of believers in this world? How might one describe their relationship to the world in which they live? According to the author of Hebrews, Christians are pilgrims, exiles in search of a homeland and of a better country, of "a city prepared by God" (Heb.

11:13-16; cf. 12:22).[11] The pilgrimage to an earthly sanctuary is replaced by people's pilgrimage to a lasting heavenly sanctuary (6:19-20). Israel's unbelief during the exodus is to serve as a warning against the Hebrews' disbelief during their new exodus (3:7-4:11; cf. 1 Cor. 10:6, 11). Abraham is presented as a model pilgrim: he set out not knowing where he was going, acting upon nothing but God's word of promise, living in tents like a foreigner, looking ahead to a permanent home, not in Palestine but in heaven (11:8-10).[12] Moses likewise scorned the fleeting pleasures of this world (11:24-29). According to the pattern set by Abraham and Moses, the readers of Hebrews were sojourners embarking on a new exodus, with their way led not by Joshua (4:8; Greek: *Iēsous*), but by Jesus (cf. 2:10; 12:2; Greek: *Iēsous*). As the author of Hebrews argues, the OT already contains the acknowledgment that, even after Israel had entered the Promised Land, there continued to remain a future rest for God's people (3:7-4:11; cf. Ps. 95:7-11). This new exodus, as well as the dispersion of believers (Heb. 1:1), is essential to the church's calling, since believers are to function as witnesses by living holy lives in the world (cf. Matt. 5:13-16).

The climactic exhortation of the entire book, transcending even Hebrews 12:1-3, is found in 13:13. After affirming that Jesus suffered outside the gate, the author exhorts his audience, "Therefore let us go out to him, outside the camp, and bear the abuse he endured" (13:13; cf. 10:25-26). Remarkably, ideas involving the "Temple" have been eclipsed in Hebrews by "tent" and "camp" terminologies.[13] Christians are to count it a privilege to follow the one "who for the joy set before him endured the cross, despising the shame" (12:2). Their mission is to have its root in this radical discipleship, which reveals itself in their close association with Christ, not just in his glory, but also in his sufferings (cf. 1 Pet. 1:11-12; 5:1).

---

[11] See Ernst Käsemann, *The Wandering People of God*, trans. Roy A. Harrisville and Irving L. Sandberg (Minneapolis: Augsburg, 1984); and Erich Grässer, "Das wandernde Gottesvolk: Zum Basismotiv des Hebräerbriefes," *ZNW* 77 (1986): 160-79. See also Raymond Brown, "Pilgrimage in Faith: The Christian Life in Hebrews," *Southwestern Journal of Theology* 28 (1985): 28-35; Robert Jewett, *Letter to Pilgrims* (New York: Pilgrim, 1981); William G. Johnsson, "The Pilgrimage Motif in the Book of Hebrews," *JBL* 97 (1978): 239-51; David W. Perkins, "A Call to Pilgrimage: The Challenge of Hebrews," *Theological Educator* 32 (1985): 69-81.

[12] Cf. Schick, "Priestly Pilgrims," 375. Schick's article is highly suggestive at many points, but in one point he surely overstates his case, i.e. when he claims that Hebrews presents believers as *priestly* pilgrims. Pilgrims they may be, but, according to Hebrews, only Christ is a priest.

[13] Ibid., 376.

### Implications

The mission of believers may take on different forms depending on the time and circumstances in which they find themselves. At times the church's mission will assume the form of some of its representatives going to other parts of the world and of preaching the gospel there. At other times believers may simply be called to identify with Christ where they live, bearing persecution for Christ's sake in a godly manner. A Christian in a communist country, for example, may not be called to go from door to door, passing out tracts, or to engage in street-corner preaching. Living with other believers in love and unity, and patiently enduring discrimination and abuse for the sake of Christ, may be what God requires of him or her. This is no less gospel preaching than verbal proclamation of the gospel. Such witness even may be more valuable, since it allows a watching world, including spirit beings, to catch a glimpse of Christ. Christ himself, when on trial, did not make use of many words; he let his attitude and actions speak for themselves, modeling his life after the Psalms' righteous sufferer and after Isaiah's servant of the Lord.

The writer's exhortation to believers to go to Jesus "outside the camp" and to bear suffering with him accentuates the call to Christians to be "outsiders," choosing not the easy road of material prosperity but the path of the cross, of self-denying, death-defying discipleship and, if called for, social ostracism. This letter's message is especially meaningful for the church when it is called to suffer for Christ's sake and when it is tempted to religious compromise in order to escape severe persecution. Of course, the message of Hebrews should not be taken to imply that it is always inappropriate for Christians to exercise influence on society's government and structures. Where this is possible, there appears no reason to preclude such efforts. This involvement, however, should not be coupled with religious compromise or used as an excuse for self-aggrandizement.

Mission does not end when people have been converted. Firmly establishing believers in their faith and instilling in them deep convictions regarding the superiority of Jesus are crucial in light of the dangers of syncretism and persecution. It appears artificial to dichotomize between internal and external aspects of mission, that is, between edification and evangelism, or between discipleship and mission. The NT consistently presents the church's internal dynamics, such as love and unity among believers, or purity and spiritual maturity (Heb. 5:14), as prerequisites for the church's external relationships (cf. John 13:35; 17:21, 23). The message of Hebrews for believers' activities within the community should therefore not be seen in isolation from believers' responsibilities to the outside world.

## MISSION IN 1 PETER

Is it accurate to say regarding 1 Peter that "the concentration on the life and strengthening of the churches is so strong that it is now largely impossible to speak of an understanding of the mission, in the sense in which the phrase has so far been used and was characteristic of the oldest Christianity"?[14] Is it true that the "Christians are harassed to the limit of their endurance, and all missionary activity is denied to them"?[15] The issue may partly be a matter of semantics, for the author continues, "While the persecution is going on the commission in relation to the world is not lost sight of: the upright conduct of Christians is required on the very ground that someone or other may be won over in this way" (cf. already 1 Thess. 4:12; 1 Cor. 10:32).[16] Indeed, the distinction between active verbal gospel proclamation and a more "passive" emphasis on Christian lifestyle "should not be too hastily obliterated."[17] It seems advisable, however, not to draw the lines too sharply either. One may rather conceive of mission broadly enough to accommodate both components, verbal gospel proclamation and life witness.[18]

The author of Hebrews envisions believers as pilgrims in this world. Peter conceives of the people of God in similar terms.[19] According to him, Christians are sojourners, "resident aliens" (1 Pet. 1:1, 17; 2:11; cf. Heb. 11:13; 11:9; and Phil. 3:20).[20] Peter's first epistle appears to

---

[14] Cf. Hahn, *Mission*, 140. Note that Hahn places the writing of 1 Peter in the time of Domitian (81-96 C.E.), which would make the document contemporary to Revelation in the estimation of many (141, n. 1).

[15] Ibid., 141.

[16] Ibid.

[17] Ibid., 142, n. 1.

[18] It should also be noted that Hahn's treatment of 1 Peter is significantly affected by his overall reconstruction of the early church's mission so that the actual statements in the epistle are often subsumed under this general model and not given sufficient weight.

[19] In the light of the explicit assertions of 1 Peter 1:1 and 5:1, not to speak of the external evidence, there seems to be no good reason to deny the Petrine authorship of this epistle. Moreover, the letter fits well with what is known of the apostle from the rest of the NT and from tradition. For a defense of the Petrine authorship of 1 Peter, see Guthrie, *Introduction,* 762-81; and Carson, Moo, and Morris, *Introduction,* 421-24.

[20] See John H. Elliott, *A Home for the Homeless: A Sociological Exegesis of 1 Peter, Its Situation and Strategy* (London: SCM, 1982). See also, idem, *The Elect and the Holy* (Leiden: E. J. Brill, 1966); idem, *1 Peter: Estrangement and Community* (Chicago: Franciscan Herald, 1979); and idem, "Salutation and Exhortation to Christian Behavior on the Basis of God's Blessings (1:1–2:10)," *RevExp* 79 (1982): 415-25. Elliott's work is highly suggestive. A

have been written to believers "dispersed" in Asia Minor at the onset of a major persecution in the early 60s C.E. Peter probably wrote from Rome (5:13), where such a persecution may already have started, in order to prepare his readers for imminent suffering (4:12).[21] By referring to the location where he lives at the time of writing as "Babylon" (5:13), Peter symbolically refers to Rome as the antitype to the nation that was responsible for Israel's exile, a metaphor developed even more fully in Revelation.[22] Peter, who identifies himself as a "fellow-witness of Christ's sufferings" (5:1), would soon be martyred himself, thus providing, like Jesus, an example of suffering that others could follow (cf. John 21:15-23).

Within the scope of salvation history Peter emphasizes the events at the end of that history, so that the mission of the church takes place in light of these soon-coming events. Peter's teaching on the continuity of the old and new covenant people, the necessity of holiness, and the suffering of Jesus serves to clarify the nature of the mission task.

### An Eschatological Framework

A strong eschatological component flavors the entire epistle, especially in the light of the church's suffering and persecution (1 Pet. 1:7, 9, 13; 2:12; 4:7, 11, 13, 17; 5:1, 10). As Dan O'Connor puts it, "There is, indeed, throughout the letter a continuing missionary orientation, in an attendant eschatological perspective."[23] Peter reminds Christians in the Diaspora of their imperishable inheritance kept in heaven (1:4), assuring them that they are, by the power of God, guarded through faith for a salvation to be revealed on the last day (1:5). Thus believers are to rejoice in their hope, even though they have to endure various trials in this world, "for a little while, if necessary" (1:6). Christians

---

caution should be issued, however, against reading sociological categories and theories into the text rather than demonstrating their existence from a historical and theological exegesis of the documents themselves. See also C. Wolff, "Christ und Welt im 1. Petrusbrief," *TLZ* 100 (1975): 333-42; Chin, "Heavenly Home," 96-112; Feldmeier, *Die Christen als Fremde*, and the review by Schutter.

[21] Senior and Stuhlmueller (*Biblical Foundations*, 298, 302) hold to non-Petrine authorship by members of an alleged "Petrine circle" in the 70s C.E. This unnecessarily removes the epistle from direct Petrine testimony, thus weakening the letter's apostolic authority of an eyewitness of Jesus' sufferings and of a member of his inner circle during his earthly ministry, not to speak of contradicting the explicit claims in 1:1 and especially 5:1. In the latter passage the author identifies himself as a fellow-elder and witness of the sufferings of Christ. But it is hard to see how such a claim could have been made by an author other than Peter without deceptive intent.

[22] Cf. O'Connor, "Holiness of Life," 17-26.

[23] Ibid., 23.

are, however, not alone in their sufferings; there is a solidarity among believers in all the world (5:9; cf. 2:21-25; 5:1).

Peter's message to his readers is that their "home"—that is, their identity—is found in the "household of God" (4:17), which is the fellowship of God's people, a "spiritual house" (2:5).[24] Paradoxically, these "resident aliens" are also God's "chosen race" (2:9; cf. 1:1-2). Peter's characterization of his recipients' identity in those terms represents an effort to equip the church for the fulfillment of its mission. Rather than being discouraged by their powerlessness, uprootedness, and abuse from the world, Christians receive hope and strength in their faith and vision.[25] Thus empowered, believers are readied to minister to an often abusive world rather than adopting a defensive "siege mentality."[26] God's people are to be "involved strangers," showing "critical solidarity" with the world,[27] loving their enemies (cf. Matt. 5:44).[28]

### *Transferal of Old Covenant Categories*

What, according to Peter, is the relationship between God's missionary mandate for Israel and the church? Does Peter conceive of the respective missions in terms of continuity or discontinuity? It is apparent that God's promises to his OT covenant people of a physical land, inheritance, and descendants are transformed in 1 Peter into expectations of eternal realities, thus putting experiences in this life into an eschatological perspective. Likewise, categories reserved in the OT for Israel are now freely transferred to God's "new people" (2:9-10).[29] It appears that Peter's entire vision of the church's mission takes its cue from the OT concept of Israel as a mediatorial body, a light to the nations, thus revealing God's glory (Exod. 19:6 and Isa. 43:20, quoted in 1 Pet. 2:9; cf. Isa. 49:6). Israel failed in this task (Rom. 2:24; quoting Isa. 52:5; Ezek. 36:20), but Christ, as Israel's representative, succeeded (Luke 2:32; quoting Isa. 42:6; 49:6), and transferred the task to the apostolic church (Acts 13:47; quoting Isa. 49:6). The implication of Peter's incorporation of the OT concept of mission into the new covenant community points to the essential continuity between mission in the Old and New Testaments, contrary to some who exclu-

---

[24] Ibid., 20, following Elliott, *Home for the Homeless*, 200-208.

[25] Cf. O'Connor, "Holiness of Life," 20.

[26] Cf. Senior and Stuhlmueller, *Biblical Foundations for Mission*, 299.

[27] J. Botha, "Christian and Society in 1 Peter: Critical Solidarity," *Scriptura* 24 (1988): 27-37.

[28] John Piper, "Hope as the Motivation of Love: 1 Peter 3:9-12," *NTS* 26 (1980): 212-31.

[29] Steuernagel, "Exiled Community as Missionary Community," 8-18.

sively stress the discontinuity between the dynamics involved in the OT and NT.

In analogy to Israel's intended function, Peter perceives the church's presence in the world from the vantage point of mission, stressing its identity as a witnessing community.[30] The transferal of covenant categories from God's old to his new covenant community in 1 Peter 2:9-10 is linked with the climactic purpose statement in 2:9, "that you may proclaim the excellencies of him who called you out of darkness into his marvelous light," a quote from Isaiah 43:21, a clearly eschatological passage. Immediately following this, the epistle's recipients are exhorted to keep their behavior excellent among the nations "so that . . . they may on account of your good deeds, as they observe them, glorify God in the day of visitation" (2:12). The proclamation of God's excellencies thus must be undergirded by "excellent behavior," now not by OT Israel among the Gentiles but by the new covenant community in the unbelieving world surrounding it.

### Holiness and Submission

The transferal of OT categories to God's new covenant people also involves the need for NT believers to be holy as God is holy. The entire section of 1:13-2:10 is devoted to Peter's exhortation to his readers to live holy, spiritually separated lives.[31] As O'Connor contends, "No part of the NT speaks out more eloquently . . . on [the] theme of holiness of life as a way of Christian witness [than does 1 Peter]."[32] Significantly, this exhortation for holiness, rather than being focused on believers' relationships with God or with one another, is directed toward believers' responsibility to reflect God's character in the midst of the unbelieving world around them. The injunction is grounded in God's command to the people he called out from slavery in Egypt to be holy and set apart for him (1:15-16; quoting Lev. 11:44, 45; 19:2; and 20:7). While the external expressions of such distinctness—dietary, ritual, and ceremonial laws—have largely been rendered obsolete, the need for God's people to live a distinct Christian lifestyle and to abstain from both physical and spiritual adultery remains (1 Pet. 1:14, 18; 2:1, 11-12; 4:3-4, 15). By living holy lives, Christians reveal to their surrounding world God's very own nature, just as Israel was called to do. A failure to do so, today as then, amounts to a failure to commend the gospel of Christ by our lives. Notably, the power for living a holy life is not drawn from one's own moral capacity, but derives from Christ's redemption (1:18-23).

---

[30] Robinson, "Missiological Perspectives from I Peter 2:4-10," 176-87.

[31] Elliott, "Salutation and Exhortation," 415-25.

[32] O'Connor, "Holiness of Life," 17.

Not only this, even believers' submission to earthly authorities, whether civil, economic, familial, or ecclesial (2:13, 18; 3:1; 5:1, 5), is necessary ultimately for mission, a frequently overlooked fact.[33] Mission provides a powerful rationale not only for believers to submit to governing authorities (2:13) or economic superiors (2:18) but also for wives to husbands (3:1) and for younger men in the church to elders (5:5). In each case, the same word, *hupotassō*, is used.[34] Christian wives may hope to win over unbelieving husbands by their submissive behavior "without a word" (3:1). In a society where women were usually expected to adopt their husband's religion, Christian wives in mixed marriages were in a very vulnerable position indeed.[35] Husbands, in turn, are to treat their wives with understanding, as fellow-heirs of grace (3:7), while the entire congregation is to humble itself under God (5:6). Indeed, Christ, the powerful one who became weak (cf. 1 Cor. 1:25-29; 2 Cor. 8:9; Phil. 2:6-8), is more than able to strengthen those in minority positions, whether Christian citizens existing in an ungodly society, Christian slaves suffering from the abuse of people in authority over them, or Christian wives living with unbelieving husbands.

According to Peter, the church is the place where exemplary relationships in proper submission are to be lived out before a watching

---

[33] The effort by Senior and Stuhlmueller, *Biblical Foundations*, 310, n. 5, to interpret "submit" in 2:13 exclusively in terms of "participation" and "involvement" in the world in contrast to "non-involvement" is reductionistic and misses the denotation of the term for a possible connotation (cf. also 300-301 and 311, n. 8). This is evident by the use of the same term used for "submit" in the context of slave-master (2:13) and wife-husband relationships (3:1-6). Clearly, for example, wives are not merely encouraged to "participate" in their marriages but to reflect, by their proper submission to authority, their Christian faith even under the improper use of authority, setting their Christian witness above their desire for immediate vindication and liberation.

[34] It will not do to set aside the implications from this passage for husband-wife relationships by reducing the thrust to a "pattern of courageous witness and redemptive suffering" (Senior and Stuhlmueller, *Biblical Foundations*, 301), nor is there any basis to argue for a shift in meaning from "subjection to authority" in 2:13 to "considerate submission to others" in 3:1. See Robert L. Richardson, "From 'Subjection to Authority' to 'Mutual Submission': The Ethic of Subordination in 1 Peter," *Faith and Mission* 4 (1987): 70-80. While the larger context is frequently not given adequate attention in the passage's interpretation, "context" should not be permitted to overwhelm the explicit teaching of the passage or empty it of its clear implications, that is, that wives are to adopt a submissive stance toward their husbands, even *unbelieving* ones.

[35] See David L. Balch, *Let Wives Be Submissive: The Domestic Code in 1 Peter*, SBLMS, no. 26 (Chico, Calif.: Scholars Press, 1981).

world. Church leaders are called to "shepherd the flock" by being examples (5:2-3), just as Christ provided an example for believers to follow (2:21). Ultimately, of course, it is God who is the "shepherd and overseer" of our souls (2:25), and Christ the "chief shepherd" (5:4). As under-shepherds, those given charge of God's people must be prepared to lay down their lives for others (cf. John 15:13).

### Jesus, the Example in Suffering

Peter presents Jesus not merely as our Lord and Savior, but, similar to the author of Hebrews, also as believers' supreme example in suffering (2:21-25; cf. Heb. 12:1-3). Indeed, patient suffering on the part of Christians may even lead some to God. This is the implication of Peter's linking of the exhortation to suffer for doing what is right (3:17) with the explanatory statement, "For Christ also died for sins once for all, the just for the unjust, in order that he might bring us to God" (3:18). While Peter's focus is on Christians' appropriate attitude toward and response to suffering, he does not therefore neglect to point to their need of being prepared to give an answer to those who ask them (3:15).

While this approach may be considered to be more defensive than, for example, the Great Commission at the end of Matthew, it is an appropriate as well as realistic perspective on the mission task in the context of persecution. As in 2:9-12, verbal proclamation is linked with the necessity of a holy life: believers are to "set apart the Lord Christ in their hearts" (3:16). Like Noah, Christians are to bear bold witness in the midst of hostile unbelievers (3:19-20). Moreover, even in a context of persecution, believers are to practice love and hospitality (4:8-9; cf. Heb. 13:1-2), and to exercise their spiritual gifts, whether of speaking or of serving, to the glory of God in Christ (1 Pet. 4:10-11). Simply put, believers are to "do good" (2:12, 15, 20; 3:6, 11, 17; 4:19).

### Implications

Peter's teaching about mission, besides being influenced by the context of suffering, presents Christianity as a "working man's religion." Lofty Christian concepts and virtues are brought down to earth and applied to everyday relationships, at work or at home. No sphere of life is to be exempt from obedience to Christ. This vision was revived during the Protestant Reformation, where great emphasis was once again placed on the living out of one's Christian faith in everyday life. However, even in this model of mission there are risks, foremost that of conforming to the world in which one lives (cf. Rom. 12:2; 13:13-14). If there is no difference between Christians and non-Christians in the way they live (as is all too often the case in contemporary North

American society), Christian witness will remain ineffectual. There will be no reason for questions concerning the hope of Christians (1 Pet. 3:15). Peter believes that the Christian lifestyle, if it is a consistently holy lifestyle, has certain unique qualities that will render the gospel proclamation attractive.

## CONCLUSION

The writings surveyed here present, each in its own way, a theology of mission that is firmly based upon the conviction that Jesus Christ is the unique Savior of all those who receive the Christian gospel. The nature of believers' witness may differ, ranging from life witness, including martyrdom, to verbal proclamation, but the belief undergirding such witness is that unless people hear the gospel and believe in Christ, they will spend eternity separated from God and Christ. To persevere until the end really matters; to resist spiritual compromise is vital indeed, since there will be eternal ramifications regarding a person's faithfulness or failure to represent the truth.

This study essentially confirmed the initial working description, which emphasized the means of either direct preaching or life witness, the importance of suffering, and the significance of believers' identity in Christ. To this may be added that mission must be carried out under the sovereignty of God, with full acknowledgment of the supremacy of Jesus, even regarding his example in suffering, and in a spirit of holiness and spiritual separation from the world. Mission is understood in an eschatological perspective, with the church as a body of pilgrims and resident aliens walking the fine line between submission to authorities and courageous witness of her Lord.

The bedrock convictions of the writings considered here expose the shallowness of recent contemporary attempts to refashion the Christian message in the image of secular societal developments.[36] The authors of Hebrews and 1 Peter gave supreme importance to believers holding fast to their faith, even if that determination severely limited their opportunity for "religious dialogue." Ultimately, it is not missionary appeal but the vindication of God's sovereign righteousness that is of supreme importance, both in Christ's first coming at the cross and at his second coming. Not human obduracy and sin, but divine righteousness will have the last word.

---

[36] For a discussion of this, see Harold A. Netland, *Dissonant Voices: Religious Pluralism and the Question of Truth* (Grand Rapids: Eerdmans, 1991); Andrew D. Clarke and Bruce W. Winter, eds., *One God, One Lord: Christianity in a World of Religious Pluralism*, 2d ed. (Grand Rapids: Baker, 1993). Contra Chester Gillis, *Pluralism: A New Paradigm for Theology*, Louvain Theological & Pastoral Monographs, no. 12 (Grand Rapids: Eerdmans, 1993).

# 12

# *Mission in John's Gospel and Letters*

## Martin Erdmann

Studies on the purpose of John's gospel must eventually examine John 20:30-31: "Jesus did many other miraculous signs in the presence of the disciples, which are not recorded in this book. But these are written that you may believe that Jesus is the Christ, the Son of God, and that by believing you may have life in his name." In drawing out the meaning of these verses, some interpreters emphasize the words "the Christ," on the assumption that difficulties existed within the Jewish section of the early church. Doubting Jewish Christians, they argue, became confused about the vital issues of their faith, because they suffered under a barrage of assaults by their former co-religionists, often leading to expulsion from the synagogue. They needed to be assured that Jesus was indeed the Messiah and to recoup their courage in asserting themselves against their Jewish critics by confidently relying on that fact.[1]

Yet there is another way of reading John 20:30-31. Instead of putting the emphasis on "the Christ" in verse 31, the stress can legitimately and more logically be placed on the phrase "that you may be-

---

[1] Two recent Johannine studies based on this hypothesis are Takashi Onuki, *Gemeinde und Welt im Johannesevangelium: Ein Beitrag zur Frage nach der theologischen und pragmatischen Funktion des johanneischen "Dualismus,"* WMANT, no. 56 (Neukirchen-Vluyn: Neukrichener Verlag, 1984); and David Rensberger, *Overcoming the World: Politics and Community in the Gospel of John* (London: SPCK, 1988). See also Raymond E. Brown, *The Gospel according to John*, AB, vols. 29, 29A (Garden City, N.Y.: Doubleday, 1966-70), 1:LXX-LXXV, LXXVII-LXXIX; 2:1055-61.

lieve."[2] This purpose clause in John 20:31 strongly suggests that John's intention was propagandistic in nature. It is instructive to compare this clause with John's purpose statement for his first epistle: "I write these things to you who believe in the name of the Son of God so that you may know that you have eternal life" (1 John 5:13). John's first epistle is clearly written to Christians for their instruction. By contrast, the purpose statement of John 20:30-31 appears to be aimed at unbelievers who need to make a decision about the identity of Jesus. Viewed in this light, John is primarily pursuing a mission objective in writing his gospel. Although John's gospel may be encouraging to believers in their faith, it is primarily directed toward unbelievers in order to move them to faith in Jesus as the Messiah, the Son of God.[3] Advocates of this position believe, in accord with W. C. van Unnik, that the Fourth Gospel was "a mission book."[4] D. A. Carson, for ex-

---

[2] At this point it would be counterproductive to engage in the discussion on whether John 20:30-31 or John 21 marks the conclusion to the gospel. Paul S. Minear ("The Original Functions of John 21," *JBL* 102 [1983]: 85-98) has more recently opened up the debate on this question again. Whether we agree with his conclusions or not, it is immaterial to the argument that this passage is significant for the understanding of the missionary emphasis of the gospel. Even R. Schnackenburg has noted that it is impossible to overestimate the importance of John 20:30-31 in interpreting the whole of the Fourth Gospel. See R. Schnackenburg, "Die Messiasfrage im Johannesevangelium," in *Neutestamentliche Aufsätze: Festschrift für Josef Schmid zum 70. Geburtstag*, ed J. Blinzler, O. Kuss, and F. Mussner (Regensburg: Friedrich Pustet, 1963), 240-64.

[3] In arguing for a primarily propagandistic purpose of the Fourth Gospel, I do not intend to discount its catechistic utility to believers. As a matter of fact, both go hand in hand, as two sides of the same coin.

[4] W. C. van Unnik, "The Purpose of St. John's Gospel," *Studia Evangelica* 1 (1959): 410. To agree with van Unnik generally about the missiological purpose of the gospel of John does not necessarily mean he is equally correct in stating that John sought to win "converts of a [localized] synagogue in the Diaspora." The specifics as to his intentions in writing the gospel are more speculative than van Unnik is ready to concede. For others who hold to an evangelistic purpose for John's gospel, see John A. T. Robinson, "The Destination and Purpose of St John's Gospel," *NTS* 6 (1959-60): 117-31; Leon Morris, *The Gospel according to John*, NICNT (Grand Rapids: Eerdmans, 1971), 855-56; D. A. Carson, "The Purpose of the Fourth Gospel: John 20:31 Reconsidered," *JBL* 106 (1987): 639-51; Miguel Rodriguez Ruiz, *Der Missionsgedanke des Johannesevangeliums: Ein Beitrag zur johanneischen Soteriologie und Ekklesiologie*, FB, no. 55 (Würzburg: Echter Verlag, 1987), 25-30; Teresa Okure, *The Johannine Approach to Mission: A Contextual Study of John 4,1-42*, WUNT, no. 2/31 (Tübingen: J. C. B. Mohr [Paul Siebeck], 1988), 232; D. A. Carson, *The Gospel according to John* (Grand Rapids: Eerdmans, 1991), 87-95; Andreas Köstenberger, "The Challenge of a Systematized Biblical Theology of Mission: Missiological Insights from the

ample, concludes his article "The Purpose of the Fourth Gospel: John 20:31 Reconsidered" by insisting on "the possibility that the Fourth Gospel is primarily evangelistic after all."[5]

Since John wrote his gospel in order to fulfill a mission task, it is logical to assume that mission is a fairly prominent theme in John's writings.[6] Such is the case. What is emphasized in John's approach to mission is the idea that the Father sent the Son. In the following discussion the sending of the Son will be examined first, since it serves as an important foundation for other topics related to mission in John's gospel. Contemporary biblical scholarship has tended to ignore the mission theme in John's gospel as well as in the rest of the New Testament.[7] Nevertheless, a study of mission in the New Testament in gen-

---

Gospel of John," *Missiology* 23 (1995): 448; Philip H. Towner, "Paradigms Lost: Mission to the *Kosmos* in John and David Bosch's Biblical Models of Mission," *EvQ* 67 (1995): 104. See also the critical survey of A. Wind ("Destination and Purpose of the Gospel of John," *NovT* 14 [1972]: 26-69), who concurs broadly, though not in all respects, with the thesis advanced here.

[5] Carson, "Purpose," 651.

[6] This chapter deals with the Johannine literature, including John's gospel and John's epistles but excluding Revelation, which is treated in the following chapter.

[7] As an exception to this general observation, some significant work has been done by Catholic biblical scholars. See James McPolin, "Mission in the Fourth Gospel," *ITQ* 46 (1969): 113-22; idem, "Studies in the Fourth Gospel: Some Contemporary Trends," *IBS* 2 (1980): 2-26; Donald Senior and Carroll Stuhlmueller, *The Biblical Foundations for Mission* (Maryknoll, N.Y.: Orbis Books, 1983). This work apparently has come about in response to Vatican II and to Karl Rahner's call for further study on the missiological data found in the NT. See Karl Rahner, "Towards a Fundamental Theological Interpretation of Vatican II," *TS* 40 (1979): 716-27. The present lack of interest within critical biblical scholarship concerning the mission theme of John's gospel is a departure from the views expressed by critics of an earlier era. See, for example, Karl Bornhäuser, *Das Johannesevangelium: Eine Missionsschrift für Israel* (Gütersloh: Bertelsmann, 1928); Wilhelm Oehler, *Das Johannesevangelium: Eine Missionsschrift für die Welt* (Gütersloh: Bertelsmann, 1936); idem, *Zum Missionscharakter des Johannesevangeliums*, BFCT, no. 42 (Gütersloh: Bertelsmann, 1941). Rudolf Bultmann ("Die Bedeutung der neuerschlossenene mandäischen und manichäischen Quellen für das Verständnis des Johannesevangeliums," *ZNW* 24 [1925]: 102) stated that "die zentrale Anschauung" or "Grundkonzeption" of the gospel is that Jesus is "der Gesandte Gottes . . . der Offenbarung bringt durch Worte and Taten." Even though the theme of mission is not explicitly mentioned in Bultmann's "Die Theologie des Johannes Evangeliums: Die Sending des Sohnes," *Theologie des Neuen Testaments*, 3. Aufl. (Tübingen: Mohr, 1958), 385-422, it still appears implicitly in his "Sendungs" terminology. Ernst Haenchen ("Der Vater der mich gesandt hat," *NTS* 9 [1963]: 208) interprets the phrase "der Vater der mich gesandt hat" as being the central statement of the Johannine "Offenbarungslehre" and the

eral and in John's writings in particular is crucial for a cohesive biblical theology. As Senior rightly observes:

> The mission concerns of the [early church] community and their
> impact on the NT writings must be given their due. Mission must
> be considered a potential part of the "horizon" that shaped the
> aim of the biblical author. The NT writings served a variety of
> community needs, among which was perspective on the church's
> universal mission.[8]

## THE SENDING OF THE SON

The concept of mission in the Fourth Gospel is encapsulated in
Christ's designation of the Father as the "one who sent me." This motif
occurs approximately forty times in the gospel, usually expressed by
different variations of the verbs *pempō* or *apostellō*.[9] Some interpreters see a shade of difference between these two verbs. Rengstorf argues, for example, that *apostellō* is used to describe the authority with
which Christ fulfills his mission and *pempō* to affirm the participation
of God in the whole process.[10] However, the case for differentiating

---

"Lieblingsformel" of the gospel. A few other scholars expressed similar views.
Joseph Kuhl (*Die Sendung Jesu und der Kirche nach dem Johannesevangelium*,
Studia Instituti Missiologica Societatis Verbi Domini [St. Augustin: Styler, 1967],
1) sees the "Sendungsidee" as a vital aspect of the Johannine theology. See also
Werner Bieder, *Gottes Sendung und der missionarische Auftrag nach Matthaeus,
Lukas, Paulus und Johannes*, Theologische Studien, no. 82 (Zurich: EVZ, 1965).

[8] Donald Senior, "The Struggle to Be Universal: Mission as Vantage Point
for New Testament Investigation," *CBQ* 46 (1984): 66.

[9] In John's gospel the term *pempō* is used approximately twenty-three times
for the sending of the Son, all in articular participial forms: eight times in the
nominative (5:37; 6:44; 7:28; 8:16, 18, 26, 29; 12:49); seven times in the
genitive (4:34; 5:30; 6:38, 39; 7:16; 9:4; 14:24); seven times in the accusative
(5:23; 7:33; 12:44, 45; 13:20; 15:21; 16:5); once in the dative (5:24). *Apostellō*
occurs seventeen times in reference to the sending of the Son, in indicative
forms only. These are *apesteilen* (3:17, 34; 5:38; 6:29, 57; 7:29; 8:42; 10:36);
*apestalken* (5:36; 20:21); *apesteilas* (11:42; 17:3, 8, 18, 21, 23, 25).

[10] K. H. Rengstorf, "*apostolos*," in *TDNT* 1:404: "When *pempein* is used
in the NT the emphasis is on the sending as such, whereas when *apostellein* is
used it rests on the commission linked with it." With reference to the usage in
John's gospel he remarks: "To denote His full authority both to the Jews and
to the disciples Jesus uses *apostellein*, since He thereby shows that behind His
words and person there stands God and not merely His own pretension. . . .
When Jesus uses *pempein* in speaking of His sending by God he does so in
such a way as to speak of God as the *pempsas me*." For Rengstorf, *apostellein*
grounds Jesus' authority in that of God; *pempein* affirms the participation of
God in his work.

between the meaning of these two terms is difficult to establish, since John uses the verbs interchangeably.[11] For example, in chapter 5 John alternates between *pempō* (5:23, 24, 30, 37) and *apostellō* (5:33, 36, 38) without any clear distinction in meaning. Not only does John use *pempō* and *apostellō* to describe the Father's sending of the Son, but he also uses these words to refer to the Father's sending of John the Baptist (1:6, 33; 3:28) and the Holy Spirit (14:26; cf. 16:7).

Further data concerning the sending of the Son is found at the different places in the gospel where the verb *erchomai* ("come") is used to portray Jesus as the one who has come into the world on the authority of the Father. In some instances Jesus himself denotes the purpose of his coming, expressed both positively (*elēlutha*: 5:43; 12:46; 16:28; 18:37; *ēlthon*: 9:39; 10:10; 12:27) and negatively (*ouk elēlutha*: 7:28; *oude . . . elēlutha*: 8:42; *ou . . . ēlthon*: 12:47). Periodically, other persons refer to the Messiah's coming; among them are John the Baptist (1:15, 27, 30; 3:31), Nicodemus (3:2), the Samaritan woman (4:25-26), and Martha (11:27). On the occasion of Christ's feeding the Galilean multitude, he is recognized as the prophet who was to come (6:14). While the Jewish crowds at Jerusalem debated about the identity of Jesus and their own expectations concerning the coming of the Messiah (7:27, 31, 41-42), the people accompanying Jesus at his triumphal entry praise God for this king who comes in the name of the Lord (12:13, 15). John also presents the subject of mission by using the verb *didōmi* to express the Father's giving of the Son (3:16; 6:32) and the Spirit (3:34; 14:16).

The terminology of sending/coming/giving is uniquely employed by the apostle John in characterizing the relationship between Christ and the Father.[12] Within this relationship, the Father is the sender. As

---

[11] An extensive treatment of *apostellō* and *pempō* can be found in Juan Peter Miranda, *Der Vater, der mich gesandt hat: Religionsgeschichtliche Untersuchungen zu den johanneischen Sendungsformeln: Zugleich ein Beitrag zur johanneischen Christologie und Ekklesiologie* (Bern: Herbert Lang, 1972; Frankfurt: Peter Lang, 1972), 8-38. This work is an unrevised edition of a 1971 dissertation at the Catholic faculty of theology at Tübingen. See also Juan Peter Miranda, *Die Sendung Jesu im vierten Evangelium: Religions und theologiegeschichtliche Untersuchungen zu den Sendungsformeln*, SBS, no. 87 (Stuttgart: Katholisches Bibelwerk, 1977), 29-38; Andreas Köstenberger, "The Two Johannine Words for Sending: A Study of John's Use of Words with Reference to General Linguistic Theory," paper presented at the annual meeting of the Society of Biblical Literature, Chicago, Ill., November 1994.

[12] It should be noted that Miranda (*Die Sendung Jesu im vierten Evangelium*, 41) objects to the interpretation of correlating the Father/Son relationship with Christ's sending by the Father on the basis that traditionally Christ's designation of being the Son of God has been differentiated from his filial relationship to the Father.

McPolin rightly states, the Father remains "the 'mission centre,' the source from which all missions derive."[13] As the sender, the Father takes the position of an authority, determining the task and message of the one who is sent into the world. As long as there is opportunity, the Son does the work of the one who sent him (9:4). He does not pursue his own goals but rather always does what pleases the Father (8:29). Repeatedly, Jesus points out that his words are not his own; instead, his message is from the one who sent him. The Son does not speak on his own, since the Father commanded him what to say and how to say it (12:49); his teaching comes from the one who sent him (7:16; cf. 3:34; 7:18; 8:26; 14:24). The Samaritan woman spoke correctly when she said that the Messiah at his coming would explain everything (4:25). Jesus comes to bring divine illumination, to give light to everyone (1:9; cf. 8:12).

In its most fundamental aspect Christ's identity is defined as the envoy of God, sent into this world on a specific mission.[14] As the sent one, Jesus seeks to accomplish the Father's work and will. The fulfillment of his obligation toward God is foremost on Jesus' mind, regardless of what this means to him personally. Jesus does the work that the Father has given him to complete (5:36; cf. 17:4), and he seeks to do the will of the one who sent him (6:38; cf. 4:34). The work of God is completed at the cross, where Jesus exclaims, "It [my work] is finished" (19:30). In that darkest of all hours, Jesus perfectly fulfills the assignment given to him by his Father. The complete obedience of Jesus is reflective of the unity between the sender and the sent one. There is a unity of purpose, so that whoever believes in the Son also believes in his sender, the Father (12:44; cf. 5:23; 8:16; 13:20), and whoever looks at Jesus sees the one who sent him (12:45).

In 3:13-19 John emphasizes the "giving" (3:16), "sending" (3:17), and "coming" (3:19) of the Son. The point stressed most sublimely in this cardinal passage of the gospel is that Christ is God's messenger who comes to accomplish a distinct and unique mission. The purpose of this mission is summed up in the statement that "God did not send his Son into the world to condemn the world, but to save the world through him" (3:17). Christ came not for judgment but for salvation (cf. 12:47), which of course does not mean that all judgment is avoided (cf. 9:39). Christ does not come to produce judgment, but those who love darkness already stand under the condemnation of God (3:18-19). Even at the final judgment in the last day, the wicked will be condemned by their own evil works (5:29) and choices (12:48).

---

[13] McPolin, "Mission in the Fourth Gospel," 114.

[14] On this point, see also Rudolf Pesch, "Voraussetzungen und Anfänge der urchristlichen Mission," in *Mission im Neuen Testament*, ed. Karl Kertelge (Freiburg: Herder, 1982), 14-16; Ruiz, *Missionsgedanke*, 20-23.

John seems to characterize most frequently the saving purpose of Christ's mission as the giving of life, which appears like a refrain throughout his gospel (for example, 3:16; 5:24-25; 6:57; 10:10; 11:25-26; 17:2; 20:31).[15] McPolin states:

> The object of Jesus' mission, then, is described in various ways— to confer life, to reveal his Father as the light and the truth, to accomplish his work, to do his Father's will. But from various texts it emerges that the primary purpose, to which all others are subordinated, is to confer life.[16]

Jesus describes himself as the bread of life, which, in contrast to the manna given to the Israelites in the desert, is capable of imparting eternal life (6:47-52). Jesus qualifies his self-identification as the bread of life by equating it with "giving my flesh" (6:51). The latter expression signified Christ's awareness that his self-sacrifice is the means by which life is infused into the world (6:51; cf. 12:24). On various occasions Jesus also proclaims himself to be the source of living water (4:10-13; cf. 6:35). At the Feast of Tabernacles, for example, Christ invites everyone yearning for the water of life to drink it to the full (7:37), promising that after his resurrection the Holy Spirit will transform the inmost being of every believer into a fountain of living water (7:38-39). Jesus' mission, therefore, involves the giving of life to believers, life that is satisfying, abundant, and eternal.

### THE OBJECTIVE OF MISSION: THE GLORY OF GOD

Christ's mission in John's gospel, however, fulfills a much higher purpose than simply to confer life to a sinful humanity. The ultimate objective for Jesus is to bring glory to God.[17] In the high priestly prayer Jesus Christ encapsulates in a brief but profound synopsis the primary purpose of his first coming (17:1, 4, 6, 26). His whole life is devoted to the glorification of God.[18] In perfect obedience to his Father's will, he reveals the majesty and glory of God against the backdrop of human ignorance and depravity. Jesus glorifies the Father by accomplishing

---

[15] See also 1 John 2:25; 3:14; 4:9; 5:11-13.

[16] McPolin, "Mission in the Fourth Gospel," 118.

[17] The glorification of God as the goal of the Christian mission is well-expressed in John Piper, *Let the Nations Be Glad!: The Supremacy of God in Missions* (Grand Rapids: Baker, 1993), 11-40.

[18] In John's gospel the Son brings both glory (*doxa, doxazō*) and honor (*timē, timaō*) to the Father. On the relationship between these two word groups, see S. Aalen, "Glory, Honor," in *The New International Dictionary of New Testament Theology*, ed. Colin Brown (Grand Rapids: Zondervan, 1976), 2:44.

the work for which he was sent (17:4) and by making the Father known
among God's chosen ones (17:6, 25-26). The high priestly prayer also
points out that the Father glorifies the Son (17:1, 5, 10, 22, 24). Jesus,
therefore, stands in contrast to those who are satisfied with self-glori-
fication and the honor of men (5:41; 7:18; 8:50, 54). John accuses the
Jewish religious leaders in particular of seeking after approval and
honor from others (5:44; 12:43). The Father's glorification of the Son
is not separate from the Son's glorification of the Father, since both
take place together (17:5). In fact, the Father glorifies the Son so that
in turn the Son might do the same for the Father (17:1). In this way
Jesus both glorifies the Father and reveals in himself the glory of God.
The Father and Son are united in the display of God's glory.

John's profound observation that Christ exhibited the glory of God,
full of grace and truth (1:14), is recognized as one of the gospel's most
fundamental propositions. Throughout his gospel John enumerates
examples of God's glory radiating forth in Jesus' character and ministry. The manifestation of Jesus' glory appears, for example, in the series of signs or miraculous events recorded by John, the first of which
takes place in Cana of Galilee at a wedding feast. When the wine for
the feast runs out, Jesus turns water into wine, providing an abun-
dance of the very best, and John labels this action as a revelation of
Jesus' glory, a revelation that encourages the faith of the disciples (2:11).
Another incidence occurs at the pool of Bethesda, situated near the
Sheep Gate on the north side of the Temple ground. Surrounded by a
large crowd of invalids who are congregating around the pool in the
hope of being healed by mysterious angelic powers,[19] Jesus approaches
a lame man who has been lying there for thirty-eight years. After a
short verbal exchange, Christ simply commands him: "Get up! Pick
up your mat and walk!" (5:8). Later that day Jesus is confronted by
the Jews who object vehemently to his performance of a miracle on a
Sabbath. In justifying his actions, Jesus states that his works (5:19,
30), testimony (5:32, 36-37), and glory come from the Father (5:41,
44). Later in the gospel Jesus sees the sickness of Lazarus as an opportunity for the display of God's glory (11:4). Indeed, Lazarus is
not only gravely ill but also dies, and his death provides an even
greater opportunity for Jesus to reveal the majesty of God's power
(11:40). Jesus shows the greatness of God by raising Lazarus from

---

[19] Bruce M. Metzger (*A Textual Commentary on the Greek New Testament*
[London: United Bible Society, 1971], 209) suggests that the editorial addition to verse 4 in chapter 5 originated probably in religious folklore rather
than in an accurate account of the healing intervention of an angel of God.
Jesus makes it clear that God heals differently, not as a capricious angelic
spirit.

the dead and in this way demonstrates that he is the resurrection and the life.

Jesus reveals God's glory not only in his activity but also in his character. The Fourth Gospel accentuates the character of Christ through the sevenfold "I am" formula (6:35; 8:12, 58; 10:11; 11:25; 14:6; 15:1, 5). In this way, Jesus signifies his oneness with God, the "I am who I am" of the Old Testament (Exod. 3:14). Whenever Jesus speaks like this, the implied message is that in him people encounter the same eternal, immutable God that Moses did at the burning bush (Exod. 3:2-22). Their longing to draw near to God is fully met by coming to him, and he satisfies every desire of the human soul.[20]

John presents the death of Jesus on the cross as the supreme moment of glorification. The request of Gentile worshipers to see Jesus (John 12:20-22) evokes in him the vision of his impending glorification. The hour has come for the Son of Man to be glorified (12:23). Jesus compares himself to a kernel of wheat that must fall to the ground and die in order to fulfill its destiny (12:24). His dying on the cross would be the ultimate manifestation of glory given to the Father, an act that would elevate Christ himself to the highest place of honor and authority. Realizing the solemnity of the hour, Jesus defines the central purpose of his life: "Father, glorify your name!" which elicits God's audible response: "I have glorified it, and will glorify it again" (12:28). Jesus speaks again of his glorification after he identifies Judas as his betrayer and instructs him to fulfill his deed quickly (13:26-32). Jesus sees in his betrayal and death the time when both the Son and the Father will be glorified. Later, Jesus begins his high priestly prayer with the recognition that in his coming death the hour of glorification has come (17:1). John's gospel views the tragedy of the cross as the majestic display of God's greatness. Viewed with the eyes of faith, the violent scene at the cross is transformed into a display of the triumphant exaltation of the dying Savior. The greatness of God's glory is defined by the depth of his love.

John's gospel also hints at the idea that believers may glorify God by fulfilling the mission that is assigned to them. In John 15:8 Jesus states that his followers bring glory to the Father by bearing fruit, and in 21:19 Jesus predicts that Peter will glorify God through his death. Jesus prays that God grant to his disciples the privilege of seeing his glory (17:24). As believers, they will enter into the presence of the Father and thus share in his glory (17:22). The followers of Jesus Christ may participate in making known the greatness of the eternal God through both life and death.

---

[20] For a similar point, see also Senior and Stuhlmueller, *Biblical Foundations*, 285.

## THE MOTIVATION OF MISSION:
## GOD'S LOVE FOR THE WORLD

Jesus Christ's death on the cross is not only the display of God's glory; the annals of history point to this event as the clearest manifestation of God's love for humanity. Jesus' mission to redeem the world and to grant eternal life to those who put their faith in him is grounded in God's continual concern for this world. At the very center of Christ's mission is God's love for all humanity. 1 John 4:9-11 expresses well God's love as the motivation for the sending of the Son and the resulting love of believers for one another.

> This is how God showed his love among us: He sent his one and only Son into the world that we might live through him. This is love: not that we loved God, but that he loved us and sent his Son as an atoning sacrifice for our sins. Dear friend, since God so loved us, we also ought to love one another (1 John 4:9-11).

God commissioned his Son to enact the most important chapter of salvation history because of his love, a love which extends to the whole world. God loved the world so much that he gave his Son (John 3:16). God sent his Son as a sacrifice not only for the sins of believers but also for the sins of the whole world (1 John 2:2; 4:10). The message of the gospel of John is that the Son of God assumed human flesh to give his life and in this way express fully the Father's love for all humanity.

Jesus fulfills his mission because of his love for his disciples. When Jesus recognizes that the time for his death and his return to the Father is at hand, he chooses to love his own to the very end (John 13:1). As the Good Shepherd he deliberately lays down his life for his sheep (10:17, 18) and in this way shows his compassion for his friends (15:13). The love that Jesus gives to his disciples reveals to them the relationship that they ought to have with one another (13:34; 15:12; cf. 1 John 4:11). If Jesus laid down his life for believers, then they should live with sacrifice toward one another (1 John 3:16).

It is easy to assume that God's love for the world would result in the grateful reception of God's grace by the world, but this is not the case. Instead, the world, in general, rejects God and his ways. In John's gospel the world is more than simply a place. It includes also the earth's inhabitants as well as the forces and thoughts that move them and determine the course of their lives.[21] So, for example, John describes in the prologue how Jesus was in the world and he made the world, but the world did not recognize him (John 1:10). He came to the earth and

---

[21] Towner, "Paradigms Lost," 107-8.

the people of this place did not know or accept him. The tragedy is that Jesus, sent by the love of God, came to his own and his own did not receive him (1:11). Jesus is portrayed repeatedly as the light of the world (1:9; 8:12; 9:5; 12:46), and although the light has come into the world the earth's inhabitants will not come to the light because they love darkness and their own evil deeds (3:19-20).

Therefore, the Fourth Gospel views the world in largely negative terms.[22] It is dominated by the ruler of this world (12:31; 14:30; 16:11), who is the antagonist standing against God's mission. The whole world lies under the control of this evil one (1 John 5:19). The ruler of the world should be identified with the devil, who is a murderer and the father of lies (John 8:44). With good reason Jesus asks the Father to protect his disciples from the evil one (17:15). The world is also characterized by ignorance, since it does not know the Father (17:25), the Son (1:10), the Spirit (14:17), or even the true children of God (1 John 3:1). This ignorance is not innocent, since it derives from an unwillingness to leave behind evil deeds in order to accept divine illumination (John 3:20). The world's condition is sinful, driven by lust and pride (1 John 2:16). The sinful character of the world expresses itself in its hatred for both Jesus (7:7; 15:18) and his followers (15:18; 17:14; 1 John 3:13).

The response of the religious leaders is typical of the attitude of the world toward God's revelation. In contrast to the positive reception of Jesus by the common people (John 12:17-19), the Jewish leaders reject him out of hand, even plotting to kill him (7:48-49; 8:40; 9:29; 11:50, 53). Instead of worshiping Christ as their divinely ordained king, they desperately hold on to their own conceit and self-importance. They come to realize that their privileged positions are being systematically undermined by Christ's forceful public appearances. Drastic measures need to be taken to guard themselves against a further erosion of power. They know too well that if the Jewish population at large continues to shift its allegiance to Jesus, it means their immediate debasement from the seat of authority (11:48). Instead of bowing their knees before the Son of God, they choose rather to seek his death (11:47-57; 19:6-7, 15-16). In their hostility toward Christ, they reveal their true allegiance with Satan (8:44). In rejecting salvation, they incur God's wrath and judgment (3:18-21, 36).

This negative picture of the world and its rejection of Christ, however, does not annul God's love for the earth's inhabitants. God still has a mission for the world, motivated by his love, a mission which involves salvation (3:16-17). Jesus dies not as a hopeless failure but as the atoning sacrifice for the sins of the world (1 John 2:2). He is the Lamb of God who takes away the sin of the world (John 1:29). While

---

[22] Ibid., 108-10.

the world, in general, does not recognize or receive Jesus, the gospel of John holds out hope that some do believe in him and therefore become the children of God (1:10-12). These find life in Jesus Christ not by their own will but by the regenerating work of God (1:13). God chooses some out of the world who belong to him (15:19; 17:6).

The reality of God's love for a sinful and rejecting world, of course, has implications for the nature of God's mission at the present time. In spite of the world's hostility, Jesus did not want his followers to be taken out of the world (17:15). They are instead sent into the world, this object of God's love, just as Jesus was sent into the world (17:18). They should not be surprised when people hate them (1 John 3:13), since after all Jesus was hated first (John 15:18). Jesus recognizes that the world is not his kingdom (18:36). The world is not just slightly off course and with a few adjustments ready to develop into the kingdom of God. The world needs to be overcome (16:33; 1 John 4:4; 5:4-5). Although Jesus is the true king, he does not come to serve as the world's ruler but rather to testify to the truth (John 18:37). Like Jesus, his disciples may face rejection but they must remain in the world to testify to the truth, always with the hope that God has his chosen ones who will believe in Jesus and find eternal life.

## THE SCOPE OF MISSION: UNIVERSALITY OF SALVATION

John reports in chapter 4 of the gospel that many Samaritans believed in Jesus and came to know with certainty that Jesus is the Savior of the world (4:42). Here the term "world" is used in a context that emphasizes the universality of Christ's work of salvation. God's mission extends beyond the Jewish people. If Jesus' encounters with the Samaritan woman at Jacob's well and later with the inhabitants of Sychar have any continuing significance, it is in the recognition that God's salvation is efficacious for members of race communities outside the Jewish nation.[23] The Samaritans rightly recognize in Jesus the Savior of the world after spending only a few days in his presence (4:42).

Jesus' encounter with the woman at the well begins with the woman's surprise over Jesus' request for a drink of water, since by this request Jesus sets aside the customary reactions of Jews toward Samaritans (4:9). Although Jews normally would have no dealings with Samaritans, Jesus the Jew continues his conversation, offering living water to

---

[23] See, for example, Edwin D. Freed, "Did John Write His Gospel Partly to Win Samaritan Converts?" *NovT* 12 (1970): 256. The point Freed makes in regard to John's intention of winning Samaritan converts is well taken, but it is unlikely that there was as much Samaritan influence on the writer of the Fourth Gospel as Freed contends.

the woman (4:10). Eventually the discussion returns again to ethnic issues. The woman at the well raises the debated issue between Jews and Samaritans concerning the proper place of worship (4:19). Christ acknowledges the extraordinary position of Israel in God's eternal economy. He emphatically states that salvation comes from the Jews (4:22). Nonetheless, Jesus foresees a time when true worshipers of God, without ethnic division, will worship the Father in spirit and in truth (4:23).

Israel has a privileged place in God's plan of salvation history, but according to John's gospel individual Jews cannot simply presume upon their ethnic heritage as though descent from Abraham alone were sufficient for a right standing before God. Jesus criticizes those who rely on their physical descent from Abraham as the decisive criterion that singles them out to be God's chosen people (8:33-41). It is inadequate simply to possess the Law of Moses. Jesus expects the people to know that Moses spoke concerning him, so that they might recognize him as the Messiah (5:45-47; cf. 1:45). For Jesus, the true Israelite is one who believes in him (1:47) and is born from above (3:3-8).

The Fourth Gospel also notes that salvation is not meant to be an exclusive commodity for the Jews. Gentiles would partake equally of it by trusting in Christ as their redeemer. The prologue of John's gospel (1:1-18) sets the tone for the remaining chapters by introducing themes concerning Christ that communicate the universal scope of Jesus' mission.[24] He is described alternately as the Word, the origin of creation, life, and light. Other terms that point to the universality of God's work include "flesh," "world," and "creation." God's desire is that all might believe (1:7). Jesus is the true light that gives light to everyone (1:9), and participation in the family of God is available to all who receive Jesus and believe in him (1:12).

The universality of salvation is a conspicuous theme in other parts of the Fourth Gospel as well. Jesus declares that many of his sheep are members of different ethnic groups (10:16). John explains that Jesus died not only for the Jewish nation but also for the scattered children of God, in order that he might bring them together and make them one (11:51-52). Repeatedly, John records that all who believe in Jesus have eternal life (for example, 3:15-16, 36; 5:24; 20:31). In this way John acknowledges the position of Israel but insists that salvation comes through faith in Christ. Köstenberger writes:

> John insists that, for Jews as for everyone else, the way of salvation is through believing in Jesus only—"no one can come to the Father except through me" (14:6). At the same time, John af-

---

[24] On this point, see Ruiz, *Missionsgedanke*, 42-44; Senior and Stuhlmueller, *Biblical Foundations*, 284.

firms that Jews have not ceased to be God's covenant people. Specifically, individual believing Jews are incorporated into Jesus' new Messianic community.[25]

At the same time that the Samaritan woman leaves to report her surprising news to the people of the town, the disciples rejoin Jesus at the well (4:27-29). The conversation of Jesus with his disciples in 4:31-38 sheds further light on the universal nature of salvation and on the missionary character and meaning of the preceding passage. Jesus reveals to his followers that he is fulfilling the mandate of the Father, the most elemental aspect of his life. His food is to do the will of the one who sent him and to finish his work (4:34). The disciples must open their eyes to the vast fields that are ready for harvest (4:35). The harvest undoubtedly includes the Samaritans from Sychar who were even at that moment walking out of the town toward Jesus (4:30), but it will include other fields as well for those who are willing to lift up their eyes and look. Jesus has already done the sowing, and now the disciples share in the reaping (4:36-38). The disciples need to understand that they are expected to carry on their master's evangelistic ministry even after his departure. Their work grows out of his labor. In concluding his interpretation of chapter 4, Schnackenburg writes, "All missionary work is in unbroken continuity with the mission and work of Jesus, and every missionary builds on the labours of his predecessors."[26]

Salvation is for all: Jews, Samaritans, Gentiles, all who believe in Jesus. However, the gospel of John is clear on one point. It rejects the idea that salvation will be automatically efficacious for every human being. Faith in Christ's substitutionary sacrifice is a precondition to being reconciled with God. The determining factor, if one would enter God's kingdom, is the acceptance of Christ's exclusive claim to be the only way to the true life in God (14:6).

## THE CONTINUATION OF MISSION:
## THE SENDING OF THE DISCIPLES

Only a relatively small band of disciples accompany Jesus Christ on his three-year sojourn throughout the land of Palestine. They are willing to share their master's company to receive from him the true knowledge of God. In his teaching Christ is often hard-pressed to dispel their self-conceived religious misconceptions. Yet even when they encoun-

---

[25] Köstenberger, "Missiological Insights," 456.

[26] Rudolf Schnackenburg, *The Gospel according to St. John* (New York: Herder & Herder, 1968), 1:454-55.

ter his hard teachings, they cling to him, for the most part, in complete loyalty. They recognize in him the Holy One of God, who has come to impart eternal life to them (6:68-69).

Three times in John's gospel Jesus explicitly commissions these faithful disciples as his "sent ones" (4:38; 17:18; 20:21). After his conversation with the Samaritan woman, Jesus sends his disciples to reap the harvest (4:35-38). Their mission's objective is to "reap fruit for eternal life" (4:36), meaning that they should introduce others to Christ as the one who confers eternal life. The earnestness to meet the challenges of this all-absorbing task is fueled by the awareness of the impending judgment upon the world (5:22, 27-30). One day the risen Christ will pass an impartial verdict over the lives of all human beings and their eternal destiny will be based upon whether or not they have believed in the gospel (3:16-18).

In the high priestly prayer Jesus does not express a desire for the Father to take his disciples out of the world but only to protect them from the evil one (17:15). Jesus asks the Father to sanctify (set aside for a specific purpose) the disciples by the truth, which they will find in the Word of God (17:17). Seemingly assured of God's answer, he continues: "As you sent me into the world, I have sent them into the world. For them I sanctify myself, that they too may be truly sanctified" (17:18-19; cf. 2 John 1-4; 3 John 3). Jesus' disciples are set apart in order that they might be sent as he was previously sent. Jesus also prays that his disciples might live with unity, since their oneness will serve as a witness to the world of the truth concerning Jesus (John 17:21-23). When believers love one another, the world recognizes that they are true followers of Jesus Christ (13:34-35).

Shortly before Christ ascended to heaven, he commissioned his disciples to evangelize the world. "As the Father has sent me, I am sending you" (20:21). Referring to this verse, John Stott remarked that the church's mission finds precise articulation in the Fourth Gospel:

> The crucial form in which the Great Commission has been handed down to us (though it is the most neglected because it is the most costly) is the Johannine. Jesus had anticipated it in his prayer in the upper room which he said to the Father: "As thou didst send me into the world, so I have sent them into the world" (John 17:18). Now, probably in the same upper room but after his death and resurrection, he turned his prayer-statement into a commission and said: "As the Father has sent me, even so I send you" (John 20:21). In both of these sentences Jesus did more than draw a vague parallel between his mission and ours. Deliberately and precisely he made his mission the *model* of ours, saying "*as* the Father sent me, *so* I send you." Therefore our understanding of

the church's mission must be deduced from our understanding of the Son's.[27]

Jesus' activity as the one sent by the Father serves as the definitive example for his followers as they seek to fulfill their mission. Jesus was always obedient, striving to complete the Father's work and to communicate the Father's message. The fulfillment of his mission came about at great personal suffering. Likewise, the disciples of Jesus must respond with faithful obedience, regardless of the cost. They continue to witness to the truth of God's message in order that others may find life and forgiveness in Jesus.

After this commission Jesus imparts to his disciples the means to fulfill their mission: "'Peace be with you! As the Father has sent me, I am sending you.' And with that he breathed on them and said, 'Receive the Holy Spirit'" (20:21-22). In the future the disciples will remain steadfast in their witness by relying on God's peace and the power of his Spirit.[28] Their ministry is to tell the world that forgiveness of sins is available in Christ. "If you forgive anyone his sins, they are forgiven; if you do not forgive them, they are not forgiven" (20:23; cf. 1 John 3:4-6).

The anointing of the Holy Spirit is a sufficient enablement for carrying on the mission. At least five times in the upper-room discourse (John 14-16), Jesus promises the Spirit's coming. Sent by the Father (14:26), he will testify about Christ (15:26) in the hearts of human beings, so that they might recognize the truth of the disciples' message about Jesus (cf. 1 John 5:6-10). John's first epistle elaborates on the witness of the Spirit by explaining that the Spirit gives assurance to believers that God has indeed granted to them eternal life (1 John 2:20-27; 3:24; 4:13). Jesus also predicts that when the Spirit comes he will convict the people of this world concerning their sin, (un)righteousness, and judgment (John 16:8-11). The Spirit will lead Jesus' followers into all truth (14:17; 16:13), and he will play an important role in calling to remembrance Christ's teaching (14:26). The Holy Spirit is permanently present within the church as its divine teacher (14:17, 26).

Although Jesus' disciples are commissioned by the Son of God and anointed with the Spirit of God, they must still expect opposition in the world as they seek to fulfill their mission. The world will hate and persecute them because of their identification with Jesus (15:18-21).

---

[27] J. R. W. Stott, *Christian Mission in the Modern World* (Downers Grove, Ill.: InterVarsity, 1975), 23. For a similar point, see Towner, "Paradigms Lost," 106.

[28] For a more extended treatment of the Holy Spirit's role in enabling Christ's followers to fulfill their mission to the world, see Senior and Stuhlmueller, *Biblical Foundations*, 285-88; Ruiz, *Missionsgedanke*, 20-23.

This is, of course, how Jesus was also treated, and it would be unrealistic for servants to expect better treatment than their master received. Near the end of his life Christ reminds the disciples emphatically of their grave responsibility to regard things eternal as of greater value than any earthly consideration. "The man who loves his life will lose it, while the man who hates his life in this world will keep it for eternal life" (12:25). To make his point unmistakably clear he took recourse to a parable, telling them that only if a grain of wheat falls to the ground and dies will it produce fruit (12:24). Death to self brings forth life in others. If the disciples truly desire to serve God, they must proclaim the gospel of revelation and redemption, even if it means to encounter their own personal Golgotha along the way. Their martyrdom would be a mark of honor, which God would personally recognize (12:26; 21:18-19).

Another difficulty that the church must face in discharging its duty is to counter the spread of false teaching. In his epistles, particularly his first, John finds it necessary to stand against false teachers. Scholars have made a number of suggestions concerning the identity and viewpoints of the false teachers opposed by John in his epistles, with an early form of Gnosticism being the most frequent suggestion.[29] What seems clear from John's writing is that some denied that Jesus was the Christ, the Son of God (1 John 2:22; 5:1, 5). Apparently this denial came as the result of their rejection of Christ's incarnation (4:1-3; 2 John 7; cf. 3 John 9-11). John recognizes in that heresy the most conspicuous product of the antichristian spirit.

> Every spirit that acknowledges that Jesus Christ has come in the flesh is from God, but every spirit that does not acknowledge Jesus is not from God. This is the spirit of the antichrist, which you have heard is coming and even now is already in the world (1 John 4:2-3).

Refusing to believe that Christ had assumed a human body during his earthly existence would be the prevalent attitude characterizing the general apostasy at the closing of the age. The only sure antidote would be a Spirit-given discernment of the truth, which would engender a consistent lifestyle on the part of the believers who would conform to it (1 John 4:1, 4-6; 2 John 4, 7-11; 3 John 3-4). By the time John wrote his first epistle, the false teachers and their followers had separated themselves from the church, presumably to set up their own rival

---

[29] For an overview of literature concerning John's opponents, see I. Howard Marshall, *The Epistles of John*, NICNT (Grand Rapids: Eerdmans, 1978), 16-22; D. A. Carson, Douglas J. Moo, and Leon Morris, *An Introduction to the New Testament* (Grand Rapids: Zondervan, 1992), 452-55.

congregation (1 John 2:18-19). This action of separation provided John with a further reason to emphasize the need for true believers to love one another (2:10; 3:10-11, 14; 4:7-8, 20-21).

The followers of Jesus serve as witnesses to the truth among people blinded by falsehood. They share light and life in the midst of darkness. Although persecuted and hated, they pursue an abundant life without despair. They have hope because they are sent into the world by a sovereign Lord who is in the process of calling out people for himself.

## THE HOPE OF MISSION: GOD'S SOVEREIGN CALLING

Given the dark portrait of the world in the Fourth Gospel, it would be easy to assume that John foresees the disciples' mission as largely ineffective. On the contrary, John maintains hope for the progress of the truth, because God sovereignly works in the lives of individuals to bring them to salvation. The emphasis in John's gospel is not on the efforts of human beings to find God but on the work of God to bring to himself those who are his own.

John presents salvation as the activity of the Father, Son, and Spirit. Only those who are drawn by the Father come to Jesus and find life (6:44; cf. 6:65). On several occasions Jesus refers to certain chosen ones who are given by the Father to the Son (6:37, 39; 10:29; 17:2, 6, 9; 18:9). To these, Jesus imparts eternal life, securely possessing them so that none of them is lost. Jesus is the Good Shepherd who knows his sheep and they know him; they hear his voice and follow him (10:3-4, 14, 26-28). Jesus also identifies some who are not his sheep, who do not believe or follow him (10:25-26). Human destiny depends ultimately not on an individual's decisions but on Jesus' choice (15:16). Regeneration, the birth of a new spiritual life, comes about by the work of the Spirit not by human choice (1:12-13; 3:3-8; 6:63). Only the one who is born from above by the Spirit is able to enter into the kingdom of God.

Nevertheless, the Fourth Gospel includes both the effectual call of God's elect and the universal offer of salvation. As Carson points out, "No New Testament book more acutely focuses attention on these essentially biblical polarities than the Gospel of John."[30] Frequently in John's gospel, salvation is offered to whoever believes in Jesus, but at the same time the axiom is established that unaided human volition is incapable of procuring salvation. In the first chapter of his gospel the apostle John states that all who receive Jesus and believe in him have

---

[30] Carson, *John*, 100. For an extended treatment of this subject, see D. A. Carson, *Divine Sovereignty and Human Responsibility: Biblical Perspectives in Tension*, New Foundations Theological Library (Atlanta: John Knox, 1981).

the authority to become God's children, but then he immediately points out that these children are not born into God's family through human choice but by God's work (1:12-13). The same truth is repeated by Jesus in greater clarity during his conversation with Nicodemus (3:3, 5-6; cf. 3:15). Jesus teaches that the only ones to come to him are those that the Father gives (6:37), but then he almost immediately states that it is the Father's will that everyone who looks to the Son and believes in him should have eternal life (6:40). The critical point is that human efforts are summarily excluded in affecting reconciliation with God. Eternal life is a gift from God that can only be received by faith. Yet it is freely available and fully efficacious to whoever wants to receive it. Whoever listens to Jesus and believes in him has crossed over from death to life, never to be condemned (5:24). At the same time, rejecting Jesus means forfeiting eternal life (8:23-24). It is a serious matter how one responds to Jesus' messianic claims, since those who refuse to believe in him are guilty and under the wrath of God (3:36). They are held accountable for their choices.

## CONCLUSION

In his writings John claims to bear witness to the truth (John 8:31-32; cf. 1 John 3:18-19; 4:6; 2 John 1, 4; 3 John 3-4). These writings reserve the right to define reality and, as a consequence, to call into question other truth claims. Truth, however, is not an abstract concept; it is embodied in the person of Jesus Christ, as the one sent by the Father to redeem humankind (John 14:6; cf. 1:14, 17).

The theology of mission in John's writings is likewise built upon a christological foundation, since God expresses his mission preeminently in Jesus. Christ assumes the role of the sent one of God, the Son of the living God who takes on an earthly existence. God would not be thwarted in his predetermined purpose for creation. God's plan for salvation through the course of history is demonstrated supremely in the events surrounding Christ's life, death, and resurrection. On the cross, Christ revealed the depth of divine grace and judgment in his own body. Suffering the final consequences of sin, death, and separation from God, he became the sinless substitute for a guilty humanity, the Lamb of God who takes away the sin of the world. Because of this death, salvation and eternal life are available to all who believe in him. Christ completes the redemptive work of God and brings salvation to the whole world. After his resurrection, Jesus sends out his followers. Empowered by the Holy Spirit, the disciples are given the privilege and responsibility of carrying the message of eternal life and the forgiveness of sins into the harvest fields of the world.

If the mission-consciousness of the modern church is lacking in fervency and conviction, it is finally because of its often superficial and

nominal adherence to the truth, which is ultimately a lack of dedica-
tion to Jesus Christ. The world needs to hear the truth and to learn
about Jesus. A weakened church will only regain its vitality by renew-
ing its commitment to proclaim boldly Jesus Christ, the true sent one
of God.

# 13

# *Mission in Revelation*

## Johnny V. Miller

The history of salvation begins in a garden, Eden, and two people communing with God. It ends in a city, the New Jerusalem, paradise regained. Between these two scenes is the account of humanity's loss of fellowship with God, and God's mission to reclaim both the lost territory and its inhabitants for fellowship with him, to his own glory. From a mission perspective, the Bible is the story of God's glorification through redemption. The book of Revelation is presented as the final chapter in that story, both bibliographically and eschatologically. It is the final phase of God's work of both redemption and judgment before time and eternity merge once again. We should expect, then, to see the unfinished strands of God's salvation history finally woven together in this account.

Such, in fact, is what one observes. History climaxes with a series of judgments upon the world system, which is unsubmitted to Christ. But that is not the highlight of the account. Rather, the chief feature is the reclamation of God's rightful territory, and the establishment of his sovereign rule over the earth and over the redeemed from every part of the earth. The missiological approach is key to understanding Revelation in relationship to the rest of the scriptures, and to the interpretation of the book itself. In the myriad of studies of Revelation, both scholarly and popular, almost no attention has been paid to its contributions to the theology of mission. It is hoped that more evangelical scholarship will explore the writing in this light.

### INTERPRETIVE ISSUES

The interpretation and application of Revelation hinge primarily on three issues: the historical background, the literary genre, and the interpretive approach to be adopted. It is assumed that the author was the apostle John, although there is divided assessment on this issue.[1] The writing is signed by John, and the weight of church history, beginning with Justin,[2] favors John the apostle. This "John" had to be well-known to the churches of Asia Minor since he needed no other description. The beloved apostle is believed to have lived in Ephesus, and the message to the Ephesians (Rev. 2:1-7) shows particular familiarity with that city.[3] He is the only John of certain identification known to that church.

## HISTORICAL SETTING

The book is addressed to seven churches in Asia Minor that were the product of and participants in missionary labor. They were spiritual oases in a hostile environment, the objects of both persecution and seduction by their religious counterparts. The setting is clearly first century, and historical evidence favors the reign of Domitian (81-96 C.E.).[4]

During the reigns of both Nero (54-68 C.E.) and Domitian the cult of emperor worship brought stress to the church. The test of good citizenship included participation in the rite of acclaiming Caesar as Lord. A Christian could not join in emperor worship and still be loyal to Christ, who brooks no rival lords (Rev. 19:16). Therefore, to be Christian was de facto disloyalty to Rome, once it demanded supreme allegiance. Eventually Christianity would be treated as treason, and its adherents executed without formality of trial.[5] However, in the first century there is no known persecution emanating from Rome and covering the entire empire.[6] Where religious persecution erupted, it was

---

[1] Donald Guthrie (*New Testament Introduction*, 3d ed. [Downers Grove, Ill.: InterVarsity, 1970], 948-49) is agnostic; D. A. Carson, Douglas J. Moo, and Leon Morris (*An Introduction to the New Testament* [Grand Rapids: Zondervan, 1992], 473) are positive. For a representative opponent of this view, see Werner Georg Kümmel, *Introduction to the New Testament*, trans. Howard Clark Kee (Nashville: Abingdon, 1975), 469-72.

[2] Justin, *Dialogue with Trypho*, 81.4.

[3] Colin J. Hemer, *The Letters to the Seven Churches of Asia in Their Local Setting, JSNTSup*, no. 11 (Sheffield: JSOT, 1986), 55.

[4] "On the principle that a strong tradition must be allowed to stand unless internal evidence makes it impossible, which is certainly not the case, the Domitian dating must have the decision in its favor" (Guthrie, *Introduction*, 957).

[5] See Stephen Benko, *Pagan Rome and the Early Christians* (Bloomington, Ind.: Indiana University Press, 1984), 1-4.

[6] Leon Morris (*Revelation*, 2d ed. [Grand Rapids: Eerdmans, 1987], 36-37) notes that emperor worship was not officially imposed before Domitian. "It was the spontaneous response of the people in the provinces to the peace and good government they owed to the Romans. There was thus a popular demand for emperor worship and the Christians would have found themselves very much out of step."

likely the work of local authorities, or else the product of animosity from local adherents of other gods who resented the exclusivist claims of Jesus Christ and the loyalty of his adherents. Significantly, during Domitian's reign a new "Caesar temple" was erected in Ephesus, increasing the possibility of persecution.[7]

It is against this backdrop of difficulty that John received his visions of the end times of salvation history. The cosmic orientation of the visions propels the reader beyond first-century experiences. Kiddle theorizes that John projected from the present persecutions of the church to a time when the cult of emperor worship was bound to be a mortal enemy of the church.[8] Ladd, however, speaks for many evangelicals in proposing that the simmering first-century problems were suggestive of the boiling cauldron of the end times.[9] What they were undergoing was paradigmatic of the eventual turmoil to be unleashed upon the earth under a ruling entity that would demand absolute political and spiritual allegiance.

## APPROACHES TO INTERPRETATION

Elisabeth Schüssler Fiorenza accurately summarizes the situation: "Despite all scholarly efforts, no generally recognized or accepted consensus has been reached in regard to the composition and the theological interpretation of the book."[10] Interpreters divide into four approaches:[11] (1) the preterist, which takes the entire message as

---

[7] See Guthrie, *Introduction*, 953; Morris, *Revelation*, 36-37; Carson, Moo, and Morris, *Introduction*, 474; Martin Kiddle, *The Revelation of St. John*, 7th ed. (London: Hodder and Stoughton, 1963), xli; Eusebius, *Ecclesiastical History*, 3.20. Will Durant (*Caesar and Christ* [New York: Simon and Schuster, 1944], 290-92) notes that Domitian initiated a project to restore the ancient religions, raising temples to Isis, Serapis, Jupiter, Juno, and Minerva, among other extravagances. Domitian required his officials to speak of him as *Dominus et Deus Noster*, "Our Lord and God."

[8] Kiddle, *Revelation*, xli. See also G. R. Beasley-Murray, *The Book of Revelation* (Greenwood, S.C.: Attic Press, 1974), 13: "For John, this foreshadowed the movement of the Antichrist, of which prophecy, ancient and modern, spoke."

[9] "For the demonic powers which will be manifested at the end in the great tribulation were also to be seen in the historical hatred of Rome for God's people and the persecution they were to suffer at Rome's hand" (George Eldon Ladd, *A Commentary on the Revelation of John* [Grand Rapids: Eerdmans, 1972], 13-14).

[10] Elisabeth Schüssler Fiorenza, *The Book of Revelation: Justice and Judgment* (Philadelphia: Fortress Press, 1985), 35.

[11] For a description of these various approaches, see Merrill C. Tenney, *Interpreting Revelation* (Grand Rapids: Eerdmans, 1957), 135-46.

immediately relevant to the first-century church, and symbolical of the issues faced by those living under the Roman empire[12]; (2) the historicist, which sees the symbols of the book unfolding the history of the Christian church from the first century through the present; (3) the idealist, which interprets the symbols as timeless truths for all church ages but unrelated specifically to any period of church history; and (4) the futurist, which views the message as relevant to the first-century church but understands the primary import of the visions to be prophetic of the last days of salvation history. While evangelicals may fit any of these camps, it is almost solely evangelicals who are futurists.

One's interpretative approach depends on one's understanding of the literary genre. Is Revelation apocalypse or prophecy? Apocalypse is most clearly identified by its pseudonymity, symbolism, and revision (fictionalization) of history.[13] Biblical prophecy, in contrast, while also employing symbolism, comes from an identified author and speaks to history in real time. The book certainly has many of the features of apocalypse, but it varies in crucial details: It is not pseudonymous or "secret wisdom," and it has an epistolary framework.[14] If it were apocalyptic, then the first-century significance of the symbols would be the key to interpretation. While it would have some enduring significance and even application, its primary meaning would be relevant only to first-century believers.

---

[12] Wilfrid J. Harrington, O.P. (*Revelation* [Collegeville, Minn.: Liturgical Press, 1993], 16) calls this "the method followed by all modern critical biblical scholars."

[13] See G. E. Ladd, "Apocalyptic Literature," in *ISBE*, ed. Geoffrey W. Bromiley (Grand Rapids: Eerdmans, 1979), 1:151-61, especially 152-53.

[14] Kümmel, *Introduction*, 418-19. See also Glenn W. Barker, William L. Lane, and J. Ramsey Michaels, *The New Testament Speaks* (New York: Harper & Row, 1969), 364: "His book is not an 'apocalypse' in the technical sense but a 'prophecy' (1:3, 22:7, 10, 18, 19)." With this Schüssler Fiorenza (*Justice and Judgment*, 151) agrees, as does Leon Morris (*Apocalyptic*, 2d ed. [Grand Rapids, Mich.: Eerdmans, 1984], 91-95). Cf. also Carson, Moo, and Morris (*Introduction*, 479) who propose that the genre is "epistle." Craig L. Blomberg ("The Diversity of Literary Genres in the New Testament," in *New Testament Criticism and Interpretation*, ed. David Alan Black and David S. Dockery [Grand Rapids: Zondervan, 1991], 523) considers it a combination of prophecy, apocalyptic, and epistle. In distinguishing the two types, George Eldon Ladd ("Apocalyptic, Apocalypse," in *Baker's Dictionary of Theology*, ed. by Everett F. Harrison [Grand Rapids: Baker, 1960], 50-54) says that no sharp line can be drawn between the two, and that there is a "prophetic and a non-prophetic apocalypse," and the Revelation is among the first type. Cf. also George E. Ladd, "Why Not Prophetic-Apocalyptic?" *JBL* 76 (1957): 192-200; David E. Aune, *The New Testament in Its Literary Environment*, Library of Early Christianity (Philadelphia: Westminster, 1987), 226-52.

However, if it is predictive prophecy, intended to be interpreted eschatologically, then the message was relevant to the first-century church with primary significance for all ages of the church, as believers look for the promised return of their resurrected Lord. All prophecy was given in the context of a larger message that had significance to its immediate recipients, even though fulfillment of certain elements of the message might be divinely determined to be still centuries in the future, such as those prophecies that related to the first advent of the Messiah.[15] Revelation claims to be prophecy (1:1), and John claims to be the channel, not the author, of its message (1:2, 11, 19; 10:4, 11; 14:13, etc.).

The key to interpretation is found in the prolific citation of Old Testament prophecy. There are repeated allusions to such books as Daniel, Zechariah, Ezekiel, Isaiah, Jeremiah, Joel, and Exodus. Guthrie notes that out of 404 verses, only 126 contain no Old Testament allusion.[16] The introduction (1:7) points this direction when the author conjoins Daniel 7:13 and Zechariah 12:10, two prophecies of the return and reign of the Messiah, in such a way as to focus on a specific future event as central to the theme of Revelation. One's approach to Revelation should be consistent with one's approach to these Old Testament prophecies.

The visions of Revelation seem to bring to culmination the yet unfulfilled prophecies prominent in the aforementioned Old Testament writings. While the language is symbolical, even "apocalyptic," behind those symbols are the same kind of literal realities that were behind similar symbolic language of Old Testament prophecy that introduced readers to world powers as beasts, their leaders as horns, and the emissaries of God as angelic horsemen. First-century readers would have been schooled in this approach to the prophetic scriptures by the Jewish apostles, who were themselves thus schooled through the teaching of Christ (Matt. 24-25).

The same Old Testament writings that promised a first and second advent of the Messiah also unfolded God's plan for a universal mission, that is, to claim from among every group of peoples on earth a distinct people for his own name who would be loyal to his Messiah. It is the confluence of these prophecies regarding the Messiah's return and global redemption that occupies Revelation. There are three major topics that connect the message of Revelation to God's global mission: the cosmic Christ, the conflict of the ages, and the consummation of the ages.

---

[15] Ladd ("Apocalyptic, Apocalypse," 52) writes: "The prophets took their stand within a specific historical situation and addressed their message to their environment."

[16] Guthrie, *Introduction*, 964-65.

## THE COSMIC CHRIST:
## THE SUBJECT AND OBJECT OF MISSION

God's mission takes place within the framework of salvation history; God works in the context of history both to judge and to redeem. According to Revelation, it is impossible to understand God's activity in history or the church's mission apart from an appropriate perspective on the Lord Jesus Christ, since he stands at the center of salvation history. The subject of mission proclamation in the New Testament is redemption by the crucified Christ and the subsequent rule of the risen Christ. The Jesus of history is the Christ of God, sovereign over all the earth.[17] The object of mission is to establish his lordship over all nations through voluntary submission of faith in his divine person and his redeeming work. In Revelation, Jesus Christ is depicted in four aspects.

First, he is an overwhelming presence at the locus of his churches (Rev. 1:12-20). The immensity and splendor of his appearance communicate both comfort and challenge to his persecuted body. He is the sovereign risen Lord, in control of their destiny (1:18). He is in their midst to empower and to purify. Mission flows from the power of his presence among his churches (chaps. 2-3).[18] The selection of seven churches and the application of each message to all of the churches (2:7, etc.) probably indicate the timeless and universal intention of each message.

Second, he is the slain Lamb, the meek sacrificial substitute, who is also heaven's Lion, the fierce and powerful prophesied ruler (5:5-6). He receives authority and worship in heaven and on earth because of his substitutionary atonement, which purchased universal redemption (5:9; cf. 1:5; 7:14; 14:3-4). If this statement of praise is proleptic, it anticipates the revelation to follow; if not, it depicts the fruit of the faithful witness of the churches. Whichever, it spotlights the heavenly celebra-

---

[17] Jesus Christ is no tribal God; he is the earth's only Lord and Savior (John 14:6; Acts 4:12). The proposition that Jesus is only one of many revelations of God is diametrically opposed to consistent biblical teaching. Cf., for example, John Hick and Paul F. Knitter, eds., *The Myth of Christian Uniqueness: Toward a Pluralistic Theology of Religions* (Maryknoll, N.Y.: Orbis Books, 1988). There is not one suggestion in the Old or New Testament scriptures that other religions gave people a knowledge of God or brought them into a relationship with God. Jesus himself said to religious Jews who knew the scriptures, worshiped at the temple, and considered themselves followers of God: "You know neither me nor my Father. If you had known me, you would have known my Father also" (John 8:19).

[18] Paulin Poucouta, "La mission prophetique de l'Eglise dans l'Apocalypse johannique," *NRT* 110 (1988): 38-57.

tion of the fulfillment of God's salvation history, in which redemption is effected to all peoples of the earth and the Son receives the worship he deserves to the glory of God (5:12-14; cf. 1:5-6; 11:17-18). Schüssler Fiorenza argues that John does not conceive of salvation as individual and spiritual but rather as political and socio-economic, relating the song of the elders (5:9) to exodus terminology and the liberation of Israel from the slavery of Egypt.[19] However, her dichotomization is unwarranted. It is the blood of the slain Lamb that makes redemption possible (7:14; 13:8), and it is because of personal salvation that one is able to enjoy the political, social, and economic benefits of the king-dom reign of Christ (21:8, 27). The power of the Lamb is the power of holy sacrifice.

Third, he is the judge of the earth (14:14), who participates in har-vesting the grapes of wrath. There are consequences for rejecting the Lamb, and his love does not cancel his righteousness. In a sense, all of the judgments visited upon the earth through the trumpets and bowls are the work of the Son, inasmuch as they are the work of God. The Father is Creator (4:11) and rightly judges the rebellious planet (11:17-18). The Son's personal role in the judgment is touched on twice—14:14; 19:11. In 14:14 the image is reaping, and the Son of Man wields the sickle (cf. Joel 3:12-13; Jer. 51:33). The context seems to presume that the reaping is judgment (cf. Rev. 14:10-11), a prophesied role of the Son of Man (John 5:27; Dan. 7:28-29). The implication of the larger scriptural context is that this judgment is manifest in the out-pouring of the bowls (Rev. 16) and the subsequent plagues. If so, then the hand of the Son is as much behind the torments on the unbelieving world as is the hand of the Father (cf. 14:7). The second scene of judg-ment is 19:11, when the Son makes war on the unbelieving armies. This answers the taunt of 13:4, "Who is able to make war against the beast?" The authority to judge is a corollary to his sovereignty.

Fourth, he is the King of kings and Lord of lords (19:16; cf. 11:15-18; 12:10). He has authority to open the scrolls and unleash judgment over all the globe, preparing the way for his return (5:5; 16:1). Jesus Christ is the returning sovereign, who slays his enemies with the sword of his mouth (19:11-16; cf. 17:14) and then gathers his redeemed into his kingdom. The establishment of this kingdom is the climax of mis-sion (7:9-12). He is also the eternal sovereign in the New Jerusalem, one with Almighty God forever (21:22-23). He shares the throne of God the Father (4:2; 5:6), and in name and attributes is equal to the "I AM" (1:4, 8; 21:6; 22:13). The purpose of mission is predominantly

---

[19] Schüssler Fiorenza, *Justice and Judgment*, 72-74. Her argument regard-ing the baptismal formula of 1:5 is unconvincing. She seems to make an error in logic, confusing purpose (spiritual redemption) with result (a new order).

to make him known, and to invite the thirsty of the nations to come to him and drink (22:17).

## THE CONFLICT OF THE AGES:
## THE NEED FOR AND CHALLENGE TO MISSION

Salvation history is the record of warfare for dominion over the globe and its inhabitants. God has declared that the Son shall rule (Ps. 2:7-9; Rev. 2:26-27; 12:5; 19:15). But just as the cosmic claims of the triune God have never gone unchallenged since the fall of Adam and Eve, so also those of Jesus have been resisted since his ascension. The gospel and the church have always met with opposition to the exclusiveness of Christ's claims and to the righteousness of his requirements. This is the nature of spiritual warfare, which climaxes in Revelation and which defines the need for and character of mission. The church's mission takes place in the context of conflict, a struggle that may easily escalate to the point of persecution and suffering for faithful believers.[20]

The visions of Revelation afford realistic perspective on the interplay between heaven's and earth's affairs in influencing world history. The apostle received glimpses behind the curtain of history into the inner sanctum of heaven and then saw the outworking of heaven's actions in the world of nature (e.g., 8:5; cf. Ezek. 10:4-5). He saw two arch foes and two warring systems: God and Satan, heaven and Babylon (cf. Rev. 12:1-6).

Babylon symbolizes throughout scripture the organized system of religion that opposes God's revealed way (Gen. 11:1-9). Roman emperor worship was an example of Babylon's system (cf. Dan. 3). And so also was the Judaic system that rejected Messiah Jesus and depended upon continuing sacrifices or works righteousness as avenues of acceptability to God (Rev. 2:9; 11:8). So also is an economic system that puts material comfort and security ahead of spiritual reality (Rev. 18). All organized religion that rejects or ignores the slain Lamb is the expression of Babylon and is destined to be defeated in the end (14:8; 18:2). In this symbolism Revelation grants insight into the true nature of such religions: they are Satanic substitutes for reality. Satan is the arch deceiver; his modus operandi is to fool or intimidate the world into worshiping him through some substitute form of god, whether spiritual or economic (12:9; 13:17-18).

---

[20] Donald Senior and Carroll Stuhlmueller (*The Biblical Foundations for Mission* [Maryknoll, N.Y.: Orbis Books, 1983], 305) write: "The Christians are to proclaim the good news of universal salvation to the world, and their pulpit is a heroic refusal to compromise with a system they see as aligned with the forces of sin and death."

It is because of this systemic warfare that mission is necessary. Mission is the invasion of Babylon, Satan's territory, in search of God's chosen (13:8). God's agents of invasion invite the earth's inhabitants to change sides, to profess a different loyalty, to submit to a different master. Mission is not the redemption of the system but the calling of people out of the system before the system is judged.

One agent of mission is the embattled church. The church is the true people of God (2:9-10), followers of the Lamb, entrusted with the exclusive message that offers eternal life, provoking the wrath of Satan (12:17). The church is God's outpost in enemy territory and therefore a target of Babylon. The seven churches in Asia Minor (2:1-3:22) experienced spiritual warfare because of their calling and placement. On one hand, there was subtle seduction to spiritual adultery, compromise with other religious systems that deny exclusive loyalty to Christ; there were syncretistic pressures (2:14, 20, meat offered to idols) and cultic perversions (2:6, 15, the Nicolaitans; 2:20, "Jezebel"). These were meant to destroy the church from within. On the other hand, there was outright persecution, designed to crush the church from without. Martyrdom (*martyr*, "witness," 1:5; 2:13; 11:3; 17:6) is the ultimate price of faithfulness to the Lamb, the most compelling form of witness. Persecution is no excuse for unfaithfulness; a church that compromises to avoid suffering has failed in its calling. Some witnesses are protected throughout their mission, while others die for their boldness (6:9-11; 12:11). The suffering church is not the exception but the rule when the church clashes with Babylon. Because death is not the end, the proclamation of God's exclusive way of salvation is more important than an individual life. The martyr has nothing to lose, while the listener has everything to gain. The followers of the Lamb are called to be victors, overcomers (chaps. 2–3; 12:11; 21:7). There is no easy triumphalism. The liberation proffered is from eternal judgment, not temporal injustice or suffering. John does not foresee the believer's deliverance from injustice or suffering this side of Christ's kingdom.

One group in Revelation, the 144,000, is especially effective as God's agent (7:4-8; 14:1-5). In an interlude to onrushing judgments the reader is introduced to this band of missionaries set apart for the final worldwide thrust. While many interpreters see no distinction between the 144,000 and the innumerable company that follows (7:9-17),[21] it seems

---

[21] For example, James du Preez, "Mission Perspective in the Book of Revelation," *EvQ* 42 (1970): 152-67. He calls the 144,000 "the Church of all nations" (156). For one among many commentators who takes this view, see G. B. Caird who concludes that "the hundred and forty-four thousand, then, are identical with the great throng from every nation" (*A Commentary on the Revelation of St. John the Divine*, HNTC [New York: Harper & Row, 1966], 95).

clear from the text that the groups are distinct. The 144,000 may represent a remnant of redeemed Jews[22] or a cadre from the church of the last days.[23] Whichever, it seems purposeful that they are identified separately from the "innumerable company" that represents "all nations, tribes, peoples, and tongues" (7:9). In fact, it is specifically the sealing and sending of the 144,000 (7:2-8) that fulfills God's global plan of salvation and elicits another overwhelming scene of worship and praise in heaven (7:9-14). Here we are given assurance that God's global design will come to fruition. These missionaries are protected by God's mark on their foreheads (7:3; 14:1; cf. Gen. 4:15; Ezek. 9:4-5) until their mission is finished (cf. Rev. 11:5-7). They wield the gospel with purity and perseverance (14:4), the marks of the missionary church. If the Savior is the example, then their most powerful weapon is the Word, which is also Christ's tool of conquest (1:16) and judgment (19:15). The message is proclaimed worldwide (cf. Matt. 24:14). A godly life is a powerful force to draw unbelievers toward the Savior (cf. 1 Pet. 3:1), but neither Revelation nor the rest of scripture knows anything of a wordless witness that saves through the impact of presence alone (cf. 1 Pet. 1:23). Faith has content—the saving revelation of Jesus Christ—and Revelation itself is part of that witness (1:1-3).

## THE CONSUMMATION OF THE AGES:
## MISSION ACCOMPLISHED

The great unfinished business of salvation history is the King's return (*parousia*) to claim his kingdom. The kingdoms of this world must become *the* kingdom of God and of his Christ. All humanity is either joined to Christ through redemption or excluded from his reign in eternal punishment. Such is the focal point of all that takes place in Revelation.

The consummation of the ages is inaugurated through global judgment. The seal, trumpet, and bowl judgments highlight the grace of God's patience during this present interim, as well as evidence his sovereignty over those who would pretend independence (6:15-16; 9:20-21; 16:9-11). The whole world fell under the sway of Satan (12:9), offering him worship (13:7-8), but that condition cannot endure. The judgments are the final temporal consequence of rebellion against God, as well as God's apologetic witness.[24]

---

[22] Joachim Jeremias (*Jesus' Promise to the Nations* [reprint, Philadelphia: Fortress, 1982], 57) proposes that one of Israel's roles is to draw the nations to Zion to share in its banquet.

[23] Ladd, *Revelation*, 43-44.

[24] Du Preez, "Mission Perspective," 160.

Angels are prominent as agents of God's judgments. They announce the judgments, sound the trumpets, pour out the bowls, and instruct the author. They even proclaim the "eternal gospel" to inhabitants of the earth (14:6) and warn them of impending judgment (14:8-10), but this angelic proclamation effects no human redemption. Apparently only human agents are channels of redemption.

Judgment gives way to blessing as Christ takes control. For a thousand years the covenant blessings as revealed to Israel will be seen upon the earth (20:1-6). The millennium will express God's reign on earth through his Messiah, David's greater Son, and all peoples of the world will live in oneness under him (20:3). Du Preez asserts that "nations" is not used in its ethnic sense but rather in its "religio-ethical connotation,"[25] but it is difficult to see how the writer could have made clearer that the universal salvation and rule of Christ, both in time and eternity, were specifically ethnic. The continual repetition of the inclusive elements of "nations, tribes, peoples, languages" (5:9; 7:9; 10:11; 11:9; 13:7; 14:6), without ever becoming formulaic, connote only ethnic, racial, political, and linguistic universalism.[26] This was always God's design for mission.

The reclamation project culminates in eternal judgment when Satan and his coworkers are assigned to the lake of fire for eternal torment, to be joined by all whose names were never written in the Lamb's book of life (20:15). Eternity is at stake in mission, for all unreached are excluded forever from the presence of God and of the Lamb (21:27; 22:15). Pilgrim resists this exclusiveness, preferring to see a "universalistic possibility" in the Apocalypse:

> It neither shuts the door completely to anyone, even the rebellious kings and their deceived followers, nor does it automatically open the door to everyone, regardless of their conduct. It allows the possibility of God's redemptive goal for all, yet leaves its actuality to God and God alone.[27]

However, it is difficult to see how the Revelation could have been clearer as to the fact of exclusion: "But the cowardly, unbelieving, abominable, murderers, sexually immoral, sorcerers, idolaters, and all

---

[25] J. du Preez, "People and Nations in the Kingdom of God according to the Book of Revelation," *Journal of Theology for Southern Africa* 49 (1984), 49.

[26] Karl Ludwig Schmidt, "*ethnos*," *TDNT*, 2:364-72. Robert H. Mounce (*The Book of Revelation*, NICNT [Grand Rapids: Eerdmans, 1977], 148) disagrees, contrasting the terms with the exclusivism of Judaism. But that exclusivism was specifically against all of the other people groups of the world.

[27] Walter E. Pilgrim, "Universalism in the Apocalypse," *WW* 9 (1989): 242.

liars shall have their part in the lake which burns with fire and brim-stone, which is the second death" (21:8).[28]

Despite this bad news, Revelation is not primarily about the defeat of the nations, even though at times they are enemies to Christ (11:18). Rather, it is about the winning of the nations. Though many are lost forever, a countless number is finally redeemed. God's purpose is not frustrated; his covenant with Abraham and with Christ is fulfilled. His sovereignty and election assure Christ's ultimate victory (13:8); they are the guarantees of the success of mission. The mission will be accomplished, and the result will be the salvation of some from every tribe, tongue, people, and nation.

The celebration of this fulfillment, first voiced in 5:9, resounds in the eternal kingdom (21:22-26). It is not a celebration of the distinction between the people of God and those not the people of God, or of Jews and Gentiles; rather, the inclusiveness of the invitation and the universality of the victory over the enemy are recognized in that *no group is missing from the kingdom.*

## CONCLUSION

The plan of God is to redeem some from every tongue, tribe, people, and nation to his own glory and in praise of his Son. Revelation comforts the church with the truth that God is bringing about this goal unto certain fulfillment. In addition, it challenges the church to stand firm, even unto death, in the face of all opposition, in order to have an effective role in the work of God and a full reward at its consummation. The present witness of the church rings out in the words of 22:17:

And the Spirit and the bride say "Come!" And let him who hears say "Come!" And let him who thirsts come. Whoever desires, let him take the water of life freely.

---

[28] See also Hemer, *Seven Churches*, 50-52, regarding the tree of paradise.

# Conclusion

## Joel F. Williams

The picture of a sower scattering seed is an intriguing metaphor for the Christian mission. Jesus uses this picture in a parable concerning four types of soil: hard, rocky, thorny, and fruitful (Matt. 13:1-23; Mark 4:1-20; Luke 8:4-15). A sower scatters seeds, and some land in places where it is impossible for plants to grow and thrive, while others fall on the good earth and yield an abundant harvest. Jesus' parable serves as a useful illustration for highlighting some of the main concerns of this book. The studies in this volume examine a number of principles and issues, but three recurring ideas are particularly significant for an evangelical approach to mission in the New Testament. These three concerns—the center of mission, the primary task of mission, and the cost of mission—are significant for a proper interpretation of the New Testament and relevant for the church's participation in the mission today. A full examination of the church's present-day missionary task would necessarily take into consideration additional information, including a study of the current world context and the history of missionary experience. Nevertheless, attention to the biblical teaching on mission is crucial for a basic understanding of the church's present task.

### GOD'S MISSION

One of the odd features of Jesus' parable is that the sower is apparently a wasteful farmer. Without a great deal of concern, the sower throws seeds along the road, on rocks, among thorns, as well as on good soil. The common practice at that time of plowing after sowing may partially explain the sower's actions. Also, some loss is simply the typical condition of farming. Yet the abundant harvest is clearly the result of God's blessing and not the sower's skill. The size of the harvest is out of proportion to the ability of the sower. Jesus tells a similar parable about a sower who scatters seeds and then goes to sleep, only to find later that the seeds sprout and grow all on their own without his help (Mark 4:26-29). An underlying principle that helps to make sense of both parables is that ultimately the harvest is the work of God.

This is God's mission. He sends, he empowers, and he produces the results. The ultimate purpose for the mission is to bring glory to God, so that a multitude from every nation, tribe, people, and language might declare the praise and honor and glory and power of God for all eternity. Believers participate in God's mission not because God needs their contribution but because they have convictions concerning the importance of God and his will and because God in his grace has stooped to include human agents in the accomplishment of his work. God stands at the center of mission as it is described in the New Testament.

The concept of *God's mission* has been understood in different ways, but in the New Testament it is wrapped up first and foremost in God's act of sending his Son, Jesus Christ. Jesus is the sent one of God, who fulfills the central task of God's saving mission through his death and resurrection. Jesus' death serves as the basis upon which a rebellious humanity might find forgiveness and a restored relationship with God. Following his resurrection Jesus commissions his followers to serve as his messengers among the nations through the power of the Spirit of God. It is impossible to join in God's mission without pointing to Jesus as the Savior of the world. In the New Testament, Jesus provides the way to God.

God's central place in mission is a theme that is repeated in a number of places in this volume. Jesus comes proclaiming the good news of the kingdom of God (Matt. 4:17; Mark 1:14-15; Luke 4:43). People must respond with repentance and faith, because the rule of God is near and is breaking into this world in the ministry of Jesus. Paul believes that God set him apart as an apostle and revealed the Son to him in order that he might proclaim the gospel among the Gentiles (Rom. 1:1-5; Gal. 1:15-17). Paul's message to the nations is the gospel of God, which functions as God's power to bring about salvation for everyone who believes (Rom. 1:1, 16-17). Paul depends on the Spirit of God to move others to accept the message of the gospel (1 Thess. 2:5-6) and to live holy lives (1 Thess. 4:7-8; 2 Thess. 2:13). Paul's letters portray him as an individual devoted to prayer, which serves as an expression of his confidence in the work of a sovereign and compassionate God. Paul's great missionary charter, the epistle to the Romans, reveals the extent to which he is committed to the preeminent place of God in his thought and mission. The gospels, especially that of John, present Jesus as the sent one of God (for example, Matt. 10:40; Mark 9:37; Luke 9:48; John 5:23-24). Jesus in turn sends out his disciples with the promise of divine presence and power (Matt. 28:18-20; Luke 24:46-49; John 20:21-22). John's gospel also emphasizes the glory of God as the ultimate objective of Jesus' mission (John 17:1), an objective for which believers may strive as well (John 15:8; 21:19). In Acts, Luke portrays the triune God as establishing and promoting mission, as participating in mission by working through human agents, and as producing the results of mission. The witnesses of Jesus Christ are able to carry out their task throughout the earth only through the empowerment of the Spirit of God (Acts 1:8). The book of Hebrews presents God as active in mission, since he still speaks through his Son (Heb. 1:1-2) and through his word, which is living and active (Heb. 4:12). The book of Revelation points to the consummation of God's mission, when the kingdoms of this world become the kingdom of the Lord and of his Christ (Rev. 11:15).

The church of Jesus Christ and a lost world are in need of sowers who will scatter seeds, seeking a harvest out of proportion to their own abilities. Such a harvest is possible because this mission is the work of God. The task of reaching the world with the gospel of Jesus Christ is too great for believers to fulfill in their own wisdom and strength. A reliance on human effort and ingenuity will keep them from attempting what can only be done in God's power. Believers must always remember that they are participating in God's work. They must depend on his grace and live for his glory. Of course, some may presume to have God's guidance and enabling, when all along they are simply mistaken. Our understanding of what God wants us to do and God's perception of our responsibilities may not always match. Nevertheless, does the church today contain too many people who move ahead in their service for the Lord without God's direction and blessing or too few people who will trust God to empower them and use them in significant ways for the kingdom of God? On the balance are we too bold or too timid in our faith? I think the answer is clear. We lack faith; we hope for so little of what God can do in and through us.

## THE PRIORITY OF PROCLAMATION IN MISSION

When Jesus explains the parable of the sower, he identifies the seed with the word. The sower spreads the word of the kingdom. A seed is a fitting metaphor for a message, since it is small and apparently insignificant but can produce a great harvest. In a similar parable Jesus compares the kingdom to a little mustard seed, which grows into a tree (Matt. 13:31-32; Mark 4:30-32; Luke 13:18-19). It may appear woefully inadequate to suggest that first and foremost the solution to the world's problems is a message about Jesus Christ, but that is the plan of the God who created seeds. For the apostle Paul, missionary work involves the foolishness of preaching about Jesus Christ and his crucifixion, because Christ is the power and wisdom of God (1 Cor. 1:18-25).

In several ways the New Testament emphasizes that the primary task in mission involves the spreading of the word about Jesus and the salvation that he brings. Jesus' basic activity during his earthly ministry is preaching, and Jesus believes that he was sent in order to proclaim the gospel of the kingdom (Mark 1:38; Luke 4:43). Jesus is anointed by the Spirit to preach good news to the poor and to proclaim release to the prisoners and sight to the blind (Luke 4:16-21). Jesus also sends his followers out to proclaim a message concerning repentance and the forgiveness of sins among all the nations (Mark 13:10; Luke 24:45-49). In Matthew's gospel Jesus predicts the proclamation of the gospel of the kingdom in the whole world (Matt. 24:14), but he also stresses the need to make disciples and to teach new followers to obey his commands (Matt. 28:18-20). Evangelism and discipleship do not stand in contrast to one another but are logically related, bound together. Both are necessary, and both, of course, depend on the spoken word.

Paul perhaps serves as the New Testament's model missionary; his ministry is the paradigm for mission work. Paul's missionary work begins with the proclamation of the gospel of Jesus Christ, a proclamation Paul uses to move individuals to conversion (1 Thess. 1:4-10). Paul urges his listeners to repent of their idolatry and disobedience and to be reconciled to God in light of the work of Christ (1 Thess. 1:9; 2 Cor. 5:18-21). The preaching of the gospel includes an appeal to respond to Christ and accept the salvation he provides. Paul develops his gospel message most fully in the epistle to the Romans. Christ's death on the cross satisfies God's righteous wrath toward sin and provides the solution to the problem of human guilt. Therefore, God is just to offer a right standing before him to all who believe in Jesus (Rom. 3:21-26). Those who put their faith in Jesus are now empowered by the Spirit to live a life that is pleasing to God, because they are no longer enslaved to sin and death (Rom. 6:16-18; 8:1-4). Also in the epistle to the Romans, Paul explains that he has a particular burden to communicate this gospel message in the unreached, unevangelized areas of the world (Rom. 15:20-22; 16:26). Nevertheless, Paul's objective is not simply to preach the gospel and gain converts left in isolation from one another. He organizes new believers into self-governing churches, so that they might be nurtured and might encourage one another toward Christian maturity (Eph. 4:11-16; Col. 1:27-28). Paul's emphasis in his missionary work is on evangelism that leads to church planting. Paul seems to have seen little or no conflict between mission and church, between the spreading of the gospel and the creation and nurturing of believing communities. Evangelism and the planting of churches are both part of Paul's missionary work. Yet Paul's ministry is also itinerant. Although Paul reports his daily burden and concern for the churches (2 Cor. 11:28-29), he also exemplifies a willingness to leave behind newly formed churches and continue on to unreached territories. He is able to move on because he possesses confidence in the work of God's Spirit within these believing communities.

The book of Acts presents Jesus' followers as witnesses (Acts 1:8). The function of witnesses is not to do or accomplish anything but rather to give testimony to what they have seen and heard. In Acts this testimony takes the form of reporting the saving activity of the Lord Jesus, including his death and victorious resurrection (for example, Acts 2:22-24, 32). Believers can witness boldly and effectively to these events because they are empowered by the Holy Spirit (for example, Acts 4:31).

The church today needs those who will proclaim the word in the power of the Spirit, especially among people who have yet to hear and consider the message concerning Jesus Christ. By God's grace the proclamation of the gospel will lead to new believers who must be instructed in Jesus' teaching and gathered into churches. It is unlikely that the task of scattering God's word will be accomplished in the way that it has been traditionally approached, with a heavy reliance on Western missionaries. The financial cost of sending missionaries from the West is outpacing the interest and determination of the increasingly self-absorbed Western church. At the same time, Christianity is growing rapidly in the Two-Thirds World, as is the number of missionaries from non-Western churches. Western agencies must pass on responsibilities and oversight to younger churches, not only because this is right but also because the church as a whole desperately needs the leadership, insight, and active involvement of two-thirds-world Christians. The church today is a world church with a worldwide missionary task.

The greatest difficulty for giving a priority to evangelization in mission is the almost deafening cry of a world in pain. An emphasis on the importance of the gospel message appears as simply a means to ignore the massive physical and social needs of the world, particularly of the world's poor. Is the proclamation of the gospel an act of hypocrisy on the part of believers, a way to see the beaten, dying victim and still pass by on the other side of the road?

First, in answer to this question, the gospel does address the human plight. The message of Jesus Christ offers forgiveness of sin, a relationship with God, and the ability to live in obedience to God. Sin and the guilt of humanity before God are not disconnected from the painful circumstances of the world. Christians must confront the sinful condition that produces selfishness, exploitation, division, and despair. The gospel deals with the root problem rather than just symptoms. Also, the gospel changes lives and gives people the motivation to love others, since they have experienced the love of God.

Second, Christians should indeed care for the poor and serve a broken world. There is ample evidence from the New Testament that believers have a responsibility to love their neighbors and to do good to all, even to their enemies who hate them. Nevertheless, it is a mistake to confuse the mission of the church with everything that Christians should do. The emphasis in the New Testament is that the mission of the church is what the church has been sent by God to do, to go throughout the world and proclaim a message about Jesus and the salvation he provides. The mission of the church and social action are not mutually exclusive choices—believers can and should do both—but neither should they be completely identified. When social action becomes the mission of the church, the temptation arises to follow a particular political ideology, whether left or right, and to allow that ideology to set the agenda for the church. When the church becomes captive to political goals, evangelism and the nurturing of the church are viewed as less significant tasks or even as distractions to the "real" business at hand. At the worst, telling people about Jesus and the eternal salvation he provides becomes regarded as a counterproductive activity to be avoided.

Third, the care for the needs of the world is not the sole responsibility of the church. Every human being has intrinsic worth and dignity as a creation of God. No one should be exploited, oppressed, and left destitute for the selfish gain of another. Therefore, God expects everyone, including those in power, Christian or not, to treat people as valuable and worthy of respect. Yet, God has given to the church a responsibility that only the church can do, the responsibility to proclaim the gospel to the world. That task must not be set aside.

## THE REALITY OF RESISTANCE TO MISSION

In Jesus' parable of the sower, the seed sometimes falls on places where there are forces at work to impede growth and fruitfulness. According to Jesus' interpretation of the parable, there are hard places along the road where Satan is able to take away the seed. Part of the resistance to the message of the kingdom is supernatural and demonic in nature. The seed landing on the rocky places represents those who fall away from their commitment in the midst of persecution. The thorns symbolize certain priorities and values that distract people from the importance of the gospel. The worries of this age, the deceitfulness of wealth, and the desire for other things may choke out the word. The gospel does not always encounter an easy reception, with the result that sowers may face difficulty in fulfilling their task.

Persecution is an aspect of resistance that is a prominent theme in the New Testament and a repeated emphasis of this book. In John's gospel Jesus states that believers can expect persecution because he experienced the same as he fulfilled his mission (John 15:18-21). Jesus' suffering is a preview of the type of difficulty his followers will encounter in the world. Jesus teaches that there is a cost for following him, which involves bearing a cross and losing one's life (Matt. 10:38-39; Mark 8:34-37; Luke 9:23-25). Jesus also predicts that some will be arrested, beaten, and put to death because of their testimony and identification with Christ (Matt. 24:9-14; Mark 13:9-13; Luke 21:12-17). For Paul, the identifying marks of a true apostle, a "sent one" of God, are not simply miracles but also suffering and weakness (2 Cor. 12:10-12). Paul proves his apostleship to the Corinthians by cataloging his imprisonments, beatings, difficulties, and hardships (2 Cor. 11:21-28). The apostles are like those who are condemned to death, a spectacle to the whole universe (1 Cor. 4:9). The witness of believers in the book of Acts often takes place in the context of opposition and adversity (for example, Acts 4:1-22). One manifestation of the Spirit's power in believers is that they are able to speak the word with boldness in the midst of threatening circumstances (for example, Acts 4:23-31). Both Hebrews and 1 Peter treat endurance in persecution as a powerful statement to the world concerning the reality of the believer's hope in Jesus (for example, Heb. 10:32-39; 1 Pet. 3:13-18). When believers maintain a godly life in the midst of adverse circumstances, they are able to silence critics (1 Pet. 2:15; 3:15-16) and to win others to faith in Christ (1 Pet. 2:12; 3:1-2). The book of Revelation presents mission in the context of the conflict between the kingdom of God and the kingdoms of this world. This conflict involves real persecution for believers with real martyrs (Rev. 2:10; 6:9-11). The followers of Jesus should be prepared to suffer, because there is no promised end to the conflict before the return of Christ (Rev. 19:11-16).

Christians may suffer for several reasons, for example, on account of their own sinful actions or thoughtless mistakes. They may face persecution because of their stand against injustice. It is dangerous to side with the oppressed against the powerful, but such a stance may be necessary and too often the church has been silent. In addition, the New Testament assumes that it is possible to suffer as a Christian, that is, to suffer because of one's identification with Christ. 1 Peter urges the faithful not to be ashamed when they suffer as Christians or are insulted for the name of Christ (1 Pet. 4:14, 16). In the Sermon on the Mount, Jesus teaches his followers that they are blessed when people persecute them and slander them falsely because of their relationship with him (Matt. 5:11). In John's gospel Jesus predicts that his disciples will be mistreated because of his name (John 15:21). For Paul, it is a gracious gift from God not only to believe in Christ but also to suffer for his sake (Phil. 1:29). God may allow believers to suffer for Christ, which in fact is the case at this time in a number of places in the world.

The suffering of Christians is part of the context in which the discussion of religious pluralism must take place. Dialogue by Christians with other religions and ideologies cannot lead to such common ground that believers no longer have the possibility of suffering for Christ. When believers accept persecution because of their identification with Jesus, they do so out of a conviction that Jesus is the only true Lord and Savior of the world. If there are many ways to reach God, then why endure hardship for Christ? To waver on the unique authority of Jesus would be a rejection of our solidarity with brothers and sisters in Christ who are in fact suffering for their commitment to Jesus and would be a refusal to prepare to suffer in the same way. This does not mean that other religions and viewpoints are empty of any wisdom or beauty, but they are useless for reaching God, since this is through Jesus alone. Neither is it appropriate for Christians to be hostile toward those with whom they disagree, since all religious and ideological persecution is wrong. Christians who desire religious freedom for themselves should uphold it for all others. This world, though rebellious, is loved by God, and believers must follow God's example and love the people of this world, even if they reject God's ways. In addition, this argument does not convey that persecution is easy or desirable for the church. Persecution is intended to be damaging to the church and it sometimes is. Persecution may impede growth, rob the church of its leaders, and leave the faithful with the difficult task of restoring those who have denied their commitment. Yet God is able to make even persecution work out for good, by producing a stronger, more sincere community of believers. Although persecution may be difficult, faithfulness to Christ is necessary regardless of the cost. Ultimately, Christians maintain their conviction concerning the truth of the gospel not to gain power or prestige but to preserve for themselves the opportunity, if necessary, to suffer for the sake of Christ. Then in our weakness, God displays his power. Jesus himself came not to be served but to serve and to give his life, and Christianity functions best when it follows its master. Believers fulfill their mission most effectively when they go the way of the cross and live with sacrificial love toward others.

It would be a mistake to dwell on the reality of resistance without also pointing to the enormity of the harvest. In Jesus' parable the seeds fall not only along the road, on the rocky places, and among the thorns, but also on the good soil, where they produce an abundant crop. We live at a time when the gospel is bearing fruit throughout the world. The church is growing rapidly, and there are many places, especially in the Two-Thirds World, where people are particularly receptive to the message of Jesus Christ. The result is that the majority of Christians now live outside of Western Europe and North America. If we look around, we will see that the fields are ripe for harvest, and we must pray that the Lord of the harvest will send workers into the fields.

In summary, the picture of mission in this book is that of weak believers sent by a great God to bring salvation to the world through an improbable means, by scattering seeds. The task may be difficult; there is no easy triumphalism. Nevertheless, God is both powerful and gracious, and he is in the process of accomplishing his will on this earth.

# Bibliography

Aalen, S. "Glory, Honor." In *The New International Dictionary of New Testament Theology*, ed. Colin Brown, 2:44-52. Grand Rapids: Zondervan, 1976.

Agnew, Francis H. "The Origin of the NT Apostle-Concept: A Review of Research." *Journal of Biblical Literature* 105 (1986): 75-96.

Allen, Roland. *Missionary Methods: St. Paul's or Ours?* Reprint, Grand Rapids: Eerdmans, 1962.

Allison, Jr., D. C. "Eschatology." In *Dictionary of Jesus and the Gospels*, ed. Joel B. Green and Scot McKnight, 206-9. Downers Grove, Ill.: InterVarsity, 1992.

Anthonysamy, S. J. "The Gospel of Mark and the Universal Mission." *Biblebhashyam* 6 (1980): 81-96.

Archer, Jr., Gleason L. *A Survey of Old Testament Introduction*. 2d ed. Chicago: Moody, 1974.

Arnold, Clinton E. *Ephesians, Power and Magic: The Concept of Power in Ephesians in Light of Its Historical Setting*. Grand Rapids: Baker, 1992.

Aune, David E. "Apocalypticism." In *Dictionary of Paul and His Letters*, ed. Gerald F. Hawthorne and Ralph P. Martin, 25-35. Downers Grove, Ill.: InterVarsity, 1993.

―――. "Magic in Early Christianity." *Aufstieg und Niedergang der Römischen Welt* II.23.2 (1980): 1507-57.

―――. *The New Testament in Its Literary Environment*. Library of Early Christianity. Philadelphia: Westminster, 1987.

Aus, Roger D. "Paul's Travel Plans to Spain and the 'Full Number of the Gentiles' of Rom. XI 25." *Novum Testamentum* 21 (1979): 232-62.

Bailey, Kenneth E. *Through Peasant Eyes*. Grand Rapids: Eerdmans, 1980.

Balch, David L. *Let Wives Be Submissive: The Domestic Code in 1 Peter*. Society of Biblical Literature Monograph Series, no. 26. Chico, Calif.: Scholars Press, 1981.

Bamberger, Bernard J. "Proselytes." In *The Universal Jewish Encyclopedia*, 9:1-3. New York: Ktav, 1969.

Barclay, William. "A Comparison of Paul's Missionary Preaching and Preaching to the Church." In *Apostolic History and the Gospel*, ed. W. W. Gasque and R. P. Martin, 165-75. Grand Rapids: Eerdmans, 1970.

Barker, Glenn W., William L. Lane, and J. Ramsey Michaels. *The New Testament Speaks*. New York: Harper & Row, 1969.

Barnett, P. W. "Apostle." In *Dictionary of Paul and His Letters*, ed. Gerald F. Hawthorne and Ralph P. Martin, 45-51. Downers Grove, Ill.: InterVarsity, 1993.

Barrett, C. K. *A Critical and Exegetical Commentary on the Acts of the Apostles*. International Critical Commentary. Edinburgh: T & T Clark, 1994.

Barth, Markus. *Ephesians 1-3*. Anchor Bible, vol. 34. Garden City, N.Y.: Doubleday, 1974.

Bauer, David R. "The Literary Function of the Genealogy in Matthew's Gospel." In *Society of Biblical Literature 1990 Seminar Papers*, ed. David J. Lull, 451-68. Atlanta: Scholars Press, 1990.

———. *The Structure of Matthew's Gospel: A Study in Literary Design*. Journal for the Study of the New Testament Supplement Series, no. 31. Sheffield: Almond, 1988.

Beasley-Murray, G. R. *The Book of Revelation*. Greenwood, S.C.: Attic Press, 1974.

Beasley-Murray, Paul, ed. *Mission to the World: Essays to Celebrate the Fiftieth Anniversary of the Ordination of George Raymond Beasley-Murray*. Didcot, England: Baptist Historical Society, 1991.

Becker, Jürgen. *Paul: Apostle to the Gentiles*. Translated by O. C. Dean Jr. Louisville, Ky.: Westminster, 1993.

Bediako, Kwame. *Christianity in Africa: The Renewal of a Non-Western Religion*. Maryknoll, N.Y.: Orbis Books, 1995.

Beker, J. Christiaan. *Paul the Apostle: The Triumph of God in Life and Thought*. Philadelphia: Fortress, 1980.

———. "Romans 9-11 in the Context of the Early Church." *Princeton Seminary Bulletin Supplementary Issue* 1 (1990): 40-55.

———. *The Triumph of God: The Essence of Paul's Thought*. Translated by Loren T. Stuckenbruck. Minneapolis: Fortress, 1990.

Benko, Stephen. *Pagan Rome and the Early Christians*. Bloomington, Ind.: Indiana University Press, 1984.

Betori, Guiseppe. "Luke 24:47: Jerusalem and the Beginning of the Preaching to the Pagans in the Acts of the Apostles." In *Luke and Acts*, ed. Gerald O'Collins and Gilberto Marconi, 103-20. New York: Paulist, 1993.

Betz, Hans Dieter. "Introduction to the Greek Magical Papyri." In *The Greek Magical Papyri in Translation*, ed. Hans Dieter Betz, xli-liii. Chicago: University of Chicago Press, 1986.

Bieder, Werner. *Gottes Sendung und der missionarische Auftrag nach Matthaeus, Lukas, Paulus und Johannes*. Theologische Studien, no. 82. Zurich: EVZ, 1965.

———. *Grund und Kraft der Mission nach dem 1. Petrusbrief*. Zollikon-Zürich: Evangelischer Verlag, 1950.

Black, C. Clifton. *Mark: Images of an Apostolic Interpreter*. Columbia, S.C.: University of South Carolina Press, 1994.

———. "Was Mark a Roman Gospel?" *Expository Times* 105 (1993): 36-40.

Blomberg, Craig L. "The Diversity of Literary Genres in the New Testament." In *New Testament Criticism and Interpretation*, ed. David Alan Black and David S. Dockery, 505-32. Grand Rapids: Zondervan, 1991.

———. *The Historical Reliability of the Gospels*. Downers Grove, Ill.: InterVarsity, 1987.

Bock, Darrell L. *Luke—Volume 1: 1:1-9:50*. Baker Exegetical Commentary on the New Testament, no. 3A. Grand Rapids: Baker, 1994.

———. *Luke—Volume 2: 9:51-24:53*. Baker Exegetical Commentary on the New Testament, no. 3B. Grand Rapids: Baker, 1996.

———. "The Use of the Old Testament in Luke-Acts: Christology and Mission." In *Society of Biblical Literature 1990 Seminar Papers*, ed. David J. Lull, 494-511. Atlanta: Scholars Press, 1990.

Boers, Hendrikus W. "The Foundations of Paul's Thought: A Methodological Investigation—The Problem of the Coherent Center of Paul's Thought." *Studia Theologica* 42 (1988): 55-68.

Boomershine, Thomas E. "Mark 16:8 and the Apostolic Commission." *Journal of Biblical Literature* 100 (1981): 225-39.

Bornhäuser, Karl. *Das Johannesevangelium: Eine Missionsschrift für Israel.* Gütersloh: Bertelsmann, 1928.

Bornkamm, Günther. *Paul.* Translated by D. M. G. Stalker. New York: Harper & Row, 1971.

Borthwick, Paul. *Youth and Missions: Expanding Your Students' World View.* Wheaton: Victor Books, 1988.

Bosch, David J. "Mission in Biblical Perspective." *International Review of Missions* 74 (1985): 531-38.

———. "Mission in Jesus' Way: A Perspective from Luke's Gospel." *Missionalia* 17 (1989): 3-21.

———. "Reflections on Biblical Models of Mission." In *Toward the 21st Century in Christian Mission*, ed. James M. Phillips and Robert T. Coote, 175-92. Grand Rapids: Eerdmans, 1993.

———. *Transforming Mission: Paradigm Shifts in Theology of Mission.* American Society of Missiology Series, no. 16. Maryknoll, N.Y.: Orbis Books, 1991.

Botha, J. "Christian and Society in 1 Peter: Critical Solidarity." *Scriptura* 24 (1988): 27-37.

Bouchoc, Raymond. "Mission in the Book of Hebrews." Seminar Paper at Southeastern Baptist Theological Seminary, Wake Forest, N.C., 1997.

Bowers, W. Paul. "Church and Mission in Paul." *Journal for the Study of the New Testament* 44 (1991): 89-111.

———. "Fulfilling the Gospel: The Scope of the Pauline Mission." *Journal of the Evangelical Theological Society* 30 (1987): 185-98.

———. "Mission." In *Dictionary of Paul and His Letters*, ed. Gerald F. Hawthorne and Ralph P. Martin, 608-19. Downers Grove, Ill.: InterVarsity, 1993.

———. "Paul and Religious Propaganda in the First Century." *Novum Testamentum* 22 (1980): 316-23.

Brawley, Robert L. "Paul in Acts: Aspects of Structure and Characterization." In *Society of Biblical Literature 1988 Seminar Papers*, ed. David J. Lull, 90-105. Atlanta: Scholars Press, 1988.

Brooks, Oscar S. "Matthew xxviii 16-20 and the Design of the First Gospel." *Journal for the Study of the New Testament* 10 (1981) 2-18.

Brown, C. "*Lytron.*" In *The New International Dictionary of New Testament Theology*, ed. Colin Brown, 3:189-200. Grand Rapids: Zondervan, 1978.

Brown, Raymond. "Pilgrimage in Faith: The Christian Life in Hebrews." *Southwestern Journal of Theology* 28 (1985): 28-35.

Brown, Raymond E. *The Gospel according to John.* Anchor Bible, vols. 29, 29A. Garden City, N.Y.: Doubleday, 1966-70.

————, and John P. Meier. *Antioch and Rome: New Testament Cradles of Catholic Christianity.* New York: Paulist, 1983.

Bruce, F. F. *The Book of Acts.* Grand Rapids: Eerdmans, 1954.

————. *The Epistle to the Galatians.* New International Greek Testament Commentary. Grand Rapids: Eerdmans, 1982.

———— *Paul: Apostle of the Heart Set Free.* Grand Rapids: Eerdmans, 1977.

————. "Paul in Acts and Letters." In *Dictionary of Paul and His Letters*, ed. Gerald F. Hawthorne and Ralph P. Martin, 679-92. Downers Grove, Ill.: InterVarsity, 1993.

————. "The Speeches in Acts—Thirty Years After." In *Reconciliation and Hope*, ed. Robert Banks, 53-68. Grand Rapids: Eerdmans, 1974.

————. *1 and 2 Thessalonians.* Word Biblical Commentary. Waco, Tex.: Word, 1982.

Bultmann, Rudolf. "Die Bedeutung der neuerschlossenene mandäischen and manichäischen Quellen für das Verständnis des Johannesevangeliums." *Zeitschrift für die Neutestamentliche Wissenschaft* 24 (1925): 100-146.

————. *Theologie des Neuen Testaments.* 3. Aufl. Tübingen: Mohr, 1958.

————. *Theology of the New Testament.* Translated by Kendrick Grobel. New York: Scribner's, 1951.

Caird, G. B. *A Commentary on the Revelation of St. John the Divine.* Harper's New Testament Commentaries. New York: Harper & Row, 1966.

————. Review of *Paul and Palestinian Judaism: A Comparison of Patterns of Religion*, by E. P. Sanders. In *Journal of Theological Studies* 29 (1978): 538-43.

Caldwell, Larry W. *Sent Out! Reclaiming the Spiritual Gift of Apostleship for Missionaries and Churches Today.* Pasadena, Calif.: William Carey Library, 1992.

Campbell, W. S. "The Freedom and Faithfulness of God in Relation to Israel." *Journal for the Study of the New Testament* 13 (1981): 27-45.

————. "Israel." In *Dictionary of Paul and His Letters*, ed. Gerald F. Hawthorne and Ralph P. Martin, 441-46. Downers Grove, Ill.: InterVarsity, 1993.

————. "The Place of Romans IX-XI within the Structure and Thought of the Letter." In *Studia Evangelica VII: Texte und Untersuchungen zur Geshichte der altchristlichen Literatur*, 121-31. Berlin: Akademie-Verlag, 1982.

————. "Romans III as a Key to the Structure and Thought of the Letter." *Novum Testamentum* 23 (1981): 22-40.

Caragounis, C. C. "Kingdom of God/Kingdom of Heaven." In *Dictionary of Jesus and the Gospels*, ed. Joel B. Green and Scot McKnight, 417-30. Downers Grove, Ill.: InterVarsity, 1992.

Carson, D. A. *Divine Sovereignty and Human Responsibility: Biblical Perspectives in Tension.* New Foundations Theological Library. Atlanta: John Knox, 1981.

————. *The Gospel according to John.* Grand Rapids: Eerdmans, 1991.

————. "Matthew." In *Expositor's Bible Commentary*, ed. Frank E. Gaebelein, 8:1-599. Grand Rapids: Zondervan, 1984.

————. "The Purpose of the Fourth Gospel: John 20:31 Reconsidered." *Journal of Biblical Literature* 106 (1987): 639-51.

————, Douglas J. Moo, and Leon Morris. *An Introduction to the New Testament*. Grand Rapids: Zondervan, 1992.

Charlesworth, James H., ed. *The Old Testament Pseudepigrapha*. Garden City, N.Y.: Doubleday, 1983-85.

Chin, M. "A Heavenly Home for the Homeless: Aliens and Strangers in 1 Peter." *Tyndale Bulletin* 42 (1991): 96-112.

Clark, Kenneth W. "The Gentile Bias in Matthew." *Journal of Biblical Literature* 66 (1947): 165-72.

Clarke, Andrew D., and Bruce W. Winter, eds. *One God, One Lord: Christianity in a World of Religious Pluralism*. 2d ed. Grand Rapids: Baker, 1993.

Conzelmann, Hans. *An Outline of the Theology of the New Testament*. Translated by John Bowden. London: SCM, 1969.

Cortes, Juan B., and Florence M. Gatti. "On the Meaning of Luke 16:16." *Journal of Biblical Literature* 106 (1987): 247-59.

Cranfield, C. E. B. *A Critical and Exegetical Commentary on the Epistle to the Romans*. International Critical Commentary. Edinburgh: T & T Clark, 1975-79.

Dahl, N. A. "Two Notes on Romans 5." *Studia Theologica* 5 (1952): 37-48.

Danove, Paul L. *The End of Mark's Story: A Methodological Study*. Biblical Interpretation Series, vol. 3. Leiden: E. J. Brill, 1993.

Davies, W. D., and Dale C. Allison. *A Critical and Exegetical Commentary on the Gospel according to Saint Matthew*. International Critical Commentary. Edinburgh: T & T Clark, 1988.

Deidun, T. "Some Recent Attempts at Explaining Paul's Theology." *The Way* 26 (1986): 230-42.

Dillon, Richard J. "Easter Revelation and Mission Program in Luke 24:46-48." In *Sin, Salvation, and the Spirit: Commemorating the Fiftieth Year of the Liturgical Press*, ed. Daniel Durken, 240-70. Collegeville, Minn.: Liturgical Press, 1979.

Dodd, C. H. *The Apostolic Preaching and Its Developments*. New York: Harper & Row, 1936.

Dollar, Harold. *St. Luke's Missiology: A Cross-Cultural Challenge*. Pasadena, Calif.: William Carey Library, 1996.

Donahue, John R. "Windows and Mirrors: The Setting of Mark's Gospel." *Catholic Biblical Quarterly* 57 (1995): 1-26.

Donaldson, Terence L. *Jesus on the Mountain: A Study in Matthean Theology*. Journal for the Study of the New Testament Supplement Series, no. 8. Sheffield: JSOT Press, 1985.

Donfried, Karl Paul. "A Short Note on Romans 16." *Journal of Biblical Literature* 89 (1970): 441-49.

————, ed. *The Romans Debate*. 2d ed. Peabody, Mass.: Hendrickson, 1991.

du Preez, James. "Mission Perspective in the Book of Revelation." *Evangelical Quarterly* 42 (1970): 152-67.

————. "People and Nations in the Kingdom of God according to the Book of Revelation." *Journal of Theology for Southern Africa* 49 (1984): 49-51.

Dunn, James D. G. "The New Perspective on Paul." *Bulletin of the John Rylands Library* 65 (1983): 95-122.

———. *Romans 1–8. Word Biblical Commentary.* Waco, Tex.: Word, 1988.

Dupont, Jacques. *The Salvation of the Gentiles: Essays on the Acts of the Apostles.* Translated by John R. Keating. New York: Paulist, 1979.

Durant, Will. *Caesar and Christ.* New York: Simon and Schuster, 1944.

Eareckson, Vincent O. "The Glory to Be Revealed Hereafter: The Interpretation of Romans 8:18-25." Ph.D. diss., Princeton Theological Seminary, 1977.

Elder, Annette. "Boomers, Busters, and the Challenge of the Unreached Peoples." *International Journal of Frontier Missions* 8 (1991): 51-55.

Ellington, J. "Send!" *The Bible Translator* 45 (1994): 228-38.

Elliott, James Keith. "The Text and Language of the Endings to Mark's Gospel." *Theologische Zeitschrift* 27 (1971): 255-62.

Elliott, John H. *The Elect and the Holy.* Leiden: E. J. Brill, 1966.

———. *A Home for the Homeless: A Sociological Exegesis of 1 Peter, Its Situation and Strategy.* London: SCM, 1982.

———. "Salutation and Exhortation to Christian Behavior on the Basis of God's Blessings (1:1–2:10)." *Review and Expositor* 79 (1982): 415-25.

———. *1 Peter: Estrangement and Community.* Chicago: Franciscan Herald, 1979.

Ellis, E. E. "Paul and His Coworkers." In *Dictionary of Paul and His Letters,* ed. Gerald F. Hawthorne and Ralph P. Martin, 183-89. Downers Grove, Ill.: InterVarsity, 1993.

Ellison, H. L. *From Babylon to Bethlehem: The Jewish People from the Exile to the Messiah.* Exeter: Paternoster, 1976.

Engel, James F. *Contemporary Christian Communications: Its Theory and Practice.* Nashville: Thomas Nelson, 1979.

Evans, Craig A., and Donald A. Hagner. *Anti-Semitism and Early Christianity.* Minneapolis: Fortress, 1993.

Everts, J. N. "Conversion and Call of Paul." In *Dictionary of Paul and His Letters,* ed. Gerald F. Hawthorne and Ralph P. Martin, 156-63. Downers Grove, Ill.: InterVarsity, 1993.

Fee, Gordon D. *The First Epistle to the Corinthians.* New International Commentary on the New Testament. Grand Rapids: Eerdmans, 1986.

———. *God's Empowering Presence: The Holy Spirit in the Letters of Paul.* Peabody, Mass.: Hendrickson, 1994.

Feldmeier, Reinhard. *Die Christen als Fremde: Die Metapher der Fremde in der antiken Welt, im Urchristentum und im 1. Petrusbrief.* Wissenschaftliche Untersuchungen zum Neuen Testament, no. 64. Tübingen: J. C. B. Mohr (Paul Siebeck), 1992.

Fitzmyer, Joseph A. *The Gospel according to Luke I-IX.* Anchor Bible, vol. 28. Garden City, N.Y.: Doubleday, 1981.

———. *The Gospel according to Luke X-XXIV.* Anchor Bible, vol. 28A. Garden City, N.Y.: Doubleday, 1985.

———. *Romans.* Anchor Bible, vol. 33. New York: Doubleday, 1993.

Ford, J. Massynbaerde. "Reconciliation and Forgiveness in Luke's Gospel." In *Political Issues in Luke-Acts,* ed. Richard J. Cassidy and Philip J. Scharper, 80-98. Maryknoll, N.Y.: Orbis Books, 1983.

Freed, Edwin D. "Did John Write His Gospel Partly to Win Samaritan Converts?" *Novum Testamentum* 12 (1970): 241-56.

Funk, R. W. "The Apostolic Parousia: Form and Significance." In *Christian History and Interpretation: Studies Presented to John Knox*, ed. W. R. Farmer, C. F. D. Moule, and R. R. Niebuhr, 249-68. Cambridge: University Press, 1967.

Fusco, Vittorio. "Problems of Structure in Luke's Eschatological Discourse (Lk. 21:7-36)." In *Luke and Acts*, ed. Gerald O'Collins and Gilberto Marconi, 72-92. New York: Paulist, 1993.

Gage, Warren A. *The Gospel of Genesis*. Winona Lake, Ind.: Carpenter Books, 1984.

Gamble, Jr., Harry. *The Textual History of the Letter to the Romans*. Grand Rapids: Eerdmans, 1977.

Garland, David E. *Reading Matthew: A Literary and Theological Commentary on the First Gospel*. New York: Crossroad, 1993.

Gasque, W. Ward. "A Fruitful Field: Recent Study of the Acts of the Apostles." *Interpretation* 42 (1988): 117-31.

Gaventa, Beverly Roberts. "'You Will Be My Witnesses': Aspects of Mission in Acts of the Apostles." *Missiology* 10 (1982): 413-25.

Gill, David H. "Observations on the Lukan Travel Narrative and Some Related Passages." *Harvard Theological Review* 63 (1970): 199-221.

Gilliland, Dean S. *Pauline Theology and Mission Practice*. Grand Rapids: Eerdmans, 1983.

Gillis, Chester. *Pluralism: A New Paradigm for Theology*. Louvain Theological & Pastoral Monographs, no. 12. Grand Rapids: Eerdmans, 1993.

Goodman, Martin. *Mission and Conversion: Proselytizing in the Religious History of the Roman Empire*. Oxford: Clarendon Press, 1994.

Grässer, Erich. "Das wandernde Gottesvolk: Zum Basismotiv des Hebräerbriefes." *Zeitschrift für die Neutestamentliche Wissenschaft* 77 (1986): 160-79.

Gundry, Robert H. "Grace, Works, and Staying Saved." *Biblica* 66 (1985): 1-38.

———. *Mark: A Commentary on His Apology for the Cross*. Grand Rapids: Eerdmans, 1993.

———. *Matthew: A Commentary on His Literary and Theological Art*. Grand Rapids: Eerdmans, 1982.

———. *A Survey of the New Testament*. 3d ed. Grand Rapids: Zondervan, 1994.

Guthrie, Donald. *New Testament Introduction*. 3d ed. Downers Grove, Ill.: InterVarsity, 1970.

———. *New Testament Introduction*. 4th ed. Downers Grove, Ill.: InterVarsity, 1990.

———. *The Pastoral Epistles*. Grand Rapids: Eerdmans, 1957.

Haenchen, Ernst. "Der Vater der mich gesandt hat." *New Testament Studies* 9 (1963): 208-16.

Hagner, Donald A. *Matthew 1-13*. Word Biblical Commentary. Dallas: Word, 1993.

———. *Matthew 14-28*. Word Biblical Commentary. Dallas: Word, 1995.

———. "Paul and Judaism. The Jewish Matrix of Early Christianity: Issues in the Current Debate." *Bulletin for Biblical Research* 3 (1993): 111-30.

Hahn, Ferdinand. *Mission in the New Testament.* Translated by Frank Clarke. Studies in Biblical Theology, no. 47. Naperville, Ill.: Alec R. Allenson, 1965.

Harrington, D. J. "Paul and Collaborative Ministry." *New Theology Review* 3 (1990): 62-71.

Harrington, O.P., Wilfrid J. *Revelation.* Collegeville, Minn.: Liturgical Press, 1993.

Hauck, F., and S. Schültz. "*Pornē.*" In *Theological Dictionary of the New Testament,* ed. Gerhard Kittel and Gerhard Friedrich. Translated by Geoffrey N. Bromiley, 6:579-95. Grand Rapids: Eerdmans, 1964-76.

Hays, Richard B. *The Faith of Jesus Christ: An Investigation of the Narrative Substructure of Galatians 3:1–4:11.* Society of Biblical Literature Dissertation Series, no. 56. Chico, Calif.: Scholars Press, 1983.

Hedlund, Roger E. *The Mission of the Church in the World: A Biblical Theology.* Grand Rapids: Baker, 1991.

Hegermann, Harald. "Christologie im Hebräerbrief." In *Anfänge der Christologie: Festschrift für Ferdinand Hahn zum 65. Geburtstag,* ed. Cilliers Breytenbach and Henning Paulsen, 337-52. Göttingen: Vandenhoeck & Ruprecht, 1991.

Heil, John Paul. "The Narrative Roles of the Women in Matthew's Genealogy." *Biblica* 72 (1991): 538-45.

Hemer, Colin J. *The Letters to the Seven Churches of Asia in Their Local Setting. Journal for the Study of the New Testament* Supplement Series, no. 11. Sheffield: JSOT, 1986.

Hengel, Martin. *Between Jesus and Paul: Studies in the Earliest History of Christianity.* Translated by John Bowden. Philadelphia: Fortress, 1983.

———. *The Pre-Christian Paul.* Translated by John Bowden. Philadelphia: Trinity Press International, 1991.

———. *Studies in the Gospel of Mark.* Philadelphia: Fortress, 1985.

Hick, John, and Paul F. Knitter, eds. *The Myth of Christian Uniqueness: Toward a Pluralistic Theology of Religions.* Maryknoll, N.Y.: Orbis Books, 1988.

Hickling, C. J. A. "Center and Periphery in Paul's Thought." In *Studia Biblica 1978: Papers on Paul and Other New Testament Authors,* ed. E. A. Livingstone, 199-214. Sheffield: JSOT, 1980.

Hiebert, D. Edmond. "An Expository Study of Matthew 28:16-20." *Bibliotheca Sacra* 149 (1992): 338-54.

Hooker, Morna D. "PISTIS CHRISTOU." *New Testament Studies* 35 (1989): 321-42.

Howell Jr., Don N. "The Apostle Paul and First Century Religious Pluralism." In *Christianity and the Religions: A Biblical Theology of World Religions,* ed. Edward Rommen and Harold Netland, Evangelical Missiological Society Series, no. 2, 92-112. Pasadena, Calif.: William Carey Library, 1995.

———. "The Center of Pauline Theology." *Bibliotheca Sacra* 151 (1994): 50-70.

———. "God-Christ Interchange in Paul: Impressive Testimony to the Deity of Jesus." *Journal of the Evangelical Theological Society* 36 (1993): 467-79.

————. "Pauline Eschatological Dualism and Its Resulting Tensions." *Trinity Journal* 14 (1993): 3-24.

Hubbard, Benjamin Jerome. *The Matthean Redaction of a Primitive Apostolic Commissioning: An Exegesis of Matthew 28:16-20.* Society of Biblical Literature Dissertation Series, no. 19. Missoula, Mont.: Scholars Press, 1974.

Hultgren, Arland J. *Paul's Gospel and Mission: The Outlook from His Letter to the Romans.* Philadelphia: Fortress, 1985.

————. "The *Pistis Christou* Formulation in Paul." *Novum Testamentum* 22 (1980): 248-63.

Hunter, W. B. "Prayer." In *Dictionary of Paul and His Letters*, ed. Gerald F. Hawthorne and Ralph P. Martin, 725-34. Downers Grove, Ill.: InterVarsity, 1993.

Hurtado, Larry W. "The Doxology at the End of Romans." In *New Testament Textual Criticism: Essays in Honour of Bruce M. Metzger*, ed. Eldon J. Epp and Gordon D. Fee, 185-99. Oxford: Clarendon, 1981.

Jeffers, James S. "Pluralism in Early Roman Christianity." *Fides et Historia* 22 (Winter/Spring 1990): 4-17.

Jeremias, Joachim. *Jesus' Promise to the Nations.* Translated by S. H. Hooke. London: SCM, 1958.

Jervell, Jacob. *Luke and the People of God: A New Look at Luke-Acts.* Minneapolis: Augsburg, 1972.

Jewett, Robert. *Letter to Pilgrims.* New York: Pilgrim, 1981.

Johnson, Jr., S. Lewis. "Romans 5:12: An Exercise in Exegesis and Theology." In *New Dimensions in New Testament Study*, ed. Richard N. Longenecker and Merrill C. Tenney, 298-316. Grand Rapids: Zondervan, 1974.

Johnsson, William G. "The Pilgrimage Motif in the Book of Hebrews." *Journal of Biblical Literature* 97 (1978): 239-51.

Jones, Donald L. "The Title *kyrios* in Luke-Acts." In *Society of Biblical Literature 1974 Seminar Papers*, ed. George MacRae, 2:85-101. Cambridge, Mass.: Society of Biblical Literature, 1974.

Kane, J. Herbert. *Christian Missions in Biblical Perspective.* Grand Rapids: Baker, 1976.

Karris, Robert J. "Missionary Communities: A New Paradigm for the Study of Luke-Acts." *Catholic Biblical Quarterly* 41 (1979): 80-91.

Käsemann, Ernst. *Commentary on Romans.* Translated and edited by Geoffrey W. Bromiley. Grand Rapids: Eerdmans, 1980.

————. *New Testament Questions of Today.* Translated by W. J. Montague. London: SCM, 1969.

————. *The Wandering People of God.* Translated by Roy A. Harrisville and Irving L. Sandberg. Minneapolis: Augsburg, 1984.

Keck, Leander E. "Images of Paul in the New Testament." *Interpretation* 43 (1989): 341-51.

Kelber, Werner H. *The Kingdom in Mark: A New Place and a New Time.* Philadelphia: Fortress, 1974.

————. *Mark's Story of Jesus.* Philadelphia: Fortress, 1979.

Kelly, J. N. D. *A Commentary on the Pastoral Epistles.* London: Adam and Charles Black, 1963.

Kelly, Joseph G. "Lucan Christology and the Jewish-Christian Dialogue." *Journal of Ecumenical Studies* 21 (1984): 688-708.

Kertelge, Karl. *"Rechtfertigung" bei Paulus: Studien zur Struktur und zum Bedeutungsgehalt des paulinischen Rechtfertigungsbegriffs.* Münster: Aschendorff, 1967.

Kiddle, Martin. *The Revelation of St. John.* 7th ed. London: Hodder and Stoughton, 1963.

Kilpatrick, G. D. "The Gentile Mission in Mark and Mark 13:9-11." In *Studies in the Gospels: Essays in Memory of R. H. Lightfoot,* ed. D. E. Nineham, 145-58. Oxford: Basil Blackwell, 1967.

Kingsbury, Jack Dean. "The Composition and Christology of Matt 28:16-20." *Journal of Biblical Literature* 93 (1974): 573-84.

Klein, G. "Righteousness in the New Testament." In *Interpreter's Dictionary of the Bible: Supplementary Volume,* ed. Keith Crim, 750-52. Nashville: Abingdon, 1976.

Koester, Helmut. *Introduction to the New Testament.* Vol. 1, *History, Culture, and Religion of the Hellenistic Age.* Philadelphia: Fortress, 1982.

Kohler, M. E. "La communauté des chrétiens selon la première épître de Pierre." *Revue de Théologie et de Philosophie* 114 (1982): 1-21.

Koop, Doug. "Mobilizing for the Millennium." *Christianity Today,* 17 July 1995, 53.

Köstenberger, Andreas J. "The Challenge of a Systematized Biblical Theology of Mission: Missiological Insights from the Gospel of John." *Missiology* 23 (1995): 445-64.

———. "The Contribution of the General Epistles and Revelation to a Biblical Theology of Religions." In *Christianity and the Religions: A Biblical Theology of World Religions,* ed. Edward Rommen and Harold Netland, Evangelical Missiological Society Series, no. 2, 113-40. Pasadena, Calif.: William Carey Library, 1995.

———. "The Two Johannine Words for Sending: A Study of John's Use of Words with Reference to General Linguistic Theory." Paper presented at the annual meeting of the Society of Biblical Literature, Chicago, Ill., November 1994.

———, and Peter T. O'Brien. *Mission in the New Testament.* New Studies in Biblical Theology. Grand Rapids: Eerdmans, forthcoming.

Kuhl, Joseph. *Die Sendung Jesu und der Kirche nach dem Johannesevangelium.* Studia Instituti Missiologica Societatis Verbi Domini. St. Augustin: Styler, 1967.

Kuhn, Karl Georg. *"Prosēlytos."* In *Theological Dictionary of the New Testament,* ed. Gerhard Kittel and Gerhard Friedrich. Translated by Geoffrey W. Bromiley, 6:727-44. Grand Rapids: Eerdmans, 1964-76.

Kümmel, Werner Georg. *Introduction to the New Testament.* Translated by Howard Clark Kee. Nashville: Abingdon, 1975.

Kurz, William. "The Function of Christological Proof from Prophecy for Luke and Justin." Ph.D. diss., Yale University, 1976.

———. "Hellenistic Rhetoric in the Christological Proof of Luke-Acts." *Catholic Biblical Quarterly* 42 (1980): 171-95.

———. "Narrative Models for Imitation in Luke-Acts." In *Greeks, Romans, and Christians,* ed. David L. Balch, Everett Ferguson, and Wayne A. Meeks, 171-89. Minneapolis: Fortress, 1990.

La Piana, George. "Foreign Groups in Rome during the First Centuries of the Empire." *Harvard Theological Review* 20 (1927): 183-403.

Ladd, George Eldon. "Apocalyptic, Apocalypse." In *Baker's Dictionary of Theology*, ed. by Everett F. Harrison, 50-54. Grand Rapids: Baker, 1960.

————. "Apocalyptic Literature." In *International Standard Bible Encyclopedia*, ed. Geoffrey W. Bromiley, 1:151-61. Grand Rapids: Eerdmans, 1979.

————. *A Commentary on the Revelation of John.* Grand Rapids: Eerdmans, 1972.

————. *A Theology of the New Testament.* 2d ed. Grand Rapids: Eerdmans, 1993.

————. "Why Not Prophetic-Apocalyptic?" *Journal of Biblical Literature* 76 (1957): 192-200.

Larkin, Jr., William J. *Acts.* IVP New Testament Commentary Series. Downers Grove, Ill.: InterVarsity, 1995.

————. "The Contribution of the Gospels and Acts to a Biblical Theology of Religions." In *Christianity and the Religions: A Biblical Theology of World Religions*, ed. Edward Rommen and Harold Netland, Evangelical Missiological Society Series, no. 2, 72-91. Pasadena, Calif.: William Carey Library, 1995.

————. "Mission." In *Evangelical Dictionary of Biblical Theology*, ed. Walter A. Elwell, 534-38. Grand Rapids: Baker, 1996.

Lea, Thomas D. *The New Testament: Its Background and Message.* Nashville: Broadman, 1996.

Legrand, Lucien. "The Missionary Command of the Risen Christ: I. Mission and Resurrection." *Indian Theological Studies* 23 (1986): 290-309.

————. *Unity and Plurality: Mission in the Bible.* Translated by Robert R. Barr. Maryknoll, N.Y.: Orbis Books, 1990.

————. "The Unknown God of Athens: Acts 17 and the Religion of the Gentiles." *Indian Journal of Theology* 30 (1981): 158-67.

Liddell, Henry George, and Robert Scott. *A Greek-English Lexicon.* Revised by Henry Stuart Jones. 9th ed. Oxford: Clarendon, 1940.

Lincoln, Andrew T. "The Promise and the Failure: Mark 16:7, 8." *Journal of Biblical Literature* 108 (1989): 283-300.

Longenecker, Bruce W. "Different Answers to Different Issues: Israel, the Gentiles and Salvation History in Romans 9-11." *Journal for the Study of the New Testament* 36 (1989): 95-123.

Longenecker, Richard N. *Galatians. Word Biblical Commentary.* Dallas: Word, 1990.

Luter, A. B. "Gospel." In *Dictionary of Paul and His Letters*, ed. Gerald F. Hawthorne and Ralph P. Martin, 369-74. Downers Grove, Ill.: InterVarsity, 1993.

Malbon, Elizabeth Struthers. "Disciples/Crowd/Whoever: Markan Characters and Readers." *Novum Testamentum* 62 (1986): 104-30.

————. "Fallible Followers: Women and Men in the Gospel of Mark." *Semeia* 28 (1983): 29-48.

Marshall, I. Howard. *The Acts of the Apostles: An Introduction and Commentary.* Grand Rapids: Eerdmans, 1980.

————. "Dialogue with Non-Christians in the New Testament." *Evangelical Review of Theology* 16 (1992): 28-47.

————. *The Epistles of John*. New International Commentary on the New Testament. Grand Rapids: Eerdmans, 1978.

————. *The Gospel of Luke*. New International Greek Testament Commentary. Grand Rapids: Eerdmans, 1978.

Martin, R. P. "Center of Paul's Theology." In *Dictionary of Paul and His Letters*, ed. Gerald F. Hawthorne and Ralph P. Martin, 92-95. Downers Grove, Ill.: InterVarsity, 1993.

Marxsen, Willi. *Mark the Evangelist: Studies on the Redaction History of the Gospel*. Translated by James Boyce and others. Nashville: Abingdon, 1969.

McDonald, James I. H. *Kerygma and Didache: The Articulation and Structure of the Earliest Christian Message*. Society for New Testament Studies Monograph Series, no. 37. Cambridge: University Press, 1980.

McGavran, Donald. *Understanding Church Growth*. Grand Rapids: Eerdmans, 1970.

McKnight, Scot. "Gentiles." In *Dictionary of Jesus and the Gospels*, ed. Joel B. Green and Scot McKnight, 259-65. Downers Grove, Ill.: InterVarsity, 1992.

————. *A Light among the Gentiles: Jewish Missionary Activity in the Second Temple Period*. Minneapolis: Fortress, 1990.

————. "Matthew, Gospel of." In *Dictionary of Jesus and the Gospels*, ed. Joel B. Green and Scot McKnight, 526-41. Downers Grove, Ill.: InterVarsity, 1992.

McPolin, James. "Mission in the Fourth Gospel." *Irish Theological Quarterly* 46 (1969): 113-22.

————. "Studies in the Fourth Gospel: Some Contemporary Trends." *Irish Biblical Studies* 2 (1980): 2-26.

Meier, John P. *Law and History in Matthew's Gospel: A Redactional Study of Mt. 5:17-48*. Analecta Biblica, no. 71. Rome: Biblical Institute Press, 1976.

Metzger, Bruce Manning. *The New Testament: Its Background, Growth and Content*. 2d ed. Nashville: Abingdon, 1983.

————. "A Reconsideration of Certain Arguments against the Pauline Authorship of the Pastoral Epistles." *Expository Times* 70 (1958-59): 91-94.

————. *The Text of the New Testament: Its Transmission, Corruption, and Restoration*. 3d ed. New York: Oxford University Press, 1992.

————. *A Textual Commentary on the Greek New Testament*. 2d ed. Stuttgart: United Bible Societies, 1994.

Minear, Paul S. "The Original Functions of John 21." *Journal of Biblical Literature* 102 (1983): 85-98.

Miranda, Juan Peter. *Der Vater, der mich gesandt hat: Religionsgeschichtliche Untersuchungen zu den johanneischen Sendungsformeln: Zugleich ein Beitrag zur johanneischen Christologie und Ekklesiologie*. Bern: Herbert Lang, 1972; Frankfurt: Peter Lang, 1972.

————. *Die Sendung Jesu im vierten Evangelium: Religions- und theologiegeschichtliche Untersuchungen zu den Sendungsformeln*. Stuttgarter Bibelstudien, no. 87. Stuttgart: Katholisches Bibelwerk, 1977.

Moessner, David P. "The 'Leaven of the Pharisees' and 'This Generation': Israel's Rejection of Jesus according to Luke." *Journal for the Study of the New Testament* 34 (1988): 21-46.

———. "Paul in Acts: Preacher of Eschatological Repentance to Israel." *New Testament Studies* 34 (1988): 96-104.

Moo, Douglas J. *The Old Testament in the Gospel Passion Narratives.* Sheffield: Almond, 1983.

———. *Romans 1–8. Wycliffe Exegetical Commentary.* Chicago: Moody, 1991.

Morgenthaler, Robert. *Statistik des neutestamentlichen Wortschatzes.* Zurich: Gotthelf, 1958.

Morris, Leon. *Apocalyptic.* 2d ed. Grand Rapids: Eerdmans, 1984.

———. *The Epistle to the Romans.* Grand Rapids: Eerdmans, 1988.

———. *The Gospel according to John.* New International Commentary on the New Testament. Grand Rapids: Eerdmans, 1971.

———. *Revelation.* 2d ed. Grand Rapids: Eerdmans, 1987.

———. "The Theme of Romans." In *Apostolic History and the Gospel: Biblical and Historical Essays Presented to F. F. Bruce on His 60th Birthday,* ed. W. Ward Gasque and Ralph P. Martin, 249-63. Grand Rapids: Eerdmans, 1970.

Moule, C. F. D. "The Christology of Acts." In *Studies in Luke-Acts,* ed. Leander E. Keck and J. Louis Martyn, 159-85. Nashville: Abingdon, 1966.

———. "The Problem of the Pastoral Epistles." *Bulletin of the John Rylands Library* 47 (1964-65): 430-52.

Mounce, Robert H. *The Book of Revelation.* New International Commentary on the New Testament. Grand Rapids: Eerdmans, 1977.

Moxnes, Halvor. *Theology in Conflict: Studies in Paul's Understanding of God in Romans.* Leiden: E. J. Brill, 1980.

Murray, John. *The Epistle to the Romans.* New International Commentary on the New Testament. Grand Rapids: Eerdmans, 1959-65.

Mussner, F. "'Ganz Israel wird gerettet werden' (Röm 11,26): Versuch einer Auslegung." *Kairos* 18 (1976): 241-55.

Nessan, Craig L. "The Gospel of Luke and Liberation Theology: On Not Domesticating the Dangerous Memory of Jesus." *Currents in Theology and Mission* 22 (1995): 130-38.

Netland, Harold A. *Dissonant Voices: Religious Pluralism and the Question of Truth.* Grand Rapids: Eerdmans, 1991.

Newsome, James D. *Greeks, Romans, Jews: Currents of Culture and Belief in the New Testament World.* Philadelphia: Trinity Press International, 1992.

Nolland, John. *Luke 1:1-9:20. Word Biblical Commentary.* Dallas: Word, 1989.

O'Brien, Peter T. *Colossians, Philemon. Word Biblical Commentary.* Waco, Tex.: Word, 1982.

———. "Romans 8:26-27: A Revolutionary Approach to Prayer?" *Reformed Theological Review* 46 (1987): 65-73.

O'Connor, Dan. "Holiness of Life as a Way of Christian Witness." *International Review of Missions* 80 (1991): 17-26.

Oehler, Wilhelm. *Das Johannesevangelium: Eine Missionsschrift für die Welt.* Gütersloh: Bertelsmann, 1936.

———. *Zum Missionscharakter des Johannesevangeliums.* Beiträge zur Förderung Christlicher Theologie, no. 42. Gütersloh: Bertelsmann, 1941.

Okure, Teresa. *The Johannine Approach to Mission: A Contextual Study of John 4,1-42.* Wissenschaftliche Untersuchungen zum Neuen Testament, no. 2/31. Tübingen: J. C. B. Mohr (Paul Siebeck), 1988.

Olsson, Birger. "Mission la Lukas, Johannes och Petrus," *SvenskExegetisk Årsbok* 51 (1986): 180-91.

Onuki, Takashi. *Gemeinde und Welt im Johannesevangelium: Ein Beitrag zur Frage nach der theologischen und pragmatischen Funktion des johanneischen "Dualismus."* Wissenschaftliche Monographien zum Alten und Neuen Testament, no. 56. Neukirchen-Vluyn: Neukrichener Verlag, 1984.

Osburn, Carroll D. "The Interpretation of Romans 8:28." *Westminster Theological Journal* 44 (1982): 99-109.

Page, S. "Ransom Saying." In *Dictionary of Jesus and the Gospels*, ed. Joel B. Green and Scot McKnight, 660-62. Downers Grove, Ill.: InterVarsity, 1992.

Percy, E. *Die Probleme der Kolosser und Epheserbriefe.* Kobenhavn: Lund C. W. K. Gleerup, 1946.

Perkins, David W. "A Call to Pilgrimage: The Challenge of Hebrews." *Theological Educator* 32 (1985): 69-81.

Pesch, Rudolf. "Voraussetzungen und Anfänge der urchristlichen Mission." In *Mission im Neuen Testament*, ed. Karl Kertelge, 11-70. Freiburg: Herder, 1982.

Peters, George W. *A Biblical Theology of Missions.* Chicago: Moody, 1972.

Peterson, David G. "Prayer in Paul's Writings." In *Teach Us to Pray: Prayer in the Bible and the World*, ed. D. A. Carson, 84-101. Grand Rapids: Baker, 1990.

Pfeiffer, Robert H. *Introduction to the Old Testament.* New York: Harper & Brothers, 1948.

Pilgrim, Walter E. "Universalism in the Apocalypse." *Word and World* 9 (1989): 235-43.

Piper, John. "Hope as the Motivation of Love: 1 Peter 3:9-12." *New Testament Studies* 26 (1980): 212-31.

―――. *Let the Nations Be Glad! The Supremacy of God in Missions.* Grand Rapids: Baker, 1993.

Plevnik, Joseph. "The Center of Pauline Theology." *Catholic Biblical Quarterly* 51 (1989): 461-78.

Polhill, John B. *Acts.* New American Commentary. Nashville: Broadman, 1992.

Poucouta, Paulin. "La mission prophetique de l'Eglise dans l'Apocalypse johannique." *La Nouvelle Revue Théologique* 110 (1988): 38-57.

Powell, Mark Allan. *God with Us: A Pastoral Theology of Matthew's Gospel.* Minneapolis: Fortress, 1995.

Pritchard, James B., ed. *The Ancient Near East in Pictures.* Princeton: Princeton University Press, 1969.

Przybylski, Benno. *Righteousness in Matthew and His World of Thought.* Society for New Testament Studies Monograph Series, no. 41. Cambridge: University Press, 1980.

Quere, Ralph W. "The AIDS Crisis: A Call to Mission Based on 1 Peter." *Currents in Theology and Mission* 14 (1987): 361-69.

Rahlfs, Alfred. *Septuaginta.* 2 vols. Stuttgart: Württembergische Bibelanstalt, 1935.

Rahner, Karl. "Towards a Fundamental Theological Interpretation of Vatican II." *Theological Studies* 40 (1979): 716-27.

Räisänen, Heikki. *Paul and the Law.* Philadelphia: Fortress, 1986.

Reicke, Bo. *The New Testament Era: The World of the Bible from 500 B.C. to A.D. 100.* Translated by David E. Green. Philadelphia: Fortress, 1968.

———. *The Roots of the Synoptic Gospels.* Philadelphia: Fortress, 1986.

Reid, Daniel G. "The Misunderstood Apostle." *Christianity Today,* 16 July 1990, 25-27.

Rengstorf, K. H. *"Apostolos."* In *Theological Dictionary of the New Testament,* ed. Gerhard Kittel and Gerhard Friedrich. Translated by Geoffrey W. Bromiley, 1:407-45. Grand Rapids: Eerdmans, 1964-76.

Rensberger, David. *Overcoming the World: Politics and Community in the Gospel of John.* London: SPCK, 1988.

Reumann, John. *"Righteousness" in the New Testament.* Philadelphia: Fortress, 1982.

Rhoads, David. "Mission in the Gospel of Mark." *Currents in Theology and Mission* 22 (1995): 340-55.

Richardson, Robert L. "From 'Subjection to Authority' to 'Mutual Submission': The Ethic of Subordination in 1 Peter." *Faith and Mission* 4 (1987): 70-80.

Ridderbos, Herman N. *Paul: An Outline of His Theology.* Translated by John Richard De Witt. Grand Rapids: Eerdmans, 1975.

Rigaux, B. *Saint Paul. Les Épîtres aux Thessaloniciens.* Paris: J. Gabalda, 1956.

Robinson, John A. T. "The Destination and Purpose of St John's Gospel." *New Testament Studies* 6 (1959-60): 117-31.

———. *Redating the New Testament.* Philadelphia: Westminster, 1976.

Robinson, P. J. "Some Missiological Perspectives from I Peter 2:4-10." *Missionalia* 17 (1989): 176-87.

Romaniuk, Kazimierz. *L 'amour du père et du Fils dans la sotériologie de S.Paul.* Rome: Biblical Institute Press, 1974.

Rommen, Edward. "The De-Theologizing of Missiology." *Trinity World Forum* 19 (Fall 1993): 1-4.

———, and Harold Netland, eds. *Christianity and the Religions: A Biblical Theology of World Religions.* Evangelical Missiological Society Series, no. 2. Pasadena, Calif.: William Carey Library, 1995.

Ruiz, Miguel Rodriguez. *Der Missionsgedanke des Johannesevangeliums: Ein Beitrag zur johanneischen Soteriologie und Ekklesiologie.* Forschung zur Bibel, no. 55. Würzburg: Echter Verlag, 1987.

Samuel, Vinay, and Chris Sugden. *Evangelism and the Poor: A Third World Study Guide.* Oxford: Regnum Books, 1983.

Sanday, William, and Arthur C. Headlam. *A Critical and Exegetical Commentary on the Epistle to the Romans.* 5th ed. International Critical Commentary. Edinburgh: T & T Clark, 1901.

Sanders, E. P. *Paul and Palestinian Judaism.* Philadelphia: Fortress, 1977.

———. *Paul, the Law and the Jewish People.* Philadelphia: Fortress, 1983.

Scaer, David P. "The Relation of Matthew 28:16-20 to the Rest of the Gospel." *Concordia Theological Quarterly* 55 (1991): 245-66.

Scheffler, Eben H. "Reading Luke from the Perspective of Liberation Theology." In *Text and Interpretation: New Approaches in the Criticism of the New Testament*, ed. Patrick J. Hartin and Jacobus H. Petzer, 281-98. Leiden: E. J. Brill, 1991.

Schick, Edwin A. "Priestly Pilgrims: Mission outside the Camp in Hebrews." *Currents in Theology and Mission* 16 (1989): 372-76.

Schmidt, Karl Ludwig. "*Ethnos.*" In *Theological Dictionary of the New Testament*, ed. Gerhard Kittel and Gerhard Friedrich. Translated by Geoffrey W. Bromiley, 2:364-72. Grand Rapids: Eerdmans, 1964-76.

Schnackenburg, Rudolf. "Die Messiasfrage im Johannesevangelium." In *Neutestamentliche Aufsätze: Festschrift für Josef Schmid zum 70. Geburtstag*, ed. J. Blinzler, O. Kuss, and F. Mussner, 240-64. Regensburg: Friedrich Pustet, 1963.

———. *The Gospel according to St. John*. New York: Herder & Herder, 1968.

Schürer, Emil. *The History of the Jewish People in the Age of Jesus Christ (175 B.C.—A.D. 135)*, ed. Geza Vermes, Fergus Millar, and Martin Goodman. Edinburgh: T & T Clark, 1986.

Schüssler Fiorenza, Elisabeth. *The Book of Revelation: Justice and Judgment*. Philadelphia: Fortress Press, 1985.

———. "Miracles, Mission, and Apologetics: An Introduction." In *Aspects of Religious Propaganda in Judaism and Early Christianity*, ed. Elisabeth S. Fiorenza, 1-26. Notre Dame, Ind.: University of Notre Dame Press, 1976.

Schutter, William L. Review of *Die Christen als Fremde: Die Metapher der Fremde in der antiken Welt, im Urchristentum und im 1. Petrusbrief*, by Reinhard Feldmeier. In *Journal of Biblical Literature* 113 (1994): 743-45.

Schweitzer, Albert. *The Mysticism of Paul the Apostle*. Translated by William Montgomery. New York: Macmillan, 1956.

Schweizer, Eduard. "Zur Christologie des ersten Petrusbriefs." In *Anfänge der Christologie: Festschrift für Ferdinand Hahn zum 65. Geburtstag*, ed. Cilliers Breytenbach and Henning Paulsen, 369-82. Göttingen: Vandenhoeck & Ruprecht, 1991.

Scott, J. Julius. *Customs and Controversies: Intertestamental Jewish Backgrounds of the New Testament*. Grand Rapids: Baker, 1995.

Segal, Alan F. *Rebecca's Children: Judaism and Christianity in the Roman World*. Cambridge, Mass.: Harvard University Press, 1986.

Senior, Donald. "The Struggle to Be Universal: Mission as Vantage Point for New Testament Investigation." *Catholic Biblical Quarterly* 46 (1984): 63-81.

———, and Carroll Stuhlmueller. *The Biblical Foundations for Mission*. Maryknoll, N.Y.: Orbis Books, 1983.

Shaw, Mark. "Is There Salvation Outside the Christian Faith?" *East Africa Journal of Evangelical Theology* 2, no. 2 (1983): 42-62.

Simpson, E. K. *The Pastoral Epistles*. London: Tyndale, 1954.

Sims, David C. "The Gospel of Matthew and the Gentiles." *Journal for the Study of the New Testament* 57 (1995): 19-48.

Spicq, Ceslas. *Les Épîtres Pastorales*. Paris: J. Gabalda, 1947.

Stein, Robert H. *Luke.* New American Commentary. Nashville: Broadman, 1992.

Stendahl, Krister. "Paul at Prayer." *Interpretation* 34 (1980): 240-49.

―――. *The School of St. Matthew.* 2d ed. Philadelphia: Fortress, 1968.

Steuernagel, V. R. "An Exiled Community as a Missionary Community: A Study based on 1 Peter 2:9, 10." *Evangelical Review of Theology* 10 (1986): 8-18.

Steyne, Philip M. *In Step with the God of All Nations: A Biblical Theology of Missions.* Houston: Touch Ministries, 1991.

Stock, Klemens. "Theologie der Mission bei Markus." In *Mission im Neuen Testament,* ed. Karl Kertelge, 130-44. Freiburg: Herder, 1982.

Stott, J. R. W. *Christian Mission in the Modern World.* Downers Grove, Ill.: InterVarsity, 1975.

Stronstad, Roger. *The Charismatic Theology of St. Luke.* Peabody, Mass.: Hendricksen, 1984.

Stuhlmacher, Peter. *Paul's Letter to the Romans: A Commentary.* Translated by Scott J. Hafemann. Louisville, Ky.: Westminster, 1994.

Stumme, Wayne C., ed. *Bible and Mission: Biblical Foundations and Working Models for Congregational Ministry.* Minneapolis: Augsburg, 1986.

Telford, W. R. "Introduction." In *The Interpretation of Mark.* 2d ed., ed. William Telford, 1-61. Edinburgh: T & T Clark, 1995.

Tenney, Merrill C. *Interpreting Revelation.* Grand Rapids: Eerdmans, 1957.

―――. *New Testament Survey.* 2d ed. Grand Rapids: Eerdmans, 1985.

Thielman, Frank. *Paul and the Law: A Contextual Approach.* Downers Grove, Ill.: InterVarsity, 1994.

Thomas, John Christopher. "A Reconsideration of the Ending of Mark." *Journal of the Evangelical Theological Society* 26 (1983): 407-19.

Tiede, David. "Acts 1:6-8 and the Theo-Political Claims of Christian Witness." *Word and World* 1 (1981): 41-51.

Tolbert, Mary Ann. *Sowing the Gospel: Mark's World in Literary-Historical Perspective.* Minneapolis: Fortress, 1989.

Towner, Philip H. "Paradigms Lost: Mission to the *Kosmos* in John and David Bosch's Biblical Models of Mission." *Evangelical Quarterly* 67 (1995): 99-119.

Trebilco, P. "Itineraries, Travel Plans, Journeys, Apostolic Parousia." In *Dictionary of Paul and His Letters,* ed. Gerald F. Hawthorne and Ralph P. Martin, 446-56. Downers Grove, Ill.: InterVarsity, 1993.

Turner, Max. "'Empowerment for Mission'? Pneumatology of Luke-Acts: An Appreciation and Critique of James B. Shelton's *Mighty in Word and Deed.*" *Vox Evangelica* 24 (1994): 103-22.

Tyson, Joseph B. "The Problem of Jewish Rejection in Acts." In *Luke-Acts and the Jewish People: Eight Critical Perspectives,* ed. Joseph B. Tyson, 124-37. Minneapolis: Augsburg, 1988.

―――, ed. *Luke-Acts and the Jewish People: Eight Critical Perspectives.* Minneapolis: Augsburg, 1988.

Van Gelder, Craig. "A Great New Fact of Our Day: America as Mission Field." *Missiology* 19 (1991): 409-18.

van Unnik, W. C. "The Purpose of St. John's Gospel." *Studia Evangelica* 1 (1959): 382-411.

Wagner, C. Peter. *Lighting the World: A New Look at Acts, God's Hand-book for World Evangelism*. Ventura, Calif.: Regal Books, 1995.

Walkenhorst, K. H. "The Concluding Doxology of the Letter to the Romans and Its Theology." *Katorikku Kenkyuu* [Tokyo] 27 (1988): 99-132.

Wanamaker, Charles A. "Christ as Divine Agent in Paul." *Scottish Journal of Theology* 39 (1986): 517-28.

———. *Commentary on 1 and 2 Thessalonians*. New International Greek Testament Commentary. Grand Rapids: Eerdmans, 1990.

Wenham, John. *Redating Matthew, Mark and Luke*. Downers Grove, Ill.: InterVarsity, 1992.

Westerholm, Stephen. *Israel's Law and the Church's Faith: Paul and His Recent Interpreters*. Grand Rapids: Eerdmans, 1988.

Wiefel, Wolfgang. "The Jewish Community in Ancient Rome and the Origins of Roman Christianity." In *The Romans Debate*, ed. Karl P. Donfried, 85-101. Peabody, Mass.: Hendrickson, 1991.

Wiles, Gordon P. *Paul's Intercessory Prayers: The Significance of Intercessory Prayer Passages in the Letters of Paul*. Society for New Testament Studies Monograph Series, no. 24. Cambridge: University Press, 1974.

Wilkins, Michael J. *Discipleship in the Ancient World and Matthew's Gospel*. 2d ed. Grand Rapids: Baker, 1995.

Williams, Joel F. *Other Followers of Jesus: Minor Characters as Major Figures in Mark's Gospel*. Journal for the Study of the New Testament Supplement Series, no. 102. Sheffield: Sheffield Academic Press, 1994.

Williams, Sam K. "Again Pistis Christou." *Catholic Biblical Quarterly* 49 (1987): 431-47.

———. "The 'Righteousness of God' in Romans." *Journal of Biblical Literature* 99 (1980): 241-90.

Wilson, Stephen G. *The Gentiles and the Gentile Mission in Luke-Acts*. Society for New Testament Studies Monograph Series, no. 23. Cambridge: Cambridge University Press, 1973.

Wind, A. "Destination and Purpose of the Gospel of John." *Novum Testamentum* 14 (1972): 26-69.

Witherington III, Ben. *The Jesus Quest: The Third Search for the Jew of Nazareth*. Downers Grove, Ill.: InterVarsity, 1995.

Wodecki, P. Bernard. "ŠLH dans le livre d'Isaïe." *Vestus Testamentum* 34 (1984): 482-88.

Wolff, C. "Christ und Welt im 1. Petrusbrief." *Theologische Literaturzeitung* 100 (1975): 333-42.

Wright, N. T. "The Paul of History and the Apostle of Faith." *Tyndale Bulletin* 29 (1978): 61-88.

———. "Putting Paul Together Again." In *Pauline Theology I: Thessalonians, Philippians, Galatians, Philemon*, ed. Jouette M. Bassler, 183-211. Minneapolis: Fortress, 1991.

Ziesler, John. *Paul's Letter to the Romans*. Philadelphia: Trinity Press International, 1989.